Eugen Seeger

Chicago, the Wonder City

Eugen Seeger

Chicago, the Wonder City

ISBN/EAN: 9783744791175

Printed in Europe, USA, Canada, Australia, Japan

Cover: Foto ©Andreas Hilbeck / pixelio.de

More available books at **www.hansebooks.com**

Chicago,

...THE...

Wonder · City.

—:::::—

...BY...

EUGEN SEEGER.

—::::—

CHICAGO:
1893.

Published by
The Geo. Gregory Printing Company
123-125 La Salle Avenue
Chicago

Elijah Wentworth's Tavern. The Miller House.

Chicago In 1832.—Wolfs Point.

Published by Rufus Blanchard, 171 Randolph Street, Chicago.

PREFACE.

To compress the history of Chicago into four hundred and fifty pages is no easy task. With what success this has been done in "CHICAGO, THE WONDER CITY," the reader must judge.

It has of late become quite a lucrative business to write histories of cities and interweave them with detailed biographies of their wealthier citizens. The present volume was not written on that plan. It is a history of Chicago, not a series of biographical notices of men whom the city's rapid and enormous growth has lifted into prominence. Nature designed the site of the city for a great metropolis, but no man or set of men has made Chicago. Chicago has made many men, but it is the great body of the people, the industrial and industrious middle classes that have brought about the greatness of Chicago.

Since the body of the book was written, it has, in true Chicago fashion, been overtaken by some important events, notably the pardoning of the anarchists, the decision in regard to Sunday opening of the World's Fair and the estimation of the present population of the city, based on the figures given in the new city directory. This volume contains five hundred and forty thousand names, which would under ordinary circumstances represent, according to the usual methods of computation, over two million people, but owing to conditions created by the World's Fair this basis of calculation is undoubtedly too large, and it is probable the two million mark has not been reached yet.

On June 26, 1893, John P. Altgeld, the present governor of Illinois, added perhaps the final chapter to the anarchist case by granting absolute pardon to the three men sent to the penitentiary in 1887—Fielden and Schwab to life terms and Oscar Neebe to a fifteen-year term. On the question of the pardon itself there has been but little discussion, most people believing that the clemency they themselves prayed for should be extended to them; but the manner of the pardon is loudly and well-nigh universally condemned. The prisoners petitioned for mercy—they were given a vindication. Governor Altgeld explained his action in a carefully prepared message of seventeen thousand words, and based his pardon on the grounds of a packed and incompetent jury, a prejudiced and unfair judge and the failure of the State to establish the guilt of the prisoners. Not content with placing the crown of martyrdom on the heads of the men convicted of a heinous offense, the governor saw fit to go out of his way to attack a co-ordinate branch of the government, to impugn the honor of a judge of untarnished reputation and insolently to override the decisions of not only the lower courts but also of the state Supreme Court. For this action on the part of the governor the people of Illinois were entirely unprepared. An official utterance such as this pardon of the governor, is well calculated to shatter the confidence of the people either in the wisdom of their laws and the justice of their execution or in the competency of their chief executive. The isolated position of Gov. Altgeld is the only redeeming feature of the situation.

The decision of the United States Court of Appeals permitting the opening of the World's Fair on Sunday, was a victory for the liberal element, and it is a matter for congratulation that the decent and orderly behavior of the Sunday crowds is fast reconciling to the new order of things those who had thought that a study, on Sunday, of human progress and achievements would necessarily prove a desecration of that day. The Fair is already a success from every point of view—even from the financial one, conservative judges estimating that shareholders will be reimbursed the larger part of their contributions.

The facts given in the chapter on the '48ers are largely taken from an essay by Emil Dietzsch, himself a '48er and a keen observer withal.

The photographs of the descedants of the Algonquin Indians who played such an important part in the early history of Chicago, were taken by Grabill (113 Monroe street), who visited the west for this purpose.

The particular acknowledgments of the author are due to Mr. Robert Kennicott Reilly for help in arranging and compiling parts of the work and assistance in editing it.

EUGEN SEEGER.

July 4, 1893.

John Dean. J. Baptiste Beaubien. Fort Dearborn Dr. Wolcott. John Kinzie.

Chicago at the Beginning of the Century.

TABLE OF CONTENTS.

	PAGE
Preface	5

Early History. PART ONE.—A chapter from Wayback—The Indians—French Navigators sail through the Straits of Belle Isle and discover Canada—Cartier, Champlain, Nicolet, Perrot—New France—The first victims of the white conquerors—Jolliet and Marquette—Bitter conflicts in the land of the Illini—An Indian Jeanne d'Arc—Robert Cavelier and his conquests—Dismal failure of the French colonization scheme—Chicagou, the Garlic River .... 1—38

PART TWO.—The rule of the English—Emigration of the French—The Pontiac War—A fateful love intrigue—Pontiac's tragic end—The Americans take the helm .... 39—44

Chicago. Early documents—A miscarriage in land speculation—The earliest settlers—Erection of Fort Dearborn—Tecumseh—Massacre of Fort Dearborn—Tedious development of the village—Black Hawk—End of Indian War in Illinois and beginning of the rapid development of the future metropolis 45—88

The City, Chicago	89
Chicago as a commercial center before the fire—The industrial develpment	91

Chicago's Progress. Early German settlers—The Forty-eighters—Social and military growth in the Fifties—Beer riots—Americans and Germans unite in opposing slavery—Early breweries—Douglas and know-nothingism—Underground railroad—Chicago's part in the war of the rebellion .... 105..120

The Chicago Fire	121
The catastrophe of October 8th and 9th	125
The beginning of the great fire on the West Side	127
The destruction of the business center of Chicago	131
Street scenes during the fire	142
The burning of the North Side	148
On the "Sands"	153
A woman's story of the fire	157
Scenes at the mouth of the river	162

xi

On the prairie	169
Incidents	171
A walk through the ruins	178
Action of the police	182
The fire department	184
Losses and insurance	187
Chicago's Architectural Development	193
Chicago's Art Development	212
The Public Library	232
The Labor Movement. History of the Eight-hour agitation	247
The Chicago Anarchists	254
The Cronin Case	272
Chicago.—The Main Exhibit	300
Libraries, Educational and Charitable Institutions	324
The Chicago Press	331
Germans and German Influence in Chicago	343
Population	353
Trade, Commerce and Manufactures	356
Miscellaneous Information. Chicago's municipal resources—Statistics—Public Schools—Municipal Health Department—The Drainage Channel—The City Government	372—382
The World's Fair	383

Early History.

PART ONE.

A Chapter from Wayback—The Indians—French Navigators sail through the Straits of Belle Isle and discover Canada—Cartier, Champlain, Nicolet, Perrot—New France—The First Victims of the White Conquerors—Jolliet and Marquette—Bitter Conflicts in the Land of the Illini—An Indian Jeanne d'Arc—Robert Caveller and his Conquests—Dismal Failure of the French Colonization Schemes—Chicagou, The Garlic River.

From the time of the great flood to a later but equally indefinite period, the territory comprising the present state of Illinois was the basin of a great inland sea, for Lake Michigan formerly extended southward far beyond its present shores.

Later through the parting waters broke the primeval forests with their clumsy inhabitants: the mastadon filled the swampy desert with its hoarse bellowing, fat and self-satisfied saurians lumbered complacently about in the rank and slimy vegetation while the primeval bird, the monstrous archæopteryx, lurched lazily through the sultry air.

It is as unimportant as it is impossible to determine how long this idyllic period lasted, but finally the future of this awkward, earliest creation lay all behind it and it disappeared from the scenes of the world-stage. Afterwards, and heaven only knows how long afterwards, the red man made his entrance, coming probably from the west or southwest, from the Gulf of Mexico or the Pacific coast; but over what roads and under what circumstances no man can tell.

The first reliable information about the northwest and its inhabitants dates from about the middle of the seventeenth century and comes from the brave French discoverers who made exploring trips from Canada throughout the region.

With the exception of the Iroquois, Hurons and Winnebagoes (the Winnebagoes belong to the Sioux or Dakota family) the Indians who at that time peopled the northwest belonged to the great Algonquin family and came from the region around the Ottawa river in Canada.

The number of Indians then living in North America is estimated at 190,000. Of these 20,000 belonged to the Huron-Iroquois and 90,000 to the Algonquin family. The Algonquins play an interesting and important part in the historical development not only of the northwest but also of Illinois and even of Chicago. Their principal tribes, each with many smaller branches, may be geographically divided as follows: in the north, above the St. Lawrence and the great lakes, the Nasquapees, Montagnais, Algarkins, Ottawas and Kilistinous or Creeks; on the Atlantic coast, the Micmacs, Abenakis, Sokokis, Massachusetts, Narragansetts, Mohicans, Delawares and Virginias; in the west, the Chippewas, Menominees, Blackfeet, Sacs and Foxes; in the south, the Shawnees.

Although united by ties of kinship and language, these tribes differed essentially as to customs and characteristics, even in regard to looks and mechanical skill. Some were peaceful and docile, others warlike and intractable. While those who first came to the southern shores of Lake Michigan beyond doubt wandered there afoot, had not the slightest idea of navigation and in more than one regard showed a strong antipathy to water and an equally strong antipathy to fighting, on the other hand their cousins, who afterwards invaded the country from the north, proved themselves daring sailors and wild and cruel warriors.

Of course none of these Indian tribes were very highly

civilized; their endeavors were directed primarily to satisfying their bodily wants, and their implements, arms and clothing were as primitive as possible. Some of the chiefs, however, were men of talent; bold,. heroic, eloquent, prudent and of great influence among their tribes.

His contact with the whites never benefitted the Indian. He is weighed down with many an evil race characteristic, but treaty-breaking and lying are not among them. These he first learned from his white brother, and by him also he was tainted by terrible, hereditary diseases, before unknown to him. After the noble priests and explorers, who came from the far east to brave the manifold dangers and privations of missionary life and to turn the savages to milder customs and instruct them in the arts of peace, followed a class of men by no means adapted to furnish the aborigines of the New World models of European civilization. Indeed, the official reports prove that for the purpose of increasing the number of its colonists the French, as well as the English government from time to time emptied its prisons and asylums and transported the wretched prisoners, sometimes even in chains, to America. Not all the western pioneers were what poets and writers of romance are wont to depict. Together with the hardy explorer, the high-minded idealist, the hard-working farmer and mechanic came many of that class of gentry one does not wish to meet after dark, ne'er-do-wells of all kinds and both sexes. Such a crowd, naturally enough, did nothing to help the Indian physically, improve him morally, or to make the intercourse between the natives and immigrants more harmonious.

At the time when the first white reached the present site of Chicago, and for the following half century, the "land of the Illini" was the home of the following Indian tribes: Illinois, Miamis. Kickapoos, Mascoutins, Pottawatomies, Sacs and Foxes, Winnebagoes and Shawnees—all, with the exception of the Winnebagoes, being members of the Algonquin family. Of their early history we know only that they claim to have lived always in America, or, as they put it, that their ancestors sprang up from the earth itself, the Shawnees alone preserving a tradition to the effect that they came originally from a far-distant land.

The names by which the Indians were designated by the newly-arrived whites were, for the most part, determined by chance or derived from the then or former dwelling places or from characteristic peculiarities of the respective tribes. The

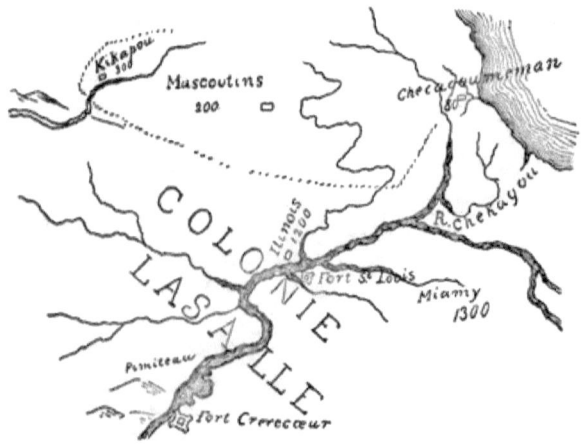

first explorers do not seem to have been at all particular as to the orthography of Indian names, for we find the same name spelled in a dozen different ways and not infrequently mutilated beyond easy recognition. Thus, for instance, the Kaskaskias, Cahokias, Tamaroas, Peorias and Mitchigamies, with characteristic Indian modesty called themselves the "Inini," an Algonquin word meaning "superior men." The French found "Inini" a hard word to pronounce and converted it into "Illini," soon thereafter affixing the French termination "ois." Thus from "Inini" were derived Illinois, Illinoies, Illinoues, Illimonek, Illiniwek, etc.

The principal settlements of the "Inini" or Illinois were in the middle and northern part of the territory now forming the State of Illinois. In La Salle county, near the present site of Utica, there formerly stood a flourishing Indian village called La Vantum, which, in 1680, contained no less than 8,000 inhabitants. In the territory mentioned there were probably twenty other villages of similar character, although smaller. The accompanying map, made for his government by the young French engineer, Franquelin, in 1684, affords a good idea of the Indian villages and the settlements and forts of La Salle and the French missionaries.

The settlements of the Illini reached along the various river banks down as far as opposite the present city of St. Louis, and at the beginning of the 18th century the farthest outpost reached even to the mouth of the Ohio. This land of the Illinois was at that time a veritable Indian paradise: luxuriant meadows, heavy forests, splendid farm land, an abundance of fish in lake and river, and of game in wood and open; buffalo, deer, bear, panther, wildcat, wolf, fox, beaver, otter, marten, ground-hog, raccoon, rabbits, wild swan, geese, ducks, wild turkeys, partridges, quail and enormous flocks of pigeons; such vegetables as the red man cared for as, for instance, maize, beans, cabbages and various roots, nuts and wild fruit in plenty—the Indian's insurmountable abhorrence of work was of small consequence in those golden days.

But no rose without its thorn, no cup of bliss without its drop of bitterness. The very blessings of the Illinois proved the cause of their misfortune. Even without the aid of telegraph and newspapers, the report of the extraordinary richness of the country spread to the farthest corners of the land, and there soon sprang up among the noble red men a socialistic-communistic warfare which would have brought joy to the soul of even the most advanced of modern "walking delegates." The first who came to "divide" were the Sioux from the far west; from the north came the Sacs and Foxes; the Kickapoos and Pottawatomies from the northeast, and last but not least from the remote east rushed in the wild hordes of the Iroquois. Then the skull-cracking began and many a worthy predecessor of Johann Most bit the dust, before the great communistic principle of division in its various stages and repetitions, first found a practical application on the virgin soil of this free country. The strongest, cruelest and wildest of course came out ahead in the deal, in this case the Iroquois, who undertook several bloody expeditions to "divide" with the Illini, till the latter were almost wiped out of existence. The history of the Indians of the northwest from the middle of the 17th till toward the end of the 18th century reads like the last act of Hamlet, bloodshed without end, a battle of all against all to annihilation. But even this wild can-can of bestial selfishness was not without romance, as is proven by the following historically authenticated incident, recounted all the more willingly as it throws some golden rays on the gloomy picture of the times and forms one of those rare exceptions where an Indian woman participated actively and triumphantly in the affairs of men. It was about the year 1673. The Iroquois had again undertaken one of their looting expeditions, had plundered a village, driven away the inhabitants and indulged in one of their beastly orgies of victory which was not interrupted even by the set of sun. Helpless and listless, the vanquished Illini watched from afar the revels of their enemies. Then the youthful Watchekee—or Watseka as the scribes of the whites were wont to call her—appeared before them. Her eye flashed with the fire of inspiration. Her cheeks glowed with righteous anger at the wrongs wrought upon her people and at their spiritless endurance of them. She besought the warriors to avail themselves of the cover of night and the disorganized condition of the victors for revenge and retaliation. But the men were not disposed to again cope with the powerful enemy and sat in sullen submission to their fate. Then Watseka addressed the women and begged them to shame the cowardly warriors and in their place to march forth against the foe. The squaws, each armed with bow and arrow, responded in hordes. Then, at last, the men bestirred themselves and, led by the brave girl, this strange band surprised the Iroquois and almost exterminated them. The place where this battle occurred more than 200 years ago is now the county seat of Iroquois county, and in honor of this Indian Jeanne d'Arc is called Watseka.

After the French took possession of the Northwest territory the history of the red man becomes blended more or less with the story of the priests and soldiers of Charles V, the explorers of the region. It was in 1534 that Jacques Cartier (or Quartier as the name is often spelled), an experienced Breton sailor, who made fishing trips from the west coast of France to the north coast of Labrador, drifted into the Straits of Belle Isle while on a voyage of discovery in the interests of the French government. His expedition consisted of two vessels, each of 61 tons burden and the crews numbered 61 men. From the Atlantic Cartier made his way down the Straits of Belle Isle, lying between Labrador and Newfoundland, to the Gulf of St. Lawrence and finally landed in the Gaspe district on the northeast point of Canada, between the Gulf of St. Lawrence and Chaleur's Bay. In this desolate spot, inhabited by only a few Indians, the French sailors erected a large wooden cross which bore the arms of Charles V and the inscription, "Vive le roi de France," and thus took possession of the newly-discovered country.

It is reported that the Indians, the Canadagnois (Nassequapes), who were much disturbed at the sight of these strange men and their mysterious ceremony, asked for an explanation, whereupon Cartier replied that the cross had been erected simply to mark the harbor and so allayed the Indians' suspicions. Alas, their first meeting with the whites had a sad sequel, for Cartier stole two of their boys and carried them back with him to France.

May 19, 1535, Cartier started on another expedition to Labrador, this-time with three ships. Again he passed through the Straits of Belle Isle, but this time kept to the west and continued up the St. Lawrence to the isle of Orleans, which, on account of its luxuriant vegetation and heavily-laden wild grape vines, he called the "Isle of Bacchus." The Indians of this island, especially their chief Donnacona, treated the French in the kindliest manner, helped them to explore the country and accompanied them up the Hochelaga (St. Lawrence) to the big Indian camp, Stadacone, on the site of the present city of Quebec. Here, too, they were received in a friendly manner, but the natives tried by artifice and persuasion to prevent the strangers from going further up the stream. Cartier, however, persisted and on October 2, 1835, successfully reached the great Indian camp at that time called, like the river, Hochelaga—to-day Montreal. Amid the blowing of trumpets and waving of flags the French landed. The Indians, who believed them of divine origin, were beside themselves with joy. They overwhelmed the newcomers with all possible proofs of their hospitality and with great pride showed them their fortified camp, consisting of about fifty immense block-houses, and finally even brought out their sick, requesting that Cartier should touch and so heal them. The clever Frenchman made the most of the situation. He made the sign of the cross over the ailing, read a few verses from the Bible and prayed for them—all in French. Then he distributed axes, knives, glass beads, looking-glasses and various small trinkets among the delighted aborigines and with another flourish of triumph left his new friends, promising to return. Highly pleased with his adventures and successes, Cartier returned to Stadacone, where he built a fort and spent the winter. His gratitude for the hospitality shown him by the Indians the Frenchman proved by capturing Donnacona and some of the other chiefs and taking them as prisoners to France. It was on July 16, 1536, when the expedition arrived at St. Malo. The Indian chiefs were immediately baptized, but this attention did not prevent their dying shortly after from homesickness. Cartier made several other voyages to the New World before his death in 1555. The country discovered by him was called Canada because its great stream, the St. Lawrence, was sometimes called by the natives the "Canada" river. According to other French explorers the word "Canada" signifies "city," and still others translate it "continent." In the writings of Cartier, however, the title "Canada" is used to designate a strip of land lying between Quebec and the Isle aux Coudres. During the sixteenth century many other explorers visited the country that Cartier had described, but the first permanent settlement was made early in the seventeenth century by the celebrated Samuel de Champlain.

Champlain was born in Brouage, on the Bay of Biscay, in 1567, of an old and illustrious family which had for generations followed the sea. In addition to being a thoroughly equipped sailor, Champlain received an excellent military training. In 1599, in command of the St. Julien, a vessel belonging to his uncle, he sailed for some time along the coast of the West Indies, Panama and Mexico, and in 1601 returned to France. While in Panama he looked into the question of a canal to join the Atlantic and the Pacific, and on his arrival in France pointed out the advantage of such a work.

He thus became the father of the great Panama Canal scheme, which was finally taken up by Ferdinand de Lesseps some years ago and which only lately, after the squandering of four hundred million dollars, culminated in the greatest public scandal of the century, and almost destroyed the French Republic. March 25, 1603, Champlain organized an expedition for North America and on May 24th landed

near Tadoussac at the confluence of the Saguenay and
St. Lawrence. From there he visited the places discovered
by Cartier in 1535. In August he returned to France, published extensive reports about his travels and the next spring
again started out on an exploring trip. He first touched at
Nova Scotia and afterwards coasted along the shore to the
Chesepeake bay. In 1607 he returned to France and agitated
the question of establishing a French trading post on the
St. Lawrence and successful in his endeavors, he returned in
1608, sailed up the St. Lawrence to the place called "Stadacone" by Cartier but then called Quebec (narrows) by the
Algonquins. Here Champlain built houses, sowed grain, inaugurated an extensive fur trade and thus founded the city
of Quebec.

As the friendly Algonquins were hard pushed by the
Iroquois who lived to the southeast of them, Champlain, in
the summer of 1609, united with them in an expedition against
their enemies. This was about the same time that the Englishman Henry Hudson, in the service of the East India Company of Amsterdam was exploring the Hudson river and in
his little vessel, the "Half Moon" first encountered the
red men.

On his expedition Champlain discovered the beautiful
lake which now bears his name, and on it swarms of Iroquois.
When the hostile forces caught sight of each other they
immediately put to shore and fortified themselves. The next
morning at sunrise the fight commenced. Awkward as the
arquebuse now appears, it proved a terrible weapon in competition with the simple bows and arrows of the naked savages.
Champlain killed two chiefs with the first shot fired and with
a second bullet mortally wounded a third. Thereupon the
Iroquois fled. This was the first Indian blood shed by the
whites in North America and in course of time the French
paid dearly for their easily won victory. As long as they were
in power in Canada and when they established colonies in

Illinois the Iroquois were persistently after them and, partly on their own account and partly as hirelings of the English, relentlessly worried and tormented them.

In the fall of 1609 Champlain visited France and in the following spring returned to America with a well equipped fleet and a considerable number of mechanics. Shortly after reaching Quebec he organized another campaign against the Iroquois and at about the same time that his king and patron, Henry IV, fell a victim to the dagger of Ravaillac, he himself, while storming a fortified camp of the enemy near the Sorel river, was dangerously wounded by an Indian arrow. He sought and found health in his native land and in 1612 was made lieutenant-governor of New France (Canada). He straightway assumed the duties of his new office and for a number of years discharged them with the greatest discretion and ability. In the autumn of 1613 he revisited France in the interest of the colony and on his return in 1615 brought with him Father Denis Jamay, two other Franciscan monks and a priest, all of whom rendered him valuable services both in his exploring voyages along the St. Lawrence river and through lakes Huron and Ontario and also in his efforts to civilize the Algonquins. These Franciscan monks were the first spiritual teachers to leave the Old World to bring to the savages of the north instruction in the Christian religion and European civilization.

At this time his old enemies, the Iroquois began to harass Champlain, and in the fall of 1615 he was not only twice dangerously wounded by them, but was even repulsed on account of the insubordination of his allies, the Hurons. The star of the new settlement seemed to be now waning. It was in vain that Champlain, after his recovery, redoubled his exertions to increase the trade of his colony and awaken in the mother country a more active interest in it. The young commonwealth could not yet stand alone, and the Italian adventurers who during the minority of Louis XIII exercised such an unfortunate influence upon the French regent, Maria de Medici, felt not the slightest concern for it. Only after Cardinal Richelieu became a member of the council of state, was there felt a decided change for the better in regard to the struggling colonies of the New World. The settlement of Quebec was energetically pushed, the commerce with the natives materially increased, and the colony itself adequately fortified. Richelieu, who paid particular attention to trans-Atlantic affairs, especially during the first year of his power, appointed the duke of Ventadour as viceroy of New France (1625), and the first official act of the latter was to send over a number of Jesuit priests to participate in the work of civilizing and converting the natives. This act, as will be soon seen, was of the greatest importance in the development of the northwest and especially of Illinois.

Shortly after the arrival of the Jesuits some lively controversies took place between them on the one hand and the Franciscan fathers and the colonial government on the other; but the Jesuits soon gained control in the affairs of the colony.

A fateful event in the history of the settlement was the arrival in July, 1628, of English men-of-war under the command of Sir David Kirk and his two brothers, who demanded the unconditional surrender of the fortress and its commander, Champlain. The Canada company, organized in Paris by Cardinal Richelieu, had at almost the same time dispatched from France several vessels laden with provisions, arms, etc., and these were anxiously awaited by the little French colony at Quebec. Before arriving at their destination, however, the vessels were intercepted and captured by the English men-of-war. In consequence of this mishap the poor colonists passed a miserable winter, and just one year after the arrival of the English, Champlain was forced to capitulate. He was taken to England and there held as a prisoner until 1632. At this time the French government had apparently lost all hope for the future of the Canadian colony, for when by the peace of

St. Germain-en-Laye the English offered to give up their claims to the settlement in Quebec the French were at first undecided as to whether they should accept the offer. But in the spring of 1633 Champlain, with three excellently equipped vessels, returned once more to his colony—this time as its governor. There was boundless joy among both Indians and whites when the old and tried leader made his appearance. Immediately after his arrival Champlain fortified Richelieu Island, founded the city of Three Rivers and established a school for young Indians. The great explorer did not, however, long enjoy the fruits of his labor, for he died in Quebec Christmas day, 1635.

The powerful impulse given by Champlain to the settlement and civilization of the New World did not cease at his death, for his companions followed the same path—toward the west. Among them was Jean Nicolet, who lived for years among the various Algonquin tribes, learning to speak their language fluently and finally becoming so thoroughly Indianized that the red men treated him like one of themselves. His services as interpreter and negotiator, in fact his whole influence on the Indians, were of the greatest value to the Canadian government. On the 4th of July, 1634, Nicolet discovered Lake Michigan, or as it was first called Lake Illinois, "Lac des Illinois," and afterwards explored a large part of the northwest, visiting the Chippewas in Green Bay, the Mascoutins on the Fox river, and the Menominees and Winnebagoes on the lake named after the latter. Wherever Nicolet went there were great Indian gatherings which the explorer invariably addressed, producing a strong impression on the red men. As a matter of curiosity it may be mentioned that on the occasion of his last visit the Indians honored this Frenchman with a banquet at which not less than 120 beavers were served. Nicolet was the first white man, whose foot touched the territory of Wisconsin and Illinois. The first white man to see the upper Mississippi was Pierre Esprit

Radisson, 1658, an indefatigable explorer and fur-trader, who on all his travels kept an accurate diary, and to whom his contemporaries are indebted for much important information. Jointly with his brother-in-law, Medart Chouart, he established a settlement on Hudson Bay, which afterwards developed into the well-known Hudson Bay company. The Jesuit fathers, Menard and Guerin, both of whom afterwards perished on an exploring tour, are also reported to have seen the upper Mississippi more than ten years before Jolliet and Marquette. The next of the French discovers was Nicholas Perrot, who from 1670 to 1690 distinguished himself in explorations of the upper lakes, the Fox river valley and the upper Mississippi. He was the discoverer of the lead mines in the west.

Louis Jolliet (frequently spelled Joliet) was the first of the French pioneers to lead an exploring expedition to the Illinois country and to set foot on the site of modern Chicago. He was a child of the New World. Born in Quebec in 1645, the son of a poor mechanic he was brought up in the local Jesuit school and destined to become a priest. But the free air of the forest had more charm for him than the close atmosphere of a monastery. In 1669, in commission of the colonial government, he visited the copper mines on the shores of Lake Superior. On his return he explored Lake Erie. Owing to his success with all his undertakings, he received a commission from Governor Frontenac to visit the "South lake in the Mascoutin country and the great Mississippi river" (from the Indian "Miche-Sepe," great river). At that time the Canadians did not know that the mighty stream discovered by De Soto in 1541 and explored from the White river to the Gulf of Mexico was identical with the "Miche-Sepe" of which they first learned from the Indians, and whose upper part was navigated by their missionaries.

In the fall of 1672 Jolliet set forth on his new expedition, accompanied by a trusty servant and four Indians. December 1 he arrived at the Straits of Mackinaw connecting Lakes Huron and Michigan. On the northern shore at that time there stood the French Jesuit Mission of St. Ignace whose superior, Father Marquette, was well-known for his zeal and success in civilizing and converting the natives. Thither Jolliet first went to invite Marquette, who spoke six Indian dialects fluently, to accompany him on his perilous trip to the far west. Marquette was only too glad to accept. On the 17th of May, 1673, they left Mackinaw and a few days later arrived at Green Bay from where they went up the Fox river. Then they got the Mascoutin Indians to guide them to the Wisconsin river down which they floated to the Mississippi, which they reached June 17, 1673. They were nearly a week on the Mississippi before discovering the first trace of human beings, an Indian trail leading from the western shore of the river to a beautiful prairie. The boats were made fast and Marquette and Jolliet went ashore and after fervently praying for heaven's blessing, marched along the newly discovered trail in anxious anticipation.

How the hearts of the two bold discoverers must have beaten as they suddenly saw three Indian villages spread out on the green meadow before them. A loud call from the new comers was the signal for a lively scene. The astonished Indians rushed out of their wigwams and from a distance carefully regarded the peculiar looking strangers. After a short pause four old chiefs approached slowly and with dignity, carrying in their hands pipes of peace. Close up to the two white men they marched, and then without saying a word stood before them. From this Father Marquette perceived that the Indians were well disposed toward their unexpected visitors and asked them in the Algonquin dialect: "Who are you?" "We are Inini," was the reply. The pipes of peace were then passed around and afterwards a regular Indian feast was held to celebrate the newly formed friendship between the whites and the redskins. The next day 600 of the natives accompanied the explorers to their boats and won from them a promise soon to return—a promise which unfortunately they were never able to keep.

Then they went further down the Mississippi—how far it is not definitely known. Marquette himself, in a report prepared much later, after a long illness, and without written notes, the diaries of both having been lost through the capsizing of the boat, maintained that he and Jolliet had gone as far south as the $32°$ of latitude, but La Salle and other contemporaries vigorously disputed this. It is a fact that Marquette and Jolliet on the 17th of July, just four weeks after their first meeting with the Indians on the Mississippi, turned homeward, so that, considering the possible speed of their boat, it would seem probable that they scarcely went further south than to the mouth of the Missouri or at most to the confluence of the Ohio, near the present site of Cairo. The reason for their return, as given by Marquette, was their fear of falling into the hands of the Spaniards. In this regard it is worthy of note that the Indians, whom they met in the southernmost part of their journey, had fire-arms, axes, knives and beads which they claimed to have received from the "Europeans in the east."

On their return voyage Jolliet and Marquette went from the Mississippi into the Illinois river as the Peorias, living at the mouth of the Illinois, told them that this was the shortest way to Mackinaw. In Kaskaskia, a village of the Illinois, they were received in the kindliest manner possible and indeed a chief with a picked band of young Indians accompanied them to lake Michigan, along whose western shore the Frenchmen rowed to Green Bay, which they reached in September.

In the Jesuit Mission at this place, Jolliet passed the winter and in the spring betook himself to Quebec. Here in Fort Frontenac he talked over with La Salle the events of his trip and made a written report to the colonial authorities who immediately turned it over to the French government,

Jolliet and Marquette in Illinois.

which in turn had it printed. His request to found a colony in the land of the Illinois was peremptorily refused by Colbert, the famous minister of Louis XIV, on the ground that Canada itself should first be more strongly fortified and thickly peopled. Jolliet thereupon devoted his attention to the north and northeast of Canada, received in 1680 from the French government the isle of Anticosti and other land grants, and was successful in all his undertakings, until death in 1700 put an end to his remarkable career.

Far more tragic was the end of his brave companion, Marquette. In consequence of his great exertions and of the privations which he endured in his travels throughout the far west, he was still sick when Jolliet returned to Quebec. He had to remain in Green Bay and not until the fall did he feel strong enough to return to the land of the Illinois. On the present site of Milwaukee, sick and exhausted, he passed a miserable winter in a wretched log-hut. In March he had so far recovered as to continue his journey to the Indian settlement at Kaskaskia, where he arrived on the 8th of April. He was received by the natives with the greatest joy. By the hundreds they listened to the words of their noble, white friend, who was able to exercise the greatest influence over them. On Easter Sunday of the same year Marquette founded an Indian mission after he had converted scores to Christianity. His rapidly increasing illness, however, compelled him to make immediate preparations for a return. Something like the premonition of death may have come to the high-minded man, as he took his departure from his Indian converts and promised to send them a friend from the north. So unwilling were the Indians to part with their teacher that hundreds accompanied him to Lake Michigan from the eastern shore of which he embarked for home. Alas, it was not permitted him to reach his lonely cloister in the far north. He became weaker and weaker, and at last so helpless that his two comrades had to carry him in and out of the boat. May 18, 1675, having reached a point about thirty miles north of the present city of Manistee, Marquette caused a halt to be made at the mouth of a little river, which long afterwards bore his name. Then he informed his friends that he felt his end was near. On a hill near the water's edge they hastily constructed a hut of bark and fir branches, and here the next night ended the blessed life of this great but still young man. After the body was consigned to earth, Marquette's companions continued their sorrowful journey to their northern home. In the winter of 1676 a number of his Indian adherents showed their gratitude and affection by disinterring the body of the missionary, placing it in a carefully constructed birch-bark coffin and taking it to the monastery at St. Ignatius, where it was reburied under one of the flag-stones of the chapel. For two hundred years the bones of the illustrious man rested in the silence of the cloister, forgotten by all, until the year 1877, when they were discovered and brought to the attention of the world.

It was no easy path they trod, who led the way for modern bank presidents, speculators, beer brewers and pork packers!

At the time Marquette founded the mission at Kaskaskia, there was among the various tribes of the Algonquins a fairly brisk trade, reaching from the St. Lawrence river to the confluence of the Ohio and Mississippi, and having its center in the region of the great lakes. The number of French hunters, fur-traders and hangers-on, having commercial relations with the Indians, was already very considerable. And while the red men were ever at loggerheads with such Englishmen as wandered thither, in regard to the French they seemed to be of Heine's opinion that even a cursing Frenchman was preferred by the Lord to a praying Englishman. The Iroquois alone formed an exception to the rule, but they were never reinforced by the other tribes, unless the English made it to their material advantage to do so.

It is worthy of note that as early as June 14, 1671, at a French-Indian conference held near the Falls of St. Marie (Sault Ste. Marie) St. Lusson, in behalf of the French government in Canada, took possession, in the name of Louis XIV, of the great lakes and the adjacent territories as well as of all land "south to the ocean that is already discovered or is still to be discovered." The ceremony was imposing, and after it was over a great wooden cross was raised in honor of the church. On this occasion were present representatives of seventeen Indian tribes, from all parts of the before mentioned territory—among them the Menominees, Pottawatomies, Sauks and Winnebagoes—and many Frenchmen, including Jolliet, Perrot, Moreau and many Jesuit missionaries. The Canadians gave the chiefs numerous presents, whose value, however, was not so great, so the chronicles tell us, but that it was offset by the rich furs and trophies of the chase which the noble red men had brought with them for their white brothers. The natives and foreigners at that time were in splendid accord.

Volumes could be written of the adventures and labors of the various travelers and explorers in the north and northwest, but to a complete understanding of certain events, especially bearing upon the development of the state of Illinois and the city of Chicago, it is especially necessary to consider the life and labors of one man whose figure stands out most clearly and prominently among the pathfinders and martyrs of his time, and whose name is closely united with the early history of the lake region: Robert Cavelier, Sieur de La Salle.

Cavelier was born in Rouen, November 23, 1643. His father, a well-to-do merchant, gave him a scientific education, and before he was twenty he held the position of teacher in a Jesuit school in his native city. Soon, however, the ambitious youth left the narrow life of his home for the broader sphere of activity offered in the new world. Thither his older brother

ROBERT CAVELIER, SIEUR DE LA SALLE.

had already gone as a teacher in the Jesuit college of St. Sulpice at Montreal. In the year 1666 he arrived at Montreal, and through the influence of his brother received from the Jesuits a large grant of land which he straightway caused to be settled by his numerous followers. Immediately upon his arrival La Salle conceived the most daring plans. He wished to find a passage to China by way of the American continent. His means were in no proportion to the magnitude of his schemes, but the courageous youth was not to be deterred on that account. From the Indians with whom he was in constant communication he learned of the great rivers of the west, and to them he first turned his attention. To gain a part of the money necessary for their exploration, he sold his lands and arranged an expedition from which he did not return for two years. He went to the south and west and discovered the Ohio, up which he went to the rapids at Louisville. On his exploring tours he did not neglect the fur trade through which he hoped to secure the means for still more extended trips. In 1672 he visited the eastern shore of Lake Michigan and upper Illinois. In the year 1673 Cavelier, taking with him the warmest kind of letters of recommendation from Governor Frontenac to Louis XIV and his powerful minister, Colbert, returned to France to obtain a letter of nobility and a grant of land and to interest influential people in his undertakings. Louis' insatiable rapacity and greed for land greatly aided the young explorer. Successful in all that he had planned, Cavelier, now Sieur de La Salle, on his return to America, took possession of Fort Frontenac and the territory belonging to it, all of which had been granted him by the French government. Henceforth he devoted himself with great activity to his colonization schemes, and especially to the fur trade from which he still had to obtain for the most part the means for his various enterprises.

His purpose to find a passage from America to China, La Salle now abandoned, and devoted himself to a plan to build forts along the shores of the great lakes as well as on the Illinois, St. Joseph and Mississippi rivers, and especially at the mouth of the latter, on the Gulf of Mexico, to unite all the Indians of the west, and thus acquire for France possession of the region of the great lakes and the Mississippi valley and to monopolize its commerce. In the year 1677 La Salle again betook himself to France in order to win over to his cause Colbert, the influential minister of Louis, and again he was eminently successful. He returned to his colony with extended authority, enormous land grants, valuable privileges, among them the monopoly of trading in buffalo hides, considerable money and trusty subordinates and business associates. Among the men under his leadership were the Italian Chevalier de Tonti, who afterwards, as La Salle's trusty friend and lieutenant, played an important role in the history of Illinois, and the Franciscan monk, Louis Hennepin, the discoverer of coal in America, (near Ottawa, Ill.) who afterwards made a reputation by his thorough exploration of the upper Mississippi and discovery of St. Anthony's Falls.

Incidental mention may here be made of the characteristic fact that in furthering La Salle's plans, the French government by no means had in view the development of the rich resources of the immense territory in which he was to rule. It hoped that the young explorer might discover an easy road to Mexico, then regarded as the inexhaustible Dorado from which Louis' ever-empty coffers might be replenished.

In November, 1678, bold, pious and joyous, La Salle's expedition started off for its distant goal. He was glad, indeed, to leave behind him the creditors who made his life a burden, and the Canadian traders, who, fearing his competition, harassed him in every possible manner. From the wild men and wild beasts among whom he was going he had nothing to fear. He was leaving his enemies behind.

The winter of 1678-79 he passed above Niagara Falls and there built a small vessel, which he called the "Griffon," and which was launched in August, 1679. September 18 he sent the "Griffon" back to Canada heavily laden with furs, which were to appease his clamorous creditors. From Green Bay, where he had laden his vessel, La Salle pushed on in four canoes, going down the west shore of Lake Michigan, past the present site of Chicago, and up the eastern shore to the mouth of the St. Joseph river, where the little band of explorers —La Salle with nineteen companions, among them two missionaries—landed November 1. Here La Salle expected to find his friend, Tonti, with twenty men who were to have made the trip down the eastern shore, but they did not appear until three weeks later. On this spot La Salle built a fortified camp (Fort Miami) in which he left a small garrison, and then continued the expedition up the St. Joseph, through the Kankakee, into the Illinois river, and to the great Indian village, La Vantum. This, however, he found entirely abandoned.

On January 4, 1680, La Salle came to Peoria lake, and on it he found a village of the Peoria Indians. The conduct of these Indians, and the fact that six of his men had deserted, caused him to erect a fort in this neighborhood, which, for obvious reasons, he called "Crevecoeur"—"Heavy Heart." From every side misfortune befell him. His patience and endurance were submitted to the severest tests. The first thing he learned after his arrival among the Peorias was that his creditors had seized his possessions in Canada, and that the "Griffon," which he had daily expected with almost indispensable supplies, had been sunk. To arrange his affairs at home, La Salle had to hurry thither as quickly as possible—hurry in winter, with the rivers and lakes covered with ice, a distance of over a thousand miles.

His trusty friend, Tonti, with a part of the men, he left in the new fort; another party he sent down the Mississippi with Father Hennepin and one Indian, and four Frenchmen he took with him to Canada. He started March 1st, reached the St. Joseph river March 24th and Fort Frontenac, his home, on May

6th, having accomplished this terribly trying journey in 65 days.

While La Salle in the north was moving heaven and earth to straighten out his affairs and to obtain new means for his various enterprises, a fateful tragedy occurred at Fort Heavy Heart. On his way to La Vantum, La Salle had noticed a

STARVED ROCK.

great rock on the Illinois river (eight miles from the present city of Ottawa), where later the Illini were overcome by their terrible fate. Since that time it has been known as "Starved Rock." It is an erratic block, 135 feet high, completely isolated, and with an upper surface of three-fourths of an acre. It is absolutely inaccessible, except by one small, steep path on the eastern side.

Appreciating the strategic importance of this point, La Salle, on his departure, commissioned Tonti to erect a fort on top of the rock. Tonti, jointly with the missionaries, Membre and Ribourde, and three other Frenchmen, immediately set to work, leaving the rest of the men with the provisions, ammunition and other supplies at Fort "Heavy Heart." To his great amazement, Tonti discovered a few days afterwards that the fort had been plundered and destroyed by its own garrison, and that the latter had fled. He immediately dispatched two messengers to inform La Salle of this new misfortune, and with the few men who had remained faithful to him retired to La Vantum, where he spent the summer. The two messengers on the way north learned that the deserters had also ransacked Fort Miami and the large fur depots at Mackinac, but succeeded in advising La Salle in time for him to capture the insurgents after killing two of them. The remainder were sent to Quebec, where they were properly punished.

Alarmed at the possible fate of his friend Tonti, La Salle, August 10th, 1680, with a force of twenty picked men, once more started on a trip to the Illinois country. Exactly a month later the blood-thirsty Iroquois again made a raid on the peaceful Illini in La Vantum, and during this attack the flourishing settlement was entirely destroyed, 1,200 of the Illini massacred, and the remainder driven across the Mississippi. Even the burying ground of their victims was not spared. The hostile Iroquois dug up the dead, scattered the bones on the ground and stuck the skulls up on long poles. Tonti and his men fled, but during their escape Father Ribourde was murdered by a Kickapoo. Completely exhausted, they finally found shelter among the Pottawatomies.

It was the 4th of November when La Salle reached the mouth of the St. Joseph and learned from the Miamis the sad fate of affairs. Crevecoeur, whither he next went, was a scene of the cruelest devastation, with wolves battling with each other over the unburied bodies of the slain. Hoping to find traces of Tonti, La Salle went down to the mouth of the Illinois. In vain. On a tree he fastened a letter for his missing friend, and near by left a canoe, some furs and an axe, and then turned back to Fort Miami, which he reached January 31, 1681. The rest of the winter he spent in allying to himself the Indians of the region, and on the 25 of May, having learned from a Pottowatomie that Tonti was still alive, hastened to Mackinac, where the two friends met again.

La Salle had reason enough to rejoice, for the dangers and difficulties which beset his undertakings were scarcely to be overcome and he more than ever needed the services of the cautious but energetic Tonti. As bad news came from Fort Frontenac the two straightway returned to Canada. Of course it was money that had caused the trouble —old debts that La Salle had contracted to further his scheme. With the aid of Governor Frontenac and rich relatives La Salle again extricated himself from his difficulties and even succeeded in raising means for another expedition to the goal of his ambition—the Gulf of Mexico. It consisted of twenty-three Frenchmen, eighteen Indians, ten squaws and three papooses and on December 23, 1681 they sailed off in Indian canoes. Their first destination was the Chekogoua river (as it is spelled in a report of La Salle) where Tonti with seven men had already gone.

The title "Chekogoua" river is here applied to the Calumet and in the early days it was very often, not only in verbal intercourse, but even in writings and on maps applied with the most varied orthography, to the St. Joseph, Des Plaines and Illinois rivers. On the oldest maps the present Chicago river does not appear at all and in later years is given simply as a canal. No especial importance was ever attached to it by the poineers. The origin of the name can be only conjectured.

By "Getchi-ka-go" the Illini meant something big and strong, by "Shecaugo," pleasant water; in the dialect of the Pottawatomies "Choc-ca-go" signified a desert; the Chippewas called the skunk "Shegog" and the wild skunkweed "Shegougawinze," and in many of the writings of the second half of the eighteenth century we find the expression "Chicagou, or Garlic creek." One can therefore attach such significance to the name "Chicago" as suits his own fancy. The fact, however, that in former times, there were in this vicinity great quantities of wild skunkweed (allium ursinum) would suggest that the Indian probably called the stream "Schegog" river (skunk river) on this account. The Calumet in those days formed the chief means of communication between Lake Michigan and the Illinois and Mississipi rivers, but sometimes, depending on the state of the weather, the time of the year and the amount of water in the streams, the St. Joseph or the present Chicago river was chosen. The chief thing to consider was always the "portage," that is, the places where on account of the interruption of the navigable waters, both boat and contents had to be carried.

But let us return to our Argonauts who had been rowing down the Des Plaines to the Illinois river and on this, past many devastated Indian villages to its confluence with the Mississippi, at which point they landed February 6, 1682.

At first detained by ice and later by his many sojourns in Indian villages along the route, La Salle finally passed the mouth of the Arkansas March 12, and at last on April 7, had the joy of reaching the valiantly and persistently fought for goal of his hopes and ambitions—the Gulf of Mexico. Amid the singing of the Te Deum and huzzas for the king of France, all of which sounded strangely enough in the magnificent wilderness, a pillar was erected bearing the French arms, and La Salle, "by virtue of his right as discoverer and with the consent of the natives," took formal possession of the spot on which he had landed (in the region which Hennepin at an earlier period had named Louisiana in honor of Louis XIV) as well as of "all the territories and provinces lying along the shores of the Mississippi and of the cities, mines and fisheries therein contained," from the Alleghanies to the Rocky mountains. (*)

The next work for La Salle was to properly fortify the newly discovered country. But here again he had to meet his old difficulties and indeed in increased measure. His means and the greatness of his undertakings were in pitiful contrast. The Canadian merchants feared that his increasing influence would prove injurious to their interests and sought to injure him. His creditors were clamorous as ever and to fill the measure of his misfortune his friend Frontenac, through the influence of the Canadian Jesuits, was relieved of his position as governor and replaced by De La Barre—a man anything but kindly disposed toward La Salle.

Two days after taking possession of Louisiana La Salle started on his homeward journey. In December of the same year he had reached that great rock in the neighborhood of La Vantum whose intended fortification had brought such disaster to poor Tonti. Now, however, the scene was joyously animated; a strange, gay picture presented itself to the view of the returning voyager. The great rock was properly fortified and called Fort St. Louis. Under its protection the chief tribes of the Indians who had allied themselves with the French had again assembled. To the south of the fort were the Illini, numbering 7,000 souls; about 2,000 Miamis had chosen a dwelling place on the neighboring "Buffalo" island on the north side of the river; to the east were 200 Shawnees and 600 Pickashaws—in all not less than 3,880 Indian warriors were gathered around the fortress. In addition there

---

* This event, so fateful in the historical development of our country, gave the French possession of the greatest and most important part of the New World, and took place scarcely six months after that great marauder, Louis XIV, had surprised the rich and beautiful city of Strassburg in the midst of peace and wrenched it from the German empire, and at the same time that his allies, the Turks, were marching on, plundering and burning as they went, to attack the walls of Vienna.

was the usual large number of camp followers and hangers on, who, despite their white skins, did not constitute the best element in the new settlement. Many of these men had become wholly savage, both in body and mind, as far as appearances went scarcely to be distinguished from the most neglected of the red skins and in their moral conduct far worse. Some, however, were honest fellows, skilled in hunting and trapping, or industrious farmers or mechanics, who carried on their various trades and so put upon the little community springing up in the far west, the stamp of European civilization. Here were the primitive elements for a future great city and the brave explorer and leader seemed at last to have a fair prospect of carrying out his bold plans. Very many western cities and future great cities were, scarcely more than a generation ago, in a worse condition than Fort St. Louis. The best understanding existed between La Salle and his Indians. He afforded them effective protection and labored to instruct and elevate them. They, on the other hand, made his profitable fur trade possible, exchanging all kinds of skins for weapons, ammunition, calico, agricultural implements, trinkets for the women and other supplies. The summer which La Salle spent in the colony which he himself had founded formed the few days of real happiness which he had enjoyed since the time when, as a youth, his heart full of high hopes, he had first touched the soil of the New World. Toward fall however his troubles returned.

First the necessary supplies from the north ceased and then his agents there were prevented from returning to the colony and it was again molested by the Iroquois. His land-grant —Frontenac—was seized upon by the provincial government under some vain pretext, and finally, to add the last drop to the cup of his unhappiness, La Salle was deprived of his command of Fort St. Louis, that child born of his sorrows, and one Chevalier de Beaugis made commandant—leaving the intrepid explorer, dishonored, robbed, homeless. It was the before mentioned Governor De La Barre who was responsible for this foul blot on the page of French history in America. That his trusted friend Tonti was allowed to remain in the colony was the only circumstance to lighten the sorrow of La Salle's leave-taking. Woodland and meadow were covered by the gray mists of autumn when the sore-tried man cast his last glance upon the young creation of his unselfish energy.

In the spring of 1684 La Salle was again in Paris. After having again triumphed over his enemies he busied himself with preparations on a large scale for a new expedition to America. Four ships were equipped and manned with 100 soldiers; mechanics and common laborers flocked to La Salle, and even a few dozen bankrupt nobles and speculators joined his standard. Their destination was the mouth of the Mississippi. A naval officer named Beaujeu commanded the squadron. But even on the voyage across the ocean some serious misunderstandings arose between this man and La Salle. When entering Matagorda bay in the Gulf of Mexico one of the vessels containing the most valuable and indispensible supplies and implements foundered with its whole cargo. Many of the men believed that this catastrophe was simply an act of revenge on the part of Beaujeu. The expedition had got about 600 miles too far west and La Salle made a fatal error in taking Matagorda bay as a western outlet of the Mississippi. After several fruitless endeavors to find the great river Beaujeu set sail with his squadron for home, leaving La Salle and the colonists on the Texan coast. The privations and miseries of the new comers increased from day to day. From day to day it was more difficult for La Salle to maintain discipline. With a courage born of despair he tried for two years to find the mouth of the Mississippi in order to obtain from Canada succor for his starving immigrants. It was in March, 1687, that, during one of his searching expeditions he got in a western outlet of the Trinity river, about the present site of Galveston, and here the bold explorer was overtaken by his tragic fate. He was murdered from ambush by one of his own men. Shot through the head he silently breathed his last, but his death marks the beginning of the end of the French rule in the New World. His contemporaries had neither the sense to appreciate nor the ability to maintain the advantages which his venturesome spirit and marvelous energy had gained for his fatherland. Besides, that crowned robber, Louis XIV and his ministers, were at that time too much busied with plundering Europe to form an idea of developing the immeasurable resources of the New World, the full extent of which they had not even a vague notion. The famous devastation of the Palatinate by the French commenced about two years after La Salle's assassination and from that time on for fully eight years, they were occupied with the work of destruction in Germany. Then up to 1714 the war of the Spanish succession prevented Louis from interesting himself in the works of peace in his trans-Atlantic possessions. Thus it was that the French never brought any of La Salle's far-reaching plans into reality.

About the same time that La Salle arrived in Paris on his last trip, the Iroquois, 2,000 strong, appeared before his rocky fortress on the Illinois river. But the stronghold proved to be a complete success and Tonti, after six days of seige, punished the hostile redskins so thoroughly that they never had any desire to return.

In the year 1686, while La Salle was wandering along the Texan coast seeking the mouth of the Mississippi, Tonti, apprehensive for his friend's fate, organized an expedition for the Gulf of Mexico, but had to come back without accomplishing anything. Returning to the fort he learned of the sad death of La Salle, whereupon he again went south, visited the scene of the tragedy and provided for the helpless immigrants. Later with fifty of his own men and 200 Indians Tonti made a successful campaign against the Iroquois in Canada. His return from there to the fort caused quite a change in the life and activity of the colonists, inasmuch as the families of many of the soldiers, hunters and traders came with him to join the settlement around the fort Their arrival was the signal for an almost endless jollification and formed the beginning of the development of family life in the new community. This does not signify however that the new commonwealth distinguished itself as a model of morals and manners. Quite the contrary. After the inhabitants were freed from the fear of the Iroquois, they, whites as well as Indians, gave themselves up to unbounded excesses. The great mistake of the French leaders was that they neglected to create a solid moral and material basis for the colony by fostering agriculture and industry. It was impossible also to keep from the colony a class of people who had left their country only for their country's good and whose intercourse with the Indians acted like the breath of a pestilence. Upon the redskins the missionaries after all never gained much hold in spite of untold efforts and terrible privations. On the whole the Indian has very little talent for Christianity and when he allowed himself to be "converted" he did so largely "for revenue only." The copper-colored aborigines were far more partial to the fire-water of the French traders than to the holy water of the French priests. All these circumstances acted against the healthy development of the young community; it was a scrofulous condition of affairs.

What a difference between this French colony and that founded by Pastorius in Germantown at almost exactly the same time! From the first the Pennsylvania settlement was a model of industry, good order, earnest endeavor and excellent morals. Not that its founders rested on beds of roses, for Pastorius himself writes that "enough can neither be written nor believed by our more favored descendants, of the extent of the poverty and destitution in which this Germantownship was founded by colonists, distinguished alike for their Christian frugality and indefatigable industry."

The German settlement received at the beginning a township organization and judiciary. Property rights were strictly regulated and official records kept. Agriculture, viticulture and various industries were developed, and in 1691 the first paper mill in America was established there. There, also, at this early period the first agitation against slavery in this country was inaugurated, an event which John G. Whittier extolled in his poem, "The Pennsylvania Pilgrim." In a comparison between the development of Germantown and Fort St. Louis lies the explanation of the historical fact that while the Germans have come to be an important element in the New World, the French influence was only transitory and local, and left no perceptible stamp on the national development, neither socially nor politically.

In 1702 Fort St. Louis, the population of which had given itself up to a happy-go-lucky mode of existence, was abandoned by the Canadian government. Poor Tonti lost his position and possessions, but afterwards participated in the colonization of Louisiana and died a poor pauper in a little settlement on Mobile bay. Fort St. Louis existed, but only as a trading post, until 1718, when it was totally destroyed by the Indians of the vicinity. It is interesting to note that the savages gave as an excuse for this act the statement that the French had become intolerably immoral. Intolerance from a moral point of view and supersensitiveness were never prominent characteristics of the Indian nature. Their peculiar act and more peculiar explanation, therefore, form a valuable commentary on the methods of life then and there prevailing. As a whole the Illini lost more than they gained by their intercourse with the French, and the brandy introduced by the latter had as demoralizing an effect as opium exerts on the Chinese. Effeminated and morally corrupted, these Indian associates of the French soon became unable to defend themselves against their robust enemies in the north and east; most of them, therefore, went south, down the Mississippi, where they dissolved their tribal relations, and, to a large extent, were lost sight of. Those that remained in their old country, the last of their tribe, were the victims of a cruel fate. Under the pretext of their having been implicated in the murder of the Ottawa chief, Pontiac, whose death was probably instigated by the English, the remnant of the Illini was surprised by his tribe (1769) and driven to their old settlement at La Vantum, where a bloody engagement took place. Beaten here, they fell back, under cover of a stormy night, to the isolated rock where once stood La Salle's formidable Fort St. Louis. Here they sustained a twelve days' seige, at the end of which their provisions were completely exhausted. Then those who still felt strength enough for the ordeal left their rocky eyrie to sell their lives as dearly as possible. They were slaughtered to the last man. With a wild war-whoop the cruel enemy, after this bath of blood, hurried up the rock, where the mad carnage began anew. Pitilessly the tomahawk flew through the air and fell upon the heads of the poor victims who, sick and exhausted, had remained behind. Only one, an Indian half-breed, escaped from the terrible butchery. Such was the end of this once numerous and powerful tribe, which has given our state its name, and which not only always kept faith with the white pioneers, but even helped them in their enterprises. Verily they merited a better fate—the poor Illini.

After the peace of Ryswick (1697), which put an end to his plundering and devastation in Europe, Louis XIV again found leisure to cultivate his trans-Atlantic colonies. He established a fort in Louisiana, but its existence was precarious. First, the garrison and settlers were attacked by yellow fever, and later, on account of being fully occupied with the war of the Spanish succession, Louis found himself unable to assist his Mississippi fort. In consequence of this the French saw themselves obliged to govern Louisiana independently of Canada, or, more properly speaking, to turn their southern possessions over to the tender mercies of a set of tax gatherers different from those who bled the colonists elsewhere.

Boomers began to turn their attention to the valley of the lower Mississippi, which they expected to find a land of fabulous wealth. The Scotchman, John Law, to whom the inflationists and silver cranks ought long ago to have reared a monument; that prince of financial jugglers and speculators, who, by his bank of issue, contributed so much to the financial and moral ruin of France in the reign of Louis XV, established the India company (Compagnie de l'Inde), which leased from the French government the exclusive right to "govern" and tax the provinces of Louisiana and Illinois, acquired the monopoly of the tobacco, slave, East India, China and South Sea Island trade, and procured the sole privilege of refining gold and silver. Under the influence of this rich and powerful company, and especially under the bold schemer Law, there began in the colonies on the Gulf, the Mississippi and in Illinois, an activity that was lively in spite of being unhealthy, forced and tainted with fraud. In 1718 New Orleans was founded and near Kaskaskia, in the Mississippi bottom, Fort Chartres, and this post, around which a flourishing, industrious and, considering the times, even fashionable little city developed, was henceforth the seat of the French government in Illinois. In that year not less than 800 immigrants landed at the mouth of the Mississippi and from then on they came at regular intervals and in great numbers. Many negro slaves were also brought to the new colonies. In 1722, in Cahokia, as well as in Kaskaskia, mills, factories and stores were erected. In Kaskaskia a stone church and a stone dwelling house for the Jesuits were erected. The settlement of the whole territory from New Orleans to Kaskaskia was so rapid that its division into nine civil and military districts was considered necessary. Illinois, the seventh district, was, next to that at New Orleans, the largest and most thickly settled. The commerce of Illinois was henceforth carried on, not by way of Canada, but via New Orleans, which city gained rapidly in importance. In the year 1732 the India Company was dissolved and from then on the colonies were again governed by French officers whose rule, if never brilliant, was at least tolerable. After an unfortunate campaign against the Chickasaws, during which the youthful commander of the Illinois district, Pierre d'Artaguiette, together with some of his officers and two missionaries, fell into the hands of the Indians and were burned at the stake, the Illinois colony enjoyed a long and profitable peace, while commerce, agriculture and manufactures developed very satisfactorily. Thus, for instance, not less than 1,000 sacks of flour were sent by them in 1745 to the New Orleans market, with a large quantity of lard, hides, leather, lumber, lead, furs and even wine. The transportation was effected in clumsy barges, which usually traveled together, and a round trip from New Orleans to Kaskaskia ordinarily lasted four to five months. But these long and slow journeys were were not devoid of pleasure. The boatmen landed in friendly settlements and enjoyed fishing, hunting and other sports. The return of these barges from the young metropolis at the mouth of the Mississippi was usually the cause for great jollification, for they not only brought new supplies of sugar, rice, tobacco, ammunition, etc., but also news from abroad and letters from home.

It can well be said that about the middle of the 18th century the French colonies in Illinois reached their highest point of prosperity. Spared the attacks of hostile Indians and other calamities since 1736, they could develop themselves naturally and according to their inherent peculiarities, and that is what they did. But the end was pitiful.

> "The last result of wisdom stamps this true:
> He only, earns his freedom and existence
> Who daily conquers them anew."

The last of the French colonial days in North America remind one vividly of these words of Faust. Here the material prosperity caused the moral downfall. Man cannot live by bread alone. The leading spirits, busied with cares for the material welfare of the colonists, neglected their spiritual and moral needs; the commonwealth lacked in ideal force, in spiritual endeavor; it stagnated and the rank growth of a coarse sensuality killed out the tender shoots of the growing state so that its total destruction was only a question of time. Bold and energetic as the French were in discovering and exploring new territories, they were weak and unsuccessful in the maintenance and organic development of the same, in state formation. For eighty long years they reigned uninterruptedly over the immense and rich domain stretching from the St. Lawrence and great lakes to the Gulf of Mexico. They erected forts, trading posts and missions; but in spite of all their efforts they did not succeed in colonizing more than 4,000 whites in their enormous possessions. While fully appreciative of their great services in the exploration of the New World and their attempted civilization of the natives, we cannot exempt the French missionaries from censure for their neglect to use their influence and means to establish public schools and to foster the education and elevation of the common people. Significant is the single fact that during the whole French rule, from beginning to end (after the battle of Quebec, September 13th, 1759), not a printing press was to be found in any of their colonies, while in the other colonies newspapers and books aided materially in the intellectual growth of the commonwealth.

The northern part of Illinois, especially the region of the present Chicago, was totally neglected by the French after the death of La Salle. Only when the Anglo-Saxon appeared, were the first foundations laid for the Wonder city of to-day.

PART TWO.

The Rule of the English—Emigration of the French—The Pontiac War—A Fateful Love Intrigue—Pontiac's Tragic End—The Americans Take the Helm.

"Short is the reign of tyrants," says an old proverb, and short was the English reign over the conquered northwest. Of small advantage was it to either the ruled or the rulers, and as far as the latter were concerned, it was anything but creditable.

At the time the British rule began in Illinois there were five settlements, having a total white population of 1600 persons, divided as follows: Kaskaskia 700, Cahokia 450, New Chartres 220, Prairie du Rocher 110 and St. Philip 120. Fort Chartres was the last French military post to pass over into the hands of the English. It was October 10, 1765, that the French flag had to yield to the English on the walls of the fortress, and thus disappeared the last symbol of French rule in Illinois.

It goes without saying that the French immigrants had no love for these conquerors. Not less than one-third of them preferred to leave the homes they had won after so many struggles and sacrifices, rather than to submit to the rule of the despised Britons. They went to New Orleans, Natchez, Baton Rouge, Genevieve and to the trading post of St. Louis. This was founded in 1764 by Pierre Laclede and about it there soon sprang up a flourishing little village which remains to mark the spot to this day. Only one man was left in St. Philip, and only a half-dozen in the neighborhood of Fort Chartres where formerly the elite of the French population had been found.

But the native population of the Illinois district was far more dissatisfied with the new order of affairs than even the French. Their opposition sprang from both heart and head. The French had never been despotic, but had lived with them on terms of friendship, almost of equality, sharing with them their joys and sorrows, instructing them and even intermarrying with them, so that it galled the redskins that their friends should quietly submit to the rule of the hated, heartless, selfish English. In regard to their own interests too, the rule of the English was very disagreeable to the Indians—so much so that they at once set about opposing them.

The seat of the English government in the northwest was at that time Detroit, which in 1763 came into possession of the English, and was put under the command of Col. Henry Hamilton, lieutenant-governor of the territory. Some of the duties of this gentleman cannot be better described than as characteristically English. Thus, for example, he was instructed to "drive back the settlers across the Alleghanies." For the English had no intention of colonizing the territory of the great lakes and Mississippi river; they wished rather, on account of import and export trade, to have the settlements as thickly peopled as possible along the coast. Another order given the commandant at Detroit, was to cause the Illinois settlers, who rebelled against the British rule, or rather misrule, and also their Indian allies, to be tantalized and opposed by Indians from the northeast, especially by the Iroquois to whom the government did not hesitate to offer a considerable reward for any scalps they brought in, whether of men, women or children.

The first result of British supremacy in the northwest, was the so-called Pontiac war, which marks the bloodiest epoch in western colonial history.

Pontiac, a chief of the Ottawas, and the recognized leader of the whole Algonquin family, an Indian of imperious nature and far more than average ability, formed the bold plan of forcibly putting an end to British rule in the northwest. His remarkable talent and his almost white skin, would suggest that this crafty warrior was a French half-breed; at any rate he succeeded, without raising the least suspicion, in forming a powerful federation of the Indians of the Ottawa, Chippewa, Pottawatomie, Menominee, Miami, Shawnee and Wyandotte tribes. He then arranged, on a certain day in May, 1763, to capture, either through force or cunning, all the forts in the northwest held by the English. This bold plan, which was executed with marvelous skill, came within a hair's breadth of complete success. Mackinac, Sandusky, Green Bay, St. Joseph, Presque Isle (Erie) and Venango fell into the hands of the Indians. But Detroit, the strongest, and strategically the most important point, whose capture Pontiac himself had undertaken, escaped a similar fate through chance. Here again it was an Indian girl who took a prominent role, and thus saved the English garrison. She belonged to the Ojibway tribe and had a love affair—not a Platonic one—with Major Gladwin, commander of the troops stationed at Detroit. Suspecting the danger in which her lover was placed, she did not rest until she had fully learned of Pontiac's plan to surprise the fort. The chief and 400 of his warriors, each with his weapons concealed under his blanket, entered the fort with permission of the commander, and according to program, started what was ostensibly to be a peaceable pow-wow. It had been arranged, however, by the conspirators that at a signal from Pontiac, the unsuspecting garrison should be attacked and murdered. But the cunning Indian had not made his reckoning with the Ojibway maiden, who had duly informed her lover of all that was going on. Pontiac in the grotesquely solemn fashion of the Indians, had begun an harangue and threateningly, and ever more threateningly addressed Gladwin, who was quietly sitting before him. The critical moment seemed to be at hand. Suddenly, however, there sounded a peal of trumpets and a roll of drums.

In a moment the amazed and dumfounded Indians were surrounded with glittering bayonets and drawn sabres. Rapid as this dramatic transition was, the change in the conduct of the redskins, and in the tone of their demands, was more so, and they thanked their lucky stars when they were finally dismissed with a stern warning, but with whole skins. This scare however did not deter them from making an attack on the fort the next day. But they were repulsed. Pontiac seemed to take his failure and humiliation at Gladwin's hands very much to heart, and for three months harrassed the fort almost daily, making several particularly desperate but unsuccessful attempts to capture it. When he finally perceived that he had underestimated the force of the English in the same degree that he had overestimated the power of the Indian federation, the embittered chief turned to the French officers, who, after the surrender of their forts, had been dismissed on parole by the English, and asked aid and support from them. Indeed he dispatched messengers as far as New Orleans, and could not comprehend that his former comrades and brothers-in-arms had to look idly on at the desperate struggle he was waging for the rights of both. Many another bitter conflict took place between the red warriors and their hated English foes, many another settlement was devastated, and many an emigrant's family killed or dragged into slavery before Pontiac finally (August 1765) made peace in the name of all the tribes commanded by him. Broken in spirit and bodily strength, the great chieftain, after his last disaster, disappears from the scene of events, and all that is henceforth heard of him, is, that in April, 1769, he was befuddled with liquor, at the instance of an English trader named Williamson, and murdered by a Kaskaskia Indian. St. Ange, the gray-haired commander of Fort Chartres, felt affection enough for the grim warrior to have his body removed to St. Louis and buried there. Thus at least his bones did not rest in hostile earth, and none of the despised English could tread upon the grave of their fallen foe.

Had Pontiac lived ten years longer, he would have had the great satisfaction of witnessing the disgraceful defeat of the English in Illinois and the final dissolution of English rule in the northwest.

George Rogers Clark, a brilliant and patriotic Kentuckian, conceived the idea in 1778, of capturing Fort Chartres, Kaskaskia, Vincennes—in short, the whole Illinois territory—from the English. On laying his plans before Virginia's great governor, Patrick Henry, he was assured arms, ammunition and the necessary authority, and at once set out on his campaign. He first captured Kaskaskia, taking the Creole commandant of the British fort by surprise, and, making friends of the French colonists, won over to his cause the inhabitants of Cahokia and Vincennes. This was in the summer of 1778 and thus far the very audacity of Clark's plans had made them successful. He had captured the Illinois territory without a struggle. But in the fall Col. Hamilton with a large force of English and Indians set out from Detroit, fully intending to capture Clark and his handful of "buckskins" and restore the British rule in short order. He reached Vincennes early in the winter and captured the town without a fight. Here he entered winter quarters, postponing his annihilation of Clark until spring. This was his great error, and the American's good luck, for in February, 1779, Clark, with 170 men under his command, attacked his fort and compelled his surrender. From that day the whole northwest territory has been in undisputed and peaceful possession of the United States. It was first incorporated as one of the counties of Virginia but that state afterwards (1782) ceded it to the general government.

In 1800 Ohio was separated from this "northwest territory" and Michigan and Indiana a few years later. There still remained the state of Illinois, Wisconsin and a part of Minnesota, with a combined white population of 12,282 souls. December 3, 1818, Illinois was admitted to the Union as a separate state with Kaskaskia as its first capital. Later Vandalia became the seat of the state government and in 1836 Springfield.

The earlier immigrants settled for the most part in the southern portion of the state and flourishing settlements of highly educated people sprung up in Vandalia, Belleville and other tows of southern and central Illinois. Among the first settlers in Belleville was Gustav Koerner, who afterwards became governor of the state. He is still (1893) enjoying robust health and is actively engaged in political and literary labors.

Chicago was, to a certain extent, avoided by the earlycomers and it was not until years after that the flood of immigration turned to the city on the southern shore of Lake Michigan.

FIRST CAPITOL BUILDING IN ILLINOIS.

Chicago.

Early Documents—A Miscarriage in Land Speculation—The Earliest Settlers—Erection of Fort Dearborn—Tecumseh—Massacre of Fort Dearborn—Tedious Development of the Village—Black Hawk—End of the Indian War in Illinois and Beginning of the Rapid Development of the Future Metropolis.

The bold deeds of Frederick the Great, the bloody Turkish war, which so violently agitated all Europe, the storming of the bastille, the murder of Louis XVI, the appearance of Napoleon on the world's stage, the important events in England, even the war for American independence and its immediate consequences—none of all these important scenes which were enacted in the drama of nations in the 18th and beginning of the 19th centuries, affected Chicago. The wonder-city of to-day was then only a geographical conception, an unimportant and insignificent meeting-place of fur-traders and Indians. At the time of La Salle and Tonti there was, of course, a comparatively active trade in Chicago and as early as September 14, 1699, the Jesuit priest Buisson de St. Cosne was warranted in making to the bishop of Quebec a favorable report on the Jesuit mission in the neighborhood. But this was given up about the middle of the last century and the trading post of "Chicagou" was soon outdistanced by those of Melwarick (Milwaukee) and St. Joseph.

Unfortunately there is a lack of reliable documents and reports on many an interesting event in the development of Illinois and its chief city and absolutely no care is being taken by the proper state authorities to gather and preserve such material as is still existing. One of the oldest documents relating to Chicago affords a glimpse of the early speculators.

A venturesome Englishman named William Murray, who had turned up in Kaskaskia eight years before, established in 1773 the "Illinois Land company" and in the presence of the civil and military officers of the town held a pow-wow with the chiefs of several of the Illinois tribes and received in trade from them two enormous tracts of land east of the Mississippi. In consideration of this cession he gave the Indians five shillings in cash, 250 blankets, 250 strouds (a thick cloth), 250 pairs of stroud-and-half-thick stockings, 150 stroud breechcloths, 500 pounds of gunpowder, 4000 pounds of lead, one gross of knives, thirty pounds of vermillion, 2000 gun flints, 200 pounds of brass kettles, 200 pounds of tobacco, three dozen gilt looking glasses, 10,000 pounds of flour, 500 bushels of Indian corn, twelve horses, twelve horned cattle, twenty bushels of salt and twenty guns.

In the deeds, which, however, were afterwards declared null and void by Congress, one of the boundary points was designated as "Chicagou or Garlick creek," and the site of the present city would be included in this grant.

The present spelling of Chicago is found for the first time in a letter of an Indian trader named Burnett, written from St. Joseph, Mich., in 1780, and containing this laconic sentence: "The Pottawatomies at Chicago have killed a Frenchman about twenty days ago. They say there is plenty of Frenchmen."

The name "Chicago" was officially recognized by the government of the United States in the treaty which Gen. Anthony Wayne made in Greenville, Ohio, in 1795, with the Indians of the northwest. The territory which the Indians at that time were forced to cede to the United States, included "one piece of land, six miles square, at the mouth of the Chicago river, emptying into the southwestern end of Lake Michigan, where a fort formerly stood."

Within this boundary, and on the northern side of the river, where Kinzie street commences, only one man lived at that time, Jean Baptiste Point de Saible, as the historians call him.

This first Chicago settler, who drifted here about the year 1779, originally came from the island of Hayti. By the peace of Ryswick, (September 20, 1697,) the western part of this island was ceded to the French and thereafter made extraordinary progress in its material development. As here in the west they had joyfully accepted the opportunity of intermarrying with the Indians, so among the negroes of the West Indies the French accepted the same privilege. Many of the half-breeds of Hayti, whose origin may be attributed to this Gallic peculiarity, were educated in the schools of France and afterwards attained positions of prominence at home, while the Spanish Haytiens, the inhabitants of Santo Domingo, led a precarious, semi-barbarous existence. The slaves formerly brought by Renault to Fort Chartres, came from Hayti.

Point de Saible (or perhaps more correctly Point de Sable or Sabre,. for there is no French word "Saible") was a French mulatto of the before mentioned type. Together with one Glamorgan, an adventurer from Santo Domingo, he came by way of New Orleans, to the Peoria Indians and later wandered up to Lake Michigan, where he met the Pottawatomies. Here he organized an extensive and very remunerative trade, reaching as far as Detroit and Mackinac. He was, therefore, the first Chicago wholesaler, and made Chicago, for the first time, a commercial center. Personally he is described as a good looking and very pleasant fellow who, in his solitude, had acquired but one bad habit, he would get drunk. In the year 1796 Monsieur de Saible retired from business a wealthy man. In spite of his material success, however, he does not seem to have liked Chicago, for after making his fortune here, he vanished from the scene and was heard of no more. His dwelling and storeroom, a large blockhouse built by his own hands, passed into the possession of a French trader, Le Mai, who in 1804 sold it to John Kinzie. During the last three years of his stay in Chicago, Saible had neighbors, three French Canadians, Guarie, Ouillemette and

Pettell, the first of whom lived on the West Side, the two others near the place on which in 1803 the fort was erected. None of these gentlemen had held himself aloof from the French-Indian race mixing process, for the four firesides in the four log-houses were presided over by four full-blooded Indian squaws.

Immediately after his treaty with the Indians of the northwest, Gen. Wayne recommended to the government at Washington, the establishment of a fort in Chicago, as a protection for American traders, and he afterwards came here himself to supervise the preliminary steps in the undertaking. Eight years, however, elapsed before the United States government acted on this recommendation. Capt. John Whistler with a small command of United States troops reached here July 3, 1803, in the government schooner "Tracy." He at once began, at the corner of the present Michigan avenue and River street, to erect a fort which was completed about the first of the following December. In honor of Gen. Henry Dearborn, at that time secretary of war, the new fort was called Fort Dearborn. Except for the French settlers and John Kinzie, who came here in 1804, there then lived between the Chicago and Des Plaines rivers, only Pottawatomie Indians, whose principal settlement was on the Calumet river near the present site of South Chicago.

A correct idea of the then existing condition of affairs may be gained from the following letter of Mrs. Julia Whistler, wife of the commander of Fort Dearborn: "The United States Schooner 'Tracy,' * * * * on arriving at Chicago, anchored half a mile from the shore, discharging her freight from boats. Some 2000 Indians visited the locality while the vessel was here, being attracted by so unusual an occurrence as the appearance in these waters of 'a big canoe with wings.' There were then here but four rude huts, or trader's cabins, occupied by white men, Canadian French with Indian wives. * * * * There was not at that time, within hundreds of miles, a team of horses, or oxen; and as a consequence, the soldiers had to don the harness, and with the aid of ropes, drag home the needed timbers."

Only once a year did the soldiers of the fort receive their supplies from the government, and then generally from a government vessel. How wise was the recommendation of Gen. Wayne, that a fort be erected in this neighborhood, the occurrences of the following year amply proved. To gain an adequate idea of the situation, it is necessary to view the Indian treaties effected by Gen. Harrison, and to note the dissatisfaction caused by them. President John Adams appointed as governor of the northwest territory, created by an act of Congress May 7, 1800, Gen. William Henry Harrison, who at that time was a member of Congress. He had formerly gained much experience under Gen. Wayne in Indian fighting, and proved himself a brave soldier. Gov. Harrison confined his efforts principally to making treaties with the Indians by which their lands came largely into possession of the United States. That the national government was ever cheated in these transactions is hardly to be believed, and the Indians always maintained the contrary, claiming to have been most unmercifully duped. Be this as it may, it is a fact that the United States government gained possession of the lands of the Indians of the northwest very cheaply, as is proved by the following figures:

DATE OF THE TREATY.	NAME OF THE INDIAN TRIBE.	NUMBER OF ACRES.	PURCHASE PRICE.
Fort Wayne, June 7, 1803	Delawares, Shawnees, Miamis, Pattawotomies, and Kickapoos	2,038,400	$4,000
Vincennes, Aug. 15, 1803	Kaskaskias, Cahokias and Mitchigamies	8,911,850	12,000
St. Louis, Nov. 3, 1804	Sacs and Foxes	14,803,500	22,234
Vincennes, Dec. 30, 1805	Piankashaws	2,676,150	4,100
Vincennes, Dec. 9, 1809	Kickapoos	138,240	2,700

In the same measure as the government succeeded in getting possession of the Indians' lands in the northwest the discontent among the natives increased. In addition is the fact, that the white settlers as well as the government agents, frequently acted with unnecessary harshness toward the Indians and that the English in Canada lost no opportunity to create discontent among the red men and incite them to begin hostilities against the federal government. In consequence of the conditions thus created it was inevitable that the decision as to the final possession of the great northwest, east of the Mississippi be left to the sword.

An important and in many respects highly interesting role in this crisis was played by Tecumseh, a gifted and influential chief of the Shawnees. He was born near the present site of Springfield, Ohio, in 1768. While he was still a child his father fell on the battle field, a fact not calculated to inspire him with any high degree of affection for the whites. His own baptism of fire he received in Kentucky at the age of 20 when at the first volley he succumbed to the "bullet fever" and ran away as fast as his legs could carry him. Through more than ordinary prudence and valor, however, he distinguished himself in the bitter conflicts which preceded the treaty of Greenville. About the year 1805 he also tried to execute the plan which had caused the downfall of Pontiac —to form a union of all the Indian tribes of the west against the whites.

He was greatly assisted in all his undertakings by his brother, Ellskwatawa, commonly called the "Prophet," who exercised a remarkable influence upon the redskins. The dissatisfaction among the Indians was, of course, favorable to the plans of the brothers. They asserted that the chiefs were unduly influenced, by brandy or bribes, to make the various treaties effected by Gen. Harrison, that the territory affected by these treaties belonged to the various Indian tribes and families and that therefore individual chiefs had no right to dispose of it or any part thereof. In spite of the most importunate warnings of Gov. Harrison the two brothers, with indefatigable zeal and persistency, labored hard to arouse a warlike spirit among all the Indian tribes from the region of the great lakes to the Gulf of Mexico.

In the year 1806 they came to the vicinity of Chicago to incite the Pottawatomies to deeds of violence and to induce them to join the federated Indians. Their failure to accomplish their purpose was due partly to the officers of the fort but chiefly to the efforts of John Kinzie, who was highly regarded by the Indians.

In August, 1810, Tecumseh was invited by Gov. Harrison to a "quiet talk" and with 400 warriors, all fully armed, betook himself to Vincennes, where Gov. Harrison's headquarters then were. He was asked to take a seat on the veranda of the governor's house but proudly refused, saying: "Houses were built for you to hold councils in and Indians hold theirs in the open air." Thereupon Gov. Harrison went out to meet the haughty chief who received him with a speech, eloquent in the true Indian fashion. At the conclusion of his harangue he was asked to take a seat beside his "father" (Gen. Harrison) but gravely refused, saying: "The sun is my father and the earth is my mother. On her bosom I will repose."

In the discussion which followed, Tecumseh deported himself in such a violent and threatening manner that negotiations were broken off. The next day he apologized for his conduct and the conference was resumed, but without result, and the agitation of the brothers, and the general discontent of the Indians continued. Soon the Pottawatomies, the savages near Chicago, began to grow uneasy; the young warriors heeded not the advice of the older and wiser chiefs, and began to listen to the schemes of the brothers. While Tecumseh was engaged in organizing the Indians of the south, the Prophet, November 11, 1811, made an attack at Tippecanoe on the troops of Gen. Harrison, but was repulsed with heavy losses on both sides.

After the breaking out of the war of 1812, Tecumseh allied

himself with the English in order to wreak his vengeance on
Gen. Harrison, whom he hated bitterly. From the English
he received command of the Indian forces, and took a prominent part in the principal conflicts of 1812 and 1813. In
recognition of his bravery and ability, he was made a brigadier-
general on the battlefield of Maguaga where he had been
dangerously wounded. The cut here given represents him
in his uniform as an English general.

His aversion to Gen. Harrison and his staff was so great
that he refused to participate in any conference where one of
them was present. This fact, however, did not deter him, after
the successful siege of Fort Meigs, where he commanded 2000
Indian warriors, from preventing the proposed slaughter of the
American prisoners. During the retreat of the British, after
the battle of Lake Erie, Tecumseh who always fought desperately, in the very front ranks, was again severely wounded.

Pathetic to a high degree is the end of this remarkable
chieftain. Even before the decisive battle on the Thames in

Canada, October 5, 1813, where he commanded the right wing of the English, he believed defeat inevitable and rather than survive the triumph of his enemies decided to seek death on the field of battle. He laid aside his sword and uniform and once more put on the regulation war dress of an Indian chief. With a wild war-whoop he dashed into the midst of the conflict and soon found the desired end. Tecumseh was indisputably one of the most prominent and intelligent of the Indian leaders, and would undoubtedly have become a statesman and soldier of renown had his earlier education been of a different character.

Closely connected with the agitations of Tecumseh, and the Prophet and the intrigues of the agents of the English, was an event which cast its awful shadows over the very beginning of Chicago, the massacre of the garrison of Fort Dearborn.

This took place in August 1812. Saturday, August 9, a friendly Pottawatomie chief, Winnimeg, hurried unexpectedly into the fort. He brought a letter from Gen. Hull, commander of Fort Detroit, to Capt. Heald, who, after the transfer of Col. Whistler, had command of Fort Dearborn. For weeks the situation of the garrison had been very critical. The Indians who hung around the fort day by day became more threatening and now bad news from the east! The letter announced that the United States had declared war against England June 12, 1812. Three weeks before Mackinac had fallen into the hands of the enemy. Fort Dearborn was to be abandoned and the garrison, if possible, was to go to Detroit by land. The supplies and ammunition in the fort were to be disposed of according to the discretion of the commander.

It was believed that the contents of the letter could be kept secret from the Indians, but Tecumseh had taken good care to fully advise his red brothers of the turn affairs had taken and they were in no mood to forego any of the advantages offered by the situation. Allured by the prospect of plunder, new bands of Indians arrived almost hourly. Besides a great quantity of various kinds of merchandise there were stored in the fort immense supplies of powder and whisky, and powder and whisky were just what the Indians desired. They decided therefore, to butcher the garrison and only awaited a favorable opportunity. Capt. Heald had only forty-five men and two officers under his command and there were but twelve militia men in addition. Part of his men were sick so that only forty of the garrison were able to bear arms. Their chief duty was to protect twelve women and twenty children. The Indians surrounding the fort were 700 strong.

After the arrival of Winnimeg a council of war was held in the fort, but on account of the decided difference of opinion no definite action resulted. Winnimeg advised leaving the fort at once, abandoning to the Indians, arms, ammunition, whisky —everything. Capt. Heald, however, wished to give the Indians in return for a promise of safe conduct, everything but what they wanted—i. e., arms, whisky and ammunition. Lieut. Helm, Ensign Ronan and a majority of the men were in favor of remaining as long as possible in the fort in hopes of reinforcements. None of the unfortunates had much hope of escape. The arrival, on August 13, of Capt. William Wells, Indian agent in Fort Wayne, with thirty friendly Miamis, cast the last faint ray of sunshine into the gloomy camp. Wells, the uncle of Mrs. Heald, had received news of the precarious condition of the garrison, and had voluntarily come to afford it relief if possible. He well knew how to deal with Indians, in peace or man to man on the battlefield. When a boy of 12, during an Indian war in Kentucky, in which his father played a conspicuous part, he was stolen by a Miami and adopted by their great chief, Little Turtle. Then he became the chief's son-in-law, having married one of the Misses Little Turtle. But he soon tired of this interesting family, and of Indian life, and one fine morning told his wife's relatives that he would take his family and return to the whites. Later, under Gen. Wayne, he distinguished himself in many a hot combat against the red men. Since the peace of Greenville, however, he lived in perfect harmony with the tribe to which his wife had belonged.

Wells urged an immediate abandonment of the fort, and agreed with John Kinzie and Capt. Heald as to the advisability of destroying the arms, whisky and ammunition. This was done. When the Indians saw keg after keg of their beloved fire water rolled into the lake, their wrath knew no bounds.

On the morning of August 15, about 9 o'clock, the gates of the fort were opened and the garrison marched out. Fifteen of Capt. Wells' Miamis march at the head. Then came the band—playing a funeral march! In the middle, in wagons or on horseback came the women, children and the sick, guarded by the few able-bodied soldiers; the other fifteen Miamis formed the rear guard. John Kinzie, although warned by a friendly Indian, also went along, hoping that if worst came to worst, his influence with the natives might prevent bloodshed. His family had already been taken in canoes by friendly Indians to a hiding place in the vicinity of St. Joseph. The last man had hardly left the fort when the Indian hordes like a pack of hungry wolves, rushed howling into the building, but of that which they most eagerly sought, whisky and powder, they found no trace.

According to an agreement with Capt. Heald 500 Pottawatomies escorted the garrison from the fort. They marched along the lake shore on an Indian trail. About 100 yards west of this trail, and perhaps a quarter of a mile south of the fort, there was a row of sand-hills which completely cut off the view to the prairie. As soon as the Indians arrived at the first of these hills they made a detour to the right, marching along to the west of them and cut completely off from the the sight of the people from the fort who continued along the shore between the lake and the hills. Availing themselves of their protection the Indians hastened on and about a mile and a half from the fort made an ambuscade and awaited the approach of the unsuspecting garrison. They did not have long to wait. Soon Capt. Wells, riding well in advance of the troop, appeared, but caught sight of the Indians almost as soon as they did of him. Realizing in a moment what had happened, he wheeled his horse and dashed back to report to Capt. Heald. Their worst fears had come to pass. The hundreds of Indians had lured them from the fort and now meant to butcher them. There was but one thing to do—sell their lives as dearly as possible and protect the helpless women and children to their last breath. The soldiers did not stop to draw up the wagons and make of them a rude shelter from the bullets of their foes but dashed on up the hill, hoping by a brilliant charge to dislodge their enemy. In this they were partially successful, but new hordes of the red devils suddenly appeared in the rear and in an instant captured the almost helpless wagon train. The soldiers came back, but too late! The wagons were already captured and the red men outnumbered the soldiers twenty to one. Around the wagons the struggle was fiercest. Hand to hand the white and red men fought and fell. Among the first who was cut down was Capt. Wells. Mortally hurt with the blood pouring from a wound in his head the brave fellow rode up to Mrs. Heald to bid her farewell and send a last message to his wife and children. Then he rode back to fight while his strength lasted. In a moment he fell dead from his horse, but the red fiends instantly picked up the body and carried it away. The head was hacked from the trunk and the brave heart torn from the breast, cut into little pieces and given by bloody fingers to the various chieftains, who ate the still warm flesh, hoping thus to gain for themselves some portion of the heroic spirit that had dwelt therein. Wells was not the only man to fall, however. The whole encounter lasted but ten or fifteen minutes and when it was over there remained of the 132 white persons, who had but a few moments before left the fort under promise of safe guidance from the Indians, but twenty-five men, two women and eleven children—all more or less severely wounded.

The most horrible incidents in this massacre were the slaughter of a whole wagon load of little children by a young buck, and later the murder by the squaws of the sick and wounded soldiers. Capt. Heald had surrendered only on the express condition that the lives of the prisoners be spared—but in spite of this many of the helpless whites were killed in cold blood, and all were cruelly treated. The scene of this horror was near 18th street where it crosses Prairie and Indiana avenues.

Besides Capt. Wells, Ensign Ronan and Surgeon Van Voorhis were among those slain. Capt. Heald, Lieut. Helm and their wives were among those severely wounded. The escape of Mrs. Helm, a daughter of Kinzie, was remarkable. A young warrior had seized and was trying to tomahawk her, when an older Indian, evidently a chief, ran up and dragged her away from her captor. He then carried her to the lake and plunged her into the water and the unhappy woman expected to be drowned. Soon, however, she noticed that the old chief was carefully holding her head above water, and looking closely she saw that her captor was Black Partridge, her husband's friend, who had used this strategy to save her life. She was afterwards taken to her parents in Detroit. Her husband also escaped with his life, but was held captive by the Indians until the payment of a heavy ransom. Mrs. Heald was wounded six times. She, with her husband, was taken to St. Joseph, and there kept until both had recovered. Capt. Heald was afterwards paroled by the English. In the evening after the massacre, the Indians celebrated their bloody work by firing Fort Dearborn.

The ruins of the fort were still smoking when the red devils left the scene of their carnage, taking their booty with them—leaving their victims unburied behind. Quiet reigned once more in the youthful settlement—a quiet as profound as when the first French explorer put foot upon the virgin soil. The log huts were desolate and deserted, the tilled fields were laid waste and the store houses empty and plundered. The only man who escaped the great disaster without injury was the French half-breed, Antoine Ouillemette, who still dwelt, as before, with his family on the West Side, tried to get his fur trade in shape again and finally founded, a few miles north of Chicago, the little villiage of Wilmette.

The plan of connecting Lake Michigan with the Illinois and Mississippi rivers, proposed by Joliet as early as 1673, came one step nearer realization in 1814 when President Madison, in a message to Congress, pointed out the great advantages to be derived from such a connection. The first direct effect of the message was the re-erection of Fort Dearborn. Capt. Hezekiah Bradley, appointed by the government for this purpose, arrived in Chicago July 4, 1816, with two companies of soldiers. The first act of the new comers was to gather the bleached bones of their predecessors and bury them in the garrison cemetery, which was then located on the spot now occupied by the Lake Front Park. The new fort was erected on the site of the old one but was built on a better plan and was considerably larger. In consequence of peace being declared between England and the United States, February 17, 1815, and the rebuilding of Fort Dearborn, trade and commerce began to flourish once more in the neighborhood of Chicago. The first to return to their deserted home was the Kinzie family (1816). The firm of Detroit fur-traders, Conant and March, founded a branch establishment in Chicago in 1817, and a certain John Crafts was their foreman. John Jacob Astor, a German of New York, who had succeeded in establishing a fur-trading business that soon rivaled that of the Hudson Bay company, sent his agent, Gurdon S. Hubbard, to Chicago in 1818. John Kinzie, who was by trade a silver-smith, and at first dealt in furs only incidentally, was among those who did business with Hubbard. The Astor branch became so successful that Conant and March could not compete with it and were compelled to sell out to Astor. In 1819 the first Milwaukee man came here and he never had cause to regret the change—this was Jean Baptiste Beaubien, an old fur-trader, who afterwards played an important role in the development of the city. He was an enterprising man and very rich, for those days.

Furs, at this time, comprised the staple article of Chicago's trade. At regular intervals the Indians brought into town the results of their hunting expeditions. The fur-traders then sent the skins in small vessels to the Atlantic coast, from where they were shipped to Europe. That this trade was carried on with any remarkable degree of honesty cannot be asserted. Those Indians who had been in constant intercourse with the whites, had become more and more demoralized since their first contact with the French, and by the beginning of the present century, were helpless slaves to alcohol. Characteristic is the following remark of Topenebe, a prominent Pottawatomie chief of not less than 80 years, who, during a public address before the great Indian meeting in Chicago in 1821 with impressive solemnity said: "We care not for the land the money or the goods; it is the whisky we want, give us the whisky."

After the conclusion of the treaty made at this gathering, the appetites of the noble advocates of fire-water were partially, at least, appeased by the government land commissioner who gave them seven kegs of whisky. During the next twenty-four hours not less then ten cowardly murders were committed in the Indian camp. Among the Americans in those days there were of course some humanitarians who tried, both by kind teaching and stern laws, to save the Indian from the terrible consequences of whisky; but the traders, who reaped their profit from the misery of the redskins, did not favor these kindly measures, nor in their time did the French officers and post commanders. In this regard the following letter, written in 1695 by Cadillac, the commander of Fort Michilimackinac, to a friend in Quebec, may be quoted as showing the attitude of the French. With true Gallic cynicism he writes: "What reason can one assign that the savages should not drink brandy bought with their own money? This prohibition has much discouraged the Frenchmen here from trading in the future. It seems very strange that they should pretend that the savages would ruin themselves by drinking. The savage himself asks why they do not leave him in his beggary, his liberty, and his idleness; he was born in it and wishes to die in it—it is a life to which he has been accustomed since Adam. Do they wish him to build palaces and ornament them with beautiful furniture? He would not exchange his wigwam and the mat, on which he squats like a monkey, for the Louvre!"

Whisky was the principal article which the traders gave the Indian in exchange for his furs—a fact due not only to the redmen's natural love of "fire-water," but quite as much to his utter inability to drive a shrewd bargain when in a mild state of inebriety. Often dishonest traders would get an Indian befuddled with liquor and then mercilessly fleece him. Naturally enough the after effects of a redman's debauch were peculiarly exasperating, for almost invariably, as his brain cleared, came the cheerful consciousness that he had been stripped of all his worldly possessions. As a result the commercial relations between the Indians and the whites were often unpleasant, and not infrequently called for government interference. Soon after Fort Dearborn was rebuilt, the secretary of war established, both there and at a fort in Green Bay, factories, so-called, or agencies through which the Indians and traders were to make exchanges on an honest basis. But the experiment was not a success. The factories fell into the hands of unscrupulous and dishonest men, and the Indian soon learned that he had merely fallen from the frying pan into the fire. Both he and the government were cheated while the whisky anarchy grew stronger than ever. So strong, in fact, that the government found itself obliged to give up its paternal and quasi-socialistic factory system, which, in 1822, passed into the hands of Astor. The Knickerbocker pelt-dealer thus got control of the fur trade of the northwest, and so made an enormous fortune.

Fortunately Chicago commerce soon outgrew these primitive business methods, and became much more diversified and healthful.

As early as August 24, 1816, a national commission consisting of Gov. Edwards, of Illinois, William Clark and A. Chouteau, met in St. Louis, the representatives of the Pottawatomies, Chippewas and Ottawas, and tried to secure the surrender by the Indians of enough land for the already projected Illinois and Michigan canal. According to the official documents, this canal was "to connect Buffalo with New Orleans," and it was in its interest that the great Indian meeting of 1821 was held in Chicago. This was a most important event in the development of the city. By virtue of the treaty then concluded with the Indians by Gen. Lewis Cass, and Solomon Sibley, with the assistance of John Kinzie and Beaubien, certain lands necessary for the construction of the canal were obtained, and the troublesome redmen crowded away from the eastern shore of Lake Michigan.

The preparations which had to be made for this meeting by the national commission and by the few residents of Chicago, were in keeping with the importance of the occasion. Fifteen thousand Indians had to be so fed and cared for that they should be satisfied and yet not so well entertained that they become unmanageable. The task of the national commission was by no means easy: to come to a satisfactory understanding with the sixty-four chiefs who represented the various tribes interested. The Indians were loath to give up the rich and fertile hunting grounds they had learned to love and they noted with grave apprehensions how, more and more they were being crowded out of the fruitful region of the great rivers and lakes of the northwest and into the inhospitable and remote sections of the country. The negotiations lasted several weeks and were not always conducted in the smoothest manner possible. Many an eloquent and poetic word was spoken by the red man, many a one which sounded like a lamentation for the inevitable destruction of a once powerful people, but there was also many a word which showed the utter demoralization into which some of the tribes had already fallen. It was on August 29 that the treaty was finally arranged to suit all parties and was subscribed to by the chiefs. The formality of their signing the document was complied with by having each chief mark a cross after his name which had already been written down in English characters. Sixteen white witnesses then signed their names and the transfer to the United States of five million acres of land was concluded. In return the Ottawas and Chippewas were to forever receive an annual payment of $1000 from the government and the Pottawatomies one of $5000, and in addition $2500 a year was to be expended by the government in providing the Indians with instruction in blacksmithing, agriculture, etc.

By this treaty the great canal project was assured and from it dates the first powerful impetus to Chicago's development.

By the ordinance of March 30, 1822 Congress gave the state the right to construct a canal through the government lands according to certain fixed plans. In addition, the state of Illinois was granted a strip of land ninety feet wide on each side of the canal and Congress appropriated $10,000 to defray the cost of the preliminary survey. Thus were made, on paper at least, the beginnings of the canal, but not until much later, July 4, 1836, was the first shovelful of earth turned in the great undertaking. In the meantime enormous financial difficulties had been met and overcome.

During this period the political history of Chicago was less important than vicissitudinous. Shortly after the organization of the territory of Illinois, the region in which Chicago lies was a part of St. Clair county, soon thereafter it was assigned to the new county of Madison; in 1819 it was transferred to Clark county, which extended to the Canadian boundary; then in 1821 it belonged to Pike, in 1823 to Fulton and in 1825 to Peoria county. The settlement, Chicago, was then scarcely deserving of a name.

The number of the settlers varied. The increase was slow and irregular. Only after the survey of the region by the canal commission, August, 1830, did the village of Chicago receive a fixed organization. It was bounded by Kinzie, State, Madison and Des Plaines streets, and contained about one-half a square mile. In 1831, Cook county was organized, and Chicago became the county seat. The county was named in honor of Daniel C. Cook, who played an important role in the history of Illinois as a politician, newspaper-man, first member of Congress from this district and as judge.

In 1823 the authorities of Fulton county levied a tax of one-half per cent on all personal property with the exception of household effects. The result of the levy was $11.42, and the value of the assessed property, $22.84. At this time the town collectors were still honest.

A tax levied in Peoria county in 1825, gave a better result $90.49. The fur company paid the highest tax, $50.00, then followed Beaubien with $10.00, Jonas Clybourne with $6.25, Alexander Wolcott with $5.72, John Kinzie with $5.00, Antoine Ouillemette with $4.00 and Beaubien's rich father-in-law, La Framboise, with $1.00.

The first election took place December 2, 1823. John Kinzie was elected justice of the peace, and two years later Archibald Clybourne, Chicago's first butcher, who had come from Virginia in the meantime, was elected constable. At an election held August 7, 1826, in the house of the Indian agent, Wolcott, a son-in-law of John Kinzie, there were thirty-five voters, almost three-fourths of whom were French Canadians or half-breeds. The judges of election were John Kinzie, John Baptiste Beaubien and a half-breed named Archibald Caldwell or Sauganash. This Caldwell is one of the most interesting figures among the pioneers—a man who served to such good advantage, both Indians and whites, that he deserves to be held in grateful remembrance by future generations.

Archibald Caldwell, or "Billy" Caldwell, as he was more commonly called, was born in 1780, and was the natural son of a certain Col. Caldwell, an Irishman, stationed in the British fort at Detroit, and a Pottawatomie maiden, who is reported to have been of remarkable beauty and extraordinary intelligence. As the son, in addition to possessing a singularly sweet and straightforward nature and a helpful and kindly disposition, had inherited all his mother's wit and not a little of her famous beauty, it is to be regretted that no picture of either has been preserved.

When a boy he attended the Jesuit school in Detroit, learned to read and write English and French, and mastered the principal Indian dialects of the northwest. But little else is known of him during his youth, except that on account of his fine, slim figure the Indians called him "Tall Tree." Later both the whites and redskins of the northwest called him merely "Sauganash" (the Englishman).

In early manhood he became a close and devoted follower of Tecumseh, and from 1807 to the latter's death on the battlefield of the Thames, October 5, 1813, he was the great chief's most trusted friend, his messenger and secretary. In all the bloody scenes through which he passed at Tecumseh's side, he distinguished himself by his strength, skill and valor. He first came to the region around Chicago as a messenger from Tecumseh to the Pottawatomies, shortly before the massacre of Fort Dearborn. As he was, like his chief, a humane man, and not inclined to the cruelties practiced by the Indians, he did his best to prevent the massacre of the whites and failing in this, he accomplished, at least, the salvation of the Kinzie family. Later, as he became better acquainted with the Americans, his love for the English grew cold, and about the year 1820 he cut loose from his former allies and settled in the neighborhood of Fort Dearborn. In 1826 he was appointed justice of the peace in Peoria county and during the early elections regularly officiated as judge or clerk. He was a true friend of the whites and exercised in their favor a strong influence upon the Indians. The threatened revolt of the Winnebagoes and Pottawatomies in 1827, which would undoubtedly have been but a repetition of the horror of 1812, was prevented only through Sauganash and his friend, Shawbonee, chief of the Pottawatomies. The fact that the Indians in the neighborhood of Chicago did not go on the war-path with Black Hawk is due solely to the healthful influence of Sauganash. He always endeavored to make the blessings of Caucasian civilization accessible to the Indians, and when in 1832 a certain Watkins established a private school in Chicago he offered to pay for the clothing, books and tuition of all Indian children who would attend it. No one, however, accepted this generous offer, for the Indians did not wish their children to be dressed after the fashion of the whites.

Sauganash also strove to check polygamy among the Indians, thereby, however, giving rise to sarcastic criticism—his red brothers alleging as the reason of his objection to polygamy, that he had been unfortunate in the choice of a wife and found one more than sufficient. His spouse was the daughter of a well known Indian chief and soon after her marriage won for herself a reputation as an Indian Xantippe. Strong and courageous as Sauganash otherwise was, before her he struck his colors, and his white neighbors were fond of relating how shrill and angry words from his wigwam used to break the stillness of the night—and the voice was not that of Sauganash. The only child of this marriage died in infancy.

In adjusting difficulties among the Indians, or between them and the whites, as well as in negotiating treaties, Sauganash rendered his contemporaries many an important service. It was in recognition of this fact that the government granted him a pension. Proof of his nobility of character is an incident which forms, as it were, the finale of his public career. In the year 1836 the government caused the Indians in the vicinity of Chicago to assemble in the town for the last time before being transferred to their new reservation on the Missouri near Council Bluffs. The Indians did not take at all kindly to this change and the plans of the government would undoubtedly have failed of peaceful execution but for the aid of Sauganash. He volunteered to give up the home near Fort Dearborn, which had grown very dear to him, and to leave his many friends in order to share the fate of his people. He then personally superintended the removal of the Indians, which was successfully accomplished.

Another kindly deed of Sauganash was to deny certain campaign stories circulated in 1840, about his former foe, Gen. Harrison, then a presidential candidate. The general was charged with cowardice, and Sauganash and his friend Shawbonee, both of whom had opposed Harrison under Tecumseh, wrote a pathetic letter, in which they speak not only of the bravery, but also of the humanity and kindness of the old Indian fighter.

Sauganash did not long survive his transfer to the "Wild West" of that day, dying when 62 years old, in Council Bluffs, September 28, 1841.

One of the first hotels built in Chicago, and the first building not a log-house, was named after Sauganash. While it was in course of construction, the friends of the proprietor, Mark Beaubien, suggested that it be named in honor of some great man. Thereupon Beaubien delighted his friends and neighbors by declaring that the new hotel should be called the "Sauganash."

Young Chicago was very proud of this frame palace, which was situated on the corner of Lake and Market streets. For nearly three decades, under various proprietors, it enjoyed an excellent reputation, but on the night of March 4, 1851, together with various other buildings, it was burned down—probably by an incendiary.

A great many historical facts are coupled with the Sauganash hotel. For years it was the center of social and political Chicago; here J. B. Beaubien founded his debating society in which the inhabitants of the young city were wont to spend many of their leisure hours. In the evening Mark Beaubien

"THE SAUGANASH," AS ERECTED BY BEAUBIEN IN 1832.

would delight the dancers with his tuneful fiddle; once in a while a ventriloquist or juggler gave exhibitions—an event which never failed to cause a joyful break in the monotony of frontier life. Finally in 1837, the "Sauganash" was even transferred into a theatre, for the use of a band of itinerant players who, having reached Chicago, determined, for good and sufficient reasons, to remain here. In spite of the protests and prayers of these pioneers of art, the relentless city fathers straightway proceeded to impose a tax of $100 on this new temple of Thespis.

Aside from the saltatory delights afforded by Beaubien's fiddle, Chicago, in the earliest days, enjoyed few social pleasures. Once in awhile there was a big wolf or duck hunt, in which all took part, but the hunting ground was usually confined to what is now the businesss center of Chicago—then but thick woods or dreary swamps.

The debating society however was not the only method of culture enjoyed by the pioneers of Chicago. In 1816 the first public school was established by a superannuated soldier, formerly of the garrison of Fort Dearborn. Besides five of the Kinzie children, he had to instruct four youngsters from the fort. In 1820, a sergeant, also from the fort, continued the work of education begun by the old private. In 1832 the school system had assumed very considerable dimensions. When John Watkins came to town and announced himself as professor of sciences and belles-lettres, Col. Richard T. Hamilton generously put a stable at his disposal. The room was twelve feet square and desks and benches were manufactured with a view less to elegance than durability, out of old dry-goods boxes. There were twelve pupils who sat at Watkins feet—four white children and eight half-breeds of various degrees.

The first baptism took place in 1821, when the Jesuit father, Stephen D. Badin, baptized a son of Beaubien. The first sermon was delivered in 1825 by a Baptist minister, Isaac McCoy, who on invitation of Indian Agent Wolcott came to Chicago on ration day of the Indians, and attempted to instruct his red brothers in the Protestant religion.

During the early '30's a certain progressive turn of affairs is noticeable in the flourishing settlement; the characteristically Indian and the half-savage began to yield to a better civilization. Heretofore the men had been in the habit of dressing more or less in the Indian fashion, and beard and hair had been neglected. At this epoch, however, modern clothing made its appearance, and there was a more frequent and general use of comb, brush and razor; and the women! Most of them now rejoiced in leather shoes and many went to church in dresses and hats of modern material, where but recently the naive barefoot, with colored kerchief and home-spun and home-made garments, had set the prevailing style.

The list of voters in 1830 contained but twenty-four names, or eleven less than in 1826, but more of the voters were American and fewer French-Canadians. Things were already getting too fine for the French half-breeds, and they commenced to seek less civilized regions. Chicago at that time contained fifteen log houses and about one-hundred inhabitants, most of whom had settled on the West Side, at Wolf's Point, where the Chicago river divides into the north and south branches. The course of the stream in these days differed from the one of to-day. There was a bend near the lake and it ran south for some distance, parallel to Michigan avenue, and finally emptied into the lake at the foot of what is now Washington street. It was as late as 1833 that the United States government straightened the stream out into its present channel, which from time to time has been made deeper and wider by the city authorities.

On the West Side also was the store of Robert A. Kinzie; on the North Side there was only the little house of John Kinzie, which stood opposite to the fort, and on the South Side, on the corner of Lake and Market streets, stood the "Green Tree" hotel, not so proud and fine, to be sure, as the "Sauganash" but fully able to satisfy all the demands at that time made of it. Commerce between the three sides was carried on by ferries of the most primitive description. They were private enterprises belonging to Samuel Miller, Archibald Clybourne and Mark Beaubien, but in spite of the high fare charged they never paid and on this account were continually neglected.

The first German settler, Johann Wellmacher, arrived in

Chicago in 1830. He was from Frankfurt, was a baker by trade and but 17 years old when he came to America. He made $2,500 working in the lead mines at Galena, Ill., and brought this sum with him to Chicago, where he went into business for himself. He was not successful however and died, years after, a pauper in Joliet. Soon after Wellmacher, the first Jew appeared, bearing the common enough surname of Cohen. His given name, Peter, was, however, rather remarkable for a Jew, but is attributable to the fact that his mother was a Christian. Nobody will be surprised to learn that in the first newspaper (Calhoun's Democrat, November 26, 1833) which appeared in Chicago, he advertised his "immense stock of winter clothing" at "greatly reduced prices" and that he thanked the public for the "enormous patronage" accorded him.

Trade and commerce developed in many directions at the beginning of the '30's and the immigration was large, everyone looking hopefully to the future. Suddenly, however, like a clap of thunder from a clear sky, came the news of a bloody Indian uprising—the "Black Hawk war" had begun.

It is greatly to the advantage of us Americans that the Indians cannot write. It is on this account, perhaps, that in our conflicts with the red men, we are ever the magnanimous heroes, the defenders of innocence, the noble victors in a strife into which we are always unwillingly forced, while the Indians, on the other hand, are so often bloodthirsty savages and treacherous cowards. In the interest of truth one could wish that there were an Indian historian who could describe the origin and course of the conflicts between his race and the whites.

We call savages those first Americans who were discovered with this country, but neither barbaric nor savage was their treatment of Cartier, Champlain, Jolliet, Marquette, La Salle, Tonti and a host of other early explorers and missionaries who were almost invaribly regarded by the natives as higher beings and whose wish was law.

Only when, with the little bands of the best people of Europe, came also the very worst classes in great numbers, did the character of the Indian become vicious and his treatment of the new comers change. The numberless Indian horrors, chronicled in the histories of the last three centuries, appear in a far milder light when it is remembered how much the Indians suffered from the greed, brutality and viciousness of those whom they had joyously welcomed as strangers but who in their turn had abused, oppressed or driven away their red hosts.

Indeed, it is not necessary to turn to past centuries to show how many Indian wars and Indian horrors have been caused by conscienceless whites, especially by rascally contractors and thievish Indian agents who have exposed the wretched redskins to death from cold or starvation in order to use the plunder thus obtained in drinking bouts, or by frontiersmen and adventurers of the wild west who, far removed from all restraining influences of civilization, lent emphasis to their passing wishes and whims with rifle or bowie-knife.

Thus, for the so-called "Black Hawk" war, the whites were in the first instance responsible, having driven the Indians to the very verge of despair; and even if, as the historians of the northwest comfortably relate at some length, the Indians deserved their annihilating defeat, still no one won any laurels in its administration. Were the pitiful causes less significant—less characteristic of the then existing conditions, and had the antecedent events less powerfully influenced the development of the northwest, it would not be worth while to detail them. For the less said about them the better for all concerned—but especially for those supernumeraries who, in the role of saviours of their country, lounged about the stage of public events and on this account long afterwards attracted undue attention by their self-assumed importance.

The cause of the war may be told briefly: "Ote toi de là que je m'y mette" (clear out of here, so I can come).

The Sacs, who for almost a century had held the eastern bank of the Mississippi, and who had once possessed the whole region between the mouth of the Wisconsin and that of the Missouri, had, a short distance above the mouth of the Rock river, their principal settlement, which they called Saukenuk. Here 500 families lived, forming the largest of all western Indian towns, and the main meeting place of the Sacs and Foxes. Here all their big pow-wows were held, their feasts celebrated, their religious ceremonies performed and their dead buried. For Indians, they had a remarkable and unusual love for this home of theirs, and were especially proud of the adjoining fields, some 3000 acres of the most fertile soil, which they cultivated as well as they knew how. There they were in no one's way; the nearest settlement of whites was more than fifty miles from Saukenuk and rich and fertile soil was at that time to be had elsewhere for the asking.

In spite of this, many of the pioneers turned greedy eyes toward the possessions of the savages, and moved heaven and earth to, either alone or with the help of the government, drive the Indians out of their homes.

Since the agitation of Tecumseh the relations between the Indians and whites had been reasonably pacific; but now on both sides numerous attacks and deeds of violence took place—none of them to be sure attaining any considerable dimensions.

To take for granted that the white population of that thinly settled region consisted at this time entirely of people of ideal characters, concerned only in honestly and honorably completng their hard days toil in the service of progress and culture, were an error. Together with the pioneers from Pennsylvania, Ohio and Indiana, who were partly hunters, partly farmers and stock-raisers, there was no lack of that class of border ruffians who even to-day form the inevitable companions of the worthy settlers of the far west and are as much a plague as reptiles and poisonous serpents in the hot zones. For this gang, which goes withersoever there is little danger of having to work, and where police and penitentiaries are still reposing in the womb of time, an Indian war forms an ever welcome diversion—for then there is blood and whisky and plunder.

But even the best of the pioneers have but little to interpose against such a war, for it brings money to the people and that

BLACK HAWK.

is what they lack, opens up new and fertile lands to be divided as soon as their red occupants are killed or driven away, and last but not least, furnishes an opportunity for wiping out all old scores and beginning over again. If, in addition to these facts, the reader will bear in mind that the English never lost an opportunity to stir up trouble between the whites and Indians, even going so far as to send agents down from Canada for this very purpose, he will be able to form a fairly accurate idea of the situation at the outbreak of the unhappy war whose inglorious course might easily have been conjectured by any one knowing the miserable condition of affairs.

From whatever point of view the Black Hawk war be considered, the facts remain that by it more than a thousand human lives were sacrificed, eight thousand militiamen and fifteen hundred regulars had to take the field to drive five hundred Indians, with their women and children, from hearth and home, that the campaign lasted for more than three months and cost several millions of dollars.

"Black Hawk," a chief of the Sacs, was the last Indian to play a prominent role in the history of Illinois, the Black Hawk war forming, as it were, the close of the Indian era in the state.

An adherent of Tecumseh, under whom he led over 500 warriors in campaigns against the Americans, Black Hawk disputed the legality of the treaties made by Gen Harrison in St. Louis in 1804. His principal contention was that the signatures of the Indians were fraudulently obtained by intoxicating chiefs before asking them to sign. Nevertheless he himself in the year 1816 was induced to sign a similar treaty, by which the Sacs and Foxes relinquished to the United States all their land east of the Mississippi river, with the proviso, however, that members of these tribes could dwell and hunt in these lands, as long and as far as they were under the sole control of the United States government. In consequence of this treaty by far the greater number of the Indians, under the leadership of Chief Keokuk, went to Iowa in 1823, settling on the west bank of the Mississippi. Black Hawk and his adherents, however, refused to quit their old home at Saukenuk. There they stayed, going out on their regular winter hunting expeditions and in the summer diligently cultivating the soil. Thus they comfortably provided for themselves and families. At the instigation of the settlers, however, Gov. Edwards induced President Jackson to order the military authorities to eject the Indians (1829) in case they should not voluntarily relinguish their lands before April 1, 1830, and take up their abode on the further side of the Mississippi river.

Black Hawk resolved to defend what he believed to be his rights and to defy the government. He did not make the slightest preparation to move. When, however, in the spring of 1830 the tribe returned from their hunt, Black Hawk found that a number of white squatters had seized the greater part of the land and had even burned down the Indians' wigwams and desecrated their graves by leveling off with plow and harrow the mounds of the dead. Without retaliation but not without protest, Black Hawk submitted to the inevitable, contenting himself with the little the whites had left him. At the beginning of the next winter he and his warriors went on their hunting trip as usual. The season was uncommonly severe, the hunt not at all successful, and it was with much discouragement that the Indians returned to Saukenuk, from which the whites straightway attempted to drive them. Black Hawk announced with much dignity that the land belonged to him and that upon it he intended to dwell. Thereupon the squatters petitioned the governor (Reynolds) to have the Indians removed by force. As a result 2500 militiamen and regulars advanced on foot and on horseback June 5, 1831, against Saukenuk and its little band of poorly armed, meanly clad and scantily provisioned Indians, numbering all told not more than 1300 souls. In the face of the imposing military array of the whites, who were more awful in appearance than in reality, Black Hawk and his people, under cover of night, fled to the western shore of the Mississippi, leaving the little village of Saukenuk to be destroyed by the brave army of white men.

Black Hawk then allowed himself to be scared into going to Gen. Gaine's headquarters, where he was compelled to sign a document by which he pledged himself never to return to the eastern shore of the Mississippi. This was the first act of the tragedy. In the second, Black Hawk and his band, almost crazed by the pangs of hunger, are found in a wilderness beyond the Mississippi. Neapope, one of Black Hawk's lieutenants has been hastily sent with a secret message to Canada and also to the Pottawatomies and Winnebagoes, and has returned with good news. The English, as well as their old Indian allies and relatives, stand ready to aid the refugees.

April 6, 1832, the chief prepared to return to Saukenuk, and with his 500 warriors, their wives and children, bag and baggage, crossed the Mississippi and marched straight toward his old home. This of course was in violation of the agreement Gen. Gaines had forced from him the year before. Black Hawk had intended, as he afterwards assures us, to obtain permission to remain in Saukenuk, and in case this was denied him, to help the Winnebagoes with their farming. Hardly, however, had he crossed the Mississippi, before he saw he had committed a fatal error. Through the influence of Sauganash, the Pottawatomies around Chicago resolved at the last minute not to join him, and of the Winnebagoes but few appeared. Without allies the struggle against the soldiers would be hopeless, and Black Hawk resolved to embrace the first opportunity to return to the further shore of the Mississippi, and if possible avoid bloodshed. But fate had willed otherwise.

The military authorities of the United States, in the person of Gen. Henry Atkinson, in Fort Armstrong, and the governor of Illinois, attempted jointly to carry out plans which would result in the suppression or annihilation of Black Hawk and his warriors. Not less than 100 militia companies and 1300 regulars, 300 from Fort Crawford and Fort Leavenworth, were gathered at Fort Armstrong, May 7, 1832. Besides these troops, 200 cavalrymen did guard duty between Rock Island and the Illinois river, and 200 more, under Maj. Stillman, patrolled the eastern shore of the Mississippi. Jefferson Davis and Abraham Lincoln each commanded companies in this campaign, and Zachary Taylor, afterwards president, was a colonel.

The army, divided into two troops, commanded by Gen. Atkinson and Gen. Whiteside, reached Dixon May 12, 1832. Here they met the two cavalry companies. While the infantrymen of the militia were scantily provisioned, the proud cavalry had good things in abundance, and not only both ate and drank their fill, but had large quantities of ammunition. On this account they wished to operate independently of the infantry, and were commissioned by Gov. Reynolds to patrol the country along "Old Man's Creek."

It was May 14; Stillman's bold horsemen had just secured a well-protected position about thirty miles northeast of Dixon, and had made themselves comfortable, and picturesquely grouped around the camp fire, they leisurely ate a copious meal, and the whisky flask was being diligently passed, when one of Black Hawk's spies caught sight of them. He immediately rushed back to camp with the news and Black Hawk, believing them to be Atkinson's army, sent three of his young warriors with a flag of truce to announce that the Indians were willing to enter into peace negotiations. Five other warriors were dispatched to watch from secluded points how the three were received. The bearers of the flag of truce were halted by the guard, taken to Stillman's headquarters and made prisoners. The five spies were discovered, pursued and shot at. Two received mortal wounds, but the others escaped to Black Hawk's camp. The chief was just getting ready to himself carry the white flag to the headquarters of the soldiers, but when he learned the fate of his emissaries he tore the flag in shreds and passionately asked his handful of warriors, some forty, who were then with him, to avenge their comrades. (*)

The little band of Indians, maddened by this treacherous treatment, hastened at once toward the hostile camp. No sooner did they come in sight of Stillman's heroes than the latter in the wildest confusion galloped forth to meet them. Black Hawk sought shelter and calmly awaited the attack. When within gunshot of the Indians the brave cavalrymen seemed suddenly to remember that discretion hath charms as well as valor, and so halted. Then far and wide resounded the the wild war cry of the Sacs, and Black Hawk galloped forth from his concealment brandishing his tomahawk. Behind him dashed his forty warriors firing at the valiant 200. Hardly ever has anyone disappeared so quickly from a scene of intended heroism. Like 200 madmen, the soldiers, agonized by a terrible fear, galloped away toward their camp; past it they flew, leaving all behind, past creeks and hills they sped and slackened their speed only when they arrived once more in Dixon where they believed themselves comparatively secure. Many, no longer burning to pluck the laurel wreath of fame, hastened directly home.

"Black Hawk has broken loose with 2000 of his bloodthirsty warriors." This cry of terror resounded through the whole state; the fear which the homeward-rushing cavalrymen had spread everywhere was unparalleled. The demoralized settlers rushed hastily to the nearest forts and there sought refuge—even up to Chicago the fugitives hurried—men, women and children, and at one time Fort Dearborn sheltered not less than 1000 of them.

No one was more surprised at the turn affairs had taken than was Black Hawk himself. The half-starved chief, who a thousand times had cursed his crossing of the Mississipi, forsaken by his former allies, sadly anxious for the immediate

---

* According to thoroughly trustworthy reports, this stupid violation of the rules of all civilized warfare, was caused by a too frequent use of the whisky bottle in Stillman's camp.

future and only too ready to surrender to the whites—had all at once become a much dreaded man, a terror to tens of thousands.

The benefit which Black Hawk and his followers derived from this change, consisted primarily in a hearty meal, for Stillman's cavalry was, as above mentioned, abundantly provisioned. Weapons also had been captured, and blankets and ammunition—the Indians were happy. After their meal they collected the spoils and set off in a northeasterly direction, up the Keshwaukee river to the swamps of Lake Koshkonong. After here concealing the women, children and baggage, Black Hawk set out on a recruiting expedition to the Pottawatomies and Winnebagoes. Then commenced the terrible guerrilla warfare from which the inhabitants of northwestern Illinois suffered so much. Divided into small bands the hostile Indians scattered in all directions and robbed and stole wherever they could. Many a dastardly murder and cowardly incendiarism marked their path. Especially cruel and feared was the murderous half-breed, Mike Girty, who led a band of Pottawatomies and was responsible for many of the terrors of the war. Meanwhile the militia had lost their interest in military life to such a degree that the enforcement of discipline was out of the question and the commander was compelled (May 28) to send them home. Gen. Winfield Scott with one thousand men was then ordered to Illinois from the east, a circumstance which was fateful to the little village of Chicago, crowded full as it was, of fugitives, for it was thus that Asiatic cholera was here introduced. It first broke out in the vessels which had transported the troops. The scenes at the landing mocks description. The sick soldiers were encamped by the hundreds along the sandy shore of the lake. Nearly half of them died at once. The news of this terrible scourge spread to all places connected with Chicago and the town was consequently avoided by everyone, commerce and trade were at a standstill and the terrified inhabitants fled. The remnant of Gen. Scott's men were transported as soon as practicable to the seat of war, but arrived there too late to participate in the slaughter of the Indians.

Besides the regular United States troops several thousand volunteers, recruited after the inglorious dismissal of the militia, were engaged in the extermination of the Indians. There were many skirmishes with the small, roving bands, but no battle. Black Hawk, knowing that he could not drive the troops before him, was clever enough to drive them after him.

Finally Gen. James D. Henry, commanding the third brigade, got reliable information from a French-Indian fur-trader as to the movements of the elusive Black Hawk. The Indians were hastening by forced marches westward to the Mississippi, evidently intending to escape to the further side and thus avoid punishment. When the soldiers learned of the flight of the Indians and of their desperate condition they could hardly be restrained. A wild chase began. Abandoned supplies scattered along the road, cloths, blankets, cooking utensils, worn-out and starved horses, Indian warriors too sick to flee, indicated the haste with which the enemy was attempting to escape. Where Madison, the capital of Wisconsin, now stands the rear guard of the Indians, commanded by Neapope, was overtaken by the soldiers about 3 o'clock in the afternoon of July 24, 1832. Fierce conflicts, lasting until late at night, then took place on the heights along the shore of the Wisconsin river. Black Hawk himself, who was satisfied that the whites had determined to completely annihilate his tribe, hastened to the assistance of Neapope with twenty warriors and fought desperately, hoping to cover the retreat of the main body of his followers. Under the cover of night several rafts were hastily constructed and, together with such boats as had been carried along, were filled with the sick and the helpless old men and a part of the women and children and sent down the Wisconsin. In spite of the capture of his flag-bearers through whom he had asked for peace and mercy and the unjustifiable killing of their comrades who had been sent out to see what had become of them, and in spite of many an other unmistakable sign that the white officers bore a bitter hatred towards the Indians, Black Hawk had hopes that the garrison at Fort Crawford, which guarded the mouth of the Wisconsin river, would let the old men and defenceless women and children pass by and so enable them to cross the Mississippi. But the people in the fort had no sooner caught sight of the boats than they commenced extensive preparations to kill the passengers. Fifteen Indian women and children fell dead in the boats and rafts after one of the murderous musketry volleys from the fort, fifty, who, during the panic had jumped into the river, were drowned, four old men and thirty-two women and children were captured and of the remainder, who succeeded in reaching the woods on the shores of the Wisconsin river, all but twelve either starved or were tomahawked by the merciless Menominees, who had been hired for that purpose by the whites

After Black Hawk and his warriors had dispatched the boats and rafts to their horrible fate, they again succeeded in eluding their pursuers and it was a week before the whites got traces of them—and such traces! The young trees and bushes had been peeled and their bark had served the Indians for food. Starved horses lay along the road in great numbers, but all had been carefully stripped of every edible portion. Many a warrior's dead body also, bore stern witness of the terrible want of the fugitives.

Finally they had reached the Mississippi—a few hours more and they were safe—but while, inspired by new hope, they were at work on rafts on which to cross the river, a new misfortune suddenly and unexpectedly befell them. The United States steamer "Warrior," which had been sent up the river with instructions to its commander to unite the Sioux against

Black Hawk, was returning and reached the camp of the fugitives before the almost exhausted Indians were able to seek shelter. In token of his surrender Black Hawk himself displayed the flag of truce, but when for lack of a boat he was unable to comply with the order of the commander of the "Warrior" to go on board, the latter ordered a volley of grape-shot to be fired at the half-dead savages, so killing and wounding many of them. The Indians returned the fire, and the captain thereupon continued on his trip to Prairie du Chien. The Indians now hastened their preparations for crossing the Mississippi. But the delay caused by the attack of the steamer was fatal. The soldiers were already hard on their heels. As long as he could, Black Hawk used his few, hastily constructed rafts to send as many of his warriors as possible across the river and then, forseeing the inevitable fate of his tribe, took advantage of night to flee, and sought refuge among the Winnebagoes.

The next morning, August 2, the soldiers finally reached the Indians and the longed-for slaughter commenced. With bayonets, clubbed muskets and cold lead the last of the Sacs were dispatched—even those who had thrown themselves into the river and those who had dragged their starved bodies into the branches of trees became the easy prey of the well-directed bullets of the sharp-shooters. Neither women nor children were spared. The Indians, intending to sell their lives as dearly as possible, killed twenty whites and wounded twelve. Of the red men, 150 lay dead on the battlefield and as many more were drowned. Forty Indian women and girls were captured and about 300 of the fugitives succeeded in gaining the western shore of the river. A more pitiable crowd of humanity has been seldom seen: sick, emaciated, starved, bleeding from undressed wounds—this was the last of Black Hawk's warriors. Here they were finally, where the government wanted them! There was nothing in the wide world that they could call their own, and most of their

Algonquin Indians of To-day.

friends and relatives had been sent by the whites to the happy hunting grounds of the great father. But the poor wretches were at least alive, and the constant race for life or the agonies of death were passed. Thus may have reasoned these creatures of sorrow who took it for granted that their cup of bitterness was full to overflowing. Alas! It was not long before they learned to what degree of beastly brutality even whites could degrade themselves; for Gen. Atkinson disgraced the name of humanity and civilization by letting loose upon the defenceless fugitives a band of bloodthirsty Sioux, who with their tomahawks and stone battle axes mercilessly crushed the skulls of all who could not run away or creep into the reeds along the swamps. More than 100 corpses covered the scene of the Sioux carnage. Many of the Sacs died from exhaustion while fleeing and of all who had left with Black Hawk in the spring but a mere handful returned to the place of banishment. The Black Hawk war was at an end and with this bloody finale the Indian era in Illinois terminated—the red dawn of a new and fairer day already glowed on the horizon.

Black Hawk was turned over by the Winnebagoes to the United States, August 27, and after the signing of the formal treaty of peace on September 21, he, the "Prophet," and Neapope, were kept for a time as hostages in Fortress Monroe. Later on Black Hawk was put in charge of the friendly Sac chief Keokuk, his former rival—a fact which more than anything else in his life pained the proud old warrior, who, when but 15 years old, had distinguished himself on the battlefield and who for forty-five years had been the most prominent leader of his people.

In the unhappy role of one deposed, he did something which the fallen great have of late often resorted to, but which before Black Hawk's time had never been done by an Indian—he dictated his memoirs to an enterprising publisher, and they appeared in book form in 1834. October 3, 1838, Black

Hawk, after almost completing his 71st year, finally found eternal repose—that is to say, he did not find it, for his body was stolen, and—sic transit gloria!—his skeleton was publicly exhibited as a curiosity. Even his bones had a remarkable career—until in 1855, when among other curiosities of the historical society in Burlington, they were destroyed by fire.

With all due deference to the reputation of his mother, it is very probable that this celebrated Indian was a Frenchman, or, rather a French half-breed. His personal appearance, the fact that he left memoirs, and the circumstance that in his native place, Kaskaskia, the relations between French and Indians were not well calculated to preserve the purity of either race, make this theory probable.

* * *

The Black Hawk war, the annihilation of the last Indians to fight for hearth and home, caused a sensation throughout the land. One result was that the crowd of officers, newspaper correspondents and speculators who had come from the east to the seat of war, called public attention in a new and almost unheard of manner, to the west and its rich resources, and an influx of interprising, energetic men soon followed. Manufacturing industries made great strides and speculation took its first bold chances. Various railroad projects, engineered by G. S. Hubbard, Chicago's representative in the state legislature, and by others, found but little favor outside, but the canal project made steady, although sometimes slow progress. In 1833, Congress appropriated $30,000 to deepen the mouth of the Chicago river and thus made that stream accessible to the commerce of the great lakes. In the summer of that same year, no less than 150 frame houses were erected. Chicago was incorporated as a village, August 5, 1833, and at an election, held immediately thereafter, 111 votes were cast. At that time the tax levy amounted to $48.90.

In 1834 was completed the first wooden drawbridge, a most important undertaking for the domestic trade of the town.

The bridge was erected at the foot of Dearborn street and connected the North and South Sides.

In 1833 but four ships arrived at Chicago, but in 1834 no less than two hundred vessels entered the enlarged and improved harbor.

The immigration, both by land and water, increased rapidly, and in 1835 Chicago could boast a population of 3265 souls. There were 398 dwelling houses, 4 warehouses, 29 dry goods

CHICAGO'S FIRST DRAWBRIDGE

stores, 19 grocery stores, 5 hardware stores, 3 drug stores, 19 taverns, 26 wholesale establishments and, also, not less than 17 law offices.

The first county court house, erected on the southwest corner of Clark and Randolph streets—a brick building, remarkably fine for the times, was opened to the public in 1836, and the same year the "Chicago American," a Whig organ in opposition to the "Democrat," issued its first paper.

Descendants of the Algonquins.

In the spring following a branch of the "State Bank of Illinois" was established in Chicago. In May, 1836, the first sailing vessel built in Chicago was launched, and on July 4th work on the new canal was formally begun. This important event was marked with a grand celebration, speeches being made by Dr. Wm. B. Egan and Gurdon S. Hubbard, after which there was a general jollification. It was in 1827 that Daniel P. Cook had put the canal project on a firm footing

FIRST CHICAGO COURT HOUSE.

by securing the passage of a bill granting the state alternate sections of land for six miles on each mile of the channel, to aid in its building. In 1836 the state legislature passed its canal bill, a measure of vital importance to the undertaking. The canal was finally completed April 19, 1848, almost twelve years after Col. Archer had "turned the first shovelful of earth."

The City, Chicago.

Wild Leek
The Emblem of Chicago.

DESPITE Chicago's characteristic trinity, the North, West and Southsiders, in mass-meeting assembled, October 26, 1836, unanimously agreed that the town should be given a regular municipal organization. Accordingly the legislature was petitioned and shortly after Chicago received its city charter. On the first Tuesday in May, 1837, the first election was held in the new city. William B. Ogden, later one of the western railway kings, was elected mayor. Chicago was at this time divided into 6 wards and the city boundaries were North avenue on the north, Wood street on the west, Twenty-second street on the south and the lake on the east, save for a part of section 10, which was reserved by the United States Government for a military post; in addition, there belonged to the city a half-mile strip, known as the old city cemetery, lying along the shore of the lake east of north Clark street and north of North avenue.

The Chicago of 1837 was laid out on a generous scale, covering a surface of about 10 square miles, although the population numbered but 4179 people. But the city soon enough covered the whole territory, and in 1847, an annexation of new territory was found necessary. The year 1853 brought a new extension of the city limits, and 1854 still another. In 1863,

Bridgeport and Holstein were annexed and the city made to embrace 24 square miles, divided into 16 wards. The ordinance of 1869, added still more territory to Chicago, which, shortly before the fire, contained 36 square miles, divided into 20 wards, each of which sent two aldermen to the city council.

That political greatness and commercial prosperity do not always go hand in hand the future metropolis was to learn to its sorrow. Soon after Chicago's organization as a city, a great financial panic swept over the land. A complete crop failure, in consequence of an extraordinary drouth, an unsound bank-note and paper money system, gross mismanagement of the treasury, cessation of work on public improvements and a malarial epidemic, popularly called canal cholera, numbering its victims by hundreds, added to the misery of the people of Illinois. Besides all this, Chicago suffered from a veritable craze for speculation. All branches of industry were affected, but the greatest havoc was wrought with real estate values. The price of property, especially of such as lay inside the city limits, increased with fabulous rapidity for a time, but finally a tremendous reaction set in. The result was complete business stagnation. Trade and commerce were paralyzed, goods in the warehouses could not be disposed of at any price, laboring men could find no employment, money disappeared from circulation, immigration ceased, contracts could not be fulfilled—in short, the only activity to be seen was in the seventeen law offices, where a feverish energy was displayed. Finally, to cap the climax, the United States Government removed (1837) the garrison from Fort Dearborn and sent it further west.

It was not until the middle of the 40's that under the influence of active, energetic men, the effects of the crisis began to wear off and a strong, healthy commercial spirit reasserted itself. In the last of the 40's and the early 50's, especially at the time of the German revolution, immigrants in large numbers, including thousands of Germans, came to the city; trade developed rapidly and a vigorous intellectual progress was noticeable.

CHICAGO AS A COMMERCIAL CENTER BEFORE THE FIRE—THE INDUSTRIAL DEVELOPMENT.

The construction of the Illinois and Michigan canal made, or rather changed Chicago into a trade center for the region commercially dependent on and tributary to the new waterway, which stretched 96 miles, from Chicago (Bridgeport) to La Salle, on the Illinois river. The influence of this water connection, however, was felt only gradually by the farmers of the district, for the work on the channel was frequently interrupted and the canal fully completed only in 1848. How cheap the future of Chicago was held, even in the first of the '40's, is shown by the fact that many of the laborers, who had been employed on the canal at 50 cents a day, preferred to invest their savings in land near Dunkley's Grove, Schaumburg and Elk Grove, settlements about twenty miles from town, and become farmers rather than buy two or three acres a few miles out on State street. Meanwhile the population of the city, except during the crisis of 1837 and the immediately subsequent stagnation, grew steadily but not as rapidly as in the beginning of the 50's—the era of the railroads. In 1848 Chicago had but 20,023 inhabitants; in 1850, 25,269; but during 1852 and 1853 not less than 22,000 new-comers settled in the city.

It was the railroads that caused Chicago's unparalleled development, that marvelous outstripping of all other western cities, which has ever produced and ever will produce the world over, such wonder and amazement.

The pioneer road was the Galena & Chicago Union Railway. Its charter was dated 1836, a time when in all the United States there were less than a thousand miles of railroad. Track laying, however, was not commenced until 1847, and as the construction of roads was still an infant industry but 42 miles, from Chicago to Elgin, were built within the next three years. Although outside capital has constructed most of Chicago's roads, local enterprise was responsible for the "Galena Union." Several times it seemed that the project would have to be abandoned, at first the line failed to pay even the operating expenses and public sentiment did not favor the innovation. Chicago's few capitalists were not daunted however and pushed the road on to Elgin. As soon as that point was reached the new venture proved a success and the earnings made handsome returns on the investment. From Elgin the road was extended to Freeport, where connections through to Galena were effected with the Illinois Central. Later the Galena & Chicago Union made arrangements with the Central to run its trains from Chicago through Galena to Dunleith, a point on the Mississippi opposite Dubuque. This was the Central's own terminal and gave Chicago the benefit of a direct railroad connection with the Mississippi river. In 1864 the Galena Union was absorbed by the Chicago & Northwestern, a powerful company, controlling even then 1176 miles of road and reaching northward to the iron region of the upper peninsula of Michigan and westward through Illinois and Iowa to Omaha, the starting-point of the first great trans-continental road, the Union Pacific.

Another early road was the Chicago, Burlington & Quincy, which in 1852 had but 15 miles of completed track, reaching from Aurora to Junction. In 1853, 45 miles, from Aurora to Mendota, were constructed, and in 1863 the road for the first time entered Chicago over its own tracks (on Sixteenth street), having previously used the right of way of the Galena Union.

Another road to reach Omaha and later to compete with the Northwestern and Burlington for the through freight of San Francisco and New York, was the Chicago & Rock

Island, now the Chicago, Rock Island & Pacific. Its costruction began in April, 1852, and by February, 1854, the line had reached the Mississippi at Rock Island, opposite Davenport.

The Illinois Central was the first road to receive, through the exertions of the Illinois senators and some of the representatives, Stephen A. Douglas, Gen. Shields, Sydney Breese and John Wentworth, a land grant from the United States. This consisted of 2,595,000 acres of land, almost all of it fertile, lying on either side of the right of way. In the course of time immense sums were realized by the road from this enormous land grant. The Illinois Central did not at first enter Chicago, but ran from Cairo in the extreme southern part of the state to Dunleith in the northwestern part. When it built its branch to Chicago it was given a right of way into the city along the lake shore. By the building of the North Pier an eddy had been created in the lake which began to eat away the shore line south of the pier. Various attempts were made to check the encroachments of the waves, but although millions of dollars worth of property was threatened no adequate defence against the lake currents was secured. The city referred the matter to the state and the state in turn referred it to the national government. Meanwhile the eddying waters had washed their way clear to Michigan avenue, and immediate action was imperative. Just then the Illinois Central appeared with its petition for a right of way into the city. It was given and accepted the privilege of building a track east of the Lake Front park, or in other words over the lake itself. The railway company straightway built, at large expense, a line of stone cribs some five hundred feet beyond the shore line and then inside the cribs drove piles on which the track was laid. Of course the cribs protected the shore from further action of the lake and at the time seemed a very happy solution of that difficulty. The right of way too, leading as it did into the heart of the city, was excellent, and both road and city were for a time satisfied. Later, however, many complications and expensive litigation resulted from the Central's claim to all the "made" land east of its tracks. Only during the present year (1893) has the Supreme Court of the United States settled the controversy by denying the claims of the road and vesting the ownership of the made lands in the city of Chicago.

Chicago's importance as a railroad center is demonstrated by the fact that the great trunk lines, connecting the Atlantic coast with the west, have always been anxious to secure terminal facilities here, while other cities, such as St. Louis, Cincinnati and Milwaukee, have had to incur heavy debts by issuing or endorsing bonds, in order to secure railroad connections.

The Galena Union in 1852, shared the railroad honors of Chicago with the Michigan Central and Michigan Southern roads, which in that year pushed through from the east. Then, after the Chicago, Rock Island & Pacific and Chicago, Burlington & Quincy in 1854, came the Chicago & Alton and Chicago & Northwestern in 1855, the Illinois Central and Pittsburgh, Fort Wayne & Chicago in 1857, and the Chicago & Great Eastern in 1861. The completion of the Grand Trunk road gave Chicago direct railroad communication with Quebec, Montreal and other Canadian points; just as the Michigan Southern and Michigan Central first connected it with New York and the Atlantic ports. During the next decade the railroad achievements of Chicago consisted mainly in the extension of its trunk lines over the territory lying west and northwest of Illinois. The completion of the Union Pacific in 1868, brought all the through business between the Atlantic and Pacific coasts under the control of Chicago, gave to commerce with Japan and China a new and lasting impetus, and made Chicago the distributing center for the Asiatic import trade for the millions of consumers of the Mississippi valley, just as it already was, the distributing point for European merchandise.

Through the Chicago & Northwestern, Chicago was enabled to make important conquests in Wisconsin and the iron and copper regions of the upper lakes. Like the other pioneer roads of Chicago, the "Northwestern" has shared the prosperity of the city, and is to-day one of the largest railroad systems in the world. It first appeared in 1854, under the name of the Illinois & Wisconsin Railroad, and ran from Chicago to Crystal Lake, hardly 40 miles away. At that time it did its whole passenger business in one coach attached to the regular daily freight train.

All told, there were shortly before the fire, 12 trunk lines and 29 branch roads terminating in Chicago, with 7019 miles of track. Each succeeding year increased the mileage of the roads, and with it the territory tributary to Chicago. Tables giving the earnings of the roads from 1849 to the fire, afford an approximate idea of the development of the city during this period. In 1849, the Galena Union stands in this table solitary and alone. It was operated only in the latter half of that year, and its gross earnings were but $27,418. In 1854, the gross earnings of all roads terminating in Chicago were but $6,330,-000; in 1855, $10,500,000; in 1857, $16,750,000; in 1861, $17,750,000; in 1863, $27,500,000; in 1864, $40,300,000; in 1867, $49,000,000, and in 1870, over $70,000,000.

Even before the fire, Chicago was the greatest railroad centre in the world.

The commerce of the great lakes of the northwest, far from being injured was first built up and strengthened by the development of the railroads. While at the beginning of the century, the schooner "Tracy" made but one trip a year, between Buffalo and Chicago, in order to provision the lonely garrison of Fort Dearborn, in 1840, Chicago's eastern horizon was white with the sails of the lake, grain and lumber fleet.

The schooner "Clarissa" had been launched here in 1836, and in 1840 the first side-wheeler, the "George W. Dole," named in honor of its builder, appeared. In 1842, the first propeller, the "Independence" left the first wharf—Averill's.

Accurate reports of the tonnage of the vessels clearing the port of Chicago before the 50's are lacking. In 1854 the total tonnage of the vessels entering the Chicago harbor was 1,092,644; in 1857, 1,453,417 and in 1864, 2,172,866. From that date a new system of registration was introduced, whereby the tonnage of each vessel was registered only once a year, regardless of the number of voyages made. According to this new system the Chicago fleet of 1323 vessels had in 1865 a tonnage of 228,115; in 1866, 251,077 and in 1867, 289,765. More than half of these vessels, including 8 sidewheelers, 13 propellers, 33 tug boats, 41 barges, 257 schooners and 227 canal boats, wintered in the Chicago river.

The development of the commerce of the great lakes may be judged from the fact that its tonnage considerably exceeds that of the whole foreign trade of the United States—and of this immense commerce Chicago receives the lion's share.

In 1838 Walker & Co. shipped the first grain from Chicago, only some 78 bushels, but before the fire the city became the world's most important grain market.

The growing problem of handling the immense masses of grain was solved by the invention of the steam elevator, which cheaply and quickly lifted the grain from the cars and canal boats by which it had been brought from the country, and loaded into the ships waiting to bear it by way of the great lakes to Buffalo and the Canadian ports. The inventor of the elevator was Capt. R. C. Bristol, who erected the first steam elevator in 1848. In January, 1855, the storage capacity of all the Chicago elevators amounted to only 750,000 bushels. In 1857 there were 12 elevators, holding 4,025,000 bushels and ten years later, in 1867, the capacity of the seventeen elevators then in use exceeded 11,500,000 bushels. These elevators could load and unload a million bushels of grain daily.

Through them passed the grain of the northwest and its value, converted in the east into manufactured merchandise of all kinds, was returned to Chicago for distribution through the western railroads to the original producers, the farmers. Thus Chicago became the great distributing center of the northwest, then containing a prosperous population of over 12,000,000 people. The "hard times" of 1857–58 were less felt by Chicago, perhaps, than by most of the cities of the country. In the United States and Canada there were 5123 bankruptcies with liabilities of $299,800,000. In New York every bank but one, the Chemical, failed, but in Chicago several stood firm. The Illinois Central and Michigan Southern roads both assigned in 1857, and temporary insolvency in all business seemed the rule. Things grew but little brighter during the next two years, but with 1861 came a change. Its cause, strangely enough, was the civil war. Far from impeding the city's growth or checking the volume of its business the great struggle caused an even more rapid development of the new western metropolis. Cincinnati, St. Louis and Louisville lost their southern trade on account of the war and a great deal of capital was transferred from them to Chicago, which in consequence soon excelled them even in branches of industry in which they had formerly taken the lead. Thus, for instance, the great packing industry of Cincinnati (Porkopolis) was transferred to Chicago and assumed enormous proportions.

Just as necessity had produced the elevator to facilitate the handling of grain, it later brought into existence the Union Stock Yards for the handling of cattle. These yards were first opened for business December 25, 1865, and covered an area of 345 acres. The pens alone covered over 100 acres, and hotels and other buildings 45 acres more. The capacity of the yards when opened was 21,000 head of cattle, 75,000 hogs, 22,000 sheep, 200 horses, a total of 118,200 animals. There were 31 miles of drains, 7 of streets and alleys, 3 of water troughs and 10 of feed troughs. There were 2300 gates, 1500 open pens and 800 covered ones. The water was supplied by an artesian well, 1100 feet deep. A "belt" line connected the yards with every railroad entering the city. Thirty years ago it seemed that these yards would prove ample for all times, but though their capacity has been repeatedly increased, the stock men and packers are still cramped for room. The advantages of the stock yards system were so apparent that the cattle business of the northwest was soon concentrated in Chicago, though other western cities, in order to save at least a part of their business, now copied Chicago's stock yards just as they had before copied its elevators.

The cattle and grain trade in Chicago is organized to such a degree of perfection and smoothness that a stranger, neither in the streets nor elsewhere, would be reminded that he is in the world's leading cattle and grain market. He sees neither wagons loaded with grain nor droves of cattle, the whole immense business being done, as it were, behind the scenes. Another of Chicago's business enterprises to early assume considerable proportions was the lumber trade and the allied manufacturing industries In 1871 the value of all imported merchandise exceeded $400,000,000. Eighteen banks, with a capital of $10,000,000 and $17,000,000 deposits were necessary to transact this enormous commerce, and the clearing house business amounted $810,000,000.

Just as the city grew in population and business, so the individual inhabitants grew in prosperity. There is no city in the world containing so many small property owners in comparison with the whole population as Chicago — no city in which the working classes are so independent.

The rapidity with which the city had been raised from the swamps, the ingenuity with which the purest water (this was before the fire) was introduced into every house and the drainage system, using Lake Michigan to cleanse that great open sewer, the Chicago river, justly attracted the attention of the world to the western metropolis.

Prior to 1840 the city had been poorly supplied with drinking water, which was either obtained from wells or was brought in from the lake in large barrels and sold by the gallon. The Chicago City Hydraulic Company, incorporated in 1836 with a capital of $2,000,000, had for its purpose the erection of public water works, but it was 1840 before its plant was put in operation.

PUMPING STATION OF 1854.

The pumping station was situated on the corner of Lake street and Michigan avenue, but its capacity was very limited —the steam pump used having but 25 horse power. In 1851, by an act of the state legislature, a board of three water commissioners was created and the city authorized to issue bonds to the extent of $400,000 for the erection of new water works. The building was situated on the lake shore at the foot of

Chicago avenue, and in 1854 the new works were put in operation. The water, however, was taken from near the shore, and was soon found to be impure at times, especially when the wind blew the contents of the Chicago river out into the lake. As a consequence it was decided a few years later to construct an inlet crib two miles from shore, and a tunnel to connect it with the pumping station, and this work, commenced in May, 1864, was completed December 6, 1866. Water was first let into the new tunnel March 8, 1867, and for a long time Chicago boasted of a water supply unequaled in purity, price and plenty.

The early 50's were cholera years, the fatal cases in 1854 being no fewer than 1424 out of 3834 total deaths in the city. From 1854, however, Chicago's development was rapid. In that year the inhabitants numbered 65,872 persons; in 1857 93,000; in 1861, 120,000; in 1867, 220,000; in 1871, 334,270.

In 1856 it was found necessary, in order to secure a better drainage system, to raise the streets of the city. On the average the grade was raised six feet, which secured sufficient "drop" for the sewers to empty by gravitation and also put them far enough underground to be protected from frost. Of course the houses had to be raised with the streets and the result was an exceedingly active, if not pleasant, operation. Even the largest and most massive buildings had to be raised. The gigantic undertaking was begun on the South Side, but the North and West Sides soon followed suit. Steam power was used to a considerable extent and the work progressed rapidly. So cleverly were the arrangements made and executed that the use of the buildings and the business in hotels and commercial houses were not interrupted even during the time the contractors were actually engaged in raising the structures. One of these contractors was George M. Pullman, who, in this manner, laid the foundations for his future fortune.

A characteristic incident took place under the administration of Mayor Wentworth, along in the 50's. On the lake shore, between Kinzie and Erie streets, there had grown up, in the course of time, a settlement of which Chicago was anything but proud. Numerous tumble-down wooden shanties, scattered helter-skelter over the beach, formed an ideal nesting place for an anarchistic proletariat,—rogues, whose lives were forfeit to the gallows, robbers and rascals of all degrees, in short, the lowest kind of men and women, who, in the open prosecution of their business, had become a public nuisance. The rough and ready mayor determined to rid the city of this precious crowd and chose a novel method to carry out his determination. He notified the shanty dwellers, that on a certain day their whole quarter would be burned down and he left it to the individuals to draw their own conclusions. The mayor was known as a man of his word and as one who could not be trifled with. Consequently very many took his hint and quietly decamped. Promptly, at the appointed time, Mr. Wentworth appeared with a full detail from the police and fire departments and caused the shanties to be fired. In a few moments the flames had completed their work of purification; the anarchistic republic was resolved into its primitive elements, which were then, as quickly as possible, rendered harmless and inoffensive.

In May, 1858, the first horse-car system was put into operation; there were five cars, and their run was from Lake street to Twelfth. In the following year a line was put in operation on West Madison street, and in 1860 a third line began running on North Clark street, going as far as Division.

Up to this time, in spite of the prosperity of the city and the well developed business activity, there had been a marked lack of public art institutions, higher educational facilities and substantial places of recreation—theatres, concert halls and the like. In 1855, however, the Rush Medical College was founded, and 1859 saw the establishment of the Chicago Medical College. Rice's theatre was opened in 1847, but ten years elapsed before there was another first-class play-house. Then McVicker's first welcomed the public, and with "Money" for its attraction, of course scored a great hit.

Aside from the temporary depreciation of paper money, trade and commerce thrived in Chicago during the civil war; money was abundant, business active, wages large—in brief, so prosperous were the times, that many a man was able to make his fortune then and there. Aside from the numerous bridges and viaducts which were constructed at this period, the tunnel under the river at Washington street was completed in 1869, and the one at La Salle street two years later. By an ordinance of the city council, passed in 1864, the Lincoln Park system was established, and a few years later the state legislature enacted a statute providing for the whole splendid park and boulevard system.

The development of the school system of Chicago, after 1850, was in keeping with the general progress of the city. In the year 1871, there were 40 school sites, on which were erected 41 buildings, and 11 other buildings stood on leased ground. The school houses and equipments represented a value of $1,200,000. There were 572 teachers whose salaries amounted to $444,635.

At this time also there were 192 parishes or separate religious communities, all but 36 of which had church buildings. Among them were 25 Catholic parishes with 12 convents and numerous parochial schools. There were also five Jewish synagogues. The value of all Chicago church property, shortly before the fire, was $10,350,000.

The development of the architecture of private houses kept even pace with that of public buildings. In 1837 Chicago consisted of 450 houses, almost all of which were frame. In 1871 the city numbered 60,000 buildings, 40,000 of which were of wood. In 1832 one could easily count the brick buildings. In 1854 the only marble building stood on the southwest corner of Clark and Lake streets, opposite the two-story brick "Saloon Building," which was pointed out as an edifice of considerable pretensions. In time, however, men ceased to look on Chicago as merely a place to make money and then desert, and began to regard it as a permanent home to whose adornment and beautification they were willing to generously contribute. Soon the streets were covered with fugitive frame houses, which, driven out of the town proper, sought a resting place on the outskirts of the city. As these outskirts constantly stretched out further and further the unfortunate houses were compelled almost yearly to begin again their peregrinations. As the frame structures yielded to the brick, so in turn they yielded to the stone and iron buildings. Palaces took the place of two-story buildings, colossal warehouses crowded out more modest stores, and simple dwellings gave place to magnificent and architecturally stylish residences. Michigan and Wabash avenues on the South Side, Washington street on the West Side and the portion of the North Side lying east of Dearborn street formed the favorite home-spots for the wealthy. Even the New Yorkers, with their Fifth avenue, had to yield the palm to Wabash avenue. The value of the new buildings erected in 1864 was $4,700,000; in 1865, $6,950,000; in 1866 over $11,000,000 and in 1870 no less than $20,000,000. Owing to the haste with which buildings were erected before the fire it was but natural that the proper building laws were not observed, and that, owing to a lack of expert, faithful police supervision, even the ordinary rules of safety were grossly violated. Thus it came about that even before the great fire Chicago, with its numerous frame houses and its enormous lumber districts, to say nothing of its location on an unprotected prairie, was known to be one of the worst fire sufferers in the Union. In 1863-64 there were 186 fires, doing over $355,560 worth of damage, and in 1869-70 the number of destructive fires reached 600 and inflicted loss to the amount of $871,000. In 1870-71 there were 660 fires, destroying property valued at

$2,447,845. During the nine years before the great fire there were 3697 destructive fires in Chicago, and the amount of loss sustained was $13,779,848, of which $10,851,942 was covered by insurance. Surely, Chicago had warning enough.

Chicago's Progress.

Early German Settlers—The Forty-Eighters—Social and Military Growth in the 50's — Beer Riots — Americans and Germans Unite in Opposing Slavery – Early Breweries—Douglas and Know-nothingism—Underground Railroad — Chicago's Part in the War of the Rebellion.

The part played by Irishmen and Englishmen in the development of Chicago, is so vital and intimate as to need no treatment separate from the story of the city itself. Allied so closely to the Americans by ties of language and kinship the Irish and English settlers of Chicago early lost their individuality as foreigners and became Chicagoans, quite after the manner of the man from Massachusetts, New York or Ohio. Their activity cannot be easily differentiated from that of the native-born citizens. The Germans on the other hand have not lost their identity as such. Had their manners and customs more nearly approached those of the Americans, the barrier of language would have still remained. It is therefore easy to point out the effect of their influence on Chicago's development.

Among the early settlers of the city, there were relatively few Germans, and these few were not, as a rule, men of culture or education. The cream of early German immigration to Illinois went to the southern part of the state. With the end of the great German revolution of 1848, however, came a change. The revolutionists were defeated and forced to flee from Germany. Thousands came to America where they were soon discovered to be very different from the earlier German immigrants. The revolutionists, as a rule, were enthusiasts, visionaries. Erratic, though the rank and file undoubtedly were, many of them were also liberal, progressive and well educated. Guided by sentiment, their mistakes had been those of youth.

They embraced all classes of men; thousands were simple artisans, but in their ranks were also found hundreds of professors, poets, musicians, artists, editors and professional men. As a rule, these latter were the leaders and many of them proved themselves remarkably clever and talented. Although radically progressive as a class, they had among them few competent leaders, no mature statesmen, no profound philosophers. Those who afterwards achieved success and fame in their new fatherland were mostly inexperienced young men when they came, and owe a great deal of what they are or have been to the conditions that surrounded them in the new world. They were able men but their ideas were impractical, immature, or at best, ahead of time. When they left Germany they hoped to put into execution in America the ideas which had been rejected in the fatherland. Eager, enthusiastic, impatient of delay, they reached their new home only to find here elements similar to those which had opposed them in Germany—the conservative elements. It was a conflict between the old German settlers and the new-comers, between the "mossbacks" and the "green-horns," as they respectively designated each other.

The Germans, who had lived for some time in the United States and become accustomed to American ways or had formed communities in which they lived according to the customs of the fatherland, looked with disdain on the newcomers, who, without waiting to learn of American institutions, wished immediately to reform and re-organize the whole country. They even held a convention for this purpose in Wheeling, W. Va., and one enthusiast actually proposed to solve the Teutonic trouble by annexing Germany to the United States. They were not, however, men who wished to upset things merely for the pleasure of it. They were in no wise like the anarchists of later days. They were simply lovers of freedom, and later became strong abolitionists. Carl Schurz, Col. Fred Hecker, George Schneider, Lorenz

Brentano, Hermann Raster, William Rapp, Emil Preetorius, Caspar Butz, Emil Dietzsch, General Sigel, General Osterhaus and Governor Salomon, were the most prominent of the 48'ers.

The conflict between the old-timers and the revolutionists was carried on here in Chicago, as throughout the whole country. The former believed that they had become pretty well informed on things American, were firmly convinced of their smartness in business matters, and were proud of the manner in which they butchered the English language. They ridiculed, in their self-satisfied way, what they considered the absurd and exaggerated political ideas of the newly arrived revolutionists, whom they were pleased to call "Latin fellows," because they were educated, and "theorists," because they had ideas of their own. The revolutionists on the other hand, looked with supreme contempt on the "moss-backs," whom they were fond of alluding to as "German-American voting cattle," because of the obstinate persistency with which they clung to the old slavery party. They did not even regard the "moss-backs" as being worthy of living in a free country, and scornfully announced that the latter were perfectly happy if some native American would clap them on the back and hail them as "Jack" or "Charley."

Among the revolutionists there were many skilled artisans, and these had no difficulty in finding work. But the professional men, the journalists, artists, doctors, lawyers and professors, had plenty of spare time to discover the evils in America, to make merry over the Yankees and to plan a great campaign of reformation. These gentlemen were forever lounging around saloons, where, at all hours, they carried on almost endless debates on weighty political and social questions and, while thinking of the old home from which they had been mercilessly driven, comforted one another and waited for happier days—in most cases, for the hour of return to the fatherland. All day long one could find in the various saloons the best of fellowship among men of good breeding and good wit. They drank and argued—criticised bitterly and praised loudly.

On Sundays, headed by a brass band, they marched through the streets of the city, delighting in parading past crowded churches, and finally reaching a suburban grove where things went merrily. Conventionalities were forgotten, and the beer flowed in streams. In short, what they claimed to be "German customs" were introduced often with more energy than discretion, and the Yankees were taught what a "free German" was. In their enthusiastic moments when all went well, the revelers would praise their meetings with the proud words: "Grad' wie in Deutschland," (just as in Germany).

Finally, however, the 48'ers carried things a little too far. While calling themselves the educated part of the community, they often forgot entirely to take any account of other people, the result of which was that a bitter hatred of foreigners sprang into existence. The know-nothing spirit made its appearance all over the country, and it was directed especially against the Germans. At this crisis there happily appeared the German newspapers to urge their readers to conduct themselves differently toward those Americans who differed from them in opinion, and on the other hand to demand of the Americans that they afford to foreign born citizens equal rights with themselves. Most of the German papers particularly and emphatically disapproved of slavery, and in time their repeated demands for its abolition won for the Germans great respect and popularity among the free-minded American element.

In 1852 the Chicago Turnverein was formed, and its members, sharing the bitter anti-slavery views of the Illinois Staats Zeitung, which had been founded a few years before, formed the first German phalanx for the future but ever nearing struggle against slavery.

The Turnverein grew and prospered. Its miserable hall on Griswold street was superseded by a splendid building, and from a band of enthusiasts the association became the most influential German organization of the city, vitally assisting in the political and intellectual development of the Germans of Chicago.

Following the Chicago Turnverein came a host of other clubs and societies. There were singing, shooting, turning and military clubs. The number grew until finally almost every German state was represented by its own turning or singing society. In some clubs all members had come from one German city, and no others were admitted. The man from Hamburg would not turn or sing with one from Frankfurt, and so on. This peculiarity, although typical of life in the fatherland, worked against the best interests of the Germans in Chicago. They became divided, and failing to act as a unit, did not exercise an influence commensurate with their numbers. The same want of harmony is still noticed among the Germans to-day, and works against them. The general effect of the clubs was, of course, good, and developed not only the social but political life of the Germans. Nor was it the Germans alone who were affected.

After the singing societies had introduced German songs into the city, it was an easy matter for German opera to follow, and thus great impetus was given to the musical development of Chicago.

The most amusing and comical feature of life in the early 50's is indisputably the extraordinary importance with which many, otherwise very worthy and steady-going citizens, invested military affairs. Those who saw in the new order of things a gentle, peaceful and practical means of advancing in business or politics, devoted themselves to Mars with remarkable ardor, but it was the gentlemanly saloon keeper who reaped the greatest profit. After the fatigues of drilling and marching, the parched throats of the warriors had to be moistened, and a saloon was always found to be the best and most suitable place for holding an important council of war. The saloon keepers all joined companies. At certain hours their white aprons were doffed and gorgeous uniforms donned, and then out they went with the other warriors to valiantly storm the saloon of some comrade — for the fatherland had called, not exactly because it was in danger, but just to test the hearts of its sons and to keep the swords from rusting in the scabbards.

On Washington's birthday, Fourth of July, at funerals and at other times of danger, the streets were thronged with brave cavalrymen on foot and infantry officers on horseback. After a "treat all around for the company" the lieutenant expected that at the next council of war he would be made a captain, for, though he had captured no breastworks, he had won the hearts of his men. Should a major buy a keg of beer, he was sure of a marshal's baton at the first favorable opportunity. Consequently the militia of Chicago, at this time, comprised about eight generals, seventeen colonels, three dozen majors, two companies of captains, a battalion of lieutenants and five privates. As the latter were for the most part hard-working men, who had no time to spare, the regiment, when it turned out on the occasion of a funeral or some event of minor importance, consisted very frequently of nothing but officers.

At the local election, held in March, 1855, Levy D. Boone, a dyed-in-the-wool "know-nothing," was elected mayor of Chicago. He firmly believed that it was his duty to make all "foreigners" fully understand that America was to be governed only by Americans. A saloon license of $300 was imposed, and the police were strictly enjoined to close all saloons on Sunday, especially if they were conducted by "foreigners." If conducted by "respectable Americans" the police might strain a point and ignore the open doors. Even before Boone's time the Sunday and temperance crusade was waged. At that time Americans did not drink beer at all; whiskey was their favorite tipple, and in 1854 the commonest grades cost but 15 cents a gallon.

On Sundays then, the Americans could wet their parched gullets, but the drink of the fatherland was denied the sons of Germany. Up to this point the Germans had fully complied with the law, but at last some of them resolved to defy it, and run their saloons without the necessary license. But Mayor Boone was not to be trifled with; he had the offending saloon keepers summoned before him and, as they refused to pay for their licenses, caused them to be imprisoned. As a consequence, the Germans of the North Side organized a relief party, armed themselves with guns, revolvers and pitch-forks, and one Saturday marched over the Clark street bridge, up to the court house and demanded the release of their countrymen, the martyr saloon keepers. A crowd of several thousand Americans, Germans and Irishmen at once collected and stood eagerly awaiting further developments. The entrance to the court house yard, which was surrounded by a tolerably high iron fence, was guarded by the police, and the great door of the court house itself was closed. Down in the basement of this building were the prisoners, and those on the outside believed they could hear a confused murmur of voices coming from the various cells. The Germans on the outside stood there for some moments, undetermined as to how to proceed, as no one appeared willing to lead the attack, when suddenly the court house doors were flung wide open, and out upon the now thoroughly frightened and demoralized mob rushed about fifty special policemen. All were armed with clubs, and every man made good use of his weapon. A few shots were fired. At the attack of the police, one of the rioters threw away his weapon and started to flee, but was overhauled and shot down. A German cigar maker shot a policeman in the arm. After quiet had been restored in the vicinity of the court house, the great militia general, A. K. Swift, felt in duty bound to call upon the soldiers to rush to arms and the rescue. They responded slowly, only about 90 men from the whole regiment appearing, and they were all pale with fear. In spite of their pallor every man of them was ready, with a lion's courage, to plunge into the struggle for whisky and against beer. But, happily, the conflict had already passed.

Two old cannon, which, rumor said, had in 1812 been abandoned as worthless by the British in Detroit, were lugged out from the city arsenal and placed, one on Clark and one on La Salle street, both pointing toward the North Side. The mayor and his council seemed firmly convinced that the chief struggle would be in the afternoon. In fact, a second and a well planned attack had been arranged, for the shameful defeat of the forenoon was keenly felt. Men gathered in all the principal streets, prepared for a bitter struggle. One rioter ran to the North Market hall and rang the alarm bell. Fortunately, however, the threatened butchery was prevented by the ready wit of an Irish bridge-tender, who, as the valiant attacking column approached the river on Clark street, swung his bridge wide open and kept the doughty warriors off the South Side. As a consequence of this simple artifice, the forces of the "Beerocrats" stood helpless and irresolute, for in this emergency their brave leaders were unable to display their knowledge of the arts and strategies of war.

The end of this rather grotesque campaign was that everyone began to laugh at the peculiar, not to say ridiculous position of the revolutionary army of the North Side. Many of the warriors themselves were right well pleased at being prevented from spilling blood, for in their rage they might have dealt too severely with the foeman. And so it came about, that within half an hour not a trace of the great army of rebels was to be seen. On the South Side, meantime, the streets had been garrisoned and were kept so until Monday morning, the militia forces increasing in numbers all day Sunday in the same measure as the reports of the likelihood of more trouble grew less frequent and emphatic.

In order to avoid further ill-feeling, the trial of the various cases growing out of this episode known in the history of the city as the "beer riots," was postponed some weeks, and then, in order that immigration might not be driven away from Chicago, the prisoners were released on straw-bail and harmony was once more restored.

Occurrences such as those just narrated, increased the feeling between the native and German born citizens. As far as business was concerned, the two dealt with each other, the Americans recognizing the Germans not only as excellent clerks and workmen, but also as profitable customers, but after business hours they separated and had absolutely nothing to do with each other. The Americans had no desire to know more intimately the "Dutchmen," and the Germans in their turn saw no necessity of making advances to the "Yankees." A prominent feature of the German is his easy adaptability to foreign habits, customs and methods of thought. If he is kindly received by strangers, he adapts himself readily to his changed conditions of life. If, however, the stranger seeks by force to forbid him his native customs or to ridicule these as barbaric, then the true Teuton rebels and clings with a remarkable persistency to the habits of his forefathers. It was rather remarkable, therefore, that the German revolutionists advocated in the German press that their countrymen should forget personal grievances and unite with Americans for the suppression of slavery. The Americans had no sympathy with the Germans. They did not understand them, and did not care to. But the German revolutionists passed all that, and with one accord, preached over and over again from the text, "Down with Slavery."

"We Germans, above all others," they cried, "should oppose as one man, this accursed institution, even if in so doing we act against our own welfare, and are forced to unite with our enemies, the know-nothings." Of course such precepts found many enemies as well as many friends, and so the conflict between the old German settlers, most of whom belonged to the democratic or pro-slavery party, and the newly arrived revolutionists waxed fiercer.

New England, where there had been but few foreigners, was, strangely enough, the stronghold of the know-nothings. There too, however, were found the great opponents of slavery, and so the two extremes met. The foreign-born German in the west opposed slavery as strongly and as vigorously as did the Yankee abolitionist in the east. For a time the native born Chicagoans paid but little attention to the German anti-slavery movement. They did not know the leaders nor their motives, and it was not until George Schneider, Caspar Butz, Ernst Pruessing, Hermann Kreisman, Ernst Schmidt, Emil Dietzsch and Fritz Bauman on the one side, and Isaac N. Arnold, Norman B. Judd, John C. Haynes, Thomas B. Bryan and "Long" John Wentworth on the other, met and learned to know each other, that the two races joined forces for a common end.

While now the Germans and Americans were coming to a better understanding on political questions, there quietly and modestly developed a branch of industry destined to strongly affect the whole social life of the American people. Up to this time, as already said, the only American tipple was whisky and it had ruined mentally and physically thousands upon thousands. But all this was to be changed, for the Americans gradually became acquainted with the excellence of the German national beverage, and beer and even wine began to share, if not usurp the place in the American heart so long held by whisky.

In spite of almost a thousand years of struggling and suffering, Germans have retained a happy and contented disposition. On the soil of their fatherland the terrible decision of the sword has settled many a question pregnant with the fate of all mankind. The German may be always dreaming, but his dreams spring from a joyous and idealistic nature, and though oftimes interrupted by the loud tocsin summoning the dreamer to a combat for existence, still in the midst of the struggle, come the pleasant clink of glasses and tender love-songs, like saving genii in the moment of anxiety. And so, inspired by the pretty and natural desire to be able here, across the sea, in his foster fatherland, in the home of freedom, to live according to his old, honorable and long-inherited customs he planted on the sunny hills of Ohio the vine brought from the Rhineland, trained the fragrant hops, and on the black, virgin soil of the prairies he sowed the vigorous barley.

It was to supply an already keenly felt demand that in the 50's even, men all over the west turned their attention to wine growing and beer brewing. In Chicago a large and ever increasing industry was founded, and the breweries later yielded almost untold riches.

Mathias Best (father of the well-known Chicagoan, Henry Best) was Chicago's first brewer. He came here from Bavaria in 1841, but found so few Germans in the city that he did not think it worth while to start a brewery, and turned his attention to the manufacture of vinegar. In 1844 he began beer brewing on a small scale, serving his customers in little wooden casks, which he made himself, and carried around on his back. About 1850 he built a small brewery, with a summer garden attachment. Later he leased his establishment to Conrad Seipp, and when Seipp started a brewery of his own, he leased it to Downer & Bemis. When they in turn built their own brewery some years later, Chicago's original brew-house stood unused until 1871, when it was destroyed in the great fire.

In 1849, in a brewery on the corner of State and Randolph streets, where the Central Music Hall now stands, Adolph P. Mueller brewed the first lager beer for Chicagoans. Among the later brewers were John A. Huck and his son Louis, Peter Schoenhofen, A. Gottfried, Busch & Brand and Bartholomae & Leicht.

German influence on Chicago business, society and art was early felt, but it was 1857 before much attention was paid the Germans by the politicians. At that time it was not deemed advisable, on account of German opposition, to again run the know-nothing mayor, Thomas Dyer, and at the suggestion of George Schneider, of the Illinois Staats Zeitung, "Long" John Wentworth received the nomination. Wentworth was triumphantly elected, and thereafter the Germans paid more attention to real politics and less to visionary plans for sweeping reforms. Under the leadership of Schneider and others they continued their opposition to slavery, and formed the nucleus of the republican party in Chicago.

January 29, 1854, George Schneider called a meeting to oppose the Nebraska bill and the extension of slavery. At this gathering, probably the first public assembly held in the United States for this specific purpose, both Germans and Americans were present.

Stephen A. Douglas, then senator from Illinois, and from 1847 a resident of Chicago, was the great opponent of know-nothingism, and marshaled the democrats against the hosts of intolerance, fanaticism and political and religious bigotry. But the majority of the Germans stood firm against slavery, and as Douglas at first wished to compromise on the question, they violently opposed him.

On the evening of September 1, 1854, Douglas called a meeting at North Market Hall, where he intended to explain his action in support of the Kansas-Nebraska bill, but a howling mob met him and prevented the "little giant" from being heard. During the afternoon flags on all vessels and buildings owned by abolitionists had been hung at half-mast, and at dusk the church bells were tolled as if for an impending calamity. Most of those in the hall were bitter know-nothings and abolitionists, and many had come heavily armed in anticipation of bloodshed. Finally, after facing the mob for two hours, Douglas yielded to the inevitable and returned to his hotel, followed by a shouting, cursing, threatening crowd.

From that day Chicago never ceased to be on the extreme verge of anti-slavery excitment, and became the center of the western movement which made Kansas a free state.

The first general anti-slavery meeting was held in Chicago in the "Saloon Building" in 1838, and in January, 1840, the Chicago Anti-Slavery Society held its first public meeting. Chicago early became one of the principal points on the "underground railroad," which was the name given to a system of co-operation of certain active abolitionists to secretly assist fugitive slaves to escape into Canada. In 1839 generous and zealous Zebina Eastman sent the first passenger on the "underground railroad" through Chicago, and Captain Blake, of the steamer Illinois, took him to Canada.

In 1860 Chicago was selected as the place for holding the republican national convention, and the hearty support of Chicago abolitionists secured the nomination of Abraham Lincoln. In the fall the election passed off quietly enough, Lincoln being chosen president. He was inaugurated in March, 1861, and in less than six weeks the roar and crash of the guns bombarding Fort Sumter ushered in the war of the rebellion. April 18 the Union defense fund was started in Chicago, and three days later, at the call of Governor Yates, Gen. R. K. Swift started for Cairo, which important post he occupied with a force of 595 men and four six-pounders, his command consisting of Companies A and B, Ellsworth's Chicago Zouaves, the Chicago Light Infantry, Turner Union Cadets, Lincoln Rifles and the Chicago Light Artillery. When the President called for 75,000 volunteers, Chicago at once raised two companies, which were assigned to the Twelfth Illinois Volunteer Infantry. The Nineteenth Illinois also contained several Chicago companies. Indeed, so rapid was the enrollment of Chicago volunteers that Governor Yates, owing to the refusal of the Secretary of War to authorize him to accept more troops than the state's pro-rata proportion of the whole number of volunteers, was unable to put many of the early companies into commission, and several Chicago companies left the state and enlisted elsewhere, principally in Missouri and Kansas. Nearly every member of Ellsworth's famous zouaves held commission during the war, but they were scattered through the regiments of various states, Ellsworth himself commanding the Eleventh New York Volunteers (Fire Zouaves).

The Twenty-third Illinois was the famous "Irish Brigade," organized by Col. James A. Mulligan, and consisted of Irish-Americans living in Chicago and neighboring towns. It was accepted by the Federal government as an independent Illinois regiment, being mustered into service June 15, 1861. After three years of service, marked by conspicuous bravery and ability, Colonel Mulligan was killed at Kernstown, July, 1864.

The Twenty-fourth Illinois, or the "Hecker-Jaeger regiment," composed exclusively of Germans, was mustered in July 8, under the colonelcy of Frederick Hecker, who 12 years before had fought for liberty in the fatherland. Afterwards Colonel Hecker resigned, and organized the Eighty-second regiment, and was succeeded in the Twenty-fourth by Geza Mihalotzy, a trained Hungarian officer, who died March, 1864, from wounds received in the service of his foster fatherland. The Twenty-fourth was largely composed of men who had served in the German and Austrian armies, and was made up of excellent fighting material.

The Thirty-seventh, "the Fremont Rifle regiment," was organized in the summer of 1861, and three of its companies were recruited in Chicago. Few regiments saw more service than the Thirty-seventh and few reaped more honors. Gen. John C. Black entered the army as lieutenant-colonel of this regiment.

The Thirty-ninth, the "Yates Phalanx," was distinctively a Chicago regiment, as were also the Forty-second, Fifty-first, Fifty-seventh, Fifty-eighth, "the McClellan brigade," and the Sixty-fifth, "the Scotch regiment."

The Seventy-second was the first, the Eighty-eighth the second, and the One hundred and thirteenth the third Board of Trade regiment.

The Eighty-second, the second Hecker regiment, was like the Twenty-fourth, largely German. Its losses exceed those of almost any other regiment in the history of the war. The Eighty-ninth was the "Railroad" regiment, the Ninetieth, the "Irish Legion," the One Hundred and Twenty-seventh, mustered in September 6, 1862, was the last of the list of the gallant Chicago regiments during the rebellion.

Besides these infantry troops, Chicago furnished many recruits to the Fourth, Eighth, Ninth, Twelfth, Thirteenth cavalry regiments and to various artillery batteries. From first to last Chicago rendered the federal government every possible assistance in carrying on the war; nor was all the loyalty displayed by the soldiers on the field, trained nurses, Sisters of Mercy and surgeons, all more or less assisted by the city proceeded to the scenes of battle and cared for the wounded and sick left in camp and hospital. Money was liberally subscribed and great work was done by the Board of Trade, Mercantile Association, Y. M. C. A., Young Men's Association and various other societies.

In September, 1861, Camp Douglas was established on the South Side, as a rendezvous for all volunteers, but it was later used as a northern prison, over 12,000 rebels being confined there at one time. In 1864 Jacob Thompson, formerly a member of Buchanan's cabinet, formed a plot to free all these prisoners of war, and with them as a nucleus, form a union of all southern sympathizers in the north, and so aid the rebels by a northern insurrection. Enough of the plot, however, was discovered to prevent any serious developments.

In November, 1860, befell the greatest single fatality Chicago ever suffered: the wreck of the Lady Elgin. The boat was one of the finest of lake steamers, and on Friday, November 7, started from Chicago for Milwaukee with 393 persons on board, most of them being excursionists returning home to Milwaukee. In the night the Lady Eigin was run down by a lumber schooner and sank within thirty minutes, carrying down with her 297 human beings. This was the inauspicious beginning of a stormy and tumultuous decade, but the end of the 60's was peaceful enough; the war was well over, new industries had sprung up and times were prosperous.

> "But with mighty destiny
> Union sure, there ne'er can be,
> Woe advances rapidly."

The Chicago Fire.

October 7th, 8th and 9th, 1871.

For fourteen weeks scarcely a drop of rain had fallen on the strong young city on the shores of Lake Michigan. Of its 60,000 buildings, 40,000 were frame, and owing to the long drouth, both the buildings and the pine sidewalks were like tinder. Broken by neither hills nor forests, the prevailing west and southwest winds swept over the prairies and burst with full force upon the city.

The days were growing shorter, and in the early falling evenings the horizon could be seen red-tinted with its reflection of distant prairie fires. In the city itself, fires had been numerous without exciting more than passing comment. In America fires concern only the firemen and insurance companies. The 335,000 Chicagoans were all busy. The end of navigation was near, and grain traffic heavy. Fall trade—the distribution of the world's merchandise to 11,000,000 neighboring people—absorbed the attention of business men. Suddenly into the feverish activity, the high nervous tension of a fully developed commercial life, entered an enormous fatality, and the heart of the young city stood still. Quiet reigned over the vast field of ruins, and a hundred thousand people, who, care-free on the evening of October 8th, laughed and sang in happy homes, found themselves on the gloomy morning of the 9th without house or goods—shelterless and homeless on the bleak prairie, struggling with relentless elements, while three hundred of their fellows, dumb in death, bore ghastly evidence to the terrors of the night of fire.

Nor was the great tragedy which laid Chicago in ashes without a fit prelude. On the evening of the 7th of October, there burned in a few hours three hundred houses on the West Side,

2500 people were made homeless; 3000 were thrown out of employment, and property worth $750,000, and but little more than half insured, was destroyed. Twenty-four hours later and the homeless were numbered by tens of thousands, the losses computed by hundreds of millions, and the insurance an unknown quantity. The fire October 7th, was the largest Chicago had ever known, but the immense conflagration that followed on the 8th made it seem insignificant. Little is heard about the great battle of Ligny, because it was followed immediately by the greater Waterloo.

But the story of the first fire is important in explaining the one that followed. South of Adams street and immediately west of the south branch of the Chicago river were numerous lumber and coal yards, planing mills and factories full of highly inflammable material, and here, at 11 o'clock Saturday evening, October 7th, fire was discovered in the planing mill of Lull & Holmes (on Canal street, a block from the river). The authorities never learned how it started, but the flames had made great headway before the fire department reached the scene. A strong wind was blowing directly from the south, and the fire spread northward with the greatest rapidity. Later the wind veered to the southwest, and the flames leaped across Canal street and worked toward the river. Within two hours they had swept over an area of more than twenty acres, completely devastating the whole district bounded by Adams street on the north, Clinton on the west, Van Buren on the south and the river on the east. Except for the National elevator, which, though on fire several times, finally escaped destruction, one saw nothing but an empty field before him—no trace of ruins or debris, a peculiarity even more noticeable in the fire of the following day. The rapidity of the conflagration even at the beginning was so great that all engines had to be called into play, and it was only by the greatest effort that the fire was checked at the corner of Adams and Clinton streets, and its progress

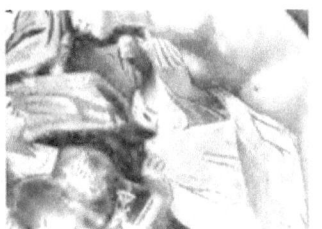

northward stopped. Had this not been done the flames would have attained sufficient force to have jumped the river—there 150 feet wide, and the terrible tragedy of October 8th would have been earlier enacted. At one time the woodwork of the viaduct on Adams street caught fire and from it the flames spread northward, threatening the many railroad cars crowded together there and the passenger and freight depots of the Pittsburgh, Ft. Wayne & Chicago and Chicago & Alton roads. The danger, however, was happily averted by tearing down one of the big freight sheds.

The wonderful spectacle had attracted hundreds of people to the bridges spanning the river, from which one could look down as from a hill upon the awful scene. Little did the spectators dream that only twenty-four hours later they would themselves be dragged to the stage and employed as actors in one of the greatest tragedies of the century. Still there was no lack of uncanny premonition. The roof of a shed from which hundreds of people looked down into the fierce sea of fire, suddenly gave way and all were precipitated to the ground and several wounded. Many of the high sidewalks on Clinton street gave way under the pressure of surging masses and caused serious accidents. A number of men in Sheriff's lumber yard and in adjacent coal yards, were so cornered by the fire, that seizing whatever pieces of lumber they could find, they leaped into the river, preferring the water and its doubtful dangers to the awful certainty of the flames. One human victim fell a prey to this earlier fire, for the next day the charred body of a woman was found on Clinton street on the spot where her home had stood. After a battle of five hours the firemen succeeded in curbing the terrible element. Exhausted, they retired to their berths above the steamers with no suspicion of the awful defeat to follow this Pyrrhus victory.

The morning of Sunday, October 8th, gave no cause for apprehension of the terrors of the night to come. Bright and beautiful shone the October sun, and only its clear light bringing the barren burnt area into bold relief, made a weird impression upon the beholder. The supremacy of the elements over human power was boldly shown. In vigorous wise fate had already knocked on the door, and thousands and thousands of spectators, who, on the bright Sunday morning gathered from all parts of the city to witness the scene of devastation, might have heard the knocking on their own doors. But the pleasure resorts in the afternoon were overcrowded, Lincoln Park was full of pedestrians and carriages. No one dreamed that he was enjoying the last day a doomed city.

THE CATASTROPHE OF OCTOBER 8th AND 9th.

Closely following the powerful prelude of October 7th, was the gigantic tragedy which forms the topic of this description. It calls to mind the old Greek tragedies, in which the chorus gives expression, not only to public opinion about the acts of the leading personages, but also on especially important occasions, takes part in the action itself; it differs only in this, that finally all parts of this divided chorus became principal actors—relentless fate involving first one division, then another, with steadily increasing effect. The three localities in which the action took place form the most natural lines on which to divide the tragedy into acts, the more so as the climaxes of feeling on the part of the people correspond to such division. As long as the fire was confined to the West Side, the South Siders, who viewed it from the bridges and eastern shore of the river, felt more pity for the repeated misfortunes of their neighbors than fear for themselves. The second act began when, about midnight, the fire leaped across the river and attacked its prey on the other side. Now the inhabitants of the South Side are hurled with frightful rapidity into the whirlpool of action. The battle between fate and heroes, between the destroying element and the saving fire department, fighting step by step the on-marching flames, reaches its climax. Buildings on Harrison street and Wabash avenue are blown up by gunpowder, and the fire is prevented from spreading further south, and by reason of this relative triumph of human ingenuity over the unchained element, the hopes of the sore-tried victims are for a time revived. The third act, the almost complete destruction of the North Side, shares with the other two the characteristic feature that the passive spectators are thrown with fearful velocity into the midst of the action—into as wild a flight as the world has ever witnessed. The army is routed—help himself who can! The retreat across the bridges on Chicago avenue, Division street and North avenue, where men, women and children, horses and wagons are precipitated in almost inextricable confusion, into the unburnt part of the Northwest Side, recalls the horrors of the celebrated crossing of the Beresina.

Even the character of the architecture varied essentially in the three divisions of the city, the flames in the first act meeting only frame buildings. Indeed, it has been argued that the rapid development of the conflagration is due almost entirely to this fact, and it may be possible that if at first the fire had had to deal with less inflammable material, its spread might have been slower and its resistance by the firemen successfully accomplished. But the complete devastation of the business center proved that a fire of such dimensions as that which finally jumped the river could not be resisted by even the most fire-proof buildings. The business center contained about one and a half square miles, bounded on the north by the main river, on the west by the south branch, on the east by Lake Michigan and on the south by Harrison street, and its buildings were chiefly of stone, iron and brick. To be sure, there were vulnerable spots—the wooden window frames, which the fire reached in spite of the iron shutters, the wooden cornices, and last, but not least, the tarred gravel roofs. The pine shelves, ornaments, fittings, the large number of newly emptied dry goods boxes, and the tinder-like interior of even the most solid and imposing stone structures, furnished abundant food for the conquering flames. The fire originated half a mile southwest of the center of the city, on the West Side, attacked the center, destroyed it and swept over the North Side, suburban in its character, until it reached the lake and bare northern prairies. The burnt district was on an average a mile wide and four miles long. The burnt buildings, placed side by side, with ten feet between each, would form a line 150 miles long. According to the estimate of Frederick Law Olmstead, a well-known New York architect, who visited Chicago immediately after the great disaster, one-third of the roof surface and half the cubic contents of all the buildings of the city were destroyed by the fire, in other words, a much greater part of the city was burned than would appear from comparing a map of the burnt district with one of the whole city, because in the business portion buildings stood close together and were from four to six stories high.

THE FIRST ACT.

The Beginning of the Great Fire on the West Side.

The wind which on Sunday afternoon had been blowing at a moderate rate, grew stronger toward evening, and finally became a terrific gale. At 9:28 in the evening the watchman in the central fire station in the court house discovered that fire had broken out on the West Side, and located it near the corner of Canalport avenue and Halsted street, and an alarm for that point was at once turned in. As a matter of fact the fire was in the rear of 137 DeKoven street, near the corner of

Jefferson, and the watchman had misjudged it by almost a mile. The neighborhood was principally occupied by Bohemians and Irishmen, their houses were of frame and cheaply constructed, and behind many of them were barns and cattle sheds filled with hay. In the O'Leary's stable in which the fire originated, the floor was covered with shavings, which were used instead of straw to bed the cattle. It was at first supposed that Mrs. O'Leary was milking her cow by lantern light, and that the cow kicked over the lantern and set fire to the stable. During the official investigation, however, the O'Leary's swore that they had not been in the stable since dark, but this fact does not prevent people from clinging to the old tradition that Mrs. O'Leary's cow kicked over her lantern. Later, the story found a champion in Chicago's well-known and efficient fire marshal, Mat. Benner, who reports as the result of his private investigations, that he believes the cow undoubtedly kicked over a lamp or lantern, but that it was not Mrs. O'Leary's. The Irish family who lived with the O'Learys had been jollifying all that Sunday in honor of a newly arrived son of Erin, and in the evening, needing milk for a punch, it is supposed that one of them volunteered to milk Mrs. O'Leary's cow. He attempted to do so, but the cow rebelled, and kicked over the lantern with dire results. Just what time the fire began it is impossible to definitely state. One engine reached the scene as early as 9:15, having been summoned by a "still" alarm. The preponderance of evidence goes to show that the fire had at that time been burning for at least half an hour, but another half hour elapsed before other engines reached the scene, and the flames were then beyond the control of the firemen. At least four of the best engines were misled by the error of the watchman in the court house tower, and this fact, taken in connection with the exhaustion of the men on account of the preceding night's fire and the crippled condition of the apparatus permitted the great catastrophe. Second and third alarms were turned in, and finally every engine in the city, with the exception of one which remained on the South Side, were summoned by the big alarm bell in the cupola of the court house. By 9:30 the flames crossed Taylor street and attacked several blocks at once, while the howling winds drowned the noise of crackling flames and crashing rafters. Vain were all efforts to check the fire, which, swelled to fearful proportions by the ever increasing fury of the southwest gale, advanced northward in two columns, one between Canal and Clinton streets, the other between Clinton and Jefferson.

All that could be done was to prevent the fire spreading west to Desplaines street, and in this the firemen were successful. Meantime the foe marched northeasterly almost unhindered. Those who tried to oppose it, soon felt its furious power. The crew of engine No. 14, having run their machine into a narrow alley, suddenly found themselves almost surrounded by flames, and were forced to abandon the steamer and flee for their lives. One block after another fell before the raging element which became stronger every minute. Polk street was reached, then Harrison, and finally Van Buren, the boundary of the burnt district of the day before. Here, had there been only an ordinary gale, the flames would have stopped. Behind were 150 acres of fire, in front 20 of ashes, and the flames had not yet strength enough to leap over the four burnt-out blocks. This empty space—that is to say, the scene of Saturday's fire—saved the West Side from destruction and proved a blessing in disguise. Had it not been checked at this point, the column of fire which progressed to the northeast would have undoubtedly destroyed the whole West Division north of Adams street, and have stopped only on reaching the extreme city limits. But just as men began to hope that the fire would burn itself out for lack of fuel, the terrible and unexpected happened: the conflagration, checked in its northward course, turned to the east, and—a thing unheard of in previous Chicago fires—the river no longer proved a barrier and protection. The flames leaped across the stream and carried along by the tempest fell upon the buildings on the opposite bank. The second and principal act had commenced. With rapid strokes, the great alarm bell announced the new and fearful change in the course of the great disaster.

Again, it is found difficult to accurately time the progress of the flames. Before 10 o'clock showers of sparks and burning brands were swept across the river into the South Side, and some were carried far into the North Division. The keeper of the crib, two miles out in the lake, testified that from 11 o'clock the sky was full of brands and that he was kept busy preventing the wooden roof of the crib from becoming enkindled. It is probable that as the West Side fire extended ten blocks along the river, the flames crossed in several places. At least as early as 11:30, the new building of the Parmelee Omnibus and Stage Co., on Jackson street, corner of Franklin, was ignited and in an instant more was literally engulfed in flame. The group of wretched wooden dwellings known as "Conley's patch," on Fifth avenue, between Adams and Monroe streets, took fire at midnight and the gas works followed immediately. The flames attacked the court house at 1:30, and at the same time, State street bridge began to burn. At 2:30, Wright's stables on the North Side caught fire, and at 3:20 the water works were in flames. "Conley's patch," the court house and Wright's stables, were in a straight line between the O'Leary shed and the water works, which were about 2¼ miles due northeast from the spot where the fire began. Such was the progress of the conflagration during the first 6½ hours! On account of eddies in the wind, however, the fire burned not only straight northeast, but also turned back, "ate into the wind" and spread on either side. Brands blown ahead, kept the flames well scattered, and at times there were ten or more different fires. But as each ate forward, all were finally united into one great element of destruction.

THE SECOND ACT.

The Destruction of the Business Center of Chicago.

From the thousands who had gone from the South Side to witness the conflagration in the West Division, burst a cry of horror when they saw that the flames had crossed the river and were burning fiercely in their rear, threatening to cut off their retreat by the bridges and imperilling their very homes. Back in a mad rush swept the people, and through them the fire engines, on their way to fight the flames in the new quarter, thunderingly forced their way. The bridge scenes at midnight were pandemonium—each narrow way choked up with a struggling, cursing mob, fighting to get beyond the line of fire.

It was 11:30 when the Parmelee building on Jackson street was attacked, and "Conley's patch," two blocks further north, was also set by brands blown from the West Side. About midnight a huge, blazing board was seized by the wind, borne across the river and lodged on the tinder-like roof of a three-story tenement on Market street. All around were low wooden buildings, saloons, hovels and sheds, the dens of the lowest classes in the city. This terror spot, the very home of crime, was to be purged by fire. Most of the male inhabitants were across the river, and, as the flames laid hold of the wretched buildings, squalid women and children rushed out in droves—awe-struck and terrified, they wandered about in hopeless, helpless bewilderment. Most of them finally escaped, but scores perished miserably in the great wilderness of flame. Some of the wretched fugitives were joined by their sisters from Fifth avenue and Jackson street and by the tribes of thieves which infested the locality; saloons were broken open, and hellish orgies added to the night's hideousness. At this time, between 1 and 2 in the morning, no one in or near the heart of Chicago slept. On the burning streets surged throngs of men and crowds of vehicles laden with property—all driving toward the lake shore. As soon as the news of the calamity reached the aristocratic mansions on Calumet, Prairie and Indiana avenues, business men hastened down-town. With dire apprehension and heavy hearts they made their way toward stores and offices. An awful sight met their gaze. Like lightning the fire rushed up the wooden sidewalks and moved simultaneously on Market, Franklin and Fifth avenue northward to Madison street, the entrance to the wholesale district. For a moment there was hope that the destroying fiend would move directly toward the lake and so skip a part of the business center. But suddenly the wind veered, and the fate of hundreds of Chicago business palaces and of millions of dollars worth of merchandise was sealed. With a mighty leap the fire reached La Salle street from Fifth avenue, and from Jackson another column of flames came rolling on to make common cause with the advance guard in the great destruction. This was the first fire which had worked its way from the Parmelee building east to the new Grand Pacific, the first of the better class of buildings to be attacked. The great hotel, stretching a block, from La Salle to Clark street, had just been roofed in and had cost almost $1,000,000. As if in anger at its imposing dimensions the fire swept over it, shone luridly from every window space and in a moment more left it tottering in ruins. Just a block to the south the splendid and massive depot of the Rock Island and Michigan Southern roads was enveloped in flames, which came from a third crossing of the river at Van Buren street. After the destruction of the depot a wing of the fire spread southward, threatening the residence portion of the South Side beyond Harrison street; but the immense stone freight depot on Griswold street offered an impregnable front and for the time at least prevented the further southward march of the conflagration. From the Rock Island depot the flames licked up some shabby buildings, and worked northeasterly toward the magnificent Bigelow House, then just completed and ready to be thrown open to the public on that very day. It stood on Dearborn street, between Adams and Quincy, and from it the all-consuming element swept grandly over Honore's two blocks and the Academy of Design, filled with noble works of art.

Now the waves of fire took on greater proportions. Hundreds of buildings far in advance of the on-rushing column were blazing pillars of fire, but the main body of the flames was all-devouring, systematic, relentless—everything fell before its wasting power. Huge tongues of flame stretched out for acres, sheets of fire covered entire blocks, enwrapping every building in a surging, seething, billowy and tumultuous sea. The heat was almost inconceivable. Six-story buildings were attacked, shone with a wild red glow, flames burst forth, and within five minutes the whole structure literally melted to the ground. The fiercest tornado ever known here was blowing, and, as William B. Ogden pointed out, its effect was like the action of a blow-pipe, causing so perfect a combustion that the brilliant blaze consumed even the smoke, and the heat was so intense as to melt iron girders and crumble into dust and ashes most of the building stones used in the city's construction. Despite its awfulness, the scene was one of wild beauty and imposing grandeur. So continuous was the crash of falling buildings that, although the ground trembled as if from an earthquake, the people paid no heed.

Hardly 20 minutes after the north-marching column from the Grand Pacific cut its swath through the magnificent buildings on La Salle street, the Chamber of Commerce, corner of La Salle and Washington streets, was reached, and soon fell a crumbling heap of ruins. An attempt was now made to check the progress of the flames by blowing up buildings with gunpowder, and the Merchants' Insurance building was leveled by a tremendous explosion. But all was in vain—the pitiless fire leaped the broad black chasm as if there had been no intervening space, and fell upon the structures beyond. The flames from the Grand Pacific spread eastward as well as to the north, and occupied but a moment in working across the Lombard and Reynold's blocks, and at 3 o'clock in the morning attacked the postoffice and custom house on the northwest corner of Dearborn and Monroe streets. This was a supposedly fire-proof edifice, but all the iron shutters had been removed from the first floor, which was filled with wooden furniture and fittings and inflammable mail matter. The blaze soon found the vulnerable points, and the first floor became a sheet of fire. The intense heat melted the iron beams supporting the floors above, and the whole inside of the building, fire-proof vaults, safes and all, fell crashing to the basement in common destruction. The building contained the United States depository, in which there were about $2,000,000. Of this amount about $1,500,000 were green-backs and national bank notes, which were destroyed. Of the specie, most was recovered, but almost all was melted and run together in a great mass of gold, silver and copper.

The burning of the court house illustrates one peculiarity of the fire; the flames did not progress continuously, but there were constantly advance fires. The court house was a substantial structure in the middle of the square bounded by Washington, La Salle, Randolph and Clark streets. The wooden cupola took fire as early as midnight, but watchmen stationed there repeatedly extinguished the blaze. Finally at 1:30 o'clock the heat grew so intense and the flames laid such firm hold upon the wooden roof and cupola that the watchmen were obliged to abandon the building — and none too soon, for both were severely burned before they made their escape. As they went down the stairs they set in motion the machinery that rang the alarm bell, which then, without human aid, continued to peal forth its terrible warnings for half an hour. Finally at 2:05 it fell, carrying down with it the iron stairs and burning rafters of the cupola. In the court house were archives, deeds, abstracts, titles to all buildings and lots, and other priceless papers, but all were destroyed. On the lower floor were the county prisoners, 150 or more, and when the building took fire all but the murderers were set free. With a wild yell the wretches, many of them half-naked, rushed out of the building, attacked a passing dray laden with ready made clothing and disappeared. Officers handcuffed those prisoners charged with murder and led them out of the building, which was already glowing like a furnace. As many as twelve different fires were now raging at once. Skirmishing lines swept forward, far in advance of the main columns, which continued more slowly their resistless march, checked now and then by a sterner battle waged around some great building, as the larger hotels, postoffice and court house. Since midnight the air had been hot with the breath of the fire demon, which shriveled and scorched all things. Cinders, ashes, coals and brands were falling in showers. The Sherman House on Clark and Randolph streets, opposite the court house, as yet withstood the attack. On its immense flat roof hundreds had gathered, who with tireless energy extinguished the fire brands which rained down thick and fast. But all endeavors were in vain. Suddenly out of the hundreds of windows burst the fiery tongues, and so rapid was the work of destruction that those in the building escaped only with the greatest difficulty.

It was 4 o'clock in the morning when this great hotel fell in ruins. The same fate overtook all the other leading caravansaries of the city. At 3 o'clock the Matteson House, corner of Dearborn and Randolph streets, was destroyed, at 3:30 the Tremont House went up in smoke, and at 4 the Briggs House followed. The course of the fire east from the court house took in Hooley's Opera House (on the site of the present Grand Opera House) the Republican office and the big newspaper buildings on Dearborn street, those of the

Post, Times, Mail, Staats-Zeitung and Evening Journal and scores of other buildings, many of them models of architectural beauty. Then Crosby's magnificent Opera House fell. It had just been renovated, and was to have been opened Monday night by the Thomas Orchestra. From it the flames spread to the St. James, corner of State and Washington streets, the last of the big hotels to crash a heap of ruins to the earth. Opposite the St. James were the First National Bank building, which resisted the flames until 5 o'clock in the morning, and the dry goods palace of Field & Leiter, which lasted but a half hour longer. These State street buildings were all north of Madison, and at 5 o'clock the fire south of Madison had not crossed even Dearborn street. The Tribune office, though threatened several times, had thus far escaped, as had McVicker's theatre and the Palmer House. As late as 6:30 in the morning it seemed that a part of Chicago — that lying between Madison and Harrison streets, east of Dearborn — was to be saved, and exhausted humanity began to seek food and rest. But the end was not yet. About 7 o'clock a sudden gust of the still raging tempest swept with fiercer violence through Dearborn street, near Jackson. The rioting elements, renewing the attack with increased fury, were to win a complete victory. Live coals were caught up from the ruins of the Bigelow House and hurled against the wooden buildings across the street, the triumphant flames swept once more to the north and east, and the last chance to bring the terrible devastation to a halt had passed unimproved. All that had been left untouched from Dearborn street to the lake shore was doomed to destruction. McVicker's theatre fell, the flames covered the Palmer House on Quincy and State streets, and finally the new Tribune building yielded to desperate assaults. This structure was of Joliet marble and of the most massive style of architecture, and had been considered really fire-proof. Up to 8 o'clock the men employed to fight the flames stood at their posts, but then of a sudden the fire burst out on all sides, seeming to come from the interior of the building itself, and so rapidly did the blaze spread that the watchmen barely escaped.

As the fury of the hurricane died down, the fire progressed to the south and southwest, along Wabash and Michigan avenues, through beautiful stores and magnificent dwellings, melting its way through the thickest masonry, right into the teeth of the wind. It seemed impossible to stop it. Past Jackson, Van Buren and Congress streets it swept, threatening to eat its way to the very limits of the city. No engines were at hand, and the only thing to do was to blow up the buildings standing in the path of the flames. Gen. Philip H. Sheridan personally superintended this work, which was begun at Harrison street. Several buildings were blown up and others were pulled and chopped down and the southward march of the fire finally checked. The substantially built Wabash avenue Methodist church also helped in the salvation of the southern end of town and its heavy, honest walls proved the turning point in the battle. Terrace Row, a palatial block of residences on Michigan avenue, between Congress and Van Buren streets, was the last group of buildings burned in the south end of the city. When its last wall fell about noon, there remained in the South Division north of it, only the Lind block at the east end of Randolph street bridge and the Illinois Central elevator, just north of the once splendid depot of the company. A large share of the costly equipments of the beautiful Terrace Row homes were transferred to safety further out on the South Side. The lake front was filled with men, women and children and property of every description. Significant of the stern mood of the people on that memorable Monday morning is the fact that the thunder of the powder explosions infused them with new courage.

Perhaps some parts of the business center might have been saved—notably, the portion of the city east of Dearborn street and south of Madison—had not the water works on the North

Side been destroyed shortly after 3 o'clock in the morning. The roof of the massive and otherwise thoroughly fire-proof water works building was a temporary affair, constructed of highly inflammable material which readily ignited from the cinders and burning brands which fell on it, after being carried by the wind for miles through the air. Soon the roof crashed in, burying in a blazing heap of debris the colossal steam pumps, and the water supply in the hydrants was soon exhausted. To add to the terror of the situation, the gas supply also gave out, the gas works on the South Side on Market street, and later, those on the North Side being burned down. From this time the fate of the still unburned portion of the business center and of all the North Side was sealed. The loss of the water works rendered useless all further resistance to the flames.

Only at some of the bridges, notably at Lake, Randolph and Madison streets, where the engines could pump water directly from the river, was the great battle still waged. It was no longer a question of saving certain South Side buildings, but the salvation of the whole West Side, threatened by the on-rolling flames, was at stake. Had the fire succeeded in re-crossing the river by means of the bridges leading into the West Division, that whole quarter of the city, with its depots, factories and numerous dwellings, reaching to the northern city limits, would have been doomed. Thousands of spectators witnessed the struggle with intense excitement and alarm. The wasting tongues of flame were already licking up two great warehouses on Market street, near Lake street, and very near the bridge. Out of doors and windows the blaze was already shooting, and the heat was as intense as in a furnace. The crowd on the west bank of the river felt the terrible glow and drew back, but the firemen did not stir. Although but forty feet from the fiery sea, they held their ground and poured streams of water upon the wooden bridge and the approach until both were fairly flooded. Finally, just as the sun appeared, blood-red and rayless, over the gray waters of the lake and looked down upon the scene of devastation as with the single eye of a demon, the heroic efforts of the firemen were crowned with success, the march of the flames checked, the West Side saved. At Madison street there was another victory over the fire. Many thought to see the flames cross the river at this point, and the situation for a time was remarkably critical. No fire engine was at hand, but before the flames reached the bridge, hose was attached to the immense steam pump of Norton's Oriental Mills (just across the river on Madison street) and for hours two powerful streams of water were thrown upon the exposed property, which was thus effectually protected.

When the court house burned, the fire-proof vaults proved of little value, and all the official records, deeds and abstracts were destroyed. This loss would have resulted in endless confusion and difficulty in establishing and re-establishing titles to property within the limits of Cook county had not some well-kept private records been preserved. These were afterwards substituted for the official records, and adequate laws were passed to that effect. The abstract firm of Shortall & Hoard saved most of their books and records, and other abstract firms saved enough to make a complete file. John G. Shortall was personally responsible for saving the books of his firm, which were to be of such inestimable value, not to himself so much as to every property owner of Chicago. When he reached his office in the Larmon block, near the court house, it was past midnight, and burning brands were falling like hail upon the roof, windows and awnings of the building. Shortall tore down the awnings, several of which were already in flames, and did what he could to fight the fire, but by 1 o'clock it was apparent that the building was doomed. In his anxiety to save his records Shortall approached no less than fifteen expressmen, offering large sums to anyone who would carry the precious books to a place of safety. Finally, when the court house began to burn, the immediate procuring of a wagon became absolutely necessary, and a friend of Shortall pressed an expressman into service at the point of a revolver. But few of the books would go into the wagon and Shortall was in despair, when help finally appeared in the shape of a heavy two-horse dray, sent by Joseph Stockton. Into it the books were piled, and with the flames roaring all around were successfully taken to Shortall's house, 852 Prairie avenue.

The fire had now destroyed all the bridges between the North and South Sides, the last to go being the Rush street bridge, which fell at 4:30 in the morning. The loss of this last bridge and the fact that smoke and steam prevented the use of the La Salle street tunnel, cut off all avenue of escape from the down-town district to the North Side, while the flames, rapidly progressing along Harrison street, checked all retreat to the south. This left the lake front as the only place of refuge for the thousands who were in the business center, and the burning of the great Illinois Central passenger station, at the foot of Lake street, and of the various buildings along Michigan avenue, literally encompassed the unfortunates between walls of fire on three sides while the cold waters of the lake lay on the other. Huddled together on this narrow strip of land the poor wretches watched the gorgeous spectacle of the burning city, with a sensation of weary despair and a grim acceptance of their crushing fate. Since the burning of Field & Leiter's magnificent store, second only in size and value of contents to one dry goods house in the land, this changed mood had come over the people. A sense of their utter helplessness seemed to weigh upon them. The heroes of a few hours before became indifferent, and thieves robbed and pillaged openly and recklessly. Thousands of valuable books were lugged away from the great book concerns on State street, only to be later thrown away or burned up. At Field & Leiter's the most elaborate

preparations for defense had been made. The whole front of the building was covered with wet blankets, and the roof filled with people ready to extinguish the falling embers and firebrands. The flames were fought back to the last possible moment, but when their victory did come, it was instantaneous. From all the numerous windows of the palatial building, the blaze shot forth its fire tongues simultaneously, the white marble fronts were illuminated with a terrible glow, and in a moment more the enormous structure fell in ruins, crushed, as a toy house would tumble under the hands of a giant.

STREET SCENES DURING THE FIRE.

The South Side streets during the fire were a panorama of remarkable spectacles. As in a shipwreck, every one showed himself in his true colors. Selfishness in all its phases and stages was seen. It was represented by the cowardly egotist who thoughtful only of his own salvation was ready to trample on every one and everything in his way, and by the daring robber who plundered large stores and carried away valuable merchandise by the car load. But there were also examples of the most noble self-sacrifice and touching readiness to assist the helpless and unfortunate. The development of the street scenes runs parallel with the development of the fire. The effects of the former increase with that of the latter. First, the streets seemed only very lively. The hundreds of fire victims who, with a portion of their hastily saved property, were looking for a place of safety, resembled a river which struggles to leap from the narrow confines of its banks into the broad ocean. But after the fire had seized the very heart of the city and the destruction proceeded with such terrible rapidity, the mass of people running to save their lives, swelled to a wild torrent over which nobody could exercise control. As soon as it became evident that the saving of the business center was out of the question, uncanny figures mingled with the multitude and began their work. First, they broke into stores under the pretext of assisting in saving goods, though most merchants preferred seeing their property burn to having it so securely saved that they would never see it again. Finally the thieves and robbers threw off every mask and used open violence. The police, of whom 150 out of a force of 450 were themselves burned out, left the streets and at most watched only the millions of dollars worth of property which was piled up in Dearborn Park, within the high fences of the base-ball club or in Lake Front Park, where it was finally overtaken by the flames.

Lake street, with its dry goods and jewelry stores, was a choice field for the operation of the robbers, who made common cause with the expressmen and operated on a wholesale plan. In aiding the thieves the expressmen reduced the number of vehicles at the service of honest merchants, many of whom, seeing their helplessness between robbers and flames, threw open their doors and invited all in to help themselves to whatsoever they fancied. The coolness of the rascals stood them in good stead, and they chose only what was of cash value. Whole car loads of precious rugs, shawls, silks and laces were carried away, and but seldom recovered, though one merchant got track of some of his property in St. Louis. Owners of wagons, with few exceptions, were grossly exorbitant in their charges for even the slightest service, and invariably demanded cash in advance. In numerous cases when a man had loaded a wagon with his most valuable property some armed villain calmly mounted the seat and drove off with it. Other richly laden wagons were looted by the mobs through which they passed.

The pillaging went on in all the stores of the city, and when a man succeeded in getting some of his most valuable possessions from his burning house or store he was not infrequently relieved of them directly afterwards at the point of a revolver. Jewels were torn from the fingers and necks of women and children. In front of Shay's magnificent store a thief drove up, and in spite of the remonstrances of the employes, proceeded to load up his wagon with valuable silks and laces. When the wagon was finally loaded some one threatened to shoot the robber if he attempted to take his plunder away, but he was not so easily cowed, and coolly said "shoot and be damned," whereupon the man put his pistol in his pocket and the thief drove away with his booty. East of Shay's store immense quantities of all kinds of fancy goods were scattered over the streets, and over them swept the streams of people and wagons until the fire burnt up what had already been crushed and ruined.

Toward morning the streets not yet reached by the fire were the scene of a veritable pandemonium. Barrels of whisky, bottled liquors of all kinds, partly given away by dealers who could not save them and in part stolen, inflamed the most beastly passions and aroused the lower classes to deeds of violence. As the fire progressed men seemed to be possessed with the idea that they needed the stimulation of liquor, and drank heavily at the great saloons and wholesale houses, where whisky was given so freely. This was true of women as well as men, and hundreds drank then who never had before. Not nearly all were drunk, but the drunken phase was terribly prominent. Among the better classes, the stimulants produced that humor of despair which in so momentous a tragedy appears as the ghastly caricature of true mirth.

An eye witness gives the following description of scenes on the South Side:

For miles around was a circle of red light. The brute creation was crazed. Horses maddened by heat and noise, irritated by falling sparks, neighed and screamed with affright and anger, roared, kicked and bit each other or stood with drooping tails and rigid legs, ears laid back and eyes wild with amazement, shivering as if with cold. Dogs ran hither and thither, howling dismally. Great brown rats, with bead-like eyes, were ferreted out from under the sidewalks by the flames and skurried along the streets, kicked at, trampled upon, hunted down. Flocks of beautiful pigeons, so plentiful in the city, wheeled up aimlessly, circled blindly, and fell into the raging fire beneath.

The people were mad. They crowded upon frail coigns of vantage, on high sidewalks, which fell beneath their weight and hurled them bruised and bleeding in the dust. They fell over broken furniture and were trampled under foot. Seized with wild panic they surged together, backwards and forwards, in the narrow streets, cursing, threatning, imploring, fighting to get free. Liquor flowed like water, for saloons were broken open and despoiled, and men were to be seen on all sides frenzied with drink. Fourth and Pacific avenues emptied their denizens into the throng. Ill-omen and obscure birds of night were they, villainous, debauched, pinched with misery they flitted through the crowd, ragged, dirty, unkempt—negroes with stolid faces, and white men who battened on the wages of shame—they glided among the mass like hyenas in search of prey. They smashed windows with their naked hands, regardless of the wounds inflicted, and with bloody fingers rifled till and shelf and cellars, fighting viciously for the spoils of the forage. Women, hollow-eyed and brazen faced, with filthy drapery tied over them, their clothes in tatters and their feet in trodden-over slippers, moved here and there, scolding, stealing, fighting, laughing at the beautiful and splendid crash of walls and the falling roofs. On Lake street bands of thieves broke into stores and threw whole bales of goods to their confederates, who fought openly for the plunder. * * * * *

When I reached Wabash avenue I found that immense street filled with objects of every possible description, and crowded with masses of fugitives. All those who had been driven from their homes by the advancing flames, had taken with them as much of their personal property as they could stagger along with, and as their onward march was getting extremely difficult—for the bridge was even more filthy jammed than the streets—many of the panic-striken mob threw their property away. Streets and sidewalks presented a remarkable scene of broken mirrors, torn paintings, ruined books and wrecked pianos. Added to this was the fact that the merchandise dragged from the stores had taken fire while the drunken rabble, having broken into a liquor store, brandished champagne bottles and executed a fire can-can. One drunken man chose a piano for his pulpit, and addressed the mob. The fire, he argued, was the friend of the poor. He wanted each to take the best liquor he could find, and in this strain continued until some one as maudlin as himself brought him down with a well-aimed bottle of whisky.

In this chaos hundreds of lost children rushed around crying and screaming for their parents. I noticed a little golden haired girl, whose long, loosely hanging locks caught fire. The child shrieked and ran past me, when someone threw upon her head a glass of brandy, which instantly caught fire and enveloped the little one in a blue flame. It was impossible for me to work my way to Rush street bridge, and I returned to Randolph street bridge, which I finally crossed in safety.

As the fire pressed on toward the lake the more difficult progress on the unburnt streets became, and the more terrible the rush for the lake shore. At 2 o'clock in the morning, people on State street south of Van Buren felt perfectly safe, but a few hours later this sense of security had so entirely vanished that from Harrison street, the final limit of the fire, to Twelfth street, everyone abandoned his house and rushed furiously toward the lake shore—there to remain exposed to the choking smoke and bitter wind all that long Monday, although as a matter of fact none of their houses had been burned.

Loss of human life added sorrow to the terrible scenes of the fire. Just how many of the wretched creatures who lived in the top stories of business blocks were surprised by the flames and burned to death in the midst of their wild orgies will never be known. Even human bones do not resist the fierce intensity of a fire which reduces stone itself to ashes. In one of the four-story windows of Speed's block on Dearborn street a man, evidently just aroused from bed, was seen to appear after the upper and lower parts of the building were on fire. The stairways were already in flames and he was 60 feet from the ground. No ladder was at hand. The suffocating smoke grew denser momentarily—some desperate chance must be tried. Suddenly the man left the window. Soon he re-appears and mechanically throws down a mattress —then some bedding. Once more he looks down the frightful depth. For a moment he halts undecided, then disappears for an instant. But there is no escape and in despair he dares all. Climbing out of the window he swings by his hands from the sill. The gleam of the flames plays on his naked limbs. Now he lets go and the next second catches the projecting cap of the third story window, another fall and he clings to the sill. The multitude below watching breathlessly this struggle for life and death, breaks out in a cry of joy. The man enters the window but can evidently find no means of escape from within for he returns again and repeats his daring feat—twice so successful. Again he succeeds and now he hangs on the window sill but 30 feet from the street. Below him the wall is smoothness itself. There is nothing to cling to and he tries to swing to the roof of a low structure adjoining, but it is too far away. The people below call to him to make the attempt once more. He does so, but it is impossible for him to swing himself so far. He tries it repeatedly, holding on with one hand and swings like a pendulum. Motionless finally, he hangs there, then slowly turns his head and looks below. The flames are hot around him and he at last releases his hold. A second later and he crashes through the flimsy sidewalk and lies in the basement a corpse. The fall has broken his neck. The mad flames rush onward and in the fierce heat the crowd

becomes panic stricken and flees. Such is the fate of one of the scores of victims to the fire.

"On to the lake!" was the cry in the business center. Whatever might become of the marble and iron blocks, Dearborn and Lake Front parks were generally believed to be secure from all danger of fire. During the whole night the most valuable merchandise from various stores was piled up there and left in the custody of reliable persons. No one thought it would burn at the very edge of the lake. Following the merchandise came thousands of people seeking refuge from the blazing streets. But the fire pursued them even here, and the property piled up in the parks became a prey of the flames. The base-ball pavilion in which the tired throng had rested, was attacked and flared up like paper — the people were finally driven into the stormy waters of the lake itself, and there at last found safety. Awful as was their position it was far more desirable than that of thousands of North Siders who were hemmed in on the narrow strip of beach north of the river, formerly notorious under the name of the "Sands." Even more dangerous was the position of those who shortly after midnight hastened to the steamers, barges, and schooners at the mouth of the river. In this crowd were many of Chicago's best citizens and the strangers who had been driven from the burning hotels. All believed the ships, and especially the steamers, perfectly safe, and no one dreamed that this place of refuge would later prove to be the most dangerous that could have been chosen.

THIRD ACT.

The Burning of the North Side.

After the citadel of a fortress is taken, the conquering army has little trouble with the outworks, whose garrison must choose between immediate surrender and hasty retreat. After the strongholds on the South Side had been devastated the North Side, with its numerous light frame houses, could offer no resistance to the victorious flames. So much the less so as the water works, although a mile from the river, were among the first buildings on the North Side to be attacked by the fire. Their destruction rendered futile all efforts of the firemen to check the great onward rush of the flames. Only in the immediate vicinity of the north branch of the river, where it saved some coal yards near the Indiana street bridge, was the fire department at all successful.

The fact that the North Side began to burn in several quarters at once—all being some distance from the main fire—gave rise to the suspicion that incendiaries had been at work. This suspicion proved entirely groundless. The origin of these separate fires was due merely to the firebrands scattered for miles by the furious gale. The water works began to burn about 3 o'clock in the morning, while the two great steam pumps were in full operation. Although the roof fell in on them, they were comparatively little damaged, and were quickly repaired, the larger pump being put in operation eight days after the fire. It was due to the heroic efforts of engineer M. Trautmann and his firemen, McKant and Prinsing, that an explosion of the boilers and the consequent ruin of all the machinery, was avoided. As soon as the building caught fire Trautmann realized the great danger from an explosion, and resolved to prevent it at all hazards. The explosion would be inevitable if the steam could not be let out of the boilers. The safety valves were opened and, although the building was on fire in a dozen places, Trautmann stood before his engines with his hand on the regulator—firm as a rock. Then the ropes by which the safety valve levers were suspended, burned off, and allowed the valves to close, but the men forced them open again. The noise of the hissing steam was drowned out by the crackling of the flames and the howling of the gale. Those outside called to the engineer to save himself before it was too late, but the officer stood true to his post. The clothes of one of the firemen began to burn while he was assisting his chief, but he did not flinch. Cinders and fire-brands fell around them like hail, but the men did not desert their engines until enough steam had escaped to save the boilers, engines and machinery from total destruction. Then, half suffocated, they rushed for the open air and barely escaped.

A terrible panic seized the North Siders when they discovered that both gas and water supply had been destroyed. There was no longer a thought of resistance — all fled. While the history of the fire on the South Side is divisible into different stages as first one massive building and then another was conquered, no similar division can be made in considering the devastation of the North Side. The fire flew on the wings of the wind, and while the main column was still busy at Kinzie street, its advance had already been mapped out by various burning buildings over a mile further north. So powerful and solid was the onward rushing mass of flames that it was impossible for spectators to remain for even an instant in any spot near the scene of action. The hot, stifling air, filled with cinders and burning brands, warned all to flee. Some wretches who had got drunk in North Water street dives were surprised by the flames, and being unable to run away fell an easy prey to the destroying demon. Because all fled, and no one had time to observe, there is a lack of reliable information concerning the progress of the fire. Uhlich's block, on North Clark street, and the big breweries near the lake were the only buildings to make much resistance to the flames. As on the South Side men deluded themselves into believing that the fire would somewhere suddenly halt, and working eastward to the lake, die out. They could not realize the terrible proportions and relentless fury of their foe. Over half the total surface of the North Side was swept by the flames, and 10,000 buildings were destroyed. The escape of the residence of Mahlon D.

Ogden, standing as it did in the very path of the flames, was remarkable. The house was isolated, occupying the center of a square, and was more or less protected by trees. In addition, the roof and side walls were covered with quilts, blankets and carpets soaked with water from private cisterns on the grounds. A large number of people assisted in fighting the flames, which finally swept on, leaving the house standing, a lone monument to dogged persistence and hard work.

Another but unsuccessful fight was made to save Unity church on Dearborn avenue, facing Washington Park. It was a massive and expensive structure and on account of its excellent construction and comparative isolation, the neighbors near and far believed it perfectly safe and an excellent repository for their valuables. Robert Collyer, the famous pastor, himself believed for a time that it would be saved. Together with a number of the younger members of his congregation he went to work to remove the wooden sidewalks and everything inflammable from the immediate vicinity of the building. Being without tools, they had to rely on their hands. From the cistern of the neighboring house of Mahlon D. Ogden water was generously furnished to wet down the frame work around the doors and windows. A part of his books Dr. Collyer removed from his studio in the church to the middle of the park. The wisdom of this action was soon seen, for within a few moments the roof of the church caught fire in a dozen places and began to burn fiercely. Collyer saw that all was lost and immediately told those about the church to flee, but he himself entered the doomed building once more and brought out the church bible.

The most characteristic feature of this third act of the great catastrophe was, as mentioned before, not the resistance to but the flight from the flames. As a rule, this flight was merely a series of retreats, the people falling back to positions of fancied security only to be driven further by the terrible blaze. Men seemed unable to grasp the fearful power of the fire. Hardly arrived at a supposedly secure point the victims were driven away again by the persecuting flames. Much of the property saved from the first attack of the enemy was lost or destroyed in these repeated retreats before the fire demon, while the price for cartage rapidly increased, $50 to $100 a load being common charges.

The loss of human life was particularly large on such streets as were suddenly and unexpectedly attacked by the fire, as Chicago avenue and Erie street. The number of victims perishing near the Chicago avenue bridge has never been determined. Early Monday morning there surged across this bridge an indescribable human chaos. Vehicles of all kinds and sizes, men and women of all ages and conditions, struggled across the narrow passage into the land of safety. Finally the bridge itself caught fire, cutting off the one means of escape still left to the poor creatures hemmed in by the advancing walls of fire. Not a few preferred death in the river to perishing in the flames and others were pushed into the water. Some tried to save themselves by running to Bremen, Townsend and Wesson streets only to learn that these streets had no outlet and death was inevitable. Many of those who remained near the burning bridge were saved by boats, which were found and bravely manned in spite of the deadly peril of approaching the east bank of the river. After the destruction of this bridge, there remained only those at Division street and North avenue to furnish transit to the fugitives hastening to the West Side. From Monday morning till late Tuesday a constant stream of people poured across the river.

Many North Siders, especially those in the northeastern part of the division, fled to Lincoln Park, where not less than 10,000 persons camped upon the graves of the old city cemetery, then incorporated as a part of Lincoln Park. But even in this place of eternal rest there was no repose for the unhappy fugitives. The fire suddenly took a northeasterly turn, and feeding on the masses of piled up household goods ate its way through the cemetery, and the refugees were once more compelled to flee—this time to the prairies to the north—or wade far out in the rough and chilly waters of the lake. In the cemetery all gradually grew still again, but it was the quietness of desolation. The ruined dead-house, the crosses and tombstones, blackened, burned and cracked by the heat—even the bark burned off the trees, which stretched out their leafless branches as if in despair. It seemed as if a demon had vented his rage on the holy spot.

Those who fled to the prairies, as the flames rushed forward all the long Monday, suffered terribly. Without protection from the bitter wind, without food, or even water, there cowered on the bare ground, tired men, exhausted women, children, invalids even—all hungry, and only a few well clothed. The clouds, colored blood-red by the fires still fiercely blazing in various parts of the burnt district, seemed to indicate that the West Side had been attacked, and thus an added horror was lent a situation already almost unendurable. About midnight the heavens finally opened their tardy flood gates, and—it rained. Drenched, shivering and cold the poor sufferers hailed the shower with unspeakable joy and gratitude. It meant that the fire must end. Unfortunately, however, the fearful exposure to the fury of the elements on the bleak prairies told on many a vigorous constitution, and diseases later developed were in countless cases traced back to the nights of the great fire. The crowd was motley. Every class, every age and condition was represented—the aged, the weak, the sick, the young and helpless—all were there. Several persons died from exposure during the night, and numerous births occurred. In short, life with its endless change went on, reckless of time or place, or circumstance.

ON THE "SANDS."

Severe as were the sufferings of those on the prairies, they were almost insignificant as compared with the hardships and anguish endured at the same time by the hundreds on the lake shore, between the mouth of the river and Erie street. When the fire first appeared on the North Side, it was principally the western part of the division that suffered while that east of Dearborn street remained unscathed for some time. This was the aristocratic residence quarter. The houses for the most part were stately mansions, isolated in fine, large grounds. Here lived, among others, W. B. Ogden, Chicago's first mayor, Julian Rumsey, also an early mayor, I. N. Arnold, Perry H. Smith, and other old settlers. Their houses were furnished with elegance, and contained remarkably fine libraries, costly paintings and priceless art treasures. But all this luxury and magnificence no more escaped the fury of the flames than the modest homes on Michigan and Illinois streets. When the fire, after devouring Lill's great brewery, finally turned its attention toward this still unburnt portion of the North Division, the flames rushed in from the north by way of the brewery and from the south over Rush street bridge. All avenues of escape, except those leading to the lake shore, were shut off by walls of fire. The shore in this neighborhood, stretching three quarters of a mile from the government pier to the pier at Lill's brewery, was the notorious "Sands," famous, when John Wentworth was mayor, as the plague spot of the city. Now it was covered with thousands of men, women, children and domestic animals of all kinds. Trunks and household furniture stood in piles round about, and there were vehicles of every description, from wheelbarrows to great four-horse trucks, each laden with property rescued, for the time at least, from the flames. Here it was that the two extremes met: wealth and poverty had dwelt side by side in the quarter of the city that had emptied itself upon this stretch of sandy waste. The aristocrat was elbowed by the pauper, the high-born dame wept with the workingwoman, and innocent girlhood was ogled and insulted by foulest vice. The air was full of smoke, cinders and brands and the red-hot sand was blown about by the furious gale until breathing became almost an impossibility. About daylight the household goods began to burn, and the smoke grew so dense that man and beast were alike compelled to enter the water to avoid suffocation. Hundreds clung to the horses and wagons standing far out from shore, and others, with their backs to the storm, stood unsupported in the waves. One woman, the wife of a well-known musician, was separated from her husband and compelled to wade out, breast deep, in the water, carrying in her arms a little child and an infant not yet three months old.

Finally the immense lumber piles to the south and southwest, along the river, began to burn, and the terrific heat, dense smoke and noxious gases threatened the very lives of the fugitives. Many succumbed. Here a family of sons and daughters mourned the mother, who had just died before their eyes, but heard no word of consolation. An invalid, brought to the water's edge on a mattress, breathed her last, but the knowledge of her death was received with stolid indifference. Not until late in the afternoon did the position of those on the "Sands" grow less precarious. At last the fury of the fire abated somewhat, and some of the more daring ventured to cross over into the West Side, others made their way out onto the pier and were rescued by tugs and steamers, but most of the unfortunates did not leave the beach until Tuesday morning.

But man himself added the greatest horror to the terrible situation, as is brought out with fearful intensity in the following description of an eye witness:

The tragedies upon the "Sands" differed from those where broader limits marked the encampment of victims of the fire. The prairies seemed to give relief to pent-up agonies and nerve the soul to silent endurance; even the park and graveyard, bleak and sombre as they were, seemed to impart an atmosphere of personal security, that was not possible upon the "Sands." There, on the scorching earth, that held the heat and sent a shimmering, ceaseless wave of blasting air and sand from underneath the feet, parching the flesh and drying up the fountains of blood and life, the spirit of infernal revelry prevailed. As in the region of the damned, told of by Dante, the evil nature of mankind glared forth to vex the tender souls of those whom fate had sent into their presence.

Imagine the scene of the horrid drama. No possibility of escape—a raging fury at the rear a pitiless expanse of lake in front, a small area filled with human creatures, maddened animals, delicate and refined women, pure and innocent children, the aged, the infirm, the weak, the dying, the despairing; young girls whose artless lives were unfamiliar with even the name of crime, men of well ordered lives and Christian minds, brutes in human form, who were not only ready to do acts of crime, but whose polluting wickedness was rank, and cast off prison fumes upon the air. All kinds and conditions and grades of life—all forms of death, from calm and peaceful passing to a welcome rest to that which follows in the train of vicious deeds. Here, huddled close and helpless, the purest girlhood was forced to endure the leering of the vile, and if a chance protector spoke in her defense, the wicked laughed and jeered and cursed until the stoutest heart grew faint with apprehension. Women whose claim to womanhood was long since lost, took fiendish delight in adding indefinable shame and terror to the misery of those who shrank from crime. Think what it would be to place a loved one in the lowest haunts of vice, and there bend over the death bed of that failing friend while all about the din of wickedness was sounding in the ears. Increase the circumstance of grim necessity and add the weight of a consciousness that home, treasures, everything was gone, and this the only, the enforced spot where death must meet the loved father, mother, sister, friend. Could all the powers of hell itself devise a keener form of anguish? Yet these lines are drawn from actual knowledge, and the shudder awakened at the recollection of sights stays the pen.

The creatures who there tortured the helpless were no longer human—vice had dulled their moral instincts and despair transformed them for the moment into demons. Their orgies were born in malice, they delighted in their sins; they shrieked aloud with glee to see the innocent rush from them and plunge into the lake, that for the instant the sight might be shut out. The dying were not always comforted with the caress of love. Upon a burned and blackened blanket lay the dead body of one poor woman whose babe lay by her side crying in shrill alarm. The crowd about this type of life and death gave no more heed than if it was the natural order of events. All night the corpse lay there untouched. If fate preserved the babe, the writer does not know of the fact. Above the terror of the fire—for that emotion grew pangless as the hours progressed; above the loss of worldly riches; above the grief of death, for death seemed then the only mercy-bringing power; above all the conditions of the scene that added elements of horror, the mingling of the two extremes of vice and virtue, and the momentary triumph of the bad, in their malicious show of wickedness, seemed the most appalling quality of this immediate spot.

Among the first to arrive at the "Sands" was I. N. Arnold, with his servants and children. He had fought the flames from his beautiful mansion to the last moment, and when finally compelled to flee, he could save only a small bundle of valuable papers. All else was destroyed—his choice library, costly bric-a-brac and fine paintings. Arrived at the lake shore he took in the situation, and resolved, if possible, to work his way out on the long pier just then being completed by W. B. Ogden. This pier, which prolonged the left bank of the river out into the lake, was not as yet planked over, and it was with difficulty that the party clambered over the rock filling to the end. A small row boat was found, and all were taken to the light-house, lying beyond the pier, and there they, with Judge Goodrich, Edward I. Tinkham and others, were hospitably received. Even here, however, the fire threatened them, and a fire company was formed to fight the flames from a burning propeller, which drifted past them, and to put out the brands blown from the lumber piles further up stream. About 4 o'clock in the afternoon the tug "Clifford" rescued the prisoners, and after a perilous voyage up the river landed them in safety on the West Side.

A WOMAN'S STORY OF THE FIRE.

* Telegraphed to the New York Tribune.

CHICAGO, October 12th.—Where shall I begin? How shall I tell the story that I have been living during these dreadful days? It's a dream, a nightmare, only so real that I tremble as I write, as though the whole thing might be brought to me again by merely telling of it.

We lived on the North Side, six blocks from the river. We were quiet people, like most of the North Siders, flattering ourselves that our comfortable wooden houses and sober, cheery New England looking streets were far preferable to the more rapid, blatant life of the South Side.

Well, on Sunday morning, October 8th, Robert Collyer gave his people what we felt to be a wonderful sermon, on the text: "Think ye, that those upon whom the tower of Siloam fell, were sinners above all those who dwelt at Jerusalem?" and illustrated it by a picture of the present life and our great cities, their grandeur, their wickedness, and the awful though strictly natural, consequences of our insatiable pursuit of worldly prosperity, too often unchecked by principle.

I came out, gazing about on our beautiful church, and so we passed the pleasant, bright day, some of us going down to the scene of the West Side fire of Saturday night, and espying

---

* By Miss Cordelia Kirkland, now living in California.

from a good distance the unhappy losers of so much property. About 5:30 o'clock our neighboring fire telegraph sent forth some little tintinnabulations, and we lazily wondered, as D—— played the piano and I watered my ivy, what they were burning up now.

At 10 o'clock in the evening the fire bells were ringing constantly, and we went to bed, regretting that there must be more property burning up on the West Side. Eleven o'clock, 12 o'clock, and I awoke my sister, saying: "It's very singular; I never heard anything like the fires to-night. It seems as if the whole West Side must be afire." One o'clock, 2 o'clock; we get up and look out. "Great God! The fire has crossed the river from the south! Can there be any danger here?" And we look anxiously out, to see men hurrying by, screaming and swearing, and the whole city to the south and west of us one vivid glare. "Where are the engines? Why don't we hear them as usual?" we asked each other, thoroughly puzzled, but even yet hardly personally frightened by the strange aspect of the brilliant and surging streets below. Then came a loud knocking at the door: "Ladies, ladies, get up! Pack your trunks, and prepare to leave your house. It may not be necessary, but it is well to be prepared." It was a friend who had fought his way through the La Salle street tunnel to warn us that the city is on fire. We looked at each other with white faces. Well we might. In an inner room slept an invalid relative, the object of our ceaseless care and love, the victim of a terrible and recurring mental malady, which had already sapped much of his strength and life, and rendered quiet and absence of excitement the first prescription of his physicians. Must we call the invalid? And, if we did, in the midst of this fearful glare and turmoil, what would be the result? We determined to wait till the last minute, and threw some valuables into a trunk, while we anxiously watched the ever approaching flame and tumult.

Then came a strange sound in the air, which stilled for a moment the surging crowd. Was it thunder? No. The sky was clear and full of stars, and we shuddered as we felt, but did not say, it was a tremendous explosion of gunpowder. By this time the blazing sparks and bits of burning wood, which we had been fearfully watching, were fast becoming an unintermitting fall of burning hail, and another shower of blows on the door warned us that there was not another moment to be lost. "Call E—" (the invalid), "do not let him stay a minute, and I will try to save our poor little birds." My sister flew to wake up our precious charge, and I went down stairs repeating, to make myself remember, "birds, deeds, silver, jewelry, silk dresses," as the order in which we would try to save our property if it came to the worst.

As I passed through our pretty parlor how my heart ached! Here lay a relic of my father's library, a copy of a bible printed in 1637, on one table; on another my dear Mrs. Browning, the gift of a lost friend. What should I take! What should I leave? I alternately loaded myself with gift after gift and dashed them down in despair. Lovely pictures and statuettes, left by a kind friend for the embellishment of our little rooms, and which had turned them into a bower of beauty — must be left? At last I stopped before our darling, a sweet and tender picture of Beatrice Cenci going to execution, which looked down at me though the dismal red glare which was already filling the rooms, with a saintly and wierd sweetness that seemed to have something wistful in it. I thought, "I will save this if I die for it," but my poor parrot called my name and asked for a peanut, and I could no more have left him than if he had been a baby. But could I carry that huge cage? No, indeed. So I reluctantly took my poor little canary, who was painfully fluttering about and wondering at the disturbance, and kissing him, opened the front door and set him free — only to smother, I fear.

What a sight our usually quiet street (Dearborn avenue)

presented? As far as I could see a horrible wall—a surging, struggling, encroaching wall—like a vast surface of grimacing demons, came pressing up the street—a wall of fire, ever nearer and nearer, steadily advancing on our midnight helplessness. Was there no wagon, no carriage in which we could coax our poor E—, and take him away from these maddening sights? Truck after truck, indeed, passed by, but filled with loads of people and goods, and carriages rushed past drawn by struggling and foaming horses, and lined with white, scared faces.

A truck loaded with goods dashed up the street, and, as I looked, flames burst out from the sides, and it burned to ashes in front of our door. No hope, no help for property; what we could not carry, we must lose. So, forcing my reluctant parrot into the little bird's cage, I took him under one arm and a little hand-bag on the other, just as my sister appeared with E—, who, thank God, was calm and self-possessed. At last the good friend who had warned us appeared, and, leaving all his own things, insisted on helping my sister save ours, and he and she started on, dragging a trunk. They were obliged to abandon it at the second corner, however, and walked on, leaving me to follow with E—. "Come E—, let us go," said I: "Go where? I am not going. What is the use?" he answered, and he stood with his arms folded as if he were interested merely as a curious spectator. I urged, I begged, I cried, I went down on my knees. He would not stir, but proposed going back into the house. This I prevented by entreaties, and I besought him to fly as others were doing; but no. A kind of apathetic despair had seized him, and he stood like a rock while the flames swept nearer and nearer, and my entreaties and even my appeals to him to save me, were utterly in vain. Hotter and hotter grew the pavement, wilder the cries of the crowd, and my silk and cotton clothing began to smoke in spots. I felt beside myself, and seizing E—, tried to drag him away. Alas! what could my woman's strength do?

There followed another shout, a wild push back, a falling wall, and I was half a block away, and E— was gone. Oh! God, pity these poor worms of the dust and crush them not utterly, was my prayer.

How I passed the rest of that cruel Sunday night, I scarcely know. Wandering, staring, blindly carrying along my poor parrot, who was too tired to make a sound, I seemed to go in a dream. Starting north to get help, running back as near the flame as I could, in the vain hope of finding E—, bitterly reproaching myself that I had ever left him for an instant, I passed three hours of which I can hardly give any account. I know that, as I turned wildly back once more, I saw the beautiful Episcopal church of St. James in flames. They came on all sides, licking the marble buttresses, one by one, and leaving charred or blackened masses. But the most wonderful sight of all was the white and shining church tower, from which, as I looked, burst tongues of fire.

Constantly faces that I knew flashed across me, but they were always in a dream, all blackened and discolored, and with an expression I never saw before. Very little selfishness and no violence did I see. * * * * Some friend—it was days before I knew who—took my parrot and forced a little bottle of tea and a bag of crackers into my hand as I wandered.

At last I found myself opposite Unity church. I was grieving enough, heaven knows, over my private woes, but I awoke to new miseries when I saw our pastor's great heart, which had sustained the fainting spirit of so many, freely give way to lamentations and tears, as his precious library, the slow accumulation of twenty laborious and economical years, fell and flamed into nothingness in that awful fire. I turned away, heart-sick, and resumed my search for the face which I now felt almost sure I should never see again. A new sight soon struck my eye. What in the world was that dark, lurid, purplish ball, that hung before me, constantly changing its appearance, like some fiendish face that grimaces at our misery? I looked and looked again. May I never see the sun, the cheerful, daily herald of comfort and peace look like that again. It looked devilish, and I pinched myself to see if I was not losing my senses. It did not seem ten minutes since I had seen the little moon look out, cold, quiet and pitiless, through a rift in the smoke cloud, from the deep blue of the sky. * * * * Exhausted and almost fainting, weeping and sorely distressed, I finally landed in a friendly house far up on La Salle street. As I stepped inside the door, E— appeared, quite composed, and almost indifferent. Burnt? Oh, no; he was all right. Did I suppose he was fool enough to stay and be burned? There was D— too, if I wanted to see her, in the parlor. Did I feel reverently thankful. Ask yourself.

SCENES AT THE MOUTH OF THE RIVER.

By midnight Sunday the down town streets were thronged with fugitives from across the river and spectators from the North and South Division. When it became evident that the city was doomed the people fled to the North and South Sides and the lake front. Thousands also, among them many of the guests of the big hotels, made their way to the mouth of the river below Rush street bridge. Here, on the very brink of the stream, with the great lake just beyond, all believed themselves safe—the more so as the spot was shut off from the flames by the massive stone depot building of the Illinois Central railroad and by the substantial brick and stone warehouses at the foot of Randolph and Lake streets. Hundreds of persons crowded on the vessels lying in the river, thinking that if the worst came, the boats would put out into the lake and so escape destruction. As long as Rush street bridge stood untouched hundreds hastened across it into temporary safety on the North Side. But when it burned those who still remained at the mouth of the river were numbered by the thousands, and not nearly all of them could crowd on the neighboring ships. The terrible flames were steadily advancing on the wretched fugitives, and there were no small boats at hand by which they could gain the opposite bank of the stream. Suddenly the great Illinois Central elevator "A" caught fire from one of the blazing pieces of wood that were borne aloft by the wind, and in an instant more the whole structure burst into flames. But a few hundred feet away stood elevator "B," and in the slip between the two were vessels which would readily communicate the flames to the further elevator. The smoke and heat from the burning building were stifling, and it seemed that all those not on the vessels were caught in an awful trap. As the flames had gradually approached the ships and steamers had crossed to the north bank of the river so as to be as far as possible out of harm's way, and now when they tried to get out into the lake it was found that the terrific southwest gale bound them as with steel cables to the bank. Then it was—in that moment of terrible need—that Providence furnished a rescuer. The saving of the vessels and people at the mouth of the river was due to the heroism of the captain and crew of the tug "Magnolia," and in those hours of brave deeds and cool courage the acts of Captain Joseph Gilson and his crew, stand unexcelled as to bravery, unequaled as to the amount of good accomplished.

Owing to the heavy southwest wind no vessels were making the harbor, and so there was no towing to be done. All the tugs but the "Magnolia" were lying up the river in the neighborhood of South Water and Wells streets. When needed at the river's mouth the burning of the intervening bridges prevented them from getting below even Clark street. The "Magnolia," however, chanced to be lying in the Illinois Central slip and her steam was up. When Captain Gilson learned of the enormous proportions of the fire he resolved to leave the tug in the hands of the engineer and fireman, Nicholas Dutcher and Joseph Sweetman, and to himself go over to the North Side to save what he could from his house. So the "Magnolia" landed Gilson on the north bank and the crew were given orders to take her well out into the lake, where she would be safe. In another moment the little tug was cleaving her way to safety. Gilson turned and started for his home. Suddenly, obeying an irresistible impulse, he looked toward the lake, and in a second more the horror of the situation flashed upon him. Providence had called this man back for the salvation of thousands of human beings. In the fierce glare of the burning elevator he saw the black masses of humanity standing on the decks of the ships and the struggling, surging mob on shore. With the quick eye of a sailor he noticed that not all the vessels were steamers and instinct told him that even the propellers could not swing clear of the river bank to which they were bound by the gale. All this came to Gilson in the twinkling of an eye, and scarcely realizing what he did, he shouted for his tug to return. The men heard his call and obeyed. Leaping aboard his boat Gilson started for the burning elevator. As he went down the stream he got two life-boats from the harbor master, and gave them to volunteer crews who straightway began the transfer of persons from the south to the north shore of the river. Gilson himself transferred several hundred people, among others, General McArthur, then president of the Board of Public Works, and Edward I. Tinkham, a prominent banker. McArthur was hurrying over to see what could be done to protect the water works, and Tinkham was trying to save a roll of money, almost a million dollars, from his bank. But soon more important work demanded the services of the "Magnolia." Gilson began to tow out the vessels in the slip between the two great elevators. It was hoped that the flames would not leap across to elevator " B." Soon, however, the fire attacked the building from the coal shed adjoining, and it seemed that nothing could save it. Some one,

Saving Vessels at the Mouth of the River.

From the Cyclorama of the Chicago Fire

however, had discovered, on a flat car near by, a new steam fire engine, marked for forwarding to Racine, Wisconsin, and had fired it up and gotten it into such a position that water could be drawn from the river. Hose was at hand, and the flames were vigorously attacked. Just as victory seemed certain the steamer stopped running for want of oil. The elevator had been shut down for some time, and no lubricants could be found in it. The "Magnolia" was finally hailed and Gilson was called upon to divide his scanty supply of oil, which he did willingly. The steamer started again, and this time the flames in the coal shed and engine room of elevator "B" were entirely extinguished and the great structure saved.

In the meantime the immense lumber piles on the north bank of the river in the yards of the Peshtigo Company began to burn. Lying near these yards were the propellers: "Ira Chaffee" and "Navarino," the steamer "Alpena," the barge "Advance" and a Canadian schooner. Not one of these boats could move from the northern shore of the river, and the various captains signaled furiously for the "Magnolia." Gilson first towed out the "Ira Chaffee," and so preserved a place of refuge for more than a thousand persons. Then he saved the "Advance," on which there were several hundred persons, among them Judge McAllister.

On attempting to move the "Navarino," Gilson found that his boat did not have power enough to stir the big propeller, and although he blew out his government valve, (raising the steam pressure on the "Magnolia's" boiler to 150 pounds, or 60 pounds more than allowed by law), he had to give her up. The refugees were transferred from the "Navarino" to the "Alpena," and "Manitowoc," and with the "Magnolia's" aid, both these vessels reached the outer harbor in safety. The "Navarino" and the Canadian schooner were now wrapped in flames and Gilson had just time to get a tow-line on the propeller "Sky Lark" and start her down the river, when the fire swept up to the very spot where she had been lying. In addition to the fugitives on board the "Sky Lark," were many valuable books and papers of the Goodrich steamer line.

The flames were now sweeping the river in one place, from shore to shore, but Gilson turned the "Magnolia" back for the last time. Ringing for full steam, he sent his boat through the sheet of fire and came out on the other side unhurt. There he picked up two policemen whom he found standing in despair on the south shore of the river. Then the little tug was turned around and the run under the flames made once more. This time Captain Gilson was not so fortunate, and the woodwork of the tug was found to be blazing in several places. The fire was finally put out, but not until after considerable damage had been done.

Nothing now remained for Gilson to do at the mouth of the river, and the "Magnolia" was turned toward Light House (or Ogden's) slip, near where the fugitives on the "Sands" were congregated. Here again Gilson's arrival was most opportune. The fierce heat had driven hundreds of people into the lake near the slip, and just as the "Magnolia" appeared the schooner "Swallow," which had been lying in the slip, caught fire, burned her moorings, and enwrapped in flames bore down upon the poor wretches in the water. Before this they were almost suffocated, and had the smoke and heat from the burning schooner been allowed to increase their sufferings, the loss of life would have been appalling. Three hundred feet away iron railroad tracks were curling up like shavings in the terrible heat, and now they were threatened with this burning vessel in their very midst! But Gilson skillfully approached the blazing schooner, got a line on her, and before it was burned off, had the boat well out of the neighborhood. Returning to the shore, the "Magnolia" began carrying people from the water and the west pier to the propellers lying out in the lake. His boat would hold only 50 or 75 persons, and Gilson was forced to make repeated trips to get all the fugitives to a place of safety. Large sums of money were offered him by the wealthy if he would save them first, but the plucky captain showed no favor and as before refused all money offers for his heroic work.

In the afternoon the "Magnolia" made her way back to the mouth of the river. It was an exploring tour to discover whether the city had been totally destroyed. Slowly the little boat made the dangerous journey. Near Rush street the groans of a man were heard, and finally a poor fellow was discovered in the river clinging to a post. He was fearfully wounded and burned about the head and arms and had been almost suffocated by the smoke. For eight hours he had been in his dreadful position, keeping under water as much of the time as possible, and lifting his face up only often enough to breathe. Gilson immediately put about and took him to one of the propellers in the lake. Then he returned and was rejoiced to find that the West Side was still unburned. On reaching South Water street he notified the various tug owners of the condition of affairs, and a fleet of forty tugs was soon at work bringing the people from the vessels in the outer harbor to the West Side.

The daring and bravery of Captain Gilson and his crew and their noble self-forgetfulness, stand out in white beauty in the darkness and gloom that had fallen around Chicago; their actions restore that faith in humanity which had been shaken by the story of the pillaging of the South Side and the terrible scene on the "Sands." •

---

* Joseph Gilson was born in Chicago in 1846 in the old "Coffee Exchange." As a mere youth he gained celebrity by the reckless daring he displayed in saving the crew of the schooner "Albany" during a terrific gale, in which none of the thousands of spectators, who lined the lake shore, dared venture forth. The schooner was being pounded to pieces on a sand bar and Gilson, in his tug, was forced to make six trips out to her before he could get near enough to rescue the men. The water was so shoal that when the tug sank in the trough of the sea, her stern post struck the bottom of the lake and heavy leaks were sprung. Gilson persisted in his efforts, however, and finally brought off every man from the vessel, which in another moment was merely a mass of wreckage, beaten about by the great billows. In 1892 Gilson, then in command of one of the World's Fair steamers, again saved the crew of a wrecked vessel, which he discovered in the lake. At present Captain Gilson commands one of the fleet of steamers which run from Chicago to the World's Fair grounds.

ON THE PRAIRIE.

Slowly and heavily rose the sun on the morning of October 10th. The air was close and sultry; smoke and vapor still lay over the whole city. It was a desolate, a heart-rending scene. There on the prairie lay many a man, broken in spirit, who but the day before had fought the battle of life with undaunted courage. But the situation had already changed—the reaction had set in. After the intense exertion of all the forces of body, mind and soul, followed a corresponding relaxation. What had been undergone was enough to severely test the moral and physical power of the strongest.

It had been a fearful night, hardly less cruel and terrible than the preceding one when the fire columns had marched relentlessly northward. Their danger had keyed the people up to the highest pitch of nervous tension but it had passed now and they broke down helpless. They could have continued their flight but this awful quiet they could not endure. With rest came reflection and the thought of horrors undergone. From the gloom of his present misery rose each man's happy past as in a vision, but when he roused himself it was to see the future barren and hopeless before him. With mental anguish came worry as to the uncertain fate of friends and families and the lack of physical necessities tortured the fugitives.

Small wonder that many lost their reason, that the eye of many a soul was blinded forever; small wonder that many a life conceived the germs of death during the horrible hours of that long Monday night, and that the number of those who languished and died only weeks after the fire was far greater than of those who met death in the flames.

Twilight should have fallen about 6 o'clock, but on that Monday evening no darkness followed the setting of the sun, for great columns of fire still illumined the scene. On the prairie lay 50,000 persons, who wondered if their cup of misery was

not already filled. Was the uncontrollable element to leap the
river for a third time, and so return to the side of the city
whence it had come? All eyes were turned toward the fire
which was working its way to the Division street bridge. It
was but a matter of moments when the flames would reach
the bridge, when at last the long-prayed for rain began. With
tears of joy the multitudes gave thanks for heaven's blessing
—the fire ceased to spread and gradually died out. All too
soon however, the wretched, houseless, ill-clothed fugitives
realized that they were exposed to the cold, drenching rain.
All night and all day they had been scorched by the heat of
the conflagration and stifled by its smoke and gases, now unfed
and unprotected, they shivered and gasped in the down-pour-
ing torrents. Side by side stood the beggar who, having had
nothing, lost nothing, and the millionaire rendered penniless over
night. Wherever the eye turned, the same picture: wagons,
laden with household goods, piles of rescued property, cows,
horses, dogs, men, women and children—all huddled together
in the greatest confusion. On her trunk sits the wife of a rich merchant, holding in her arms some saved trinket, and on her trunk
sits the wife of a poor laborer, and in her arms holds the babe
whose eyes reflect all her happiness and all her misery. Happy
he who can count his dear ones all. Many a family is separated to remain so for days. The stronger had stayed behind
to fight the flames or to try to save property while the weaker
had gone on in advance. In the great throng on the prairies
search for missing friends is a fruitless task.

Meanwhile the rain has formed little puddles and pools of water,
and these serve to moisten parched lips and cleaving tongues.

Dire necessity stimulated as ever the genius of invention.
Tents were made from carpets and blankets, and held up by
such sticks and branches as could be found. Hundreds found
some shelter under sidewalks and in culverts, and every inch
of neighboring houses and barns was occupied. But the
great mass of the people on the prairies was unprotected.

They were crowded together, but on the whole behaved well. Misfortune purified their instincts. While contemplating his own loss, no one could forget that his neighbor's was as large. All were equally miserable. After a time the men became resigned to their fate, and later felt a certain recklessness as to what the future might have in store. The women distinguished themselves by greater energy, and proved their greater mental elasticity. They had their children to care for, and it was ever the mother who, when the camp fire burned low, kept it going, or, when the rain fell mercilessly, covered her loved ones as best she could—even with her own body. So the night wore on, and before darkness fell again almost every one had found more comfortable shelter.

INCIDENTS OF THE GREAT FIRE.

Most of the human lives sacrificed to the flames on the North Side were lost on Wesson and Townsend streets. This, to a certain extent, is explained by the fact that these streets were short and narrow, terminating abruptly in culs-de-sac. As soon as Chicago avenue bridge became impassable—first because of the congestion of vehicles there, and later in consequence of the fire sweeping away the bridge itself—a great many wagons and pedestrians started north for Division street bridge, on Wesson and Townsend streets, but were caught in a fiery trap, from which escape was almost impossible. Scores perished; but in almost all cases the charred remains of the victims could not be identified. Besides those who came down these streets from Chicago avenue, the flames surprised not a few of the persons who lived in this locality. On Townsend street lived a Mr. Geyerstanger, publisher of a German humorous paper. With his wife and his four children he succeeded in saving a part of his household goods. While three of the little ones and his wife went to the West Side with what had already been saved, he and his twelve year old daughter attempted to save some books from his splendid library, but the flames were down upon them before they were aware of it, and they were unable to escape. Of the seven bodies afterwards found in this locality, it was impossible to tell which were those of the unfortunate man and his little girl. A neighbor, named Hecht, met his death in the same manner, while attempting to save his old invalid father-in-law. When the fire attacked his home, Hecht, Aneas-like, took the weak old man on his shoulders, and carried him from the burning house. In the yard he put down his precious burden, and, as it is supposed from the position of the bodies when found, returned to the house for some valuables. While inside he was overtaken by the flames, and the unfortunate old man also fell a victim to the fury of the fire.

A horrible incident occurred near the water works. Three men had stayed too long in the brewery near by and on coming out were forced to seek instant shelter from the flames. They crept into some large water mains which were lying in the street, but the fierce heat of the conflagration turned the pipes into iron shrouds, and the next moring the bodies of the men were found roasted almost beyond recognition.

The loss of an occasional life aroused but little attention. Alexander Frear, a New York alderman, was crossing Lake street bridge, the rail of which had been torn away. In front of him was a man with a heavy load of clothing. Suddenly he noticed the poor fellow stumble and fall into the water. The crowds on the bridge rushed madly on, and no one in the many passing boats paid the slightest attention to the drowning wretch, who finally disappeared, swallowed up in the black waters of the river. A driver fell from the high seat of his heavily laden truck, striking his head on the stone street and breaking his neck—the horses dashed on and the crowds passed by heedless of the corpse lying near at hand. A woman near the St. James hotel knelt in the street holding a crucifix before her. Her dress skirt blazed up, but she did not notice it. In another instant a runaway truck dashed her to the ground. On another bridge the crushing mob lifted a young girl from her feet and literally forced her over the handrail of the bridge. For a moment she clung feebly to this slight support, but was soon brushed off, and with a despairing cry, fell into the water below. No action to save her was taken either by those in boats on the river or by those hurrying across the bridge. Terror had banished every feeling of chivalry, even of common humanity.

At the Sherman House three hundred guests were quartered Sunday night. Among them were many ladies without escorts, and five single ladies were sick in bed. Early in the evening the night clerk and his assistant had all the valuable papers of the hotel conveyed to a place of safety, and when the flames threatened the hotel the guests were all aroused. The ladies were taken to the lake shore and put in charge of police officers. The sick were put in a carriage and started off, when suddenly the clerk was seized with an awful foreboding. A glance through the carriage windows showed but four persons inside and he knew there were five invalids in the house. Wrenching an axe from the hands of a fireman, and with a cry to his assistant, he rushed back through the smoke-filled corridors of the great hotel. Reaching the door of the room where he believed the fifth sick woman lay, he forced an entrance with a couple of blows of his axe. The woman was there, sitting up in terror in her bed, having had no previous knowledge of the fire. The men hastily threw a heavy dress and cloak about her, dashed the contents of the water pitcher on a woolen blanket, and wrapping the woman up in this and protecting their own heads as well as they could, hurried down stairs with the invalid in their arms. The clerk was quite badly burned, but all finally reached the street. In a few moments more the upper stories of the hotel had fallen into the fiery embraces of the basement.

The saving of the Lind block, directly east of the Randolph street bridge, was due to the energetic efforts of Alderman Walsh and I. C. Richberg, a well known attorney. These gentlemen saw at a glance the danger the West Side would be in the moment Lind's block should be attacked. They immediately organized a volunteer corps, and after considerable difficulty induced the crew of the engine "R. A. Williams" to take their steamer from Canal street, where it was lying idle, to Market street. By keeping the exposed side of the building drenched with water, drawn from the river, and by tearing down all awnings and wooden signs the structure was finally saved. This prevented the flames from crossing to the West Side by the Randolph street bridge, but there was also great danger that the fire would leap the river at the foot of Erie street, or cross by means of the Chicago avenue bridge. The prevention of this calamity was largely due to the efforts of John Buehler, the banker. He took charge of the firemen sent down from Harvard station and of a part of the Milwaukee fire department. He also had the local steamer "Chicago" put on a tug boat and in this way secured excellent service. When the burning tar from the gas works, on the east side of the river, drifted across the stream, Buehler pressed the spectators into service and extinguished the flaming mass. After all danger to the West Side was over, Buehler took his steamer to the North Side pumping station to render such aid as was possible.

Several men on the top of the big Wheeler elevator tried to save it by throwing from its roof the burning shingles and brands which rained upon it, but despite their efforts the flames attacked the building from a lower story, and they suddenly found it necessary to flee for their lives. Four of the eight on the roof dashed through the fire and smoke of the interior and reached the ground safely; the other four were cut off from the skylight by the flames. One piece of the roof after the other fell into the fiery sea below, leaving smaller and smaller the spot where the men huddled together. Repeated attempts were made to throw them a rope, but all failed. Flames and dense black masses of smoke were now pouring from the elevator. At times the men were concealed from the view of the anxious spectators. Finally a piece of brick was fastened to a long twine and thrown them. By means of the twine, the heavy rope was pulled up and the end quickly made fast. In another moment all were in safety—but none too soon, for the last man touched the ground just as the rope, burned through at the top, fell in coils around him.

Besides the mansion of Mahlon D. Ogden but one house stood in the burnt district of the North Side after the fire. This was the little wooden cottage on Lincoln place, belonging to Bellinger, a policeman, who saved his property only after a terrible struggle. He made every preparation for defense—tearing up the wooden sidewalk, raking up and burning the dry leaves in his yard, and finally covering his little home with carpets and blankets soaked with water. At the critical moment the water supply gave out, but Bellinger had a quantity of cider in his cellar, and with this he kept the blankets and carpets drenched until the fire had swept past.

The last house to burn was probably that of Dr. John H. Foster, on Fullerton avenue, near Lincoln park, which was attacked at 10:30 Monday night, about twenty-six hours after the fire began. Some authorities give the house of John A. Huck, north of the city limits, as the last one to burn; but the flames raged in coal and lumber yards and in other places where there were piles of combustible material, until far into Tuesday.

An unfinished stone building in the South Division, corner of La Salle and Monroe streets, did not burn, as there was absolutely no wood work about it, even the partition walls and floors being of brick.

The scores of people, who found temporary safety on the old North Pier, were furnished with some food by the crib keeper, but this provision was soon exhausted, and the prospects for a very hungry night seemed most excellent. Finally a true American remedy was tried: a meeting was held, with Judge Goodrich presiding. It was proposed to send a tug up the river in search of provisions, and all being agreeable a tug was hailed, and two young men were sent with an order in blank from Judge Goodrich and E. I. Tinkham, the banker. Supplies were in this manner procured, and the hungry hundreds relieved.

About 3 o'clock Monday morning, when the Washington street tunnel was crowded with men trying to get to their down-town stores and offices, to personally satisfy themselves of their losses, and with others trying to get from down-town to the unburnt West Side, the gas lights suddenly went out. The gas works had exploded, and Stygian darkness reigned in the long, narrow pathway. The danger of a collision between the streams of humanity running in different directions was the greater, as many of the fugitives from the South Side were heavily laden with effects saved from the conflagration. All at once a man with remarkable presence of mind called out in a stentorian voice: "Keep to the right," which cry immediately passed from mouth to mouth, from one end of the tunnel to the other, and all confusion was averted.

Hundreds of children were lost during the fire, and for days afterwards the police were kept busy finding parents to match the various youngsters who filled the station houses. One officer found a baby, three months old, alone in a blazing street. Two children of H. Claussenius, the German consul, were separated from their parents, and it was Wednesday evening before they were heard from. A friend of the family had found them and taken them to his home in Evanston.

Property was saved with the greatest difficulty. A bank officer got $600,000 from his vaults, and had to pay an expressman $1000 to take him to the depot, where he could take a train for Milwaukee. Ex-Lieutenant Governor Bross saw a wagon standing in front of his beautiful home, and supposing that some member of the family had hired it, filled it with the most valuable property from his house, but when the wagon was loaded the driver quietly drove away, and was never heard of again. Louis Ibach had just furnished a new hotel on Wells and Randolph streets, and when he went to save some few of the fine blankets he had just purchased, he found thieves already looting the place. On introducing himself and good-naturedly asking for a blanket or two, the rascals gave him one and told him to clear out.

When the roofs of a block of houses on State street, near Van Buren, suddenly flared up, a ghastly scene was witnessed. The occupants of the upper stories, anxious to save their property, began to throw things down into the streets below. Out flew books, pictures, looking glasses, beds and finally, a coffin, containing the body of a man. A procession of men, carrying elegant coffins down to the lake front, was one of the strange sights of the fire. They were saving the contents of an undertaking establishment, but when the lake shore was reached every coffin was filled with some tired mortal, eager to enjoy a few hour's repose in the soft upholstery. The appearance of these coffins, filled with sweetly sleeping men and women, presented a singular picture as dawn broke over the lake.

Of course there were ludicrous as well as pathetic incidents. Before the burning Bigelow House an old lady marched up and down, shouldering a cavalry sabre. Another old lady, wanting more light on the subject, paraded through the streets with a burning lantern in each hand. The mania for saving something—no matter what—was epidemic. Men and women were seen with empty bird cages, old boxes and dirty baskets, with bedding, tinware and wash tubs. Women, who supposed they were saving their jewel boxes, often found, after a time, that they were hugging some bundle of worthless rubbish. Many carried anything that was forced upon them, and one well-known banker was found carefully treasuring a cast-away frying pan.

A WALK THROUGH THE RUINS.

It was a dismal, wet morning which dawned on the unfortunate city after the terrible night of the 9th. A stiff northwest wind was blowing over the still smoking ruins, but the copious rain which had fallen had stopped the spread of the flames. The picture presented by the burnt district was that of gloomy waste and overthrow. Now for the first time the immensity of the calamity was realized. When the fire was driving the fugitives from place to place, no other thought than that of self-preservation entered men's minds. But now the poor victims could comprehend in its full extent the terrible blow which so quickly and unexpectedly had fallen upon them.

From so small an elevation as the top of a wagon one could see men standing on the ground three miles away, across what had been the most densely and substantially built portions of the city. In awful desolation the spectacle was one to boldly challenge that which burned Rome or Persepolis once displayed. Of the proud marble buildings that had seemed built for all time, there remained but shapeless piles of debris. Here and there portions of a church still stood with bald walls rising sadly to heaven. Only with great effort can one work his way through the blackened ruins which blockade the streets.

Yesterday this was South Water street. Here lay the treasures of all zones, brought by the ships of enterprising merchants to the banks of the Chicago river. Here were the immense storehouses in which the products of the world were heaped up. This formless mass is wet with precious wine from the Rhine and Burgundy; in it, destroyed and buried, lie sweet fruits ripened by the sun of the tropics, the spices of the

After the Fire.

From the Cyclorama of the Chicago Fire

West Indies, boxes of tea from China, rich stuffs from the Orient. It is difficult to keep the right road. Of the splendid court house the four walls still stand, but "in the windows gloom abideth." Where but yesterday the hum of busy multitudes was heard, where deliberative bodies held session, where justice had her seat and an army of men kept the machinery of the local government in operation, all is now grewsome and deserted, and only the storm howls through the empty window openings and threatens to shake down the tottering walls. Clark street is leveled flat. From a distance the federal building seems still intact, and one thinks that here at last some work of man has defied the elements. Mere delusion! In the interior all is burnt out. The walls stand, but unfit for future use. Even the "fire-proof" vaults are destroyed. Only the Tribune building is found to have made any real resistance to the flames. The interior is completely wrecked, but the walls are not damaged, and can be used again in the erection of a new home for the paper. With the exception of the walls of the postoffice and of the buildings mentioned, nothing meets the eye of the beholder but shapeless heaps of rubbish. Where formerly stately edifices, stood, signs are now being put up bearing the laconic inscription: "——— ——— REMOVED TO ——— ———."

A walk down Wabash avenue seems a dream—this vast chaotic field was once Chicago's " Broadway." The branches of half-burned trees which once ornamented the Corso of the Garden City and made this street particularly attractive, stretch dismally upward. Where is Michigan avenue—the Faubourg St. Germain of the city? The overthrown pillars which only a few hours ago adorned the palaces now strewn in dust, alone answer the question. They have shared the fate of the modest frame houses—the fierce flames have leveled all. The place where once stood the great hotels, the Palmer, the Sherman, the Fremont, the St. James and the others, are now marked only by smoking debris.

The picture of the burned North Side is not as interesting as the modern Herculanum of the South Division. It is more pathetic however, to all who know how many happy homes once stood upon this scene of barren desolation. There are few picturesque ruins—the frame houses and stores that had stood there are swept away, leaving no trace behind. Here and there stands a wall of a church or brick building—everything else is bare and level from the river to Lincoln Park.

But already the sound of the carpenter's axe fills the air and strong arms are erecting little shanties in the midst of the fire's havoc. American pluck and self-reliance, undaunted by disaster, start out at once to repair the work of devastation—to rebuild a city. Men do not await help from outside, but begin at once to help themselves. They had built a great metropolis on a swamp and are now determined that Chicago shall rise again more splendid than before.

Hundreds of men have lost everything and are glad to earn a penny in any way. One man, dressed in the broad-cloth suit he had on when the fire drove him from his home, and with a pasteboard sign fastened to his high silk hat, is peddling cigars, another has dug up various odd things from the ruins and is selling fire relics. Here the way is blocked by a group of men trying to open a safe just drawn from a basement. The face of the owner is a study. His whole future depends on the condition of the contents of the safe—his money, papers and valuables. The door is at last wrenched open and in a moment more he sees the inside is nothing but charred paper and ashes, which the wind whirls away into the air. Then the strain is over and the man knows he has to begin life again with nothing but his two hands and his own energy. One can turn to no spot in the burnt district without finding evidences of activity, courage and hope. The gas and water works are quickly repaired and one great source of inconvenience and discomfort is done away with.

ACTION OF THE AUTHORITIES.
THE POLICE.

On the day after the fire the popular excitement resembled a panic. For a time most persons firmly believed that the great disaster was the work of a band of incendiaries. Vigilance committees were formed on the South and West sides and absurd rumors of the capture and summary disposal of the incendiaries filled the city. Every citizen claimed to have seen one of the wretches strung up to a lamp post or shot down in the act of firing a building, and the newspapers contained numerous rumors of the application of "Lynch law." On the West Side it was dangerous to light a cigar on the public street. While it is not to be denied that various attempts were made to start another general conflagration, and that several men were killed for so doing, still the majority of the rumors of lynching, etc., were due to the overheated imagination of the narrators. When a great disaster has occurred it is but human nature to seek for some tangible object to hold accountable for all the misery caused, and to punish accordingly. The people demanded a sacrifice, and as they could not call Providence or any other abstract being to account, they sought some living creature on whom they could revenge themselves for the misery that had befallen them. In consequence of this feeling among the people, the police authorities swore in 1500 special policemen, but this force had to be disbanded very shortly, as a number of thieves and criminals were found in its ranks. Allen Pinkerton, chief of detectives, issued a characteristic proclamation informing the public that the police had orders to shoot on the spot any man who touched property that did not belong to him. At 3 o'clock on the 10th, Mayor Mason issued his first bulletin as follows:

PROCLAMATION.

Whereas, in the providence of God, to whose will we humbly submit, a terrible calamity has befallen our city, which demands of us our best efforts for the preservation of order and the relief of the suffering, be it known that the faith and credit of the city of Chicago is hereby pledged for the necessary expenses for the relief of the suffering.

Public order will be preserved. The police and special police now being appointed will be responsible for the maintenance of the peace and the protection of property.

All officers and men of the fire and health departments will act as special policemen without further notice.

The mayor and comptroller will give vouchers for all supplies furnished by the different relief committees.

The headquarters of the city government will be at the Congregational church, corner of West Washington and Ann streets.

All persons are warned against any acts tending to endanger property. All persons caught in any depredation will be immediately arrested.

With God's help, order and peace and private property shall be preserved.

The city government and the committees of citizens pledge themselves to the community to protect them and pave the way for a restoration of public and private welfare.

It is believed that the fire has spent its force and all will soon be well.

R. B. MASON, Mayor.
CHARLES C. P. HOLDEN, President Com'n Council.
F. B. BROWN, President Police Board.

Never before had Chicago stood in so great need of a strong, firm hand at the municipal helm, and never had a more incapable man stood at the head of the city government.

In his private capacity the aged mayor was worthy of the highest esteem, but he could not fulfill the demands of his public position in those hours of need. He completely lost his head, and no longer knowing how to help himself, and cherishing the absurd idea that the ruins of Chicago were overrun with robbers and cut-throats, he sought military protection, "entrusting the preservation of the good order and peace of the city to Lieutenant-General Philip H. Sheridan, United States Army." This act, contrary to the sovereign rights of the State of Illinois, caused considerable friction, as Governor Palmer had already dispatched to Chicago his adjutant-general, with several hundred state troops. Soon the control of the military proved an intolerable nuisance, the more so in view of the fact that exemplary order and quiet prevailed. Among the private citizens enlisted for guard duty were a lot of youngsters, with no idea of the seriousness and responsibility of their position.

The culmination of the bitter feeling against martial law was reached on October 20th. On the evening of that day Col. Thomas W. Grosvenor, a universally esteemed citizen, who had served throughout the civil war with honor and distinction, was shot and killed by a Douglas University student, named Treat, who was acting as guard. Colonel Grosvenor was returning home about midnight, and when the guard called to him to halt and give the countersign, he passed on without reply. The guard called to him again, and as no answer was returned, he was shot down. Treat was tried for murder but was acquitted, as the jury decided he had acted in good faith and that the responsibility for the affair devolved upon those who had organized the body of militia, to which Treat belonged. A lively correspondence sprang up between Governor Palmer and Mayor Mason and President Grant, but without definite result. At the time many people believed that the United States troops, which Sheridan ordered to Chicago, were of the greatest use in preserving order, but the emergency was one which the state militia could have met fully, and there was not the slightest necessity for the regular troops. The result of the action of the mayor in putting the city under martial law, was to spread abroad false impressions of the real state of affairs in Chicago. There was no anarchy here, there were no lynching outrages; the people of the city deported themselves with the most admirable conservatism and discretion. The police did their full duty, and public recognition of their bravery and faithfulness is the more due them as there was at one time a tendency to make scape-goats of them and the firemen. Neither department was in any way responsible for the great calamity which had befallen Chicago; both had done all that men could do.

THE FIRE DEPARTMENT.

Owing to the unprotected position of Chicago on the flat prairie, storms from whatever direction swept over it with full fury. This circumstance and the fact that, like other quickly constructed American cities, it consisted largely of wooden buildings, so greatly increased the danger of fire that a most excellent fire department was organized. It consisted of twenty-one steamers, with the necessary hose carts and hook and ladder trucks. The men had given repeated proofs of their courage and ability, and the populace placed the greatest confidence in this department of the local government. As a matter of fact Chicago owes it to the excellence of the fire department that the catastrophe of October 8th and 9th, 1871, was so long deferred.

On the day of the fire the firemen did all that could have been expected of resolute, brave, efficient men. They yielded to the flames only when their clothes began to burn. During the fire eight steamers, three carts and three trucks were abandoned, as the men had kept up their stubborn resistance to the flames so long that these machines could not be gotten away before the fire was upon them. An official account of the fire and the work of the department fully exonerates the men from any cowardice or inefficiency. In an interview after the fire, Chief Fire Marshal Williams said: "When I got to the fire, I should think there were six or seven buildings ablaze—sheds and out-houses. We got it under control, and it wouldn't have gone a foot further, but the next thing I knew they came and told me that St. Paul's church, two squares north, was on fire. The 'Rehm' stood on the corner of Church and Mather streets, working that plug, and it was so hot the engineer had to put up a door to protect himself. The 'Gund' was on the east side of the church, and the 'Coventry' on the north. * * * * The next thing I knew the fire was in Bateham's planing mill. When I got there I found that the match factory was going, as was the lumber just north of it. We got two streams in there, but couldn't do any good, as the fire was thick and heavy, and ran along to another lumber yard, north, and spread east to the old red mill. I went north to head it off, and found it was down to Harrison street. Commissioner Chadwick came to me, and said: 'Don't you know the fire is ahead of you?' I told him it was getting ahead of me in spite of all I could do; it was just driving me right along. I got down to Van Buren street and was working the engines there, but it was so hot the men were obliged to run for their lives, leaving their hose on the ground. They came to me and asked what they were to do about hose. I said, 'God only knows.'

We got the 'Gund' located at the corner of Van Buren and Canal streets. * * * * The flames rolled over the men who were with the engine on the corner, and I told the foreman to get her out or we would lose her. I asked some citizens to help, and we ran up to uncouple the suction from the plug, and others commenced to uncouple the hose. Just then a wave of flame came rolling over the street, and I was obliged to get away. Hose was afterwards attached to the axle of the 'Gund,' and the citizens pulled her up on the sidewalk, where she was burned up.

"I met Alex. McGonigle, fireman of the 'Long John,' and he told me there was a fire on the South Side. I told him to go for it, and I jumped on a hose cart and went over too. I got the 'Economy' to work on the corner of Washington and La Salle streets and lead the hose in through the stairway opposite. We were not in there three minutes before a sheet of flames rolled over us and the boys dropped the pipe and ran for their lives. The wind was blowing so hard that the water would not go ten feet from the nozzle of the pipe. We could not strike a second story window. I then went to work and got my two engines to play on the Sherman house. I thought we would be able to save it on account of the open space opposite. But, my God! there was a piece of board six feet long that came over and landed right on top of the old Tribune building on Clark street, and it was not two minutes before that row was on fire. While I was wetting down the Sherman house, I heard that the water works were on fire. I jumped into my wagon and drove over to see if it was true, and when I got near there I saw that the roof was all on fire, and the flames rolling out of every opening of the building. I saw that the fate of the city was sealed, that we could no more save the North than the South Side."

The facts here given will prove to those who did not witness the catastrophe, that nothing but a cloud burst or the cessation of the hurricane could have checked the flames. The water works were a mile from the Sherman house, but both were on fire at the same time. Even the strongest and best fire department must yield to a gale which carries burning brands for miles and scatters them on frame houses that a long continued drouth has turned to tinder.

LOSSES AND INSURANCE.

The losses occasioned by the great fire were enormous—Chicagoesque. To give the area of the burnt district, the number of houses destroyed or of persons rendered homeless, affords but little idea of the enormity of the catastrophe. Although, for example, the burned buildings were less than a third of the whole number of buildings in the city—17,450 burning and 42,000 remaining—still the value of the ones destroyed equaled that of those which were uninjured.

The most authentic report as to the area burned over and the amount of property destroyed, states that in the West Side, where the fire originated, the number of acres burned over was 194. There were 500 buildings, mostly of an inferior class, destroyed, which were inhabited by about 2500 persons. The burned area in the South Division comprised 460 acres. This district, though comparatively small in extent, was the business center of the city. It contained a majority of those structures which were costly and magnificent, and were filled with the merchandise which made the city the great emporium of the northwest. All the wholesale stores of considerable magnitude, the daily and weekly newspaper offices, the principal hotels, the public halls and places of amusement, the great railroad depots and a large number of the most splendid residences, in short, the great bulk of the wealth and the chief interests of the city were located in this district. In this division alone, there were 3650 buildings destroyed, which included 1600 stores, 28 hotels, 60 manufacturing establishments and the homes of about 22,000 people. In the North Division, not less than 1470 acres were swept by the flames, destroying 13,300 buildings—the homes of 75,000 people, about 600 stores and 100 manufacturing establishments.

The total area burned over in the city including streets, was 2124 acres, or nearly 3⅓ square miles. This area contained about 73 miles of streets, 18,000 buildings and the homes of 100,000 people.

The loss on buildings amounted to $53,080,000; on produce, $5,262,000; on merchandise, not produce, $78,700,000; on personal property, $58,710,000; miscellaneous losses, $378,000; making a grand total of $196,000,000. In foundations and available building material there was a salvage estimated at $10,000,000. The municipal losses—city hall, bridges, sewers, water works, mains, etc., police and fire department buildings and sidewalks—amounted to $2,415,180.

Eighty of the destroyed business blocks had been worth $8,515,000; the value of the burnt railroad depots, warehouses and Chamber of Commerce was $2,700,000; of the hotels, $3,100,00, and of the churches and contents, $3,000,000. Of the church losses the Catholics suffered to the extent of $1,350,000; the Methodists, $355,000; Baptists, $80,000; Episcopalians, $337,500; Presbyterians, $465,000; Unitarians, $175,000, and the various Jewish synagogues, $55,000.

Of Chicago's total loss of almost $200,000,000, about $50,000,000 was made good by the insurance companies. The great eastern companies discharged their obligations promptly and paid dollar for dollar; but the Illinois, and especially the local Chicago companies made a wretched showing. The poorer classes had insured in these local companies and received, on an average, less than 10 per cent of the value of their policies.

In addition to the insurance, Chicago received large contributions of both money and supplies. The whole world showed its sympathy and kindly interest. While the fire was still burning relief trains were on their way to the unfortunate city. At 7 o'clock Monday, October 9th, two car loads of provisions arrived in Chicago from Milwaukee. Cleveland, Cincinnati, St. Louis and New York followed suit. Not since the fall of Fort Sumter had the heart of the nation been so touched. More than 10,000 meetings were held in behalf of the fire sufferers. The governors of the various states issued proclamations and relief committees were organized over the whole Union. It was through the wonderful instrumentality of the press that the sympathy of the nation was so forcibly appealed to. As men ate their breakfast, dinner or supper, they read the dispatches in the papers which told them that at that very minute 100,000 of their fellow-men were wandering comfortless, shelterless and destitute over the still smoking ruins of their homes. Of the hundreds of eloquent appeals made in Chicago's behalf, the following delivered in Faneuil Hall in Boston, by Edward Everett Hale, is typical:

MR. MAYOR AND GENTLEMEN:—It is but a single word that I have to say here. I have simply to remind you that this is no mere matter of voting in which we are engaged. I have to remind you that these people, our people in Chicago, by their munificence, by their generosity, by their strength, by their public spirit, have made us debtors to them all. There is not a man here the beef upon whose table yesterday was not the cheaper to him because these people laid out that world-renowned and wonderful system of stock-yards. There is not a man here the bread upon whose table was not also cheaper because these people in the very beginning of their national existence invented and created that marvelous system for the delivery of grain, which is the model of the world. And remember that they were in a position where they might have said, that they held a monopoly. They commanded the only harbor for the shipping of the five greatest states of America and of the world, and in that position they have devoted themselves now for a generation to the steady improvement, by every method in their power, of the means by which they were going to answer the daily prayer of every child to God, when we pray that He will give us our daily bread. We call it their misfortune. It is our misfortune. We are all, as it has been said, linked together in a solidarity of the nation. Their loss is no more theirs than it is ours. In this great campaign of peace, in which we are engaged, there has fallen, by this calamity, one of our noble fortresses. Its garrison is without munitions. It is for us, at the instant, to re-construct that fortress and to see that its garrison is as well placed as it was before, in our service. Undoubtedly it is a great enterprise, but, as our friend has said, we can trust them for that. We are all fond of speaking of the miracle by which there in the desert there was created this great city. The rod of some prophet struck it, you say, and the city flowed from the rock. Who was the prophet? What was the rock?

It was the American people who determined that the city should be there, and that it should rightly and wisely and in the best way distribute food to a world. The American people has that duty to discharge again. I know that these numbers are large numbers. I know that when we read in the newspapers of the destruction of a hundred million dollars worth of property, those figures are so large that we can hardly apprehend them. But the providence of God has taught us to deal with larger figures than those, and when, now not many years ago, it became necessary for this country to spend not one hundred, not one thousand millions, but more than one thousand millions of dollars in a great enterprise, which God gave this country in the duty of war—this country met its obligations. And now that in a single year we have to re-construct one of the fortresses of peace, I do not fear that this country will be backward in its duty. It has been truly said, that the first duty of all of us is that the noble pioneers in the duty that God has placed in their hands, who are burned and suffering, shall have food; that by telegraph and railroad they shall know that we are rushing to their relief; that their homeless shall be under shelter, and their naked clothed; that those who, this forty-eight hours, have felt as if they were deserted, should know that they have friends everywhere in God's world. As God is pleased to order this world, there is no partial evil, but from that partial evil is reached the universal good. The fires, which our friends have seen sweeping their western horizon over the plains in the desolate autumn, only bring forth the blossoms and the richness of the next spring and the next summer.

I can well believe that on that terrible night of Sunday and all through the hours of yesterday, as those noble people, as those gallant workingmen threw upon the flames the water that their noble works—the noblest that America has seen—enabled them to hurl upon the enemy, that they must have imagined that their work was fruitless; that it was lost toil to see that stream of water playing into the molten mass and melt into steam, and rise innocuous into the heavens. It may well have seemed that their work was wasted, but it is sure that evil shall work out its own end, and the mists that rose from the conflagration were gathered together for the magnificent tempest of last night, which, falling upon those burning streets, has made Chicago a habitable city to-day. See that the lesson for this community, see that the lesson for us who are here, that the horror and the tears, with which we read the dispatches of yesterday, shall send us out to ministries of truth and bounty and benevolence to-day.

The work of properly caring for the donations which came pouring into the city, and of distributing the money and supplies among the needy and worthy, assumed so great proportions that on October 13th, Mayor Mason turned the whole thing over to the Chicago Relief and Aid Society—a local organization long established, and possessing in the highest degree the confidence of all classes of citizens. At first the homeless were sheltered in the churches and school houses of the unburnt portions of the city and suburbs and in the tents furnished by the national government and state authorities.

As soon as possible the Relief and Aid Society began the erection of cheap frame houses for the poor, and by November 17, 5226 houses were put up. The Ladies' Relief Society co-operated with the general society and rendered most efficient services.

Within the first three months after the fire over $4,200,000 was contributed to Chicago sufferers as a practical expression of the sympathy of the world. These contributions came not only from the United States and Canada, but from Europe and even Africa, Japan and India. The Common Council of London voted 1,000 guineas, and the great London bankers and railroads sent $35,000. The Liverpool Chamber of Commerce voted $25,000, and Edinburg, Berlin and Frankfort-on-the-Main contributed generously

Of the larger American donations may be mentioned the following: A. T. Stewart, of New York, $50,000; Brooklyn, $100,000; New York Stock Exchange, $50,000; District of Columbia, $100,000; President Grant, $1000; London, Canada, $5,000; Kansas City, $26,000; Montreal, $20,000; Toronto, $10,000; St. Louis, $300,000; Boston, $400,000; Pittsburg, $300,000; Buffalo, $100,000; Cincinnati, $225,000; Rochester, N. Y., $70,000; San Francisco, $100,000; New Orleans, $30,000; Philadelphia $260,000; Baltimore, $200,000; Indianapolis, $75,000; Portland, Oregon, $20,000; Quincy, Ill., $15,000; Newark, N, J., $30,000; Trenton, N. J., $17,000; Bloomington, Ill., $15,000; Erie, Pa., $15,000; Detroit, $30,000; Lancaster, Pa., $25,000.

From the State of Illinois, the Chicago authorities received $3,000,000—a sum large enough to again organize the public works and police and fire departments. The spirit of the people may be judged from the fact, that within six weeks after the fire 212 permanent stone and brick buildings were in course of erection in the South Division alone.

Typical of the mood of the people were the brave words which Robert L. Collier, pastor of the Church of the Messiah, delivered the week after the fire. After scouting the idea, advanced by certain fanatics, that Chicago had been visited by the wrath of God on account of her sins, he concluded with these words:

> What is lost? First, our homes. Thousands of families are homeless and penniless. Second, our business. This is temporary. Third, our money. This is a great misfortune, but one which we can repair. We have not lost—First, our geography. Nature called the lakes, the forests, the prairies together in convention long before we were born, and they decided that on this spot, a great city should be built The railroads and energetic men have aided in fulfilling the prophecy. Second, we have not lost our men noble, generous, and of genius. Third, we have not lost our hope. The city is to be at once rebuilt, and " the glory of the latter house shall be greater than that of the former."

Rev. Dr. Robert Collyer, of Unity church, also met his people the Sunday after the fire. Their church was burned, but they met fronting the ruins, sang some hymns, read a few passages from the bible and formally resolved to rebuild their beloved church. In a recent letter to a friend making inquiry as to what he had said on that gloomy Sunday, Dr. Collyer replied: "I doubt if there was any true report of the words I said—or could be, because so much of it came thick through the pain and tears. But we grew cheerful, I remember, before we got through and went home with our heads up, and our hearts made good our resolutions, and the last dollar of the debt was paid when I left Chicago."

Chicago's Architectural Development.

THE FIRST STAGE—TO 1852.

The following article on the architecture of Chicago was written expressly for this book, by Frederick Baumann, in a double sense one of the city's first architects.

The earliest survey record as to a settlement near Fort Dearborn bears date of August 4, 1830. It was made for the canal commission, by James Thompson, and shortly afterwards was used as a record for the incorporation of the village.

The accompanying chart shows a plan of this "original town." The site is flat—generally, but three to four feet above the level of the lake; near and parallel to the shore of which is a sandy ridge, with an added height of five or six feet. Before the construction of piers and other shore protections, this ridge, as a product of the water's motion, was ever subject to change, being increased at shielded places and broken into at others by the violence of the rolling waves. The bi-forked Chicago river is, as a matter of fact, but a narrow bayou, with standing water. It has no current from any source beyond the occasional floods produced by heavy rains or melting snows. But these occasional floods may be severe and destructive, for the area of level ground about Chicago, inclusive of that tributary to the upper course of the neighboring Des Plaines river, comprises fully seven hundred square miles. Sometimes heavy snows fall, and do not melt until the latter part of March. This was the case about the middle of the 80's, but nature was gracious. The spring was backward, the snow melted slowly, and over a week elapsed before all the water had run into the lake. As a result no serious damage was done, the high water not assuming the proportions of a flood. In 1849 however, under similar conditions, spring began with a sudden, warm rain, and melted in twenty-four hours the masses of snow with which the plains were covered. The consequence was a terrific rush of water through the narrow channel of the river, which overflowed its banks and carried away, not only all the vessels lying in the stream, but even the bridges which spanned it. Everything was swept clean by the flood, which, if repeated to-day—and what is there to prevent its recurrence?—would destroy millions of dollars' worth of property. The present Drainage Board is, however, giving attention to this problem, and, when the drainage channel is completed, it is understood that ample provision will have been made for these flood waters.

Chicago's first actual settlement was upon the sands of the north bank of the river. Later—in 1845 or thereabouts—a large hotel was erected on the spot. It was built of brick, and stood as a landmark until destroyed by the great fire. Many smaller buildings had been erected on both sides of the river, some of brick, two or three stories in height, but the greater part of them small frame houses. It was the general custom to construct the frame buildings of scantling and boards, in the so-called "balloon-frame" fashion, as distinguished from the heavy timber frame, in use in the old country. The "balloon-frame" is distinctively an American invention, saving material, and, above all, time. Foreigners are always astonished at the short time required for the construction of an American frame building.

The speculative tendency of the villagers soon widened the boundaries of the "original town." Kinzie's addition, the school section addition and Fort Dearborn addition were made, and numerous other additions followed in the course of time.

During Chicago's early years the construction of buildings was, as a matter of necessity, entrusted entirely to the mechanics and builders. Business convenience, however, soon required

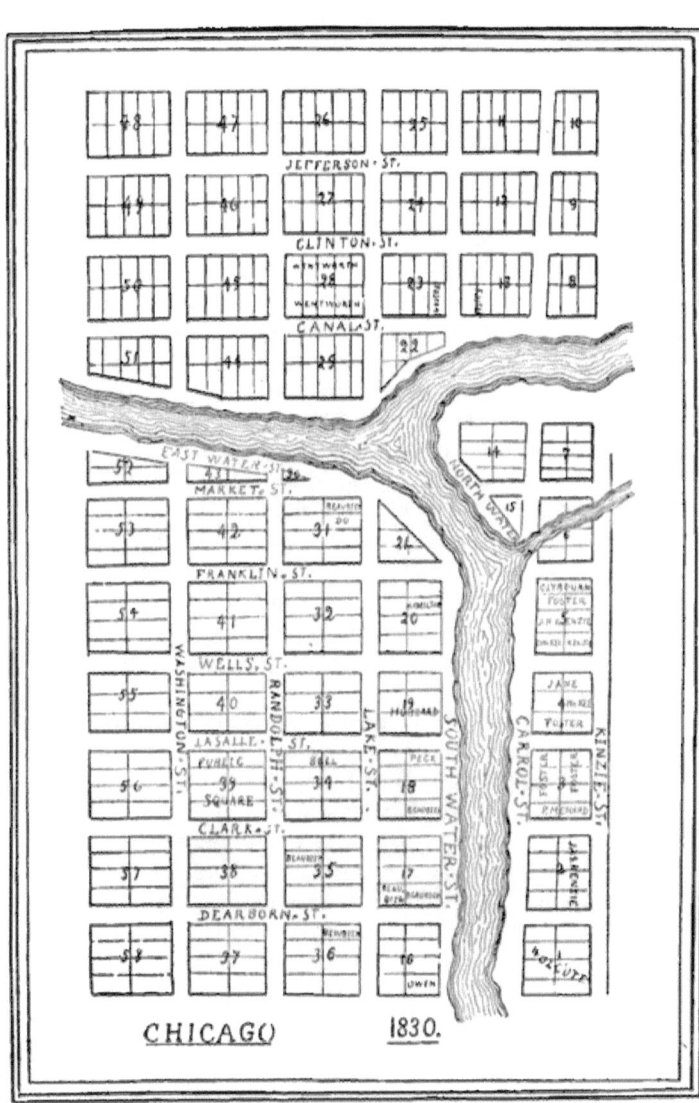

that the foremost among these men—that is those who understood something about drawing and making specifications—establish themselves as professional architects. The lead was taken by John M. Van Osdel (died in January, 1892), Edward Burling (died March, 1892), and Asher Carter (died in 1876). Each of these gentlemen enjoyed a large and prosperous business to the end of his days. The writer hereof, having arrived at Chicago in July, 1850, became associated with Mr. Burling, in February, 1852. Two years thereafter other architects settled in Chicago, and at the time of the fire there were in all twenty architects in the city. The number has increased to fully three hundred at the present time.

The first Chicago settlers were not, as a matter of course, men of wealth. They had come here to make their fortune. Hence the earliest buildings were, with very rare exceptions, of the plainest and simplest character. Common bricks were made from beds of clay which were found in several parts of the city. Pressed bricks were shipped from Indiana and Wisconsin. Lumber came from the shores of the great lakes. The lumber trade soon assumed gigantic proportions and made Chicago the greatest lumber market in the world. Cut stone caps and sills came from Joliet and from eastern points, notably from Buffalo.

The narrow waterway which divided the city into three parts necessitated the early establishment of ferries and later the erection of bridges. The ferries were propelled by pulling on a line, which ran from one shore to the other, and was dropped for the passage of vessels. It sometimes happened that owing to carelessness a vessel broke the line and in some cases even ran down the ferry with its passengers. In one instance sixteen persons were drowned owing to a collision between the ferry boat and a passing vessel. Bridges were soon built to span the river at Clark, Wells, Randolph, Kinzie, Madison, Van Buren and Twelfth streets. The bridges were constructed in three pieces, the central section was movable, one end resting on a scow in the river and the other being pivoted to one of the bridge abutments. When it was necessary to open the river for navigation, the scow was swung around close to the shore and left an opening in the bridge large enough for a vessel to pass through. This method of bridge opening soon proved too primitive and slow for early Chicago and in 1853 the first swing bridge was erected at Lake street, not, however, without the solemn protest of a large majority of the property owners on Randolph street, who were afraid that such "competition" in river crossing would depreciate the value of their property. The present steel, steam swinging bridges of Chicago are but an outgrowth of the Lake street bridge of '53.

From the first the traffic of the city—dirty even while little—was very active. The streets were crowded with people who had no leisure. Every one in Chicago was always in a hurry. Hundreds of wagons crowded the unpaved streets which, in order to secure drainage for the buildings, were laid out lower even than the average level of the city's site. Narrow wooden sewers, discharging into the river, were laid directly under the planks which covered the streets in place of a real pavement. Sometimes the sewers became choked up, and the heavy rains were not drained off. The planks, when loosened by heavy travel, floated away on such occasions, and citizens marked the places where there were no planks with signs inscribed "no bottom."

In the winter Chicago was very quiet, for there were no railroads, and the extensive fleet of the city lay still and fast in the ice-bound river. Only a few farmers, coming to town with their products, enlivened the deadness of the streets. In the second stage,

CHICAGO TO 1871,

all this was changed. Numerous railroads were built and kept the city's trade and commerce lively the year round. Excellent water works were established and their development has kept pace with the city's growth, until now (1893), a new 9-foot tunnel, running out for four miles into the lake, supplies the city with pure water.

Extensive quarries were opened at Athens, 20 miles south of Chicago, in beds of Silurian limestone, large deposits of which are found throughout the state. These beds vary in thickness from four inches to three feet, and the stone was for many years used on the best buildings in the city. It did not, however, prove durable, disintegrating on its exposed surfaces and splitting easily when quarried in large blocks. Its use, therefore, is now confined to footings, flaggings, copings and the like. Other kinds of stone were soon brought from different states; oolitic limestone from Indiana; many kinds of sandstone from Ohio, marble from Vermont; granite from New England, Missouri and Wisconsin. The trade in such building-stone has so materially increased that at this day there are probably more than a hundred kinds of free-stone and granite on the local market, certainly as many—if not more—than could be had at any other city in the world.

Brick making was soon done by machinery and the demand is at present so great that probably not more than five per cent of the bricks used are produced in the old-fashioned way. Face-bricks of all kinds and colors came gradually into demand; St. Louis, Baltimore and Philadelphia, supplied the first brick of superior quality, but now they are manufactured in scores of places.

More and more attention was being paid to architecture, although appearances were still, to a large extent, sacrificed to economy. In 1852 the six-story Exchange Bank building, corner of Lake and Clark streets, was erected in a style of Greek Renaissance, with both fronts of Athens limestone. The next year the four-story Marine Bank, corner of Lake and La Salle streets, was put up, likewise with both fronts of Athens limestone, though the style was not as consistent and elaborate as in the case of the other bank building. Several

Unity Church.

other buildings for store and office purposes were erected before 1857, when the great financial crisis put an end for several years to all building activity. None of these early buildings could bear judgment purely from the standard of high art. They resulted from productive energy and that conscious pride which has at all times been the father of art, but their development was slow. It may well be doubted, however, whether the ablest architect, under the same circumstances and with the same means, could have produced results essentially different. Most of the better buildings were in the style of the Renaissance, but greatly simplified in order to save expense. One of the finest buildings was that of the First National Bank, corner of State and Washington streets. Residences of luxurious elegance were exceedingly rare as yet.

In 1871 Chicago had become the metropolis of the northwest, and was endowed with a feverish activity. Its inhabitants numbered over three hundred thousand. Great things were expected from the future, but all at once the city was almost wiped from the face of the earth by the great fire. Nothing but a portion of the South and West Divisions remained to mark the spot where the young giant had stood. The very elements had conspired for the city's annihilation. The peculiar dryness of the atmosphere and the remarkable fierceness and power of the flames gave rise to a scientific theory that the air of the earth had become impregnated with gaseous exhalations from Donati's comet, which at that time was in its nearest approach to our planet. Another attempted explanation of the great catastrophe assumed that the near presence of the comet had generated a large amount of atmospheric electricity, and that this contributed to the rapid spread of the flames.

THE CHICAGO OF TO-DAY.

The smoke had not lifted from the burnt city when, in the heart of every patriotic citizen, it had been decided that Chicago should be rebuilt. Within a year the down-town

Prairie Avenue Homes.

quarter had been well nigh rebuilt, and before two years had passed almost all the scars of the great conflagration had been effaced. Where formerly there had been vacant lots, or two and three story frame buildings, large brick and stone structures were now erected. In fact, so active was the building that more stores and offices were put up than were needed, and only those first constructed were filled with tenants. For buildings not centrally located no adequate rents could be obtained. As the insurance in the burnt district was light, most of the buildings were put up with borrowed money, and the scarcity of tenants proved a great embarrassment to owners. All buildings had been erected at an increased cost, owing to the high prices of material and labor. The panic of 1873 caused numerous failures, and fortunate indeed was the landlord who could keep himself afloat by the assistance of a magnanimous mortgagee.

As a matter of course the new buildings erected just after the fire did not differ materially from those they replaced. Artistically considered, the new structures were no improvement on the old. For nearly ten years after the panic, building was very dull, and it was the latter part of the 80's before it grew active again. Since 1890, however, the amount of money annually expended on new buildings, is in excess of that used the first year after the fire. Since 1871 the architects of Chicago have steadily increased in number, and have done great work in the re-construction of the city. Many of these men have graduated from the best schools in the east, and not a few have been educated in Europe. Local education in architecture has been provided for in the new University of Chicago, where careful instruction will be given in this art.

Chicago architecture in general is that of the English school, which is in vogue in the east as well as the west. Only lately has the French school made its influence strongly felt on American architecture. It is, nevertheless, not too

View on Michigan Avenue.

much to say that the English architects have not equaled their French, Italian and German competitors. The ideas of the Renaissance were neither so kindly received nor so fully understood in England as on the continent—in fact, the influence of the late so-called classic Renaissance of the first decade of this century, was but slightly felt in England. Greek art and all art derived therefrom and thereon depending, can by no means, be attained by a series of mechanical measurements with rule and compass. It is so subtle, so delicate in essential details, that it requires the genius of the true artist. In recent years, however, English architects have been quite happy in their work—to a degree that one might speak of it as belonging to a new school, that of the modern English. Their style abounds in odd and abnormal forms, which sometimes go so far as to violate the principles of sound construction, and yet the result is pleasing to the eye. This modern English school has had great influence on Chicago, particularly in so far as residences are concerned. Chicago homes are not only handsome and elegant, but likewise solid and comfortable. They take an endless variety of forms, and all monotonous repetitions are avoided. Even in solid rows of dwellings, each individual house bears, on its narrow front, some peculiarity of design that relieves the general similarity.

Modern office buildings are of immense size; running from twelve to twenty stories in height. They are built with an iron or steel skeleton, which upholds the various floors and gives solidity to the structure. The facings, walls and floors are made of stone, brick and terra cotta. Numerous elevators are an essential part of the equipment of all high buildings. The interiors of the modern buildings are a vast improvement over the style of a decade ago, being clean, light and airy; but the immense windows and certain other fixed details involve the sacrifice of the frontal beauty of many of the great structures. In frequent cases the architect,

Woman's Temple.

despairing of giving the large, uniform fronts any strength or expression, has simply built a plain wall, regularly pierced with windows. Some exceptions to this rule are to be noted: first, the "Insurance Exchange," which, though not a remarkably costly structure, has a front that is clever in spite of its severity and a portico which is charming, then the "Rookery" and "Phenix" buildings, both of ornate design and pleasing exterior, and finally the "Woman's Temple." The Rookery and Phenix are independently conceived in forms derived from medieval productions, and are cheerful and pleasing. Probably no other office building in the country compares with them. They give evidence of the fact that the true architect is the inventor of his designs. The rudiments of these forms are in existence and it is for the thinking mind to work them up and so assign them as to produce a work of art.

The store buildings are not as high, on the average, as the strictly office buildings. All those of recent construction are fire-proof so far as possible, but it is doubtful whether they could withstand the heat that would be generated by the merchandise which they contain if a fire ever got well started. Their fronts are massive and imposing. Chicago theatres are numerous, the largest being the famous "Auditorium," which has the greatest seating capacity of any theatre in the world. The new "Schiller" is a model of beauty and elegance.

The city's hotels are for the most part, fire-proof, and are built in splendid style and of the best materials. One of the new hotels is fourteen stories high. The numerous apartment buildings are a feature of the city. These are beautiful structures, fire-proof, of excellent construction, and ranging from six to twelve stories high.

THE CHICAGO OF THE FUTURE.

Chicago now has a population of one and a third million, and judging the future by the past, it is safe to assume that the city will enjoy an annual growth of at least 80,000 souls. At this rate the population of Chicago in 1940 would be five millions. But what changes and improvements will have to be made to accommodate such an enormous increase in population! As to sewers, it may be confidently asserted that the new drainage canal will forever dispose of that question. The new four-mile tunnel will provide a fair supply of water for the immediate future, but the demand will in time exceed the supply, and new works will have to be constructed and new tunnels made. Still with the great lake at its doors the question of Chicago's water supply is not serious. The streets of the city are filled with underground sewers, gas, water and steam pipes, wires, cables and pneumatic tubes. The pavements are constantly being torn up to lay new pipes or wires or to repair old ones. All this must be changed, and the best way to arrange for all interests concerned is to construct large tunnels under the principal streets, and in them all the wires, pipes and sewers can be placed.

Chicago's enormous street traffic offers a problem difficult of adequate solution. This traffic is constantly increasing, while the size of the streets is fixed. No proposition to widen downtown thoroughfares can be seriously entertained. Two solutions of the difficulty have been suggested. The one provides for tunnels under the streets, the other for elevated roads. With proper construction, the elevated road seems to offer the most satisfactory means of intra-mural communication. The present elevated road, with its cumbersome trestle and dirty, noisy engine, must be done away with, and a light, graceful one substituted. Electricity—the power of the future—must be used to silently and rapidly move the cars of the new road, which would then prove entirely adequate to the demands of a great city, and underground railroads, with their many disadvantages, would not be seriously considered.

The bridge nuisance also demands early solution. At present the three divisions of the city are connected by swinging bridges, elevated on an average fifteen feet from the surface of the river, so as to afford passage without opening the bridges to tugs, scows and canal boats. For all large vessels, however, the bridges must be swung open while all neighboring street traffic congests and much valuable time is lost. So inconvenient has the swing bridge been found, that it has been seriously proposed to establish a new harbor for the city, somewhere on the lake front, and to abandon the river. This suggestion has been met with the greatest opposition from river dock-owners and vesselmen. The latter declare that no lake front harbor could provide facilities equal to the river with its sixteen miles of docks. A better solution of the question is to build stationary bridges the full width of the street at a reasonable height—say thirty feet from the water. The greater width of the new bridges would counterbalance the objection to the increased grade and the fact of their being stationary would permit elevated roads to cross them without difficulty. On the other hand, vesselmen would find that the inconvenience of the new arrangement would be more than off-set by its advantages. With fixed bridges, the masts of vessels would have to be so constructed that they could be laid flat on the decks when the harbor was reached. This arrangement could be provided for by the use of a little ingenuity, and the cost of the installation and maintenance of the new arrangement would not amount to so much as would be saved by the increased rapidity of river communication. There would be no tedious delays in waiting for bridges to open and the river channel, now blocked up with the great center pier of the swinging bridges, would be free and open, for the new fixed bridges could span the river without support except from the two banks.

Another reform demanded by the Chicago of the future is the removal of railroad tracks from the street level. The tracks must be either raised or depressed. The loss of life at grade crossings is so great—some three hundred lives being sacrificed yearly—as to imperatively demand a change.

Popular clamor is for the elevation of tracks, although the roads themselves protest that they cannot afford to make the change, and the enormous interference with all business seems to be entirely overlooked. But granted that the tracks were raised, what would be the benefits? The streets are even now overcrowded and cable cars, although already occupying most of the down-town thoroughfares, are proving unequal to the demands of the present population. One elevated road has been completed and others are being constructed. Relief is already being sought. Elevated railroads and elevated sidewalks are regarded as the only means of relieving the present congested condition of the streets. All this now, with a population of 1,300,000—what then will be the condition of affairs with a population of five or ten millions? The question must be squarely met and answered.

If we are to face the future, let us do it with unbandaged eyes. Our city is unparalleled. It has become a mighty metropolis in less than a half century, and within the next fifty years its progress will be no less wonderful. The questions it presents for solution are of a peculiar character. They have not been dealt with by other large cities, but are new with Chicago. We must solve our own problems, and to that end the writer makes these suggestions:

1. Do away, as far as possible, with all railroad tracks in the central part of the city, leaving only those that are absolutely necessary for the handling of freight.

2. Depress, to the level of the lake, those that are allowed to remain.

3. Put permanent bridges on all streets crossing these depressed tracks.

4. Put tramway tracks about twenty-four feet above the level of the streets.

5. Make the bridges across the river fixed, and so provide for the elevated tramways between different divisions of the city.

6. Locate the railroad depots at the outskirts of the city, and allow passengers to take the elevated roads to their hotels or homes. If these suggestions were adopted, the incoming traveler in 1940 might thus describe his experiences: "The train stopped in the suburbs, for the depot is situated several miles from the heart of town, and I was directed to an elevator, which took me to the second story of the depot building. This is on a level with the elevated tramway tracks. My car soon appeared and I boarded it, and in ten minutes reached the center of the city. We were not delayed by open bridges, for the new Chicago has done away with its swinging bridges, and the river is now spanned by fixed ones, under which the vessels pass with lowered masts. I got off the car onto a platform, from which I went down about eight feet, and then found myself on an elevated or second story sidewalk. I observed that most of the retail business was done on this second story level, and that the display windows in the stores were on this floor. I crossed the street by a narrow bridge, went down a flight of stairs, and for the first time reached the real sidewalk on the original street level. I called a cab, and started for my destination in another quarter of the city. We passed over several depressed railroad tracks, and under numerous elevated tracks, which were of such a light and graceful construction as to be neither disfiguring to the city nor objectionable on the ground of darkening the streets. The electric cars ran noiselessly and rapidly, and I soon saw that these people had solved the questions which, thirty-five years ago, had threatened to check the growth of the city."

Chicago's Art Development.

It is self-evident that so young a city as Chicago can have no history of art proper, for art can flourish only where there are firmly established conditions of life, and wealth and comfort generally prevail, for only then is there a desire to adorn and to improve life by art culture. All these conditions were wanting in the arduous life of the pioneer, and had first to be created by the hard work of many years. Notwithstanding this, we find, shortly after the foundation of Chicago, pioneers of art at work, preparing the rough and barren ground to the best of their ability. Among the first blossoms thus obtained were those which showed themselves on the field of music. Though the work was never so hard and the prospect never so discouraging, the innate energy of the true pioneer, his enthusiasm undampened by disappointment, successfully overcame all difficulties.

The Chicago Harmonic society gave a concert of considerable pretensions as early as December, 1835, and in 1844 there were two music instructors in the city. P. T. Barnum brought a concert troupe with Italian artists to Chicago in November, 1840, and in 1845-46 there was given a series of concerts of real merit. The Choral Union was founded in 1846, with J. Johnson as leader. In 1849 it was reorganized as the Mozart society, with W. N. Dunham and Frank Lumbard as musical directors. An effort to give regular concerts was made in 1848-1849, when Mr. Christopher Plagge organized the Philharmonic society, by which popular compositions for the piano, violin and flute were performed. But the meager support given to his enterprise so discouraged Mr. Plagge that he gave up the attempt and returned to the east. Mr. Julius Dyhrenfurth, an accomplished amateur, and, for those times, an excellent violinist, was the next who tried his luck with concerts. He induced twelve good musicians to remove from New York, and with their assistance gave, in Tremont Hall (1850-1852), popular or promenade concerts. To Mr. Dyhrenfurth, therefore, belongs the honor of having made the first attempts to give orchestra concerts, although on a smaller scale. However, it soon became clear to Mr. Dyhrenfurth that in Chicago a mercantile career promised more than an artistic one, and he relinquished art and devoted himself to business. The musicians then living in Chicago founded the Great Western band, which under their leaders, A. T. Vaas and C. Romanus, did good work, both as a military band and as a string orchestra. Soon after the great immigration of '48 there was formed an association in which social as well as artistic ends were to be cultivated. This was the Chicago Mænnergesangverein, which was formed 1852, and at first under Emil Rein, and later on under Julius Unger, did excellent service, giving in 1855 three operatic performances in the Deutsche Haus: "Mordgrundbruck," "Czar and Carpenter," and "Alexandro Stradella." The great musical event of the year 1853 was the first Chicago appearance of Adelina Patti and Ole Bull, who gave concerts in April, in Tremont Music Hall.

The splendid Germania Orchestra was disbanded in Boston in 1853, and its eminent conductor, Carl Bergmann, was induced to come to Chicago to take up the concerts abandoned by Mr. Dyhrenfurth. But Chicago life did not suit him, and after one season he went back to New York without having accomplished much of anything. Henry Ahner, a former member of the Germania Orchestra, came to Chicago in 1856 and conducted the newly established singing society, "The Freie Sængerbund." For several years he gave successful orchestra concerts (evening and afternoon), at Metropolitan Hall, corner of La Salle and Randolph streets. Ahner was a genuine musical pioneer. He had great energy, a never-tiring perseverance and that degree of enthusiasm which easily overcomes all difficulties. Besides this, he was a good musician. The whole fashionable world of Chicago patronized his concerts, and it seemed as if they would become a lasting success. Unfortunately, his rather delicate constitution proved unequal to this exacting mode of life, and he died in the summer of 1858.

During this period (1855–60), excellent chamber concerts were given, first at Tremont Hall and later on in Metropolitan Hall, by the pianists Paul Becker and Mrs. Henry Band, later Mrs. Kloss, the violinist, Henry De Clerque, and the violoncellist, Albert Melms. These concerts, in point of merit, would favorably compare with similar entertainments of the present time. The Nordwestliche Sængerbund, which had been founded in Milwaukee the year before, gave its second great Sængerfest in Chicago, in June, 1857. Besides three Chicago societies, there participated in this festival, societies from Milwaukee, Manitowoc, Madison, Dubuque, Davenport and St. Louis. All the singers, numbering 250, were quartered in private families. The orchestra, of thirty-five, was composed of Chicago musicians. The festival consisted of one principal concert at Metropolitan Hall, with orchestra and choral numbers, and one popular concert at the "Deutsche Haus," with solo singing by the different societies, on which occasion the Milwaukee musical society won the highest distinction by singing Kuecken's chorus, "On the Rhine." Mr. Christian Wahl was the president, and Mr. Hans Balatka the musical director of the festival. The principal numbers of the concert in Metropolitan Hall were: Jubilee Overture for orchestra, by Weber; a fantasia, for cornet, by Vivier, played by Mr. H. Ahner, and Weber's Concertstueck, played by Mrs. Henry Band. The grand choruses were: "Warrior's Nightwatch" with orchestra, by Eckert, Zoellner's "Mountain March," and "The Alps," by T. Froehlich.

In 1859, another American choral society was organized, the "Musical Union." It was under the musical direction of Mr. C. M. Cady, who, one year later, transferred it to Mr. George F. Root. Choruses from oratorios, cantatas, and, later on, Haydn's "Creation," but with piano accompaniment only, were produced by this society. Its accompanist, Mr. A. W. Dohn, to whom the progress of the Musical Union appeared too slow, founded the "Mendelssohn society," which entered into successful competition with the "Union," and produced Sterndale Bennett's, "May Queen," Mendelssohn's 42d psalm and other choral works by the same master.

The drama, even in those early days, was flourishing. Rice's was the first theater building, and while some of the entertainments given there were crude and with but little artistic merit, others were given by the best actors in America. Joseph Jefferson and his wife and their boy, the celebrated Joseph Jefferson of to-day, appeared in Chicago in 1837. "Hamlet" was first produced in 1839. An early Chicago favorite was Mrs. Hunt, now Mrs. John Drew—one of America's oldest and most famous actresses. Junius Brutus Booth made his first appearance in 1848.

In 1855, under the auspices of the Mænnergesangverein, the "Deutsche Haus" was built, corner of North Wells and Indiana streets, where, it was hoped, the German drama would find a lasting home. In the beginning, everything went well and the Deutsche Haus became the center of German art and society. But dissensions and jealousies soon made their baneful influence felt and gradually the Deutsche Haus, theatre and all, went to ruin.

In regard to painting, the advent of two famous artists is to be noted; the German, H. Merkle, and the Irishman, E. Healy. Healy stood very high in Paris and Rome, where he was honored by an order to paint the portrait of Pope Pius IX.

Music in Chicago received a new impetus by the production, in the Cathedral of the Holy Name, of Mozart's

"Requiem." Miss Emilie Garthe, soprano in the cathedral choir, had conceived the idea, but there was at that time no one in Chicago to undertake the work. Hans Balatka, of Milwaukee, who had already gained a national reputation by his success with the Milwaukee musical society and his management of several large Sængerfests, was suggested as the proper person to direct the production of the "Requiem." He was accordingly invited to come to Chicago and undertake the work. He accepted the invitation, and about the middle of September, 1860, the "Requiem" was given under his direction, by a chorus of sixty voices, with an orchestral accompaniment of thirty pieces. The soloists were Miss E. Garthe, soprano; Miss L. Farrel, alto; A. Maus, tenor, and Messrs. Christian Sonne and H. de Passio, bassos. The performance was, in every particular, an unqualified success. A committee of the most influential musical people, among them Messrs. E. I. Tinkham, J. G. Shortall, E. Stickney, Otto H. Matz and Dr. Brainard, invited Mr. Balatka to make Chicago his future home, and to take charge of a new musical organization. Mr. Balatka accepted this invitation also, and in October, 1860, the Philharmonic Society of Chicago was formed. In November its first concert was given in Bryan Hall—now the Grand Opera House—and from that time concerts took place monthly. Their success was unprecedented. Almost all of Beethoven's symphonies were performed, as were several from Mozart, Haydn, Mendelssohn, Gade and Hugo Ulrich. There were also rendered a great number of important overtures and other orchestral works of the modern school, alternating with vocal and instrumental solos. The demand for tickets was so great that several weeks before the beginning of a new season, every seat in the hall was taken. In 1862, Balatka accepted the leadership of the Musical Union, and in the spring of 1863, produced the oratorio of "Elijah." In 1864, he produced at McVicker's theater the opera "Czar und Zimmermann,"

(Czar and Carpenter). At this time, Mr. Paul Becker gave numerous successful chamber concerts at Lyon & Healy's, and Mrs. Kloss, piano, Dr. Fessel, violin, and Balatka, cello, gave a series of classical concerts in the First Methodist Church.

The musicians of Chicago, early in the 60's, had separated into two rival organizations, the Great Western band and the Light Guard band, but in 1864 all were re-united under the name Great Western Light Guard band, and instituted the popular Sunday afternoon concerts, in North Side Turner Hall, which still continue.

The erection of Crosby's Opera House, in 1864-65, and of Farwell Hall, marked a new epoch in Chicago musical history. Crosby's Opera House was opened with a four weeks' season of Italian opera, given by such famous artists as Zucchi, Morensi, Kellogg, Mazzoleni, Massimiliani and Bellini. The Philharmonic society transferred its concerts to the new opera house, but owing to the greater popularity of the opera the patronage of the concerts gradually diminished and they were finally abandoned. From 1866 to 1868, Balatka gave symphony concerts in Farwell Hall and supplemented them with several series of afternoon concerts, but the financial success of the new departure was indifferent and these concerts, too, were given up.

In the realm of vocal art things went somewhat better. The Musical Union was re-organized under the name of the Oratorio society, and gave, in Farwell Hall, a series of brilliant performances, with a chorus of 400 voices, and such soloists as Parepa Rosa, Nielsson, Cary, Nordbloom, Whitney and Rudolphson. Not only the artistic, but even the financial success of these concerts was complete. The Maennerchor societies now received a new impetus. Hans Balatka assumed the directorship of the Germania Maennerchor and worked to make the society the center of all German art and society in Chicago. His remarkable talent for organization soon brought about the desired result and the Germania Maennerchor compared favorably with the Liederkranz and Arion societies of New York. At the time of Lincoln's funeral, the Germania Maennerchor rendered several German choruses. Later some members of the Germania, under Otto Lob, formed the Concordia Maennerchor, and now a healthy and profitable rivalry sprang up between the two societies. The result was a series of highly enjoyable concerts and other musical enterprises, which, in 1870, culminated with the performance, by the Germania, of the operas "Der Freischuetz" and "Stradella" and the rendering of the "Magic Flute," by the Concordia. The solo parts were given by amateurs only, but so much care had been bestowed upon them that the performances were fully equal to all requirements of art. The mounting of the operas and the ensemble were much better than Chicago had ever seen before; for the Italian and Parepa's English opera troops had had a chorus of but forty voices and an orchestra of twenty-five or thirty pieces, while the choruses of these societies numbered over one hundred singers and the orchestras consisted of sixty musicians. The great Saengerfest of the North American Saengerbund, which was held in Chicago in the month of June, 1865, formed an important episode in the musical life of the city. It was distinguished from other festivals of the kind by being not only of a national, but also of an international character. Thirty-six clubs belonging to the American Saengerbund, and the two leading New York societies, the Arion and Liederkranz, were represented. Mr. Emil Dietzsch, the secretary of the festival, was instructed by the executive committee to send invitations to every singing society in Germany. A delegation of German singers actually took part in the festival. The three grand concerts were given in the skating rink, corner of Wabash avenue and Jackson street. The chorus consisted of 1200 singers, while the grand orchestra, for the first time on such an occasion, numbered one hundred musicians.

Germania Maennerchor Club House.

The artistic and financial successes were equally great. The receipts of the concerts gave a surplus of about $4000, which sum was divided among the seven Chicago societies that had arranged the festival. Encouraged by the great success of its concerts and operas, the Germania Mænnerchor, celebrated, December 17, 1870, the one hundredth anniversary of Beethoven's birth by the production of the master's immortal Ninth Choral Symphony.

Meanwhile the number of theatres had increased from two to seven, and the character of their general work was excellent. The German drama still languished in a state of total impotency, but Chicago became well known among American cities for its high standard of dramatic art. The stock company system was still in vogue. The great stars traveled from city to city, where they were supported by local companies. Chicago's stock companies were from the first composed of actors of the highest ability. Many a man who graduated from one of McVicker's stock companies has since achieved a national reputation. Though not the pioneer of the Chicago drama, James H. McVicker has contributed more to the city's development in that line than any other half dozen men. Himself a comedian of the highest ability, he made his first appearance in Chicago in April, 1848. At that time Rice's theatre was the home of the dramatic muse, and young McVicker was engaged as the comedian. He was very successful, but in 1851 left the city and began a starring tour through the United States. In 1855 he went to England, where he continued his successes. In 1857 he returned to Chicago, and on November 5th opened McVicker's theatre— the most costly, substantial and convenient theatre in the west. Its seating capacity was 2500, its stage of ample size, and its properties and scenery complete. From the first, plays of standard merit were performed by actors of no mean ability. Mr. McVicker organized a stock company that made his theatre famous, not only in America, but even in England.

Occasionally McVicker himself appeared, as was the case when the celebrated actor, James E. Murdoch, visited Chicago in December, 1857, giving a repertoire of Shakespearean plays. In the January following, Charlotte Cushman played at McVicker's, and in May Edwin Booth made his first appearance. Miss Mary McVicker, afterwards Mrs. Edwin Booth, appeared at her father's theatre in August, 1859. The celebrated Adah Isaacks Menken, the elder Sothern, J. Wilkes Booth, Edwin Forrest, J. H. Hackett, America's most famous "Falstaff," Daniel E. Bandmann, the German tragedian, and Lawrence Barrett were other stars who played at McVicker's before the fire.

Among Chicago artists at this time were G. P. A. Healy, S. P. Tracy, Howard Strong, E. Schwert, Daniel F. Bigelow and Leonard W. Volk. In May, 1859, the first Art Exposition was held in Chicago. The contributors numbered seventy, and the catalogue showed twenty pieces of statuary, twenty works in water color and over three hundred in oil on exhibition. So great was the success of this enterprise that the local artists formed the Chicago Art Union. Shortly before his nomination for the presidency, Abraham Lincoln sat for L. W. Volk, the sculptor, who executed an excellent bust, which was afterwards exhibited at the Paris Exposition of 1867. In 1866 the Chicago Academy of Design was founded by several professional artists who were eager to foster local art.

During the war George F. Root gained a national reputation by his war songs, "The Battle Cry of Freedom," "Tramp, Tramp, Tramp," "Marching Through Georgia," and others.

The great fire wiped out of existence most of Chicago's musical societies. The Oratorio Society had just finished rehearsing the two great oratorios of "Eli," by Costa, and "Judas Maccabaeus," by Handl, which were to be produced about the middle of October, when both the music and instruments of the society were lost in the fire. The society was re-organized in the fall of 1872, with J. A. Butterfield as conductor, and the Handl and Haydn Society of Boston came to its assistance with a donation of several hundred volumes for its library. A concert was announced in the spring of 1873 in the Congregational Church, near Union Park, on the West Side, but on the night before the concert the church was destroyed by fire, with all the music and instruments of the society. Some steps were taken to keep up the organization, but its misfortunes had been too great, and it ceased to exist. But soon there was a new ray of hope. The inhabitants of Chicago had quickly recovered from the effects of the terrible blow, and showed unexampled energy in rebuilding the city. As if by magic new residences and commercial palaces arose from the debris and ruins, trade and commerce revived, wages were high, and the newly-acquired wealth created a desire for adorning life by the fine arts. The Germania Mænnerchor, under Julius Fuchs as director, found a new home in the Greenebaum building, and resumed its former activity, although on a smaller scale.

Of especial importance in the musical development of Chicago was the organization of the "Apollo Musical Club," early in the summer of 1872. George P. Upton was its president, and S. G. Pratt the conductor. The office of conductor afterwards passed into the hands of Mr. A. W. Dohn, a thorough musician, who tried to make the Apollo club a Mænnerchor after the fashion of the German societies. Of the original number, no one ever dreamed that the club would attain the exalted position which it enjoys at present, not only in Chicago, but in the whole country. Its first concert was given January 21st at Standard Hall, and the singing was so excellent that none of the German societies could have competed with it. Mr. Dohn soon resigned the conductorship of the club to W. L. Tomlins. Under the new leader its development was rapid. Mr. Tomlins was not only a thorough musician, but had the personal magnetism necessary to make a great society. He soon developed the highest ability as a choral leader, and to-day stands unrivalled in this line of work. He not only changed the whole style of the club's singing, but made it a mixed, instead of a male chorus. The popularity of the concerts was phenomenal and constantly increased. They were given exclusively for its associate members, and the number of these rapidly grew. The society dedicated McCormick's Hall, in the North Division, then the Central Music Hall on State street, and in 1889 the great Auditorium. In its repertory are to be found nearly all the standard works of the great masters of ancient and modern times, and it produced recently some new works for the first time in America—among them Becker's "Reformation Cantata," Sullivan's "The Golden Legend," the "Te Deum," by Berlioz. Not content with such brilliant achievements, it instituted in 1882–1884, in connection with Theodore Thomas, grand musical festivals at the Exposition building, with the assistance of such celebrities as Materna, Nielsson, Cary and Winkelmann Toedt, Remmertz, Whitney, Scaria. It had a chorus of one thousand singers and an orchestra of 120 musicians. The club is at present in the most flourishing condition, giving to its associate members several concerts every season. These concerts are always repeated for the wage workers. The number of its active members is five hundred. It can successfully compete with any similar European organization, and probably surpasses them all in efficiency. To George P. Upton, the club's first president, the cause of art in Chicago is much indebted. Mr. Upton is an art critic of rare ability and has always given the heartiest support to the advancement of the musical interests of the city. His just criticisms and his keen appreciation of all that is excellent, have been a source of inspiration and encouragement to local artists, especially.

Balatka returned from Milwaukee in the fall of 1873 and organized the Chicago Liederkranz, which not only inaugurated successful concerts at the North Side Turner Hall, but in 1874, produced at McVicker's theatre, the opera of "Masaniello," which was equally successful from an artistic and financial standpoint. About the same time another American society, the "Beethoven Society," came into existence. Mr. Carl Wolfssohn, the leader, was a musician of excellent taste, a fine pianist and a great admirer of Beethoven. The society existed for about six years, during which period it produced such works as: Mendelssohn's "Elijah" and "Loreley" and Verdi's "Requiem," Bruch's "Odysseus" and "Lay of the Bell," and Hoffmann's "Melusine" and "Cinderella." Although the society prospered at first, the rivalry of the Apollo Club at length proved too much for it and it disbanded.

The great commercial crisis of 1873 was not without its influence upon matters of art. The general necessity for strict economy left nothing for the support of the arts. The Liederkranz went under and the other German society languished. A new musical club, the "Abt Society," was organized in 1876 from the ranks of the best American singers, with C. Loesch as director. It was, however, composed of only solo singers, who would not submit to the indispensable choral discipline, and disbanded in 1879, after having given several good concerts at McCormick's Hall. In 1877, the first series of summer night concerts was inaugurated by George B. Carpenter at the Exposition building, with Theodore Thomas as conductor. These concerts proved very successful until 1891, when the Exposition building was torn down to make room for the new Art Institute. Ten years ago chamber music received particular attention in Chicago. The Trio evenings, given by Carl Wolfssohn, the classical concerts of Adolph Liesegang and the chamber music soirees of Mr. Clarence Eddy and William Lewis, in connection with Miss Agnes Ingersoll, were especially noteworthy. Mr. Wolfssohn's concerts are still an attraction every season. In the year 1881, Chicago was again honored with the authority to organize another of the great musical festivals of the North American Saengerbund. Besides the usual male choruses a grand mixed chorus was to participate in the event. The president of the festival was Lewis Wahl, and the conductor was Hans Balatka. Singers of great reputation were engaged; among them, Madam Peschka-Leutner, soprano; Miss Cary, alto; Messrs. Candidus, tenor; Remmertz, baritone; Whitney, basso. The first concert was given Wednesday, June 29th, in the Exposition building, when Bruch's "Odysseus" was produced with a mixed chorus of 1200 singers from Chicago, Milwaukee and Cincinnati, accompanied by an orchestra of 150 pieces. On the following Thursday the male chorus sang alone. When the grand chorus of 2200 men opened with Moehring's "Prayer before the Battle," an indescribable enthusiasm prevailed in the audience. Such an overpowering body of sound nobody had ever heard before. Equally effective was the singing of the other choruses: "Salamis," by Max Bruch, and "The Consecration of Solomon's Temple," by Titl. Everything indicated the grand success of the festival. But fate had decreed otherwise. On Saturday morning, July 2d, during rehearsal, came the terrible news of the assassination of President Garfield, and all enthusiasm was at an end. The concert in the evening, at which Beethoven's ninth symphony and scenes from Wagner's "Lohengrin" were given, found no sympathetic ear, although the most famous soloists in the world took part in it.

It seemed now that the idea to give Chicago a society after the manner of the Liederkranz and Arion of New York was about to reach its fulfillment. A movement was set on foot to combine the German singers in the Germania Mænnerchor, which had given much encouragement to the festival of 1881. But opposing elements arose and defeated the plan, at the same time striking a blow at the cultivation of German song in Chicago. For, whereas the vocal forces of native

Americans became more and more united until the Apollo club grew to be the one great exponent of choral music, the German forces have gradually scattered. There are remaining, however, some good German societies which give occasional concerts. Among them are: The Germania, Concordia, Sennefelder Liederkranz, Orpheus Mænnerchor, Teutonia, Fidelia, Liedertafel Vorwaerts, Frohsinn and North Chicago Liedertafel.

A leading feature of Chicago's musical life is the Amateur Musical club, members of which are exclusively ladies highly accomplished in music. It numbers about two hundred active and five hundred associate members. It arranges fourteen concerts every season, seven of which are for the active members only, and the other seven for the entire membership. Besides these concerts, this club gives several entertainments each season for the benefit of charitable institutions. Among the musical events of the last period, the three of overshadowing importance are the grand opera festival of three weeks' duration at the Exposition building in 1885, with Patti as prima donna; the opening of the Auditorium, December 9, 1889, by the Abbey and Grau Italian opera company, with Patti again principal; and the organization of the Chicago Orchestral association under Theodore Thomas.

The Auditorium is one of the largest and best equipped opera houses in the world. Its interior is not surpassed in elegance and comfort anywhere, and its acoustics are admirable. For large political meetings it will accommodate an audience of 5000, but by an ingenious contrivance this capacity can be reduced for purposes of grand opera and for ordinary plays. The Chicago Orchestral association was formed in 1891 by fifty citizens of Chicago, who guaranteed its expense for three years by subscribing a fund of $150.000. The trustees of the association are N. K. Fairbank, C. N. Fay, E. B. McCagg, E. D. Hamill and A. C. Bartlett. The officers are: N. K. Fairbank, president: C.

Auditorium and Old Art Institute.

N. Fay, vice-president; P. A. McEwan, treasurer, and Milward Adams, manager. Theodore Thomas was engaged to take the orchestra in charge, and now makes Chicago his home. The orchestra gives twenty first-class concerts annually, each of which is preceded by a so-called public rehearsal, at which the entire programme of the following concert is given. The first season was financially unsuccessful, but the second showed a great improvement in this respect. From the first, the work of Chicago's new orchestra was, artistically considered, most excellent. The entire credit for its accurate conception and splendid execution is due to its celebrated leader, Theodore Thomas, who resigned the leadership of the Metropolitan Orchestra in New York to organize the greater Chicago institution. Under Mr. Thomas' management the work of Chicago's orchestra compares favorably with similar organizations both in Europe and America. His fidelity to the Wagner school and his marked preference for the severer classical music at first detracted from the popular appreciation of the work of the great orchestra under his control. But the masses were quick to feel the educating stimulus of his work and the result must be highly gratifying to Mr. Thomas.

Owing to his position as one of America's leading musicians, Mr. Thomas was chosen as the musical director of the World's Fair. Mr. Tomlins was made choral director. They have made extensive arrangements for the work in their department, and the cause of music in Chicago will receive the greatest impetus during the World's Fair period.

As disseminators of musical taste and culture, the numerous music schools and art institutes finally deserve a special mention, most of them being provided with excellent and conscientious teachers. The prominent among these institutes are the American Conservatory of Music, Apollo Musical school, Athenæum, Balatka Academy of Musical Art, Chicago Conservatory, Chicago Musical Col-

New Art Institute.

lege, Gottschalk's School of Lyric Art, National Conservatory of Music and F. W. Root's Music school. One of the potent promoters of musical art and education in Chicago is the Newberry Library. It was endowed by Walter L. Newberry, and a great part of the endowment is devoted to the enlargement of its musical equipment. The works there that have an especial interest for musicians include a great number of oratorios, operas, cantatas, symphonies and chamber music, in most cases, with vocal and instrumental parts, biographies, histories of music, musical dictionaries, history of instruments and instrumentation, letters and writings of musicians, special editions of rare volumes and all prominent works published by subscriptions. The rarest work in the whole collection is probably the original edition of the opera of "Euridice," by Taiopo Peri, printed at Florence in 1600. It was the first opera that was ever performed, and it is believed that the Chicago copy is the only one of the edition of 1600 now in existence. It was purchased at Florence at a high price. The great advantage which this library offers to the student is that he can study musical literature and history from original sources, without the necessity of going abroad. For the cultivation of the drama the later Chicago has erected over twenty new theatres of great splendor, in which many works of true art are performed. More than one of the modern stock companies have favored Chicago with the first productions of some of the cleverest English and American comedies, which afterwards found great favor with audiences in the east and in England. Enterprising dramatic managers have thus recognized Chicago's importance among American centers for the drama.

The fine arts have enjoyed for many years a fostering care from the Chicago Art Institute, formerly situated at the corner of Van Buren street and Michigan avenue, but now about to occupy a magnificent new building on the Lake Front at the foot of Adams street. This new temple of art is a pride to the eye of every citizen of Chicago, and will be one of the enduring forces to turn the public mind toward higher culture, and to enlarge and dignify the artistic and æsthetic element in Chicago life. Valuable works of art, both in painting and sculpture, are collected there (some original and more copies, ancient and modern) through the munificence of wealthy patrons. The rooms, which are certainly designed with as much wisdom as those of any art building in the world, are open to the student as well as to the general public every day. On Sundays access to the galleries is free. Among the greater works there are original masterpieces by Murillo, Van Dyke, Rembrandt and Rubens.

It is apparent that Chicago's growth in lines of the fine arts has been an arduous progress, impeded by many reverses and painful disappointments, but crowned often with a flattering degree of success. No small glory has the city won in its efforts to cultivate matters of art and keep them apace with its development in commerce and industry, but the future has much to accomplish in order to place the city at the head of American centers of art. The past four years have been years of marvellous strides in that direction and give reason, not only for hopefulness in the work yet to be accomplished, but also for pride in the work already done.

The Public Library.

There is perhaps no public institution in this country that has had so wonderful a development as the public library. While as yet we have not the largest libraries, we have the most useful. Collections of books for the use of the masses are justly called "the universities of the people," and their educational influence upon the people cannot be measured. The knowledge books impart is, as a rule, concise and compact, and libraries have, therefore, an advantage over schools. Schools need the positive individual learning of the teachers and their practical skill to impart it, and in proportion to these they are successful in accomplishing their ends, while mere technical knowledge and skill on part of the administration suffice to make a library comparatively useful. This, in conjunction with the energy and generosity of the American people, explains the marvellous development of the American libraries.

It is perfectly natural that the public library of Chicago should have surpassed those of its older sister cities. Its history is but a parallel to the history of the city itself. The library is to-day by far the most used in the land. The use of a library—that is, its conditional usefulness—is dependent partly on the completeness of its collection and partly upon the character of its administration. The Chicagoans, then, have every reason to be proud of the former and to be satisfied with the latter. But the Chicago Public Library can show in its favor, besides these subjective conditions, also objective proofs of its excellency and superiority. Among these it will suffice to mention the fact that the library received the award of a gold medal at the Paris International Exposition of 1889, the only distinction ever awarded to an American library at any competitive international exposition. But the library speaks best for itself. The beginnings were small and the conditions the most adverse imaginable. We will have to go back somewhat beyond the beginnings of the present institution in order to understand how it grew. Just as a private library, collected and used by its owner, indicates the degree of the latter's mental acquirements, so public libraries indicate the mental status of a community. The history, then, of the efforts of a community in this direction is of the utmost importance, and it may even be said to be its actual history, since the visible happenings are but the effects of the invisible causes in the life of entire communities as well as of individuals. It is natural that the material interests of the young city required at first all the time and energy of its inhabitants. But no sooner was the material existence of the commonwealth assured than the mental needs of the people began to assert themselves. Those who recognized and were in position to do anything towards satisfying these needs, made various efforts in that direction. How numerous were the obstacles and how great the difficulties in a young community working out its own existence, can be understood only by those who know the circumstances produced by entirely new political and social conditions. The population of the young city was very peculiar, and, in a commonwealth of such magnitude, without precedent. It had not grown in the normal way and was not composed of elements of kindred descent and homogeneous nature. The majority of those to whom the city is indebted for what it is to-day, had come here in riper years from other parts of the United States and from foreign countries. What this heterogeneous mass of people possessed in the way of intellectual treasures was as different as their outward qualities, and, in the case of a great many of them was very insignificant. The schools sufficed, it is true, to give to the children of the settlers a common, practical education, but they could not do anything toward satisfying the mental needs of the adult portion of the population. The less so as these were compelled as yet to employ their entire time for their material necessities. Churches, too, of all denominations, grew up rapidly, but the church and other similar moral institutions have but a one-sided educational influence upon the mental faculties of man.

Public lectures which have for their object the mental development and training of the masses, and public institutions of like tendency, as the theatre, the museum and other "high schools of the liberal arts," can nowhere do less than in a young community in which the fermentation is still going on—and this is so partly because their efforts must needs be of a general nature, requiring in all the same grade of mental culture, and partly because they consume more time than the people can spare. Under such conditions, then, no educating power is left but literature, and no other means to make it accessible to all the people but free public libraries. And it is in this direction, therefore, that we see turned the efforts of those who had recognized the mental needs of Chicago's early population. Before the great fire these efforts were only occasional and individual, and being often prompted by personal ambition or other egotistic motives, met with but little success. There were, in fact, but three libraries worth mentioning, and after the fire, which destroyed them all, none were re-opened. These libraries, those of the Chicago Historical Society, the Young Men's Christian Association and the Young Men's Library Association, had in no way been adequate to the needs of the people. The Young Men's Library Association had had a very promising beginning, and was fairly under way to become what a public library should be. Its first president was Walter L. Newberry, who by his later bequest of over three million dollars, has given the city the great Newberry Library, which, under the able and experienced management of Dr. William F. Poole, is rapidly coming to the front rank of American libraries. Quite a number of Chicago's best, most cultured and wealthiest citizens also belonged to the association that had established this library. But Illinois had at that time no library law and the Chicago Library was, therefore, a subscription library, and, having no certain income adequate to its requirements, was of but limited usefulness and unable to comply with the increasing demands upon it. At the time of the fire it was heavily in debt. That the unsatisfactory condition of affairs was fully appreciated will be seen from the following extract from the Chicago Tribune, of September 10, 1871, a month before the fire:

> "We are a community of nearly 330,000 inhabitants, and have absolutely no public library deserving the name. Not only is there no library in this city where a scholar could solve a difficult question in literature, or art or science, or where an educated man, to whom reading and study are a necessity, could find books to satisfy his modest desires, but there is not even one where he who wants to get a common education could find the means to this end. * * Chicago has no lack of educated people, but they are chiefly among those classes who do not enjoy the means necessary to acquire a library of their own. But even if that were not so, the blame would nevertheless be attached to us as a civilized community, for not being in possession of a public library."

But the agitators for a public library had not rested. Just before the fire, strenuous efforts had been made, and a bill presented to the State Legislature by William H. King, of Chicago. This provided that free public libraries be established in the larger cities of the state, to be maintained by general taxation. But the intended results of all these efforts were frustrated by the vigilant and active opposition of a strong minority of the tax-payers, who lacked that unselfishness and public spirit which are the very essence and foundation of a democratic commonwealth. Then came the fire and wiped out of existence the makeshift libraries that had, in a measure, hidden the urgent necessity for a first-class public institution. But it did more. It also paralyzed the opposition to a free public library by widening the bonds of sympathy on the one hand, and by directing the attention of some of the opponents to their own interests on the other. Schiller says that "man grows with his higher aims," and this applies also to communities of men. The new city had to be built up again upon a broader basis and in accordance with a higher plan. Some were still in hopes that the "Chicago Library" could be re-established. Mr. Robson, the former librarian of that institution, took the utmost pains to revive the interest of the officers of his association. Fortunately it was soon recognized that a city like Chicago must have a public library, and Mr. Robson himself was quite willing to go to England, his native land, in the interest of the free public library, which it was proposed to establish. Meanwhile the great misfortune that had visited Chicago had called forth the warmest sympathy in England, where it was decided to send to Chicago a miscellaneous collection of books, to form the nucleus of a new library. At the head of this movement stood Thomas Hughes, assisted by men like Disraeli and Burgess, and high and low, from the Queen down to the most humble man of the people, took an interest and part in it. Many a comparatively poor man contributed towards the noble and lasting monument his country was about to erect to itself in the new world. Contributions poured in upon a call from Hughes and Burgess, the president and secretary of the executive committee, that had been at once formed. During this time, however, the people in Chicago were by no means idle. A plan for the proposed people's library was worked out and the necessary steps were taken for its immediate execution. A number of competent and experienced men drew up proper bills to be substituted to the Legislature, so that the cause might not be delayed when the proper time came. The first public action was January 5, 1872, when twenty-eight prominent citizens requested Mayor Joseph Medill to call a general mass meeting of the citizens of Chicago, for the purpose of establishing a free public library.

On Monday evening, January 8, 1872, a meeting was held in Plymouth Church, and the matter thoroughly discussed. Many thought that such a library could be supported only through private munificence, but Mr. Daniel L. Shorey, an experienced lawyer and later president of the library board, expressed himself decidedly and strongly in favor of public taxation for the purpose. This brought decision and clearness into the deliberations. No one, perhaps, had given the subject as much thought as Mr. Shorey, so his arguments, ably and clearly presented, convinced all. Thereupon Mr. E. C. Larned presented a resolution, which was at once adopted, giving it as the sense of the meeting that "a free public library was of the utmost importance to the best interests and welfare of the people of Chicago, and that the present time was the most favorable for its establishment." The resolution further called upon the people of the city for active assistance in carrying out the plan, and expressed to Mr. Hughes and the English friends associated with him, the warmest thanks of the meeting. It is a remarkable fact that Mr. Larned, in his speech introducing his resolution, expressed himself very decidedly in favor of Dearborn Park as the best site for the library—the very place where now, twenty-one years after that meeting and after long years of struggle for the spot, the new library building is being erected. By another resolution the mayor was empowered to appoint a committee to at once take steps necessary to the establishment of such library, to prepare bills for the Legislature, and to further the project with all possible energy and speed. This committee consisted of Messrs. Thomas Hoyne, W. E. Doggett, E. C. Larned, S. S. Hayes, James Warrack, D. L. Shorey, J. M. Walker, W. B. Ogden, Henry Greenebaum, George S. Bowen, Judge Henry Booth, Levi Z. Leiter, George Schneider, Edwin L. Brown, Wm. Bross, Jno. V. Farwell, C. H. McCormick, Julius Rosenthal, J. Y. Scammon, Carter H. Harrison. Now the work was begun in good earnest. All the gentlemen on the committee were men of great experience and uncommon energy, and were well acquainted with all legal forms and requirements. The first great result of their work was a law passed by the Legislature of the state as early as

February 22, 1872, which empowered the council of each incorporated city in Illinois "to establish and maintain a public library and reading room for the use and benefit of the inhabitants of such city, and to levy a tax of not to exceed one mill and in large cities one-fifth of one mill annually." The law provided further that every such library was to be governed by a board of directors of nine members, to be appointed by the mayor and confirmed by the council. The law went into effect the 7th of March of the same year, and immediately thereafter the city council of Chicago adopted an ordinance creating a "free public library" and providing for its establishment and maintenance in every particular. At the next meeting the mayor sent in the names of nine of the most prominent citizens of Chicago, whom he had appointed to compose the first board of directors of the public library. These gentlemen were: Thomas Hoyne, Robert T. Queal and Daniel L. Shorey, to serve one year, Willard Woodard, Elliott Anthony, Julius Rosenthal, to serve two years, and Hermann Raster, James W. Sheehan, Samuel S. Hayes, to serve three years. The unequal terms are explained by the provisions of the law requiring the appointment of three directors each year, the term of office to be three years. The appointment of the nine gentlemen mentioned was promptly confirmed by the council. A great deal more than might be supposed depended on the first work in the direction of making the library a real public library—a library for the people.

The present admirable condition, popularity and usefulness of the institution is in no small degree due to the foundation laid by the first board. Literature is of universal character; it is the common property of mankind and its mission is therefore an international one. A large library cannot confine itself to a particular language, except, perhaps, in the lines of common, domestic literature. The board of directors of the Chicago public library met for its first session, March 11, 1872, and organized by electing its officers and appointing its standing committees. Mr. Thomas Hoyne, who had shown himself very zealous in the cause, was elected president, and within a short time the services of a capable secretary were secured in the person of William B. Wickersham, who has faithfully served the board and the library to the present time (1893). Everything being ready for action, great zeal and energy were used to open the library to the public at as early a date as possible. The first aim was to equip a good reading-room, where the best newspapers and journals of the world could be consulted by every one. As early as January, 1873, such a room was opened and became at once popular. So large was the attendance on the part of the general public that no less than 50,035 persons visited the room during the first five months. But this was only the beginning! Meanwhile, the books began to pour in from England, Germany, France, Ireland and Scotland. Among them were very valuable gifts, as, for instance, the English patent reports, a complete collection of 2800 volumes sent by the commissioners of British patents. This collection is annually augmented by 140 volumes. Learned institutions, among them the universities of Oxford and Cambridge, sent costly contributions, and so likewise did a number of prominent individuals. Most of the books coming from England bear the inscription on a special book-plate: "Presented to the city of Chicago, towards the foundation of a free library, after the great fire of 1871, as a mark of English sympathy." In all, these gifts amounted to 7000 volumes from England and about half that number from other countries, chiefly from Germany; 5000 additional volumes were purchased the first year, so the library proper could be opened to the public on May 1, 1874. In January of that year, the foremost of American librarians, Dr. William F. Poole, who was called from Cincinnati, assumed charge of the institution. When the Newberry library was organized, Dr. Poole resigned his position to go to the new institution, and Frederick

Hild was made librarian, with E. F. L. Gauss, assistant. How great and how general the need of a free public library was at that time, and how heartily it was welcomed by the masses, is shown by the experience of the institution during its first weeks. An average daily circulation of 138 volumes in the first week had nearly doubled itself in the second, and in the fifth amounted to 555 volumes daily. This unparalleled growth is the more remarkable when it is known that the Boston public library, until recently, the most prosperous and most patronized library of the land, circulated at the close of its fifth year only 310 volumes daily. A few further figures illustrating the wonderful development of the library, will be of interest:

Year.	No. of Vols. in the Library.	No. of Vols. circulated.
1874	18,183 [first month]	7,359
1875	39,236	399,156
1876	49,024	424,030
1877	51,408	428,090
1878	57,984	429,306
1879	60,423	558,428
1880	67,722	416,751
1881	77,140	408,801
1882	87,272	479,977
1883	94,606	525,883
1884	100,341	622,313
1885	111,621	651,469
1886	119,510	766,056
1887	129,129	835,295
1888	132,946	993,339
1889	140,116	1,078,210
1890	156,242	1,225,784
1891	166,475	1,265,117
1892	177,178	1,414,469

At present the library contains 187,000 volumes. In the preceding figures the number of periodicals used in the several reading rooms is not included. From June 1st, 1891, to June 1st, 1892, the number of these circulated, was 700,917. Besides the above there were also used in the reading rooms 51,846 bound volumes of periodicals and other books. In point of use the Chicago public library is now the first in the United States. In the year 1888 it surpassed the Boston public library, until then the foremost, by 58,746 volumes in the annual circulation of books. In proportion to the respective number of volumes the two libraries then contained, this difference appears still greater—the Boston library's book collection amounting to 492,596 volumes and that of our own to but 132,946.

When an institution, coming into life under such great difficulties and by such heavy sacrifices, has finally been successfully established, and enters upon a merely natural development and existence, the more interesting part of its history has come to a close, and further interesting features can be found only in the line of its work proper—either in method or effect.

Of utmost interest is the modus operandi of a large library, and it was the illustration of the same, in all its details, by a systematic arrangement and display of the various blanks used, that secured for the Chicago library the before mentioned reward at the Paris Exposition of 1889.

A library that is not complete is chiefly dependent for its selection of further books upon the catalogues of antiquarians, book auctions, sales of private libraries and occasional opportunities to purchase stray books. As a rule, current publications are not the most valuable, nor are they the most numerous purchases of a growing library. Large libraries find it necessary to have permanent agents at the several book-centers of the world. To them, the orders made up from various sources, are sent for collection. The books are generally allowed to accumulate and are then shipped in consignments of several cases. When the books arrive, they are carefully examined as to their condition and correspondence with the order and are then checked with the bill or other list accompanying the shipment. The lot, when found to be in order, is entered in the so-called "accession catalogue," each single book or work receiving a separate number. The Chicago public library has improved and perfected its accession catalogue as experience suggested, until now it is not infrequently copied. The several items that are here entered referring to each book or work, are the following: after the number, are columns for the author and title, the place of publication, the year, the number of copies of the book or work, the number of volumes comprising the same, either new or replacing worn out and lost books, number of pamphlets, size of book or pamphlet, kind of binding, source of acquisition, purchase price and remarks, such as discount, nature of accession, if not purchased, etc. In this way a complete description of the book is recorded, and can be looked up any time by means of the "accession number," which, together with the date of entry, is written on the back of the title page of the entered book. Thereupon the book is catalogued upon slips of even size, according to established rules. These slips, arranged alphabetically under their main parts, comprise the so-called card catalogue, an American invention, and by far the most famous and important of late years in the line of library economy. It would fill a volume to go into all the details of cataloguing, which is often very difficult and intricate, requiring great care, untiring pains, good judgment and large knowledge. It will suffice to mention here the main features and principles of the system. The first slip or card bears upon the upper line the name of the author of the book or work, with complete surname, if obtainable; upon the second line the title of the work, and on the next the imprint of it, i. e., place and year of publication, and in addition, the number of volumes composing the work. This "author card" is distinguished from the others referring to the same work by also containing the "accession number,"— that is, the number under which the book was originally entered. Other cards are either "title cards," "subject cards," or "reference cards," which terms explain themselves. On them the title or subject or that to which "reference" is made, is the main feature, followed by the author and the same descriptive detail as was placed on the "author card." If several subjects are treated of, in one and the same work, "subject cards" are made under each. Every card also bears the shelf letter and number. A single example will make this clear:

12568	SEEGER, EUGENE. B 1764 Chicago and the Columbian Exposition. Chicago, 1893. 3 v. in 2. 8vo.

CHICAGO, B 1764 and the Columbian Exposition. E. Seeger. Chicago, 1893. 3 v. in 2. 8vo.

COLUMBIAN EXPOSITION, 1893. B 1764 Chicago and the. E. Seeger. Chicago, 1893. 3 v. in 2. 8vo.

It is seen from this example that the cataloguing of books requires also their classification and numbering—the former being usually signified by means of letters under which main classes are arranged, the latter by successive numbers under each letter. This arrangement permits of a general and sub-classification. To this end the books are again entered in the "shelf lists," under a certain number, but only under the author and title, the number of volumes and number of copies. A memorandum of the shelf-letter and number is also made upon the back of the title page. The books then go to the printer, where they are stamped and otherwise marked, labeled and numbered; here also the circulating books receive a card-pocket on the inside of the front cover, which securely holds the book borrower's card. The books are then ready for use in the several departments of the library. In the reference and reading rooms any respectable person is admitted and books and periodicals are given out for temporary use in the rooms. To draw books from the library for home use a card is necessary, which is issued to residents of Chicago and those regularly employed there, upon the guarantee of a responsible tax-paying resident of the city. The card entitles the holder to draw books from the library for the term of two years, one volume at a time, or in case of small-sized volumes, two of the same work. Each book may be retained two weeks, and may be renewed once. If a book is not returned or renewed on time, a fine of three cents for each day is charged. This fine is an absolute necessity to insure the prompt return of books, since popular works are always in great demand. The amount received in fines last year was not less than $5,943.31. The method of changing books is, in its simplicity, exceedingly interesting, especially when it is borne in mind that the daily average circulation is in the neighborhood of 4000 volumes. Whoever desires a book, presents his card with the shelf-letters and numbers of several books, any one of which he wishes to draw, or the letter and number of a specific book he wants. The attendant procures the book desired and charges it on a little slip which bears the number of the book. These slips are afterwards arranged in numerical sequence and so kept that they can be easily found when the books are returned. A new and ingenious device has recently been introduced by which is determined the percentage of books used in the various departments.

Recently the library has extended the sphere of its usefulness by establishing five branch reading rooms in various parts of the city. Another and far greater step in the development of the institution is the securing of a suitable site for the erection of a new library building. The library has long needed a home of its own, and in fact its usefulness has to some extent been impaired by the inadequacy of its quarters. For ten years the board of directors have been indefatigable in their efforts to secure a site for the new home of the institution. No suitable site could be purchased, for there were

New Public Library Building.

Now being erected in Dearborn Park.

no funds available for such a purpose, but when, recently, the ownership of Dearborn Park, a half block bounded by Washington and Randolph streets and Michigan avenue, was vested in the city, the friends of the library secured the right from the municipal authorities to build on this property. No better location could have been secured, and after a compromise was effected with the Grand Army of the Republic, which claimed certain rights in the property, preparations for building were at once made. It was agreed that the library board should put up a building covering the entire ground, and that a suitable part of the same should be set aside for a "Soldiers' and Sailors' Memorial Hall" for a term of fifty years, after the expiration of which time the entire building and site is to revert to the public library.

After the first victory, a still greater question was to be solved by the library authorities: How are the means for building to be procured? To this question there was but one answer—by taxation. To this the legislature was induced to give its sanction by special law, giving the city the power to increase the tax for the library from $\frac{1}{2}$ mill to two mills annually for the term of five years. This gave the library a little over one and one-half million dollars for building purposes, and insured a fine and well equipped structure. Then the work began in earnest. A prize was offered for the best plan and the competition was free to all. The best design was submitted by Rutan, Shipley & Coolidge—the plans calling for a severely classic structure which will, nevertheless, prove a model of convenience and excellence. The foundations, already laid, are remarkably heavy and massive and will worthily uphold the beautiful building, which, according to present plans, will be ready for occupancy in the fall of 1895.

The Labor Movement.

HISTORY OF THE EIGHT-HOUR AGITATION.

Chicago is even now enjoying the material blessings of the future, in that here mechanical industry has reached that high development which promises to coming generations a prosperity unknown to those of the past. In use of labor-saving machinery and in juster distribution of the benefits derived therefrom, Chicago is in advance of the age. In former times the working man had no empiric knowledge of the word leisure; he may acquire it in busy, pushing, practical Chicago to-day.

The very fact that capital has attained such enormous strength in commercial Chicago has had a powerful tendency to secure to labor its full rights, and has paved a way for a general perception of the truth that the interests of capital and labor are identical. It is not only organized labor which won from capital its just dues, but an enlightened public opinion would no longer tolerate starvation wages. More than any other industrial center, Chicago proved the falsity of the law —"das eherne Lohngesetz" (iron wage law)—that the raising of wages necessarily raises the price of the manufactured product. Wages were increased in Chicago and it was found that the standard of labor had been correspondingly raised, and that consequently the productive capacity of the laborer was increased. The manufacturers also learned that by raising wages and so increasing the purchasing power of the laboring classes, they likewise increased demand, and, therefore, stimulated production and cheapened its methods. Nor have the relatively high wages which Chicago's working people receive, even in such industrial branches as come in competition with the products of other manufacturing towns, weakened in the least the city's competitive ability. On the other hand, these high wages have proved the basis for the city's general welfare, a welfare in which the immigrants— the Germans, Irish, Poles, Bohemians, Scandinavians and Italians—have not been slow to participate. More than three-fourths of the present population of Chicago are of European birth or are the children of immigrants. They have all fallen into the American habit of expecting material prosperity and have learned to a greater or less extent, the American trick of realizing their expectations. They not only expect meat three times a day and some leisure, but they also have these things.

Chicago's laboring classes are at the head of legitimate, healthy labor movements in the United States. The reason for this is first, the powerful impulse given to local industries; and second, that Chicago's foreign (especially the German) workingmen and their friends, aided by a powerful press, have taken the lead in the intellectual development of the laboring classes. Legitimate labor movement, which on the whole is but an attempt to attain a rational and natural end in harmony with the development of modern machinery and methods of manufacture, should be sharply distinguished from its morbid outgrowth—the anarchistic and communistic madness. The first and the real purpose of the labor movement is to secure shorter hours of labor. The demand for the adoption of the eight-hour day comprises most of the other demands of the wage workers in regard to the adaption of the old economic life to the newly created conditions—so much so that it can be permanently obtained only by a general international organization of wage workers. The agitation for shortening the hours of labor dates as far back as the beginning of this century. Then, as now, the leaders in the movement were the workingmen engaged in the building trades. The ship-builders of New York established a union in 1803, and in 1806 the carpenters followed suit. At that time the master builders were in the employ of the merchants, who regarded these organizations and their demand that ten and not fourteen hours should constitute a working day, with anything but a friendly spirit and relentlessly persecuted all members of unions. The movement, however, gained strength, and in 1832-3 the carpenters and plasterers of New York and Philadelphia were successful in their attempt to secure the ten-hour day. How strong and popular this idea was, even then, is proved by the fact that in 1840 President Van Buren proclaimed the ten-hour day for all workingmen in the government navy yards. In June, 1845, workingmen held great mass meetings in Pittsburg and Alleghany City, which were followed by a very general strike, which, however, did not result in favor of the strikers. The first national convention of workingmen took place in New York, October 12, 1845. At this convention the formation of a secret brotherhood was proposed. In the winter of 1845-6 the general demand for a ten-hour day was proved by the numerous mass meetings held in New England, New York and Philadelphia and by the many strikes which took place. The establishment of a ten-hour day in England by an act of Parliament in 1847, greatly strengthened the movement in this country. In 1848 petitions fairly poured in on Congress in favor of a general ten-hour day and of a law forbidding the working of children more than eight hours a day and requiring employers to provide such children with a certain amount of schooling.

In June, 1850, the National Congress of workingmen met in Chicago. Many new trades assemblies were organized and it was decided to enforce the ten-hour day in all large cities by means of strikes. In 1853 in many cities of the country an eleven-hour day was introduced. In spite of this, however, the majority of the manufacturing towns continued the fourteen-hour day in force as late as 1865. After that year the eleven-hour day was generally adopted as a result of repeated and bitter strikes. Massachusetts, Rhode Island and other eastern states passed laws enforcing the ten-hour day, and in 1868, Congress passed a law fixing ten hours as the working day for all laborers in the employ of the government. Two years before, in August, 1866, a labor congress in Baltimore resolved to organize the workingmen independently of political parties and to create a national labor party for the purpose of bringing about the eight-hour day. The next year saw many strikes, but none of them resulted favorably to the workingmen. In 1869, the Boston Eight-hour League was established, and in the winter of the same year the order of the Knights of Labor was founded in Philadelphia.

The participation of the German Social Democrats in the American labor movement began in the years 1870 and 1871, when the International Labor Association in Europe resolved to establish a branch association in the United States. From that time the influence of the German workingmen in this movement has steadily gained strength. In the summer of 1872, about 100,000 men in New York organized a strike, and the following trades won the eight-hour day: The brick-layers and their assistants, the stone-cutters, carpenters, plasterers, plumbers, paper-hangers, painters and wood carvers.

During the winter of 1873-74, which was unusually severe and caused much misery among the poorer classes throughout the country, great labor demonstrations took place in New York, and finally terminated in bloody conflicts with the police. From 1873 to 1878 there were repeated large strikes in New England, Pennsylvania, Illinois, Indiana, Missouri, Maryland, Ohio and New York.

Of the actual existence of the "social question," of strong, unreconciled differences between capital and labor, the people of the United States were forcibly reminded by the great Pittsburg riot of 1877. In July of that year the organized laborers throughout the country believed the time had come for the introduction of the eight-hour day, and they wanted no decrease, but rather an increase in wages. They wished to begin operations with the railway companies. In several eastern cities strikes were organized which caused considerable bloodshed, and in Pittsburg several hundred people were killed. The local militia having refused to aid the city authorities in the maintenance of order, several regiments of militia from other parts of the state were ordered to the seat of trouble. They were undoubtedly badly commanded. Notwithstanding the fact that they were not strong enough to cope with the thousands of rioters, they attacked them indiscreetly and were repulsed. Finally the strikers drove the militia to the round-houses and car shops of the railroads, and afterwards burned the railroad property—cars, depots and other buildings.

From there the fever spread to Chicago. On July 23, a great mass meeting of laboring men took place on Market square, and several speakers advised forcing a strike of all workingmen of the city. The next day (Tuesday) troops of laborers went through Chicago demanding that all their fellows should strike. Railroad traffic was suddenly brought to a complete standstill. In the evening another mass meeting was to be held, but the police prevented it. Mayor Heath issued a proclamation to the citizens, telling them to organize for the protection of property, and the militia was called to the armories. Gen. Joseph T. Torrence commanded the militia. Many Union veterans volunteered their services. Mayor Heath ordered the police to report to Gen. Torrence for duty. On Wednesday there were serious encounters between the police and the strikers near McCormick's factory, on the Van Buren street bridge, near the Burlington & Quincy round house, on Sixteenth street and at other points in the city. It was evident that the police could not successfully cope with the rioters, and so Gen. Torrence ordered out the militia. It was of the utmost importance that the water works should be protected, and also the railroads, when they should again be put in operation. On Thursday, July 26, the First regiment was ordered to go into camp near the Exposition building on the lake shore, and the Second regiment was quartered near the Rock Island depot. Lackey's Zouaves, the North Chicago Light Guard and one company from the First regiment were despatched to the corner of Milwaukee and Chicago avenues, where the police were in great danger. At 11 o'clock in the morning the First regiment occupied Twelfth street bridge, and the Second regiment were assembled at the Twelfth street police station. In the evening the troops held the following positions: Four companies of the Second regiment were at Halsted street viaduct, three were between the viaduct and Twelfth street, two companies of the First regiment on Twelfth street bridge, two on Jefferson street and two near the Twelfth street Turner Hall. The main body of the rioters had been earlier concentrated on the Halsted street viaduct, but were driven away by a clever movement on the part of the militia assisted by a company of the mounted veteran volunteers. During the day two companies of United States regulars arrived in the city, coming directly from an Indian war in the northwest. Although they were not accoutred in the highest military style, as regards uniforms, every man had a rifle on his shoulder and a full cartridge belt around his waist. Few of them showed even a vestige of army blue, and there were not a dozen "soldier caps" among them. They had just come from a hard and exhaustive campaign, but the long, swinging stride, soldierly bearing, bronzed, bearded faces proclaimed them the "regulars," and every man who saw them felt impressed with the knowledge that they represented the strength and dignity of the United States government. Their influence was remarkable. Strikers realized that these men made war their business, and they were not be trifled with. The militia were brave, energetic and willing, but the mob held them in contempt. The appearance of a militiaman too often acts on a rioter as a red flag does on an angry bull, but the appearance of "regulars" always has a wonderfully soothing effect on law-breakers, who, naturally enough, are quickest to judge accurately of the forces opposing them. Finally, however, the display of legal power subdued the strikers. The excitement lasted seven days and then with the return of good order, everything seemed to be forgotten.

This outgrowth of the Pittsburg riots is interesting more as local history than for any bearing it has on the labor movement as such. It is in the nature of things that in every modern metropolis there will gather people who cannot control themselves or be easily controlled by others. In times of public excitement, insignificant saloon brawls may finally lead to as serious conflicts with the police as could have been instigated by the incendiary speech of some hair-brained demagogue. In such riots there is no trace of system. But few of the workingmen who tried to bring about the eight-hour day and dreamed of a social millennium, thought seriously of riot and revolution. The whole uprising fell flat, and the few who had fled the city, fearing plundering and bloodshed, were, later, the target of much ridicule.

But the general labor disturbances throughout the land, especially the riots in Pittsburg, brought the "social question" prominently before the people. In 1878, Congress appointed a committee of seven to investigate the labor troubles. On July 4, 1878, and again in 1879, there were large labor demonstrations in favor of the eight-hour day. The year 1880 was of especial interest as regards the labor movement, owing to the establishment of the "Federation of Organized Trade and Labor Unions of the United States and Canada." This most important association adopted the English trades unions as a model for organization, and fashioned its demands after those of the conservative German socialists.

In October, 1884, the convention of the Federation met in Chicago and fixed May 1, 1886, as the day on which the adoption of the eight-hour day should be widely demanded. As a result, a general strike ensued in Chicago on that date, and members of the building trades, cigar makers, plumbers and painters' unions succeeded in obtaining the eight-hour day, which theretofore, in Chicago, had been enjoyed only by the stonecutters. In the states of California, Connecticut, Illinois, Pennsylvania and New York, the eight-hour day was established by law, and laws for the regulation of woman and child labor were passed. Such laws, however, are of practical value only where labor organizations are strong enough to secure their enforcement. Otherwise they are largely dead letter.

THE CHICAGO ANARCHISTS.

The eight-hour movement—and in fact all legitimate labor movements—received a terrible set-back in May, 1886, by the dynamite throwing in Haymarket Square in Chicago. The attack was the direct result of the riot which had occurred at the McCormick Reaper works, Monday, May 3; but was the outgrowth of a long and violently radical agitation against law and the established order of society by certain anarchists belonging to an organization called the "International." The leaders of this organization had for over a year been preaching to the laboring classes the most radical form of anarchy and had done everything in their power to bring about the general strike of May 1—not that they wished to secure to labor shorter hours, but that they hoped the strikers might be induced to join the ranks of the anarchists. The "International" was represented in Chicago by eight "groups," and two papers—the "Arbeiter Zeitung," a daily afternoon paper published in German and an English semi-monthly, called the "Alarm"—were its organs. These two papers, their editors and other prominent members of the "groups" advocated, openly and persistently, the use of dynamite to overthrow society and bring about anarchy. At the time of the trial of the anarchists this was not even denied.

The trouble at the McCormick works dated back as far as Feb. 16, 1886, at which time the works were suspended owing to the demand of the several thousand workmen there employed, that wages be increased and that only Union men be given work. In April the company granted the first request and resumed operation, refusing, however, to discriminate between union and non-union men. May 1 was the day set for the general strike for obtaining the eight-hour day. On Monday, May 3, several thousand strikers congregated near Cormick's works and after listening to an inflammatory speech by August Spies, editor of the "Arbeiter Zeitung," proceeded to attack the factory and the police guarding it. In the struggle that followed, twenty or more of the strikers were wounded by the police, several probably fatally. As soon as he had the mischief well started Spies took a street car and hied him directly to the newspaper office where he wrote his celebrated "Revenge circular," later translated for use at the anarchist trial as follows:

"Revenge! Revenge! Workmen, to arms! Men of labor, this afternoon the bloodhounds of your oppressors murdered six of your brothers at McCormick's! Why did they murder them? Because they dared to be dissatisfied with the lot which your oppressors have assigned to them. They demanded bread, and they gave them lead for an answer, mindful of the fact that thus people are most effectually silenced. You have for many, many years endured every humiliation without protest; have drudged from early in the morning till late at night; have suffered all sorts of privations, have even sacrificed your children. You have done everything to fill the coffers of your masters—everything for them; and now when you approach them and implore them to make your burden a little lighter, as a reward for your sacrifices, they send their bloodhounds, the police, at you, in order to cure you with bullets of your dissatisfaction. Slaves, we ask and conjure you, by all that is sacred and dear to you, avenge the atrocious murder which has been committed upon your brothers to-day, and which will likely be committed upon you to-morrow. Laboring men, Hercules, you have arrived at the crossway. Which way will you decide? For slavery and hunger, or for freedom and bread? If you decide upon the latter, then do not delay a moment; then, people, to arms! Annihilation to the beasts in human form who call themselves rulers; uncompromising annihilation to them! This must be your motto. Think of the heroes whose blood has fertilized the road to progress, liberty and humanity, and strive to become worthy of them.   YOUR BROTHERS."

May 4, Adolph Fischer, a prominent anarchist, had distributed circulars in German and English, reading as follows:

"Attention Workingmen! Great mass meeting to-night at 7:30 o'clock, at the Haymarket, Randolph St., bet. Desplaines and Halsted. Good speakers will be present to denounce the latest atrocious act of the police, the shooting of our fellow-workmen yesterday afternoon. Workingmen, arm yourselves and appear in full force!
        THE EXECUTIVE COMMITTEE."

In response to the circular several hundred men and boys gathered in the Haymarket and listened to Albert R. Parsons, August Spies and Samuel Fielden—all well known anarchists and labor agitators. In an alley opening on the square stood a truck, from which the speakers addressed the meeting. After harangues by Parsons and Spies, Fielden addressed the assembly. Following is a short-hand report of a part of his speech:

"There are premonitions of danger. All knew. The press say the anarchists will sneak away; we are not going to. If we continue to be robbed, it will not be long before we will be murdered. There is no security for the working-classes under the present social system. A few individuals control the means of living, and hold the workmen in a vice. Everybody does not know. Those who know it are tired of it, and know the others will get tired of it, too. They are determined to end it, and will end it, and there is no power in the land that will prevent them. Congressman Foran said: 'The laborer can get nothing from legislation.' He also said that the laborers can get some relief from their present condition when the rich man knew it was unsafe for him to live in a community where there were dissatisfied workingmen, for they would solve the labor problem. I don't know whether you are Democrats or Republicans, but whichever you are, you worship at the shrine of rebels. John Brown, Jefferson, Washington, Patrick Henry, and Hopkins said to the people: 'The law is your enemy. We are rebels against it.' The law is only framed for those that are your enslavers. [A voice: 'That is true.'] Men in their blind rage attacked McCormick's factory, and were shot down by the law in cold blood in the city of Chicago, in the protection of property. These men were going to do some damage to a certain person's interest, who was a large property-owner; therefore the law came to his defense. And when McCormick undertook to do some injury to the interest of those who had no property, the law also came to his defense, and not to the workingman's defense, when he, Mr. McCormick, attacked him and his living. [Cries of 'No.'] There is the difference. The law makes no distinction. A million men own all the property in this country. The law has no use for the other fifty-four million. [A voice, 'Right enough.'] You have nothing more to do with the law except to lay hands on it, and throttle it until it makes its last kick. It turns your brothers out on the wayside, and has degraded them until they have lost the last vestige of humanity, and they are mere things and animals. Keep your eye upon it. Throttle it. Kill it. Stab it. Do everything you can to wound it, to impede its progress. Remember, before trusting them to do anything for yourself, prepare to do it for yourself. Don't turn over your business to anybody else. No man deserves anything unless he is man enough to make an effort to lift himself from oppression. Is it not a fact that we have no choice as to our existence, for we can't dictate what our labor is worth? He that has to obey the will of any is a slave. Can we do anything except by the strong arm of resistance? Socialists are not going to declare war; but I tell you, war has been declared upon us, and I ask you to get hold of anything that will help to resist the onslaught of the enemy and the usurper. The skirmish-lines have met. People have been shot. Men, women and children have not been spared by the capitalists and minions of private capital. It had no mercy, so ought you. You are called upon to defend yourselves, your lives, your future. What matters it whether you kill yourselves with work to get a little relief, or die on the battle-field resisting the enemy? What is the difference? Any animal, however loathsome, will resist when stepped upon. Are men less than snails and worms? I have some resistance in me; I know that you have, too. You have been robbed, and you will be starved into a worse condition."

Just at this stage 180 policemen, led by Inspector John Bonfield and Captain William Ward, appeared. The inspector had been advised of the nature of the speeches by detectives who had been at the meeting, and resolved that it would be for the interest of the city to disperse the gathering—and under the law of Illinois it was his duty to do so.* It was late at night and men were being incited to deeds of violence by speakers who had long preached the most radical kind of anarchy.

When within a few feet of the speaker Capt. Ward said: "I command you, in the name of the people of the state of Illinois, to immediately and peaceably disperse," to which Fielden replied, "We are peaceable," but a second later a bomb, thrown from behind, whizzed through the air and fell with a terrible explosion in the midst of the police. Sixty-seven officers were wounded—seven of them fatally, but they closed their ranks immediately, and drawing their revolvers, proceeded to clear the streets. But little resistance was offered them and order was at once restored. The first officer to die of his injuries was Mathias J. Degan, and it was for his murder that the anarchists were later punished. Arrests began at once—the police throwing out their drag-nets for all suspected of being leaders in the supposed anarchistic conspiracy, or of being tools of these conspirators. Of the large number arrested many were immediately discharged. Some were held as witnesses, and the following men were indicted for murder: August Spies, Samuel Fielden, Louis Lingg, George Engel, Adolph Fischer, Michael Schwab and Oscar Neebe. Albert R. Parsons fled the city, but at the beginning of the trial voluntarily appeared in court and gave himself up in a very theatrical manner—an event which confirmed many people in the belief that the defendants could not be

---
*Section 253, Chapter 38, Revised Statutes, provides that "when twelve or more persons, any of them armed with clubs or dangerous weapons, or thirty or more, armed or unarmed, are unlawfully, riotously, or tumultuously assembled in any city . . . it shall be the duty of each of the municipal officers . . . to go among the persons so assembled . . . , and in the name of the state command them immediately to disperse."

legally connected with the bomb-throwing, and so punished for murder.

Police investigation soon discovered in the haunts of the defendants, many bombs and quantities of bomb material, and it was a matter of general knowledge that the accused had openly and publicly advocated the use of dynamite and the wholesale slaughter of the rich and the introduction of anarchy. The files of the "Alarm" and "Arbeiter" gave ample evidence of the teachings of the accused, but it was impossible to prove that any of the defendants had any direct connection with the bomb-thrower. It was generally believed that Schwab's brother-in-law, Rudolph Schnaubelt, really hurled the bomb, and although he was at one time in the hands of the police, he was later released, by accident, and disappeared.

His connection with the case was not proved, however, and in the absence of the identification of the bomb-thrower, many believed that it would be impossible to convict the accused. Others maintained that there was ample evidence to prove that the bomb-throwing was the result of a conspiracy. In June the trial began, and 21 days were consumed before the twelve jurors were selected from the 981 men who had been summoned for the purpose. The trial proper began July 14, and August 20 the jury rendered a verdict, finding all the defendants but Neebe guilty of murder and fixing the penalty at death. Neebe was found guilty of murder, but the penalty attached was but 15 years in the penitentiary, as the States Attorney had said that he did not think this defendant should be punished with death.

The fate of the seven was sealed from the time that the presiding judge, Joseph E. Gary, gave the decision that to prove that the defendants were guilty of murder, it was not necessary to prove that any of them threw the bomb or suggested positively that that particular bomb be thrown at that particular time. Having repeatedly advocated the use of dynamite to overthrow society and to kill the rich, the anarchists, so soon as their advice was followed, became murderers—co-conspirators in a plot and morally responsible for the deed. The defense made the objection that the accused had given only general advice as to the overthrow of law and that they could not therefore be charged with the responsibility for a specific crime which they did not personally execute. The point came up when the prosecution attempted to show that the defendants had had bombs in their possession at various times. The defense objected to the testimony unless it was to go to prove that the accused furnished the particular bomb that caused the death of Degan. In deciding the point, Judge Gary said:

"If it is agreed to use violence for the destruction of human lives upon an occasion which is not yet foreseen, but upon some general principle on which the conspirators substantially agree; for example, if a large number of men agreed to kill the police if they were found in conflict with the strikers, leaving the date to the agencies of time to determine; whenever the time and occasion do come for the use of that violence, and when that violence is used, are not the parties who have agreed beforehand to use the means of destruction equally guilty? Suppose that there was a general agreement that weapons of death should be used if the police got into conflict with the strikers; that is, if the police undertook to enforce the laws of the state and prevent a breach of the peace and destruction of property—if the police undertook to do so, that then they would attack and kill the police, but the time and occasion of the attack itself were not foreseen; the time and occasion being to be determined by the parties who were to use the force when in their judgment the time and occasion were to come; and then, when the police were found attempting to preserve the peace, some persons who have been parties to this agreement do kill them, are not all of these persons equally guilty? If there was a general combination and agreement among a great number of individuals to kill policemen if they came into conflict with parties with whom they were friendly—meetings of workingmen, and bodies of strikers; if it was the combination and agreement to kill the police in their attempt to preserve the peace; if there was such a combination and agreement among a great number of men, the object of which was something beyond mere local disturbance, whether it was the object to offer a new form of civil society or not, if there was such an agreement to kill the police upon some occasion that might occur in the future, whether the proper time had arrived being left to their judgment, then if that violence was used and resulted in the death of the police, then those who were party to the agreement are guilty of the death. It is entirely competent for the state to show that these several defendants have had such missiles in their possession to be used on occasions that they might anticipate. There need not be an agreement that they should be used on this specific occasion, but on some occasion that might arise in the future. Any one case where such violence was used may involve the showing of the entire conspiracy from beginning to end."

This position of the court, undoubtedly correct under the Illinois statutes and Supreme Court decisions*, was the turning point of the trial. The stand taken by Judge Gary was

---

* In the case of Brennan vs. The People (15 Illinois Reports, 511), the Supreme Court of Illinois held: "There is a fatal objection to the eighteenth, twenty-first and

made still clearer in his remarks upon refusing to grant the defendants a new trial. After reading from the "Arbeiter" and "Alarm," copious extracts to prove that the defendants had attempted, in a long series of public articles, to incite the working classes to make unlawful attacks on persons and property, Judge Gary said:

"The jury were not instructed to find the defendants guilty if they believed that they participated in the throwing of that bomb, or encouraged or advised the throwing of that bomb, or had knowledge that it was to be thrown, or anything of that sort. The conviction has not gone upon the ground that they did have actually any personal participation in the particular act which caused the death of Degan; but the conviction proceeds upon the ground, under the instructions, that they had generally, by speech and print, advised large classes of the people, not particular individuals, but large classes, to commit murder, and have left the commission, the time and place and when, to individual will and whim or caprice, or whatever it may be, of each individual man who listened to their advice, and that in consequence of that advice, in pursuance of that advice, and influenced by that advice, somebody not known did throw the bomb that caused Degan's death. . . . . Perhaps I can make my view upon that subject clearer by an illustration. Suppose that the radical temperance men should, for a long period of time, by speeches and publications, declare that there was no hope of stopping the evils of the liquor traffic except by blowing up saloons and killing saloonkeepers; that it was useless to expect any reform by legislation, that no prohibition laws nor high license laws nor any other laws would have any effect in their estimation, and that therefore they must blow up the saloons and kill the saloonkeepers—and justify that course; suppose that in addition to that, they taught means by which saloons could be blown up and saloon-keepers killed, and then called a meeting in West Lake street, in front of No. 54 West Lake*, and while some speakers were denouncing the liquor traffic, and saying to an audience, 'If you are ready to do anything, do it without making any idle threat,' and another speaker says,'Throttle, kill, stab the saloon business, or it will kill, throttle and stab you,' and then, while that speaking is going on, some unknown man out of the crowd, with a bomb of the manufacture of the temperance men, explodes No. 54 Lake street, and kills the occupants of the house—I apprehend that none of the parties who are objecting to the insufficiency of this proof in this case would have any hesitation in saying that the men who had advised that conduct were guilty of it."

Had Judge Gary not given this interpretation to the law, the conviction of the defendants would have been impossible.

twenty-second instructions asked by the prisoners. These instructions required the jury to acquit the prisoners unless they actually participated in the killing of Story, or unless the killing happened in pursuance of a common design on the part of the prisoners to take his life. Such is not the law. The prisoners may be guilty of murder, although they neither took part in the killing nor assented to any arrangement having for its object the death of Story. It is sufficient that they combined with those committing the deed to do an unlawful act, such as to beat or rob Story, and that he was killed in the attempt to execute the common purpose. If several persons conspire to do an unlawful act, and death happen in the prosecution of the common object, all are alike guilty of the homicide. The act of one of them, done in furtherance of the original design, is in consideration of law, the act of all, and he who advises or encourages another to do an illegal act is responsible for all the natural and probable consequences that may arise from its perpetration. . . Nor need the advice or encouragement that may make one an accessory to crime be by words, but by any word or act, sign or motion done or made for the purpose of encouraging the commission of a crime.

*Many of the meetings of the anarchists were held in the saloon at No. 54 West Lake street.

260

They could not be directly connected with the bomb-thrower, but, according to Judge Gary's interpretation, this was unnecessary. The prosecution had to prove only that the defendants had systematically and for a considerable time, in word and by writing, advocated the very crime which the bomb-thrower put in execution. This proof was easy to establish. Indeed, the defendants and their counsel so strongly felt their inability to contradict it, that they made their strongest fight to overthrow Judge Gary's interpretation. Spies, Parsons and Fielden had preached their crazy doctrines publicly and persistently; they had never hesitated in their advocacy of open rebellion against law and order and the destruction of all established institutions. They repeatedly declared that recourse to violence, bomb-throwing and the like, was the only salvation of the proletariat. Their past and the indisputable fact that they had formed "armed groups" to use dynamite against the officers of the law, stamped the accused, according to the court's interpretation of the law, as the moral instigators of the Haymarket massacre. The jury could do nothing else than find them guilty. The assertion that the jury and state's attorney were bribed by capitalists is too silly to merit attention.

Notwithstanding Judge Gary's ruling, the state's attorney, Julius S. Grinnell, tried to make assurance doubly sure by proving—especially through informers, states' evidence men, who tried thus to save their own necks—that the accused had actually belonged to an anarchist conspiracy which had plotted to make a bomb attack on the evening of May 4, that 300 bombs were to have been thrown, but that later, the plan was changed and that the bomb actually thrown was hurled by a conspirator who had not been advised of the change. It was also alleged to be a part of this plot, to take advantage of the terrible panic caused by the bomb explosions to rob the banks and proclaim anarchistic dictatorship under the sceptre of August Spies. From pieces of the bomb actually thrown, it was conclusively proved, by chemical analysis, that the engine of destruction was the work of Louis Lingg, one of the accused, and it was also shown that Lingg and others were busy all the afternoon of May 4 with filling bombs which were afterward distributed to various conspirators. But notwithstanding this proof, the state's attorney would doubtless have acted more wisely had he not insisted in carrying out his prosecution on this general line, for justifiable as was his moral conviction that the anarchists had planned a fiendish and diabolical attack for the evening of May 4, the evidence he furnished before the court was not sufficient to dispel all doubts on the subject. The existence of the plot was not definitely proved, and although this proof was unnecessary to establish the guilt of the defendants, it gave a pretext for criticism on the part of anarchistic sympathizers.

It was probably another error of the prosecution to allow an utterly irresponsible fellow named Gilmer to take the stand and pose as an eye-witness to the alleged fact that Spies himself lighted the bomb. The character of this witness imprinted on all testimony of the state—so far as it sought to establish a direct connection between the accused and the bomb-thrower—the stamp of manufactured evidence. Nor was there anything gained by it, for the guilt and liability of the defendants could not have been thereby increased by the weight of a feather, for the mere fact that they had advised the act was sufficient, under the statutes of Illinois, to hold them guilty as charged.

After the verdict the defendants asked for a new trial, which was denied. Then the opportunity to say why sentence should not be pronounced was afforded each man, and three days were consumed in speech-making. Then Judge Gary addressed the condemned men for the last time: "I am well aware," said he, "that what you have said, although addressed to me, has been said to the world; yet nothing has been said which weakens the force of the proof, or the conclusions therefrom, upon which the verdict is based. You are all men of intelligence, and know that, if the verdict stands, it must be executed. The reasons why it shall stand, I have already sufficiently stated in deciding the motion for a new trial. I am sorry, beyond any power of expression, for your unhappy condition, and for the terrible events that have brought you to it. I shall address to you neither reproaches nor exhortations. What I shall say will be said in the faint hope that a few words from a place where the people of the state of Illinois have delegated the authority to declare the penalty of a violation of their laws, and spoken upon an occasion so solemn and awful as this, may come to the knowledge of, and be heeded by, the ignorant, deluded, and misguided men who have listened to your counsels and followed your advice. I say in the faint hope; for if men are persuaded that because of business differences, whether about labor or anything else, they may destroy property, and assault and beat other men, and kill the police, if they, in the discharge of their duty, interfere to preserve the peace, there is little ground to hope that they will listen to any warning.

"Not the least among the hardships of the peaceable, frugal and laborious poor, is to endure the tyranny of mobs, who with lawless force dictate to them under penalty of peril to limb and life, where, when and upon what terms they may earn a livelihood for themselves and their families. Any government that is worthy of the name, will strenuously endeavor to secure to all within its jurisdiction, freedom to follow their lawful avocations in safety for their property and their persons while obeying the law. And the law is common sense. It holds each man responsible for the natural and probable consequences of his own act. It holds that whoever advises murder, is himself guilty of the murder that is committed pursuant to his advice; and if men band together for forcible resistance to the execution of the law and advise murder as a means of making such resistance effectual, whether such advice be to one man to murder another, or to a numerous class to murder men of another class—all who are so banded together are guilty of any murder that is committed in pursuance of such advice.

"The people of this country love their institutions. They love their homes. They love their property. They will never consent that by violence and murder those institutions shall be broken down, their homes despoiled, and their property detroyed. And the people are strong enough to protect and sustain their institutions and to punish all offenders against their laws; and those who threaten danger to civil society, if the law is enforced, are leading to destruction whoever may attempt to execute such threats.

"The existing order of society can be changed only by the will of the majority. Each man has the full right to entertain, and advocate, by speech and print, such opinions as suit himself, and the great body of the people will usually care little what he says; but if he proposes murder as a means of enforcing them, he puts his own life at stake; and no clamor about free speech, or evils to be cured, or wrongs to be redressed, will shield him from the consequences of his crime. His liberty is not a license to destroy. The toleration that he enjoys he must extend to others, and not arrogantly assume that the great majority are wrong and may rightly be coerced by terror or removed by dynamite.

"It only remains that for the crime you have committed, and of which you have been convicted after a trial unexampled in the patience with which an outraged people have extended to you every protection and privilege of the law which you derided and defied, the sentence of that law be now pronounced." Then on the 9th of October, 1886, Judge Gary pronounced sentence upon the defendants.

The contemptible remnant of the anarchistic societies of course impugned the justice of the trial and hurled calumny at those who had assisted in the prosecution of the murderers. Despite the sensational stories about the anarchists, their pure and lofty purposes, etc., they were, as a matter of fact, a very cheap crew. Spies, who is generally regarded as the leader, was phenomenally vain, and was far more inspired by newspaper notoriety than by capitalistic outrages. His salary as editor of the "Arbeiter" was a mere pittance, and yet he lived like a prince. He was famous for his connection with numerous labor picnics, which were invariably characterized by so fine an adjustment of expenditures to receipts that there was never a surplus. All the anarchists regarded Johann Most as a leader, and justice must certainly hold him responsible for the Haymarket outrage. He had been driven out of Austria, Russia and England, only to come to the United States to spread broadcast his infamous doctrines and establish his anarchistic "groups." The organization of the "groups," to which Spies, Parsons, Lingg, Fielden, Engel and the others belonged, is traceable directly to Most. It dates from his visit to Chicago in 1884, when, after winning Spies to his cause, he completely changed the policy of the "Arbeiter Zeitung," which theretofore had been only socialistic in tendency. After Most's visit, however, it became a pronounced anarchistic organ, and its pernicious activity was largely responsible for the subsequent catastrophe. Most's writings were the gospel of his Chicago followers, whom he taught to believe that they could control the whole labor movement. Most's damnable "Handbook on Anarchistic Warfare," with its minute receipts, was the direct cause of the manufacture, in Chicago, of dynamite bombs. This unique work contains not only exact formulas for the manufacture of dynamite and other explosives, but also directions "for easily setting policemen on fire from behind, chemically and without danger of discovery," for making and using fire-bombs, for poisoning "capitalistic beasts," and for other enterprising methods of anarchistic activity. During the trial this book was introduced as evidence, but its author, though morally responsible for the bomb-throwing, remained unmolested in New York. Many prominent lawyers were of the opinion that Most should have been indicted and that he could have been convicted with the others, but Chicago's states attorney thought otherwise. Justice sometimes has strange fancies! The anarchists were condemned to death for being morally responsible for the murder of Degan, but their teacher, the actual head of all anarchists in the United States, was not even indicted—simply because he happened to be in New York. It would seem that fate wished to spare the doomed men the further infamy of being in death the companions of him whose tools and dupes they had been in life.

A romantic incident of the trial was the proxy marriage of August Spies to a girl named Nina Van Zandt. The girl regularly attended the trial, and became attached to Spies, who was a rather good-looking young fellow. She was, of course, unable to marry Spies himself, but finally united to him by proxy, his brother standing in his place, for August could not be reached even by the hand of love. At the time it was generally supposed that the girl had merely a morbid craving for notoriety, but she afterward stated—shortly before a subsequent marriage—that one of the principal attorneys for the defense had made use of her passing sentimental emotion to mislead her into such sensational deportment as he hoped would arouse for his client the interest and sympathy of influential and sentimental women of Chicago and of the men controlled by them.

The supreme court of the state affirmed the judgment of the criminal court, and the day of execution first set having passed, fixed November 11, 1887, as the day for the execution of the sentence. The friends of the doomed men left no stone unturned to secure their pardon from Gov. Oglesby, and for one reason or another received support and assistance from even those who believed the sentence just. The firmness displayed by Gov. Oglesby was admirable. He was deeply affected by the entreaties of the relatives of the anarchists, but in his decision was guided not by feelings of personal pity, but by regard for the general welfare of the community He commuted the death sentence of Fielden and Schwab to imprisonment for life, after receiving from these two men a petition for mercy, in which they expressed their profound regret for the catastrophe. Parsons, Spies, Engel and Fischer atoned their crime on the gallows; Lingg, the day before the execution, killed himself by taking a dynamite cartridge in his teeth and exploding it. The execution of the sentence was without interference or demonstration, although the apprehension that something tragic might happen was not wholly causeless. In spite of the vigilance of the jail authorities, Lingg succeeded in smuggling into his cell quite a number of dynamite cartridges and bombs, but all were discovered before the day of execution. Lingg's personal courage was remarkable, and had opportunity afforded itself he would undoubtedly have blown up the jail, and if necessary all within it.

For so celebrated a case there has been a vast deal of popular misunderstanding in regard to the anarchist trial. In an article published in the "Century Magazine," for April, 1893, Judge Gary alludes to this fact, and adds: "The anarchists were not tried for being anarchists, but for procuring murder to be done, and being, therefore, themselves guilty of murder." The distinguished jurist feels called upon even to explain his motives in publicly discussing the case, and states that the principal one was "to demonstrate to my own profession, and to make plain to all fair-minded, intelligent people, that the verdict of the jury in the case of the anarchists was right; that the anarchists were guilty of murder; that they were not the victims of prejudice, nor martyrs for free speech, but in morals, as well as in law, were guilty of murder," and further, "to show to the laboring people, of whom the anarchists claimed to be the especial friends, that that claim was a sham and pretense, adopted only as a means to bring manual laborers into their own ranks; and that the counsel and advice of the anarchists, if followed by the workingmen, would expose them to the danger of becoming, in law, murderers," and, finally, to "show that the real passions at the bottom of the hearts of the anarchists were envy and hatred of all people whose condition in life was better than their own, who were more prosperous than themselves."

As to the guilt of the accused, Judge Gary, in the same article, says that "the publications in the 'Arbeiter' and 'Alarm,' and the speeches of Spies, Parsons, Schwab, Fielden and Engel (whose speeches were proved at great length on the trial, all of them advising their hearers to arm themselves, among other things, with dynamite) were acts in furtherance of the design and purpose of the conspiracy, by conspirators, and therefore, upon legal principles, acts of the whole body and each individual of the co-conspirators; that the general advice given to all readers and hearers was advice to each and every individual of those readers and hearers; that advice to pursue a course of conduct embracing or including a particular act is advice to do that act; that it is inconceivable that the man who threw a bomb made by Lingg, one of the conspirators, was not by some of those publications or speeches encouraged so to do, and therefore the whole body of the conspirators were accessories to the act of throwing it, and responsible for it, whether it was thrown by one who was himself a member of the conspiracy, or who was some hair-brained fool, or some criminal who wished to avenge himself for some grievance, real or fancied, that he had suffered at the hands of the police."

In speaking over the graves of the anarchists, two days after the execution, William P. Black, of the counsel for defence, said:

> "I loved these men. I knew them not until I came to know them in the time of their sore travail and anguish. As months went by and I found in the lives of those with whom I talked the witness of their love for the people, of their patience, gentleness and courage, my heart was taken captive in their cause. . . . . I say that whatever of fault may have been in them, these, the people whom they loved and in whose cause they died, may well close the volume, and seal up the record, and give our lips to the praise of their heroic deeds, and their sublime self-sacrifice."

Referring to this speech in the magazine article already quoted, Judge Gary writes as follows:

> "If these words have any meaning, they refer to the acts of the anarchists which I have, in part, told; 'the people whom they loved' they deceived, deluded, and endeavored to convert into murderers; the 'cause they died in' was rebellion, to prosecute which they taught and instigated murder; their 'heroic deeds' were causeless, wanton murders done; and the 'sublime self-sacrifice' of the only one to whom the words can apply was suicide, to escape the impending penalty of the law incurred by murder. For nearly seven years the clamor, uncontradicted, has gone round the world that the anarchists were heroes and martyrs, victims of prejudice and fear. . . . . . Right-minded, thoughtful people, who recognize the necessity to civilization of the existence and enforcement of laws for the protection of human life, and who yet may have had misgivings as to the fate of the anarchists, will, I trust, read what I have written, and dismiss those misgivings, convinced that in law and in morals the anarchists were rightly punished, not for opinions, but for horrible deeds."

The last development in the case occurred in April, 1892, when the United States Supreme Court gave its decision in the appeal which had been made to it by the attorneys for Schwab and Fielden. A reversal of judgment was demanded on the technical ground that the defendants had not been present, in person, when the State Supreme Court had rendered its decision, affirming the judgment of the lower court; but the United States Supreme Court decided against the appellants.

As a monument in honor of the policemen who fell in the discharge of their duty, on the night of May 4, 1886, the grateful citizens of Chicago have erected a statue—the figure of an officer in heroic size—on the very spot where the bomb fell. A more emphatic expression of their resolution to suppress every attack against law and order was the request of Chicago citizens that the federal government establish, near the city, a fort with an adequate force of United States troops. In addition to their request the citizens donated to the government a site suitable for the desired fort, and within a few months Fort Sheridan—on the lake shore, an hour's ride from the city—was established. To one familiar with Chicago's history the following comparison must occur: Fort Dearborn, in its time, was erected to protect the little settlement on the Chicago river from the attacks of the barbarous red man, and when the danger from the Indians ceased, the fort was done away with. In 1886, red anarchy threatened Chicago with another form of barbarism, and Fort Sheridan was erected to protect civilization and maintain peace. In three decades Fort Dearborn had outlived its usefulness. Fort Sheridan will doubtless endure for a longer period, although from it can never come the final answer to the social question. It will stand as a stronghold of peace, an imposing demonstration of the force and power of the state-conserving elements.

The oft-repeated assertion that anarchy in the United States is a curse for which the Germans are particularly responsible, is entirely erroneous. In judging a morbid social condition which, like anarchy, makes its appearance in all states of Europe as well as in America, there should be no room for national prejudices. It was owing to the lax administration of the city's laws and to demagogy in local politics that the anarchists of Chicago dared prepare for a "propaganda of deed." There was a time, before the bomb-throwing, when certain local politicians truckled to the anarchistic element. One must not too closely scrutinize the causes which warranted a Parsons or a Spies in believing that he was a power in the commonwealth if one does not wish to come to the logical conclusion that anarchy, in the form in which it prevailed in Chicago, was strictly of American development, and that nowhere else in the world could it have attained so rank a growth. Demagogy alone was responsible for the Haymarket massacre. There the political demagogue and the labor demagogue lent each other helping hands. Parsons and Spies were typical leaders of the anarchists—Parsons who boasted his descent from the Englishmen who landed in Narragansett Bay in 1622, and Spies who confessed to becoming first a socialist and then an anarchist after coming to the United States. But it is immaterial what language madness speaks. Anarchy has no fatherland. It breaks out in France, Spain, England and Germany as well as in America. Only, owing to the national institution of demagogy, it was for a long time not only tolerated in Chicago, but was even fostered as a legitimate political institution.

The story of the Haymarket massacre and the anarchist troubles in Chicago is here incorporated in the chapter on the general labor movement—not because the anarchists had any legitimate connection with labor development but for purposes of contrast. As has been stated, legitimate labor movement consists principally in the absolutely justifiable and almost necessary strife for a reasonably short working-day. Only when the time made free by ingeniously contrived machinery, which replaces human power and human skill, is given to productive laborers of the world, will there be a just and general participation of all mankind in the material blessings which have resulted from the reformation of industrial affairs through modern technic. Calamitous, indeed, would be the result of any attempt to artificially prohibit the adaptation of things to the new economic conditions of existence, but still more pernicious would be the effect of unduly hastening this change. There must first be developed a social basis upon which the working world may be granted its share of leisure time and increased material comforts made possible by modern machinery. The question can never be adjudicated one-sidedly or sporadically, but only in the slow and difficult way of international co-operation. Never with force—ever in peace and harmony.

The labor movement in Chicago is healthy and has met with great success. It is legitimately progressive, and the intelligent foreign workman has his full share in its development. Great reforms cannot be brought about over night, but must be achieved with patience, self-denial and persistence. Such is the way of the world, and he who knows it not, suffers for his ignorance.

The Cronin Case.

The history of the development of cosmopolitan Chicago is rich in extraordinary features, which strongly reflect the character of the elements that have formed the city. It is in this connection that the Cronin tragedy is to be considered here. The murder of Dr. Cronin, aside from its peculiarly brutal and cowardly execution, is particularly remarkable as it is closely connected with the Celtic movement in America for the freedom of Ireland. Not that the crime was the natural or legitimate result of Irish agitation, for it was not, but because it brought to public notice the magnitude and theretofore almost hidden power of a movement in which a large number of American citizens were interested.

May 4, 1889, in a lonely little cottage in the northwest part of Chicago, Patrick Henry Cronin, an Irish patriot and American citizen, was beaten to death by a band of assassins. His accusing voice forever stilled, the murderers disposed of their victim's body, and turned to the work of assassinating his character. Their plans were cunningly laid. Every detail of the cowardly conspiracy had been fixed in advance. There seemed no chance of failure. But somebody blundered—crime always blunders. And so the mutilated body of the man they martyred was discoved in the Lake-View sewer; the plot to kill his character failed; some of the conspirators were punished, others died miserably, and Cronin, dead, became a greater power than Cronin living.

Irishmen killed him, but no thoughtful man will sympathize with those Americans, or Englishmen, or Germans who hold the Irish race responsible for Dr. Cronin's death. No Irishman worthy the name but condemns the brutal murder. John F. Finerty spoke for his countrymen, when at a meeting, in the interest of the Irish National League in August following the murder, he said:

> I would deem it under other circumstances quite unnecessary to emphasize before the American people the unwavering devotion of Irish American citizens to the government of the United States, but a tragedy was recently enacted in our midst, the victim of which was one of our own race, that has been made the occasion of venting upon us as a people, and upon our society as a body, the spleen and venom of persons who, claiming to be super-loyal to the republic, have not the claim to honest loyalty which we, as a race, hold upon this continent.
>
> It has been asserted by those instrumental in covering us with defamation that we wish to screen the murderers of Dr. Cronin. We meet here to-day, among other reasons, for the purpose of vehemently denouncing his atrocious murder in our capacity as American citizens; but we claim that, as Irish Americans, we should no more be held responsible for that foul atrocity, than any other element of the body politic for crimes committed by persons to whom they are kindred. We devoutly hope that the officers authorized by the law will succeed in bringing to justice the assassins of Dr. Cronin.
>
> We repudiate, both as American citizens and as Irish-Americans, the claim made by the enemies of our race that the Irish element has any desire, or any purpose, to make the soil of America the theatre of acts of vengeance because of feuds, factions or disagreements growing out of political differences or personal heartburnings.

Mr. Finerty was right. The Heights of Abraham, red with the blood of Montgomery; the waves of Champlain, brilliant with the victory of McDonough; the plains of Chalmette, still radiant with the martial fire of Jackson; the convent of Cherubusco, still ringing with the war shout of Shields; the sunken road at Antietam, that saw the green flag of Meagher's Irish brigade rise and fall beside the stars and stripes as color-bearer after color-bearer went down before the withering breath of the rebel front of flame; the valley of Cedar Creek, in which the heroic figure of Phil. Sheridan lives as immortally as that of Napoleon at Marengo—all these examples and more could be summoned to the bar of public opinion, if it were necessary, to convince the American people that the Irish-Americans do not lack patriotism.

Fiction furnishes no tale of crime so sinister, so cold-blooded, so cowardly as the murder of Cronin. Gaboriau never conceived a plot so intricate, Dumas never told a story of more enthralling interest. But why was the "removal" of Cronin desired? Who were his enemies, and how had he gained their enmity? How would his death benefit them? These were the questions that confronted the officers of the law upon the disappearance of the physician. They found a theory ready on the tongues of Cronin's friends, that he had had fallen a victim to a political conspiracy, the conspirators being scattered over two continents, the ramifications of the plot extending in several directions, involving people of high reputation and their tools of no reputation. The motto of the conspirators was "Dead men tell no tales;" their object was the deliberate taking-off certain men, Cronin among the number, in order that certain secrets affecting the reputation of Irishmen of great power and high standing might not be made public. Upon the discovery of the body the officers of the law adopted this theory, the coroner's jury and grand jury subsequently indorsed it, and finally, upon circumstantial evidence of its correctness, twelve men sentenced three of the tools who did the bidding of the arch-plotters to the penitentiary for life. Here the officers of the law rested. But Cronin will not down. While they live, his friends will continue the search for evidence against his murderers.

Patrick Henry Cronin was an Irish enthusiast. Born in the town of Mallow, in County Cork, August 7, 1846, he was brought to the United States while a babe in his mother's arms. His childhood was spent in New York City, his education gained in the Christian Brothers' Academy, of St. Catherine's, province of Ontario. Manhood found him running a drug store in St. Louis and studying medicine at the Missouri College. He was identified with the state militia, and in 1877 did valiant service during the labor riots in St. Louis. After a year in Europe he returned to Missouri, accepting the professorship of materia medica in the St. Louis College of Physicians and Surgeons. He came to Chicago in 1882 and continued to practice successfully

He was identified with many political, secret and social societies. At the time of his death he was president of the Celto-American Club of Chicago, Deputy Grand Regent of the Royal Arcanum, Past Commander of the Knights of Pythias, Chief Ranger of the Catholic Order of Foresters, member of the Royal League, Legion of Honor, Ancient Order of Hibernians and Ancient Order of United Workmen.

Personally, Dr. Cronin was a typical Irishman—brave, loyal and warm-hearted; impulsive, vindictive and relentless; a friend for life and a foe till death. His only surviving relatives are a sister, Mrs. Carroll, living at St. Catherines, Ont., a brother John, living on an Arkansas farm, and two nieces, Sisters in a Canadian convent. Dr. Cronin was nearly six feet tall, well proportioned, of dark complexion, with black hair and eyes.

IN THE CLAN-NA-GAEL.

All his life Cronin was identified with organizations having for their object the liberation of Ireland. The most powerful of these organizations was—and is—the United Brotherhood (Clan-na-Gael). It counted its camps by hundreds, its members by thousands and tens of thousands. Its agents were everywhere. Its strength was enormous, its wealth great and its movements as silent as the grave. Founded in 1869, in ten years it had penetrated every part of the North American continent. The membership of the organization was divided into districts and the districts into local lodges or "camps." Each district had its general officer, to whose authority each local camp was subject, and the district officers in turn made up an executive board. This body possessed absolute control of the organization.

In 1881 the United Brotherhood held a national convention in Chicago. It had never been so powerful—so prosperous. Irish patriots, by the thousand, had become associated with it, moved by its principles. Irish politicians, in almost like numbers, were attracted to it by the secret political influence it wielded. Irish vagabonds joined, where they could, for what there might be in it. The Chicago convention changed the system of government of the Brotherhood, confiding the supreme control to an executive board of five men, three of whom formed a quorum. Alexander Sullivan, of Chicago, Michael Boland, of Kansas City, and D. C. Feeley, of Rochester, were elected to this board, and, working together, controlled it. From the day the convention adjourned, this "triangle" assumed a despotic sway over the order. Although they found a full treasury they soon promulgated an order that each camp should forward to the national executive committee nearly its entire receipts in lieu of the ten per cent formerly demanded. As a result of this order it has been estimated that the "triangle" had placed at its disposal between three and four hundred thousand dollars.

About this time true friends of Ireland were shocked at the inauguration of what was termed a "physical force" policy. In the next few years there occurred in various parts of England dynamite explosions, each followed by the capture and subsequent imprisonment of the men supposed to be primarily concerned. In almost every case the apprehension and arrest of the foolish tools were made under such circumstances as to indicate clearly that the dynamitard was betrayed. In the five years, between 1881 and 1885, twenty-nine Irish revolutionists were sent from America into English prisons. A prominent Irish-American has declared that each of these men was betrayed to the British government before he landed on British soil. The fact that few of the men got far enough along with their missions to do any damage, supports this theory. The conclusion was that men in the confidence of the friends of Ireland in America were plotting to wreck the Irish cause. They found plenty of ignorant tools who could be persuaded that no crime was too dreadful if done to free Ireland. The plotters told the tools what to do and how to do it, and at the same time warned their English allies as to what was going on. A record of the arrest and conviction of these deluded men was compiled and published by Henry M. Hunt, in his story of the Cronin case. It is here reproduced:

DATE OF SENTENCE.	NAME.	CRIME.	SENTENCE.
1881. May.	James McGrath. James McKevitt.	Attempt to blow up Liverpool town hall.	Life. 20 years.
1882. Jan. 31.	John Tobin.	Illegal possession of nitroglycerine.	7 years.
July 31.	Thomas Walsh.	Illegal possession of nitroglycerine.	7 years.
1883. May 28.	Thomas Gallagher. A. G Whitehead. H. H. Wilson. John Curtin. William Tansey. Pat Noughton. Pat Rogerson. James Kelly.	Illegal manufacture of nitroglycerine at Birmingham and transfer of it to London Exposition at Weston house in Galway.	Life. Life. Life. Life. 14 years. 8 years. 12 years. 2 years.
July 30.	Timothy Featherstone. Dennis Deasy. Pat Flannigan. Henry Dalton.	Illegal possession of infernal machines.	Life. Life. Life. Life.
Dec. 21.	James McCullough. Thomas Dewanney. Peter Callahan. Henry McCann. Terrance McDermott. Dennis Casey. Pat McCabe. James Kelly. James Donnelly. Patrick Drum.	Outrages at Glasgow in January, 1883.	Life. Life. Life. Life. Life. 7 years. 7 years. 7 years. 7 years. 5 years.
1884. July 29.	John Daly. J. F. Egan.	Illegal possession of infernal machines.	Life. 20 years.
1885. March.	Patrick Levy.	Explosion at Mill street Barracks.	1 year.
May 18.	J. G. Cunningham. H. Burton.	Explosion at Tower of London.	Life. Life.
Nov. 14.	J. Wallace.	Murder at Solihall.	20 years.

Cronin and his associates attributed the "physical force" policy to the executive board of the United Brotherhood.

They also believed that the poor fellows who had been commissioned to perform the deeds of violence were betrayed. The sentiment of the civilized world was turning against Ireland. On the heels of this feeling, which was giving the loyal members of the United Brotherhood the greatest concern, came a call from the executive committee for more money. No member of the order, save the "triangle" and its few confidants could understand the dissipation of the vast sum that had filled the treasury at the time of the Chicago convention. An investigation was asked. The "triangle" refused it. The refusal served to heighten the suspicions of the men who were foremost in the opposition to the Messrs. Sullivan, Feeley and Boland. Cronin, with John Devoy, of New York, and Luke Dillon, of Philadelphia, led in the attack. In the Clan-na-Gael camp of which he was a member, Dr. Cronin read a letter from a camp that had been expelled by the "triangle." For this he was tried in 1885, pronounced guilty of treason and expelled from the order.

Other expulsions followed, but these radical methods did not quell the rising storm. The United Brotherhood was split in twain. Hostility to Sullivan, Boland and Feeley crystallized rapidly. Men of ability and force directed the opposition, and gradually the "triangle" gave ground until it was completely out of office. Cronin, Devoy and Dillon kept up their attack, directing it personally against Sullivan. In 1888 an attempt was made to reunite the Brotherhood. Leaders of both wings of the society met in Chicago. It was decided that the acts of the executives of the Brotherhood from 1881 should be investigated and that its accounts be audited. A trial committee, composed of three men from each faction, was appointed. The men named on this committee were:

Dr. P. H. Cronin, Chicago.
Dr. P. McCahey, Philadelphia.
James J. Rogers, Brooklyn.
Christopher F. Byrne, Saxonville, Mass.

P. A. O'Boyle, Pittston, Pa.
John D. McMahon, Rome, N. Y.

The trial board met in New York in September, 1888. Boland, Feeley and Sullivan were on hand. The latter filed a statement alleging that Cronin was his personal enemy, that he had expressed opinions in the case, and that he was a perjurer, unfit to sit on the trial board. His protest was overruled. Then the trial began. John Devoy and Luke Dillon filed charges against the "triangle." They alleged misappropriation of funds of the Brotherhood, desertion of men sent on the society's business, illegal manipulations of conventions and the like. The trial, of course, was secret. At its conclusion, McCahey and Cronin were the only members of the board who voted "guilty." The majority acquitted the "triangle," and voted that every record of the trial be destroyed. Cronin demanded that the evidence be written up and sent to every camp of the Clan, together with the verdict. This being voted down, he refused to surrender his private notes of the trial. He and McCahey prepared a minority report, and demanded that it be published. This demand was also refused. Cronin still insisted on publicity, and, finally, announced his intention of making an open statement of the whole affair at the meeting of the Irish National League of America, which was to assemble at Philadelphia in 1889. On his return to Chicago he read the report of the minority in his own camp. From this time until his death, Dr. Cronin was active in his determination to publish to the world what he believed to be the treachery of the Sullivan wing of the United Brotherhood to the cause of Ireland. If the men the physician accused were innocent of treachery—as the law has held them to be innocent of his death—the murder was a greater misfortune to them than to the victim. In the minds of a majority of his fellows Cronin was a martyr—the men he accused must live and die under a cloud.

THE PHYSICIAN DISAPPEARS.

Dr. Cronin had not been missing from his home twenty-four hours when his intimates declared their belief that he had been murdered. The Monday following his disappearance—he was killed Saturday night—Patrick Cooney, one of the actual instruments in the physician's death, was in New York, attempting to lure John Devoy to a similar fate. Luke Dillon and P. McCahey, of Philadelphia, completed the quartette marked for "removal." The blunder in the disposition of Cronin's body seems to have unnerved the plotters; its discovery and the active investigation that followed completed their rout; exposure and conviction followed, and such of the murder gang as escaped sought their holes.

As has been said, the plan for the "removal" of Cronin was carefully matured; every detail was thought out and failure seemed impossible. A lonely cottage was rented from an ignorant landlord. A plausible business agreement was arranged between a man who lived near the cottage and Cronin, in order that the physician would respond to a call at any time without telling his friends where he was going. An officer of the law, who could do so without attracting attention, hired a horse and buggy to carry the victim to his doom. A stranger in Chicago was found to do the driving. Human tools were secured who would beat to death any one they were told to—providing only that they could strike from behind and in the dark. Other human tools were told off to strip the body, stuff it in the trunk and hurry it through the darkness to the lake shore. A tug in charge of "trusty" men was assigned to meet the body and sink it in the lake. The clothes were to be shipped to London. "Witnesses" were assigned who remembered, after the disappearance, of seeing Cronin on the way to a railroad depot the night of May 4. Other "witnesses" were chosen who saw him in Canada the following week. Still others were selected who should see him in New York and on the ocean and in Paris. Finally a body, dressed in his clothes and bearing documents making him out a traitor to the Irish cause, was to be found in the river Thames. And then the men whose reputation he had assailed would be "vindicated."

Condemned to die by a secret court from whose decision there was no appeal, Dr. Cronin sat in his office in the Windsor theatre building on the last night of his life, dismissing a patient preparatory to attending a meeting of the Celto-American club, of which he was president. There came a hurried ring at the door; Mrs. T. T. Conklin, the landlady, answered the call. A rough stranger brushed past her into the house, demanding to see Dr. Cronin. His manner was excited, his eye furtive, his nervousness ill-concealed. In the physician's presence he produced a printed business card from the O'Sullivan Ice Company.

"Doctor," he said, "one of P. O'Sullivan's workmen has been terribly injured. Unless a physician sees him at once, he will die. O'Sullivan is out of town, but he has often told us to come to you if any of the men got hurt."

The physician hesitated, glanced at his watch, and said: "I'll be with you in a moment."

"I have a fast horse at the door," said the stranger. Cronin seized his instrument case, donned his hat and coat, and led the way to the sidewalk. At the curb stood a buggy, with a white horse in the shafts. As the doctor started to climb into the waiting vehicle, Frank T. Scanlan approached. "I cannot be at the meeting to-night, Frank," he said, "there has been an accident out in Lake View, and I have been sent for." In another instant he was in the buggy, the ill-favored stranger sprang to his seat beside him, gathered up the reins, and they rattled away northward. His friends never saw the physician alive again, but the first link of evidence against his murderers was already forged. Scanlan and Mrs. Conklin, from the window of the flat above, had seen the mysterious driver and the white horse.

All that long Saturday night the Conklins listened in vain for the home-coming of their tenant. Mrs. Conklin told her husband of the mysterious caller. The tell-tale card was found on the doctor's office table. Early Sunday morning Conklin drove to Lake View, and sought out O'Sullivan. The iceman denied all knowledge of the affair. Conklin's fears were verified. He and his wife had been Cronin's confidants. They knew his life had been attempted on previous occasions. The police were notified. The services of the Pinkertons were enlisted. The search for the white horse and the mysterious driver began.

Two policemen on duty in the vicinity of Clark and Diversey streets reported that soon after midnight of Saturday, a light wagon, drawn by a bay horse, with three or four men and a large trunk in the wagon passed north on Clark street at a rapid rate. Several hours later the wagon rattled past them again, this time headed toward the city. The trunk was not then in the wagon, but the next day a trunk, the interior stained with blood and partially filled with bloody absorbent cotton, was found near Evanston avenue and Sultzer street. The trunk was new, and large enough to hold the body of a man six feet tall. The lock of the trunk had been smashed, and in their haste to remove the body of their victim the murderers had thrown the cover back with such force as to break the sheet-iron hinges. On closer examination of the bloody cotton, a lock of black hair, evidently torn from the scalp of a man, was found. This hair was declared by Dr. Cronin's friends to be from the missing man's head.

An examination of the neighborhood about the spot where the trunk was found, developed a fresh trail of wagon tracks to the lake shore, near Hollywood and Bryn Mawr avenues. The next day Officer Wade, of the Edgewater police, reported that about 1 oclock Sunday morning he saw a horse and wagon standing on the lake shore, at the point indicated by the wagon tracks. Wade asked the men in the wagon what they were doing there at that hour. One of the men replied that they were looking for the Lake Shore Drive. When the officer told them that they were two miles off the road, they turned their horse's head toward Evanston avenue and drove hurriedly away. Wade saw the trunk in the wagon.

Stimulated by the evidence thus gathered, the police pushed their investigations with energy. All the livery stables on the North Side were visited, in an attempt to locate the white horse and his mysterious driver, described by Frank Scanlan and Mrs. Conklin. The search proved of no avail. The man who could have furnished the desired clue held his peace for the time. The lake shore was examined for traces of a grave. Ponds in the neighborhood were raked, and, finally, the river was dragged for a distance of several hundred feet, either way, from the Fullerton avenue bridge, over which the wagon with its bloody freight was supposed to have crossed. No further clue was found. Dr. Cronin had disappeared as magically as if the earth had yawned and swallowed him up, and the bloody trunk promised to remain a mystery.

Thursday, May 9, five days after Cronin disappeared, the West Side police arrested Frank J. Black, alias Woodruff, who was attempting to sell a horse and wagon for $10. When put upon the rack the horse-thief told a lurid story about being hired to haul a trunk from the rear of 528 North State street at 2 o'clock Sunday morning. He stole the horse and wagon from Dean's livery stable, where he was working, and claimed to have been horrified when he discovered that he was hauling the corpse of a young woman. His story was so worded as to implicate Dr. Cronin as one of the men who employed him. He claimed to have driven over the route already known to the police and to have thrown the bloody trunk from the wagon at the point where it was found. His story did not hang together on cross-examination, but the police were satisfied that he knew something of the crime and he was detained.

Although there had been a blunder in the disposition of the

body of their victim—the expected tug not having met them on the lake shore—Dr. Cronin's murderers now proceeded to carry out their scheme of assassinating his character. Vague rumors from various sources began to find their way into the newspapers. It was hinted that he had left the city of his own free will and that his alleged mysterious disappearance was a scheme of his own, conceived for the purpose of attaining a sensational notoriety. He was represented as being an erratic, ambitious individual who thirsted for sensationalism. These innuendoes were echoed by certain members of the police force—then as now honey-combed with the triangle influence. Following hints came alleged statements of facts. Miss Annie Murphy, an employe in the Recorder's office, an elocutionist who had figured on programs at Irish entertainments with Dr. Cronin, and who would consequently be able to readily identify him, came forward the day after Woodruff's alleged confession with a statement that she had seen the physician on a Clark street car about 9 o'clock on the night of his disappearance. He had his instrument case in his hand, she said, and was bound down-town. Next came William Dwyer, a North Chicago street car conductor, who corroborated Miss Murphy's statement in detail.

When the body of the doctor was found two weeks later it was learned that Miss Murphy's father was a member of the triangle wing of the United Brotherhood and an officer in a local camp. Conductor Dwyer was not known to be a member of the Clan, but he suddenly threw up his position with the street car company and went to Canada "for his health." But we anticipate.

On the night of Friday, May 10, several Chicago newspapers received from Toronto dispatches to the effect that Dr. Cronin had been seen in the Canadian city, alive and well. These dispatches were from Charles T. Long, whose father was publisher of a Toronto newspaper. Previously Long had been a reporter on one or more of the Chicago dailies; he knew Dr. Cronin well, and thus his reports were looked upon as practically clearing up the disappearance of the physician. Saturday morning the Chicago Herald printed the following:

> Dr. P. H. Cronin is in Canada. He was seen, recognized and spoken to here to-day by a former Chicagoan, and in return told of his troubles, bitterly denouncing a number of Garden City people, Alexander Sullivan particularly. The missing and supposed-to-be murdered physician seemed to be slightly deranged, C. T. Long, who for three years was intimately acquainted with Dr. Cronin in Chicago, was walking down Yonge street shortly after 11 o'clock this morning, and when opposite the Arcade, came face to face with the missing Irish nationalist. He was accompanied by a man of shorter stature.
>
> "Hello, Doc, what are you doing here?" was Long's greeting.
>
> To this the doctor answered "Hello," and then pausing and drawing himself up in an injured manner, continued: "You have me at a disadvantage, sir. What do you want?"
>
> "Why, Cronin, is it possible that you don't remember me?"
>
> "I do not know you, sir, and shall have you handed over to the police in case you bother me further."
>
> Having thus delivered himself the doctor turned the corner of the Arcade and quickly followed the retreating footsteps of his friend, who turned down Victoria street, and together they were soon lost in the crowd. While on the way to police headquarters Long again caught sight of the pair walking rapidly down Toronto street. Slipping into a doorway he waited until they had passed, and then noticed that Cronin had adjusted a pair of goggles, but otherwise was attired precisely the same as when seen on Yonge street. Stepping up to the doctor, Long put the point-blank question: "Cronin, what are you doing in Toronto when your friends in Chicago are hunting the earth for you?"
>
> "Now, look here, Long," he replied, "for God's sake, let up on me. I have already had enough notoriety and don't want to be bothered."
>
> "Come in and let us talk the matter over," said Long, leading the pair into a convenient saloon. Cronin appeared to be out of his head. He talked in a rambling way about Chicago affairs and wound up by denouncing in frenzied terms Alexander Sullivan and other prominent Irishmen. His friend here whispered to him and thereafter he refused to talk.

A more circumstantial story followed the next day. The public began to turn against the physician. Woodruff's story was recalled, and it was hinted that Cronin had fled the city to escape the consequences of a criminal operation. In another direction it was charged that the doctor was a second Le Caron. One of his enemies gave out for publication a statement that agents of the English government were about to put another American informer on the stand in the Parnell inquiry. Cronin was said to be the man. His Chicago friends were staggered but not deceived by the Toronto dispatches. Patrick McGarry was sent to Canada. He enlisted the services of the Toronto police. Long's circumstantial story was torn to shreds. It was a tissue of lies.

FINDING OF THE BODY.

May 14, there came a complaint to the Lake View Board of Public Works that the sewer catch-basin at the corner of Evanston avenue and North Fifty-ninth street was stopped up, and that the stench arising from the stagnant water was a nuisance in the neighborhood. For nearly a week the complaints continued to come in, and finally, on May 22, workmen were dispatched to the scene to clean out the basin. They found the ditch that was supposed to drain into the basin choked with sand, and spent the better part of the day in clearing it. Just at dusk the job was completed, and before knocking off work, the foreman knelt on the iron grating that covered the basin to see that all was clear.

"There's a dog in here," he said, "and that's what's making this stench."

"That's strange," said one of the workmen kneeling beside him, "how the deuce could a dog get in there?" He pressed his face close to the bars for an instant.

"My God," he cried, "it's a corpse."

The heavy plank top of the trap was wrenched off and there, in the foul slime of the sewer, floated the bruised and bloated body of Patrick Henry Cronin. It was naked, save for a towel tightly knotted about the neck. At the morgue, where identification by friends was instantaneous, the physicians found five wounds, any one of which would have probably proved fatal. The absence of wounds on the hands showed that the first blow was delivered unawares.

In the catch-basin, where the body was found, a human finger was picked up. In his guilty haste, one of the murderers had replaced the heavy cover with a crash, crushing off his own finger. This man was not apprehended at the time of the trial, but Cronin's friends know who he was, and probably could convict him to-day if he were alive. He died of delirium tremens not many months after the murder. With the discovery of Dr. Cronin's body, the county authorities took charge of the case.

Chief of Police Hubbard issued the following order to his captains:

> In view of the fact that the mutilated body of Dr. Cronin has been found in a catch-basin in the town of Lake View, and that much public comment will be aroused, you will instruct your officers to note the nature of any such comment that they may overhear, and follow up all clues that may thus be obtained. This order is sent out, because some person, having some criminal knowledge of how Dr. Cronin came to his death, may be indiscreet enough to make some statement, when excited, that would lead to the solving of the mystery.

The above order is re-printed here to show that the police had awakened to the magnitude and extent of the conspiracy with which they had to deal.

Following the autopsy, ordered by Coroner Henry L. Hertz, Dr. Cronin's body was buried. The funeral was imposing. The murdered man's brother, John T. Cronin, and his sister, Mrs. John Carroll, were the only relatives present, but friends were there by the hundred. The day before the funeral, the body lay in state in the Cavalry Armory on Michigan avenue, guarded by Knights of St. Patrick. Twelve thousand passed before the catafalque, between the hours of noon and midnight. Sunday, May 26, at 10 o'clock, ten thousand men, members of the many societies with which Dr. Cronin was identified, formed in procession, and followed the hearse from the Cavalry Armory to the Roman Catholic cathedral on North State street, where the requiem mass was celebrated. The burial was at Calvary cemetery.

While Dr. Cronin's body lay in state in the Cavalry Armory, evidence against his assassins was accumulating rapidly. Spurred by the rising indignation of the people, the officers of the law redoubled their efforts to reach the murderers. The day after the discovery in the Lake View sewer, the police located the slaughter-pen where Cronin was beaten to death. Patrick O'Sullivan, the iceman, resided at the corner of Bosworth and Roscoe streets, in Lake View. On Ashland avenue, less than two hundred feet from O'Sullivan's home, stood a vacant cottage, one story and basement, with entrances to the main story by flights of wooden steps at front and rear. Fifty feet behind that gloomy cottage was a smaller building, occupied by Jonas Carlson, his wife and son John. Mr. Carlson owned both buildings, renting the Ashland avenue structure when he could. Only the Carlson cottages and O'Sullivan's house stood in the space, as large as the average city square, and the neighborhood was sparsely built up in every direction. The day following the discovery of the body, Captain Schuettler, of the city police, Captain Wing, of the Lake View police, and States Attorney Longenecker held a consultation. They decided to send for O'Sullivan. The iceman weakened under a rigid examination. He said he believed that something mysterious had been going on in the Carlson cottage. In March, he said, two strangers had leased the place of Carlson, telling him they were going to work in O'Sullivan's ice-house. They paid a month's rent, but had not occupied the building. He declared that he did not know the men, and had made no agreement to give them employment. He reiterated his earlier statements, that he knew nothing of Cronin's disappearance.

Schuettler and Wing ordered that O'Sullivan be detained while they drove to the mysterious cottage. Even before they entered the building, evidence of a crime was noted. Blood-stains were to be seen on the planks that spanned the ditch from the sidewalk to the road. Dark stains marked the planks of the sidewalk, and a trail of blood led up the wooden steps to the cottage door. Bursting open the latter, the two officers followed the gory trail into the front room of the little building. Here the evidence of a life-struggle was sickeningly plentiful. Blood-stains were everywhere, and from the fact that they were not as heavy as those outside the building, it was argued that the blood had soaked through a carpet that had since been taken up. In the room were a bedstead, dressing case, washstand, with pitcher and bowl, and a cheap rocking chair, one arm of which was broken off and lay on the floor. After the blood was shed, a man in bare feet had made a hurried and bungling attempt to conceal the stains by smearing them over with reddish brown paint. In the basement of the cottage were found the paint pot and brush, dropped by the wretch who had made such an ineffectual attempt to cover up the traces of the bloody struggle.

Leaving the slaughter pen, the two policemen sought the Carlsons. They did not need any urging to tell what they knew. March 20, a young man giving his name as Frank Williams, had called and rented the cottage, paying a month's rent in advance. He said his two brothers and a sister, who were coming from Baltimore in a few days, would live with him, took the keys and departed. Three days later the new tenant moved some cheap furniture into the building. Nothing was seen of him after that, until he called April 20, and paid the second month's rent. In explanation of his failure to occupy the cottage, the man said his sister was sick. Monday,—May 13, Dr. Cronin had then been missing nine days— a stranger called at the Carlson's home and tendered the third month's rent, although it would not be due for a week. By this time the Carlsons began to suspect something was wrong, and they refused the proffered money unless Williams should occupy the house. May 18, Carlson received a note dated Hammond, Indiana, signed "F. W," which read as follows:

My sister is low at present and my business calls me out of town. If you will please put the furniture in your cellar for a few days, I will pay you for your trouble. My sister told me to paint the floor for her so that it would not be so hard to clean. I am sorry now that I gave the front room one coat.

That afternoon Carlson went over to the cottage to examine it. The condition, as found by the police, filled the ignorant man with alarm. The first impulse was to notify the officers, but after a family council the old landlord decided to do nothing until Frank Williams called for his furniture. Questioned by Captain Schuettler, Carlson remembered that, when his mysterious tenant first secured the keys from him, he walked across the prairie towards O'Sullivan's house. The iceman was standing by his buggy, and Carlson heard the stranger say, as he approached him: "Well, the cottage is rented." Later, when Carlson complained to the iceman about the mysterious actions of his tenant, his neighbor assured him that the man was "all right."

The next step of the police was to trace the furniture found in the cottage. It bore the trade-mark of A. H. Revell & Co. Investigation at the furniture establishment showed that a bill of goods, corresponding to the articles found, was sold February 17 to a man giving the name of J. B. Simonds, and delivered to rooms 12 and 15, 117 Clark street. This building was directly opposite the Chicago Opera House block, where Dr. Cronin had his down-town office. It was developed that the Clark street flat was deserted March 23—the day Frank Williams moved into the Carlson cottage—and with the location of the expressman, who hauled the goods to Lake View, another link in the chain of evidence was forged. It is conjectured that the assassins originally intended to lure Dr. Cronin into the Clark street flat and murder him there, but that the idea was abandoned because of the hazard in disposing of the corpse.

When the news of the discovery in the Carlson cottage was made public, William Mertes, a Lake View milk dealer, came forward with a story that confirmed the theory that here Dr. Cronin had met his death. Mertes was passing down Ashland avenue about 8:30 o'clock on the night of May 4, and, when near the corner of Roscoe street, a top buggy, drawn by a white horse, drew up in front of the cottage. A man, answering the description of the murdered physician in every particular, jumped from the buggy and hurried up the steps. He was expected, for Mertes heard a bolt fly back as the tall man reached the door. He had no sooner passed inside than the milkman was astonished to see the man who remained in the buggy bring the whip down on the back of the white horse and rattle off in the darkness. As he passed down the street, Mertes heard a crash, like the fall of a heavy body, in the dimly-lit and closely-shuttered front room of the cottage, followed by angry voices. In an instant all was still. The murder had been accomplished.

THE WHITE HORSE LOCATED.

About the time Milkman Mertes came to police headquarters with the story of what he had seen, Patrick Dinan, a liveryman, in business at 360 North Clark street, called upon Chief of Police Hubbard, with what proved to be the most important single bit of evidence in this remarkable case. Attached to the East Chicago avenue police station, then commanded by Captain Michael J. Schaack, who did brilliant work in the anarchist case, was Detective Daniel Coughlin. On the morning of the fateful Saturday that Dr. Cronin disappeared, Coughlin is reported to have gone to Dinan's stable, and said: "I want you to reserve a rig for a friend of mine, who will call for it to-night. Say nothing to any one about it. I will be responsible."

Coughlin often hired rigs of Dinan when on detective duty, and the request of secrecy seemed natural to the liveryman. Between 7 and 8 o'clock that night Coughlin's friend appeared. Dinan's description of him tallied with the description given by Mrs. Coughlin and Frank Scanlan of the man who drove Dr. Cronin away. The stranger called for the rig that Coughlin had ordered. He was given a white horse in a top buggy without side curtains. He objected to the color of the horse and the absence of curtains, but Dinan was in a surly mood and would make no change. Finally the man climbed into the rig and drove north on Clark street in the direction of the Windsor theatre building. About 9:30 o'clock the stranger drove back to the barn, tossed the reins to a hostler and hurriedly disappeared. The horse was warm, and had evidently been driven hard.

The following Monday the newspapers, in telling of the disappearance of Cronin, minutely described the horse and buggy that had driven him away. Without thinking there was anything wrong, Dinan concluded to report to Captain Schaack. The first man he met at the police station was detective Coughlin.

"Hello," said Coughlin, "Who are you looking for?"

"Captain Schaack," said Dinan.

"What for?" demanded the detective.

"Well," replied the liveryman, "there are so many inquiries made about the white horse that was out Saturday night—the one I let your friend have—that I think I had better tell him about it."

"Now, look here, Dinan," said Coughlin, "there is no use making a fuss about this thing. You keep quiet about it. Me and Cronin have not been good friends, and if you go to talking you may get me into trouble. Everybody knows him and me were enemies."

Dinan appeared to acquiesce in the detective's plan, but later in the day he called at Captain Schaack's house and told his story. That officer questioned Coughlin closely in the matter, but accepted the detective's statement that he had hired the rig for a man named Smith, from Hancock, Michigan, who was "all right."

Dinan finally carried his story to Chief of Police Hubbard. Hubbard at once sent for Coughlin. He was subjected to a rigid cross-examination. His replies were evasive and unsatisfactory. Frequently he contradicted himself and at times refused to answer at all. When he left the room he was under arrest. Later, at the trial, Dinan testified to the facts as given above in his statement to Chief of Police Hubbard.

In the meantime, Patrick O'Sullivan's contract with Dr. Cronin was being investigated. The fact developed that, although no employe of the iceman had been injured in four years, he had recently agreed to pay the physician $8.00 a month regularly, the latter to respond to a call whenever one of O'Sullivan's cards should be presented him. To disarm suspicion the contract had been negotiated through Justice Mahoney, of Lake View, a particular friend of Cronin's. The stranger who drove the doctor away with Pat Dinan's white horse had presented the stipulated card. The stranger who rented the Carlson cottage hurried to apprise O'Sullivan of the fact. The meshes of the law were tightening about the iceman. May 27 he was arrested on complaint of Dr. Cronin's brother. May 28, after hearing the evidence thus far gathered, the grand jury indicted Daniel Coughlin, detective; Patrick O'Sullivan, iceman; and Frank J. Black, alias Woodruff, the horse-thief, for conspiracy to commit murder.

Following the indictments by the grand jury came the coroner's inquest. The jurors visited the catch-basin where the body of Dr. Cronin was found, the Carlson cottage, and examined the furniture and the bloody trunk. Mrs. Conklin, Frank T. Scanlan, Patrick Dinan, Jonas Carlson, Justice Mahoney, Milkman Mertes and others told their stories. Captain Schaack's testimony before the jury was of such nature that Chief of Police Hubbard, yielding to a popular clamor, suspended him from the force on which he had served with such distinction. He has since, however, been reinstated and now occupies a position of honor in the police department.

One of the main obstacles in the path of the men who set for themselves the task of hunting down the murderers of Cronin was the police force. Every station in the city had its spies. Every move of the detectives who were honestly striving to unravel the mystery was promptly communicated to the other side. On one occasion, Patrick Cooney—who is known to have been one of the men in the cottage at the time of the murder—was located in a New Jersey town. Two hours after an officer left Chicago to arrest him, Cooney had received a warning. Dr. Cronin's friends aver that the man who gave the warning was a high official of the police department, who has since retired on a pension.

The sensational feature of the coroner's inquest was the attempt to show that Alexander Sullivan desired, and probably directed the physician's "removal." So strong was the circumstantial evidence of Thomas F. O'Connor, Patrick McGarry, J. G. Hagerty, Luke Dillon and others that the coroner's jury recommended that Sullivan be held to the grand jury along with Coughlin, O'Sullivan and Black. He was arrested on the night of June 12, but three days later Judge Tuley admitted him to bail in the sum of $20,000. November 8, the case against him not having been pushed, his bondsmen were released and he himself declared discharged.

In 1886, there came from Ireland to the United States, an athletic young man named Martin Burke. He reached Chicago in 1887, and soon joined the Clan-na-Gaels. He was admitted to Camp 20, of which John F. Beggs, a lawyer, Daniel Coughlin and Michael Whelan, city detectives, were the leading lights. Beggs, through Alexander Sullivan, got Burke a position in the city sewer department. He was naturally a loafer and spent much of his time in bar-rooms, where his mouthings soon earned for him the reputation of being a tool of the triangle. After the murder, he disappeared. Burke was not unknown to the police force, and it occurred to officer John Collins, who was detailed on the Cronin case, that he might know something of it. His disappearance only confirmed the theory. Collins finally procured a group picture, in which the fugitive's face was shown. The Carlsons unhesitatingly picked him out of the group as Frank Williams, the man who rented the cottage. The expressman, who hauled the furniture from the Clark street flat to Lake View also recognized the picture as being that of the man who employed him. Descriptions of Burke and copies of the photograph were scattered over the United States and Canada. June 16, Chief of Police McRae, of Winnipeg, Manitoba, arrested the suspect as he was leaving the city to take ship for Liverpool. After a legal struggle that lasted six weeks, during which time Burke was mysteriously supplied with money and able counsel, a warrant of extradition was issued, and officer Collins brought his prisoner back to Chicago.

While this was going on, the police began a search for Patrick Cooney, known to his intimates as "the Fox." Cooney came from the west of Ireland and was a bricklayer by trade. He answered the description of the man who bought the furniture and rented the Clark street flat. For a month previous to the murder he was frequently seen with Coughlin and Burke, and he had been heard to denounce Dr. Cronin as a British spy. The week after the murder he was seen in New York, and twice after the search for him began he was located, but each time eluded arrest.

June 24 the grand jury learned from reliable witnesses that there was an inner circle in Camp 20 of the Clan-na-Gael, and that a trial of Dr. Cronin was ordered by this inner circle in February, 1889. For a year or more he had been denounced in this camp by Coughlin, O'Sullivan, Burke, Cooney and others as a British spy. A case was finally manufactured against him, and the trial ordered. John F. Beggs, senior guardian of Camp 20, selected the trial committee. The committee met in secret, and rendered its verdict to the senior guardian. Dr. Cronin's friends say that on May 4, 1889, the verdict was executed.

The final result of the long deliberations of the grand jury was the indictment of John F. Beggs, Daniel Coughlin, Patrick O'Sullivan, Patrick Cooney, Martin Burke, Frank J. Black and John Kunze. Kunze was believed to be the man who drove the white horse. He had done some "stool-pigeon" work for Coughlin, and thus fell under suspicion. At the trial he was first sentenced to three years in the penitentiary, but he was afterwards acquitted. By an agreement of the prosecution Black was granted a separate trial, and, finally, as he was wanted in Kansas for horse stealing, and the police had no evidence against him but his numerous confessions, he was taken to Olathe, Kansas, where he was convicted and sentenced to two years in the penitentiary. At the conclusion of this term, he was taken to Lansing, Kansas, on another charge of horse stealing. He was again convicted, and this time sentenced to five years in prison, where he died of typhoid fever, October 10, 1892.

The Kansas prison officials say that Black talked freely during his last illness. He said it was a fact that he drove the wagon containing the corpse of Dr. Cronin. The Chicago police evidently blundered in letting Black go. Had he been tried, he might have revealed the names of the men who were with him the night of May 4. Certain it is that the murderers have not all been brought to book.

ON TRIAL AT LAST.

Friday, August 30, less than four months after the murder, the trial of Beggs, Coughlin, O'Sullivan, Burke and Kunze was commenced in Judge McConnell's court. Able lawyers represented the accused men, and the states attorney was supported by some of the foremost men of the bar. Nearly two months were consumed in securing a jury. When the case had been on hearing for more than a month, a sensational development, indicative of the powerful and sinister influence at work in behalf of the prisoners, was made public by the states attorney. Two court bailiffs had been discovered in an attempt to bribe the jury. One man had been offered $5000 if he would get on the jury and stand out for an acquittal. A number of citizens had been similarly approached. Happily, for the cause of justice, the bailiffs approached the wrong men, and the plot failed. As a result of the discovery six men were indicted by the grand jury, and sent to jail for a term of years.

To rehearse, or even summarize the evidence heard at the trial would be but to repeat the story, as here set down. It was on Monday, December 16, that the jury returned a verdict. Beggs was acquitted, while O'Sullivan, Burke and Coughlin were found guilty of murder, and sentenced to the penitentiary for life. January 20, 1893, the supreme court granted a new trial on a technicality. The court reviews the evidence presented at the trial, and dwells upon the fact that it is purely circumstantial. The theory of the prosecution, that a conspiracy was hatched by Coughlin and others to bring about the murder of Dr. Cronin, is recited, together with the connection which it sought to establish between the crime and the Clan-na-Gael, of which all save the defendant Kunze were members. The supposed purposes of that organization, the declaration that Dr. Cronin was a British spy and the investigation set on foot by the members of Camp 20, are considered. The matter of the competence of Jurors Bontecou and Clark, who admitted, on examination, that from what they had read in the newspapers, they believed the prisoners guilty, was taken up and reviewed at great length. Their examination is repeated, and the propriety of the challenge for cause made in each case by defendant's counsel and refused by the court, is taken under consideration. Many authorities are quoted to show what is and what is not a competent juror. The conclusion is reached that Jurors Bontecou and Clark were disqualified by prejudice, and that, therefore, the defendants did not receive a fair trial. The decision declares that the evidence fails to show that the Clan-na-Gael was an unlawful or criminal organization, or that, as an organization, it had anything to do with the murder. The court forbears to express an opinion as to the other questions presented to it, but reverses the judgment of the lower court in the case, and remands it to the criminal court of Cook county for a new trial. Justices Magruder and Scholfield dissented from the opinion.

Thus Coughlin is now, April, 1893, in the county jail, awaiting a new trial. Martin Burke and Patrick O'Sullivan died in prison. The fatalities connected with the Cronin case have been singularly numerous. In addition to the death of the two principals, while serving life sentences in Joliet penitentiary, and that of Black in the Kansas prison, more than a score of suspects and witnesses have been called before a higher court. Martin Burke died December 9, 1892, of consumption. The same disease carried off Patrick O'Sullivan May 5, 1892. John F. Beggs, the senior guardian of Camp 20, died April 5, 1892, and Patrick Dinan, the owner of the white horse, died March 28, 1892.

Edward Spellman, the wealthy distiller, of Peoria, whose evidence on the stand stamped him a bitter enemy of the Doctor, died in December, 1891, literally losing his head in a frightful fall from a ladder. He was a prominent Clan-na-Gael, and contributed largely to the defense fund. Thomas Desmond, of San Francisco, another Clan-na-Gael, who came to advise and assist the defense, is a permanent cripple, sustaining a compound fracture of the leg on Clark street by a fall one night while on his way to a secret meeting. Matthew Dannehy, of Camp 20, kept a saloon on Chicago avenue, which the Clan-na-Gaels were known to frequent. He was an alibi witness for the defense. He never prospered after the trial, his place being finally closed up, and he died soon after. Michael Gannon was a bartender in Patrick Dolan's saloon, another resort of the order, and is supposed to have known a good deal, his testimony, however, being unimportant. During the trial he caught a severe cold one night while intoxicated. It quickly developed into pneumonia, and while in a fit of coughing he choked to death and died without the services of a priest. Frank Shea was another pneumonia victim. It is supposed his part in the trial was that of drilling alibi witnesses. A horrible death was that of Peter McGeehan, the Philadelphian, who was accosted on the street by Dr. Cronin about a week before the murder, and charged with being in the plot to murder him. He died some time between the coroner's inquest and the trial. He had obtained employment at a South Side rolling mill and fell into a pit, sustaining severe injuries. He was taken to the County Hospital and died shortly after, a raving maniac. Like Gannon, he is said to have had no priest to console him in his dying moments, and there has always been a mystery about his burial place. The death of Robert Gibbons, who was an alibi witness for Burke, was tragic and violent. Two years ago, while in the Lake View Exchange, near Hooley's Theatre, he attacked Captain Schuettler, of the police force, who had been active in running down the conspirators. Schuettler shot and fatally wounded him, and, as proven in the coroner's inquest, was fully justified in doing so.

With the new trial of Coughlin still pending, it is, of course, impossible to give the finale of the great tragedy.

"Chicago—The Main Exhibit."

Under the above heading, Mr. Julian Ralph, in an article appearing in the February, 1892, number of "Harper's Monthly," gave, in epitome, many Chicago characteristics, which, while hardly the proper subject-matter for a history of the city, still complete and supplement that history and enable the stranger to form a more correct idea of the distinguishing traits of Chicago and Chicagoans. His treatment, however, was so generous, his praise so unstinted, that only the fact that he is a New Yorker permits the reproduction, in a Chicago book, of the following extracts from his article:

"Chicago will be the main exhibit at the Columbian Exposition of 1893. No matter what the aggregation of wonders there, the city itself will make the most surprising presentation. Those who go to study the world's progress will find no other result of human force so wonderful, extravagant, or peculiar. Those who go clear-minded, expecting to see a great city, will find one different from that which any precedent has led them to look for.

"While investigating the management and prospects of the Columbian Exposition, I was a resident of Chicago for more than a fortnight. A born New-Yorker, the energy, roar, and bustle of the place were yet sufficient to first astonish and then to fatigue me. I was led to examine the city, and to cross-examine some of its leading men. I came away compelled to acknowledge its possession of certain forceful qualities which I never saw exhibited in the same degree anywhere else. I got a satisfactory explanation of its growth and achievements, as well as proof that it must continue to expand in population and commercial influence. I acquired a respect for Chicago

Clark Street from Washington.

such as it is most likely that any American who makes a similar investigation must share with me.

"The city has been thought intolerant of criticism. The amount of truth there is in this is found in its supervoluminous civicism. But underlying the behavior of the most able and enterprising men in the city is this motto, which they constantly quoted to me, all using the same words: 'We are for Chicago first, last, and all the time.' To define that sentence is, in a great measure, to account for Chicago. It explains the possession of a milllion inhabitants by a city that practically dates its beginning after the war of the rebellion. Its adoption by half a million men as their watchword means the forcing of trade and manufactures and wealth; the getting of the World's Fair, if you please. In order to comprehend Chicago. it is best never to lose sight of the motto of its citizens.

"I have spoken of the roar and bustle and energy of Chicago. This is most noticeable in the business part of the town, where the greater number of the men are crowded together. * * * The whole business of life is carried on at high pressure, and the pithy part of Chicago is like three hundred acres of New York Stock Exchange when trading is active. European visitors have written that there are no such crowds anywhere as gather on Broadway, and this is true most of the time; but there is one hour on every week-day when certain streets in Chicago are so packed with people as to make Broadway look desolate and solitudinous by comparison. That is the hour between half past 5 and half past 6 o'clock, when the famous tall buildings of the city vomit their inhabitants upon the pavements. Photographs of the principal corners and crossings, taken at the height of the human torrent, suggest the thought that the camera must have been turned on some little-known painting by Dore. Nobody but Dore ever conceived such pictures. To those who are in the crowds, even Chicago seems small and cramped; even her street-cars, running in breakneck trains, prove far too few; even her streets that

Corner Wabash Avenue and Washington Street.

connect horizon with horizon seem each night to roar at the city officials for further annexation in the morning.

"We shall see these crowds simply and satisfactorily accounted for presently; but they exhibit only one phase of the high-pressure existence; they form only one feature among the many that distinguish the town. In the tall buildings are the most modern and rapid elevators, machines that fly up through the towers like glass balls from a trap at a shooting contest. The slow-going stranger, who is conscious of having been 'kneaded' along the street, like a lump of of dough among a million bakers, feels himself loaded into one of those frail-looking baskets of steel netting, and the next instant the elevator-boy touches the trigger, and up goes the whole load as a feather is caught up by a gale. These elevators are too slow for Chicago, and the managers of certain tall buildings now arrange them so that some run 'express' to the seventh story without stopping, while what may be called accommodation cars halt at the lower floors.

* * * * *

"The cable cars of Chicago make more than nine miles an hour in town, and more than thirteen miles an hour where the population is less dense. These street cars distribute the people grandly, and while they occasionally run over a stray citizen, they far more frequently clear their way by lifting wagons and trucks bodily to one side as they whirl along. It is a rapid and a business-like city. The speed with which cattle are killed and pigs are turned into slabs of salt pork has amazed the world, but it is only the ignorant portion thereof that does not know that the celerity at the stock-yards is merely an effort of the butchers to keep up with the rest of the town.

"I do not know how many very tall buildings Chicago contains, but they must number nearly two dozen. Some of them are artistically designed, and hide their height in well-balanced proportions. A few are mere boxes, punctured with window-holes, and stand above their neighbors like great hitching

State Street, Near Monroe.

posts. The best of them are very elegantly and completely appointed, and the communities of men inside them might almost live their lives within their walls, so multifarious are the occupations and services of the tenants. The best New York office buildings are not injured by comparison with these towering structures, except that they are not so tall as the Chicago buildings, but there is not in New York any office structure that can be compared with Chicago's so-called Chamber of Commerce office building, so far as are concerned the advantages of light and air and openness and roominess which its tenants enjoy. * * * With their floors of defty-laid mosaic work, their walls of marble and onyx, their balustrades of copper worked into arabesquerie, their artistic lanterns, elegant electric fixtures, their costly and luxurious public rooms, these Chicago office buildings force an exclamation of praise, however unwillingly it comes.

"They have adopted what they call 'the Chicago method' in putting up these steepling hives. This plan is to construct the actual edifice of steel framework, to which are added thin outer walls of brick or stone masonry, and the necessary partitions of fire-brick and plaster laid on iron lathing. The buildings are therefore like enclosed bird-cages, and it is said that, like bird-cages, they cannot shake or tumble down. The exterior walls are mere envelopes. They are so treated that the buildings look like heaps of masonry, but that is homage paid to custom more than it is a material element of strength. The Chicago method is expeditious, economical, and in many ways advantageous. The manner in which the great weight of houses so tall as to include between sixteen and twenty-four stories is distributed upon the ground beneath them is ingenious. Wherever one of the principal upright pillars is to be set up, the builders lay a pad of steel and cement of such extent that the pads for all the pillars cover all the site. These pads are slightly pyramidal in shape, and are made by laying alternate courses of steel beams crosswise, one upon

another. Each pair of courses of steel is filled in and solidified with cement, and then the next two courses are added and similarly treated. At last each pad is eighteen inches thick, and perhaps eighteen feet square; but the size is governed by the desire to distribute the weight of the building at about the average of a ton to the square foot.

"This peculiar process is necessitated by the character of the land underneath Chicago. Speaking widely, the rule is to find from seven to fourteen feet of sand super-imposed upon a layer of clay between ten and forty feet in depth. It has not paid to puncture this clay with piling. The piles sink into a soft and yielding substance, and the clay is not tenacious enough to hold them. Thus the Chicago post-office was built, and it not only settles continuously, but it settles unevenly. On the other hand, the famous Rookery building, set up on these steel and cement pads, did not sink quite an inch, though the architect's calculation was that, by squeezing the water out of the clay underneath, it would settle seven inches.

*   *   *   *   *

"Chicago's great office buildings have basements, but no cellars. I have referred to the number of these stupendous structures. Let it be known next that they are all in a very small district, that narrow area which composes Chicago's office region, which lies between Lake Michigan and all the principal railroad districts, and at the edges of which one-twenty-fifth of all the railroad mileage of the world is said to terminate, though the district is but little more than half a mile square, or 300 acres in extent. One of these buildings—and not the largest—has a population of 4000 persons. It was visited and its elevators were used on three days, when a count was kept, by 19,000, 18,000 and 20,000 persons. Last October there were 7000 offices in the tall buildings of Chicago, and 7000 more were under way in buildings then undergoing construction. The reader now understands why in the

Masonic Temple.

heart of Chicago every work-day evening the crowds convey the idea that our Broadway is a deserted thoroughfare as compared with, say, the corner of Clark and Jackson streets.

"Four-story and five-story houses that once were attractive are no longer so, because their owners cannot afford the conveniences which distinguish the greater edifices, wherein light and heat are often provided free, fire-proof safes are at the service of every tenant, janitors officer a host of servants, and there are barber shops, restaurants, cigar and news stands, elevators, and a half-dozen other conveniences not found in smaller houses. One of the foremost business men in the city asserts that he can perceive no reason why the entire business heart of the town—that square half mile of which I have spoken—should not soon be all builded up of cloud-capped towers. There will be a need for them, he says and the money to defray the cost of them will accompany the demand. The only trouble he foresees will be in the solution of the problem, what to do with the people who will then crowd the streets as never streets were clogged before.

"This prophecy relates to a little block in the city, but the city itself contains 181½ square miles. * * * The true reason for the enormous extension of municipal jurisdiction is quite peculiar. The enlargement was urged and accomplished in order to anticipate the growth and needs of the city. It was a consequence of extraordinary foresight, which recognized the necessity for a uniform system of boulevards, parks, drainage and water provision when the city should reach limits that it was even then seen must soon bound a compact aggregation of stores, offices, factories and dwellings. Chicago, in her park system, makes evident her intentions. Chicago expects to become the largest city in America—a city which, in fifty years, shall be larger than the consolidated cities that may form New York at that time.

* * * * *

"Without either avowing or contesting any part of the

View in Jackson Park.

process by which Chicago men account for their city's importance or calculate its future, let me repeat a digest of what several influential men of that city said upon the subject. Chicago, then, is the center of a circle of 1000 miles diameter. If you draw a line northward 500 miles, you find everywhere arable land and timber. The same is true with respect to a line drawn 500 miles in a northwesterly course. For 650 miles westward there is no change in the rich and alluring prospect, and so all around the circle, except where Lake Michigan interrupts it, the same conditions are found. Moreover, the lake itself is a valuable element in commerce. The rays or spokes in all these directions become materialized in the form of the tracks of thirty-five railways which enter the city. Twenty-two of these are great companies, and at a short distance sub-radials, made by other railroads, raise the number to fifty roads. As said above, in Chicago one-twenty-fifth of the railway mileage of the world terminates, and serves thirty millions of persons, who find Chicago the largest city easily accessible to them. Thus is found a vast population connected easily and directly with a common center, to which everything they produce can be brought, and from which all that contributes to the material progress and comfort of man may be economically distributed.

"A financier, who is equally well known and respected in New York and Chicago, put the case somewhat differently as to what he called Chicago's territory. He considered it as being 1000 miles square, and spoke of it as 'the land west of the Alleghanies, and south of Mason and Dixon's line.' This region, the richest agricultural territory in the world, does its financiering in Chicago. The rapid increase in wealth of both the city and the tributary region is due to the fact that every year both produce more, and have more to sell and less to buy. Not long ago the rule was that a stream of goods ran eastward over the Alleghanies, and another stream of supplies came back, so that the west had little gain to show.

But during the past five years this back-setting current has been a stream of money, returned for the products the west has distributed. The west is now selling to the east and to Europe and getting money in return, because it is manufacturing for itself, as well as tilling the soil and mining for the rest of the world. It therefore earns money and acquires a profit, instead of continuing its former process of toiling merely to obtain from the east the necessaries of life.

* * * * *

"When we understand what are the agricultural resources of the region for which Chicago is the trading-post, we perceive how certain it was that its debt would be paid, and that great wealth would follow. This midland country, of which Chicago is the capital, produces two thousand million bushels of corn, seven hundred million bushels of oats, fifty million hogs, twenty-eight million horses, thirty million sheep, and so on, but in no single instance is the region producing within fifty per cent. of what it will be made to yield before the expiration of the next twenty years. Farming there has been haphazard, rude and wasteful; but as it begins to pay well, the methods begin to improve. Drainage will add new lands, and better methods will swell the crops, so that, for instance, where sixty bushels of corn to the acre are now grown, at least one hundred bushels will be harvested. All the corn lands are now settled, but they are not improved. They will yet double in value. It is different with wheat; with that the maximum production will soon be attained.

"Such is the wealth that Chicago counts up as tributary to her. By the railroads that dissect this opulent region she is riveted to the midland, the southern, and the western country between the Rockies and the Alleghanies. She is closely allied to the south, because she is manufacturing and distributing much that the south needs, and can get most economically from her. Chicago has become the third manufacturing city in the Union, and she is drawing manufactures away from the east faster than most persons in the east imagine. To-day it is a great Troy stove-making establishment that has moved to Chicago; the week before it was a Massachusetts shoe factory that went there. Many great establishments have gone there, but more must follow, because Chicago is not only the center of the midland region, in respect of the distribution of made-up wares, but also for the concentration of raw materials. Chicago must lead in the manufacture of all goods of which wool, leather and iron are the bases. The revolution that took place in the meat trade when Chicago took the lead in that industry affected the whole leather and hide industry. Cattle are dropping 90,000 skins a week in Chicago, and the trade is confined to Chicago, St. Louis, Kansas City, Omaha, and St. Paul. It is idle to suppose that those skins will be sent across the Alleghanies to be turned into goods and sent back again. Wisconsin has become the great tanning state, and all over the district close around Chicago are factories and factory towns, where hides are turned into leather goods. The west still gets its finer goods in the east, but it is making the coarser grades, and to such an extent as to give a touch of New England color to the towns and villages around Chicago.

"Chicago has in abundance all the fuels except hard coal. She has coal, oil, stones, brick—everything that is needed for building and for living. Manufactures gravitate to such a place for economical reasons. The population of the North Atlantic division, including Pennsylvania and Massachusetts, and acknowledging New York as its center, is 17,401,000. The population of the northern central division, trading with Chicago, is 22,362,279. Every one has seen each succeeding census shift the center of population farther and farther west, but not every one is habituated to putting two and two together.

"Chicago is distinctly American. I know that the Chicagoans boast that theirs is the most mixed population in

Cottage Grove Avenue, near Drexel Boulevard.

the country, but the makers and movers of Chicago are Americans. * * * The dominating class is of that pure and broad American type which is not controlled by New England or any other tenets, but is somewhat loosely made up of the overflow of the New England, the Middle and the Southern states.

"But the visitor's heart warms to the town when he sees its parks and its homes. In them is ample assurance that not every breath is 'business,' and not every thought commercial. Once out of the thicket of the business and semi-business district, the dwellings of the people reach mile upon mile away along pleasant boulevards and avenues, or facing noble parks and parkways, or in a succession of villages green and gay with foliage and flowers. They are not cliff dwellings, like our flats and tenements; there are no brown-stone canons, like our up-town streets; there are only occasional hesitating hints there of those Philadelphian and Baltimorean mills that grind out dwellings all alike, as nature makes pease and man makes pins. There are more miles of detached villas in Chicago than a stranger can easily account for. As they are not only found on Prairie avenue and the boulevards, but in the populous wards and semi-suburbs, where the middle folk are congregated, it is evident that the prosperous moiety of the population enjoys living better (or better living) than the same fraction in the Atlantic cities.

* * * * *

"A peculiarity of the buildings of Chicago is in the great variety of building-stones that are employed in their construction. Where we would build two blocks of brown-stone, I have counted thirteen varieties of beautiful and different building material. Moreover, the contrasts in architectural design evidence among Chicago house owners a complete sway of individual taste. It is said, and I have no reason to doubt it, that the clerks and small tradesmen, who live in thousands of these pretty little

Residences on Michigan Avenue.

boxes, are the owners of their homes; also that the tenements of the rich display evidence of a tasteful and costly garnering of the globe for articles of luxury and virtu. A sneering critic, who wounded Chicago deeply, intimated that theirs must be a primitive society where the rich sit on their door-steps of an evening. That really is a habit there, and in the finer districts of all the western cities. To enjoy themselves the more completely, the people bring out rugs and carpets, always of gay colors, and fling them on the steps that the ladies' dresses may not be soiled. As these step clothings are as bright as the maiden's eyes and as gay as their cheeks, the effect may be imagined. For my part, I think it argues well for any society that indulges in the trick, and proves existence in such a city to be more human and hearty, and far less artificial than where there is too much false pride to permit of it.

* * * * *

"It is in Chicago that we find a great number of what are called boulevarded streets, at the intersections of which are signs bearing such admonitions as these: 'For pleasure driving. No traffic wagons allowed;' or, 'Traffic teams are not allowed on this boulevard.' Any street in the residence parts of the city may be boulevarded and turned over to the care of the park commissioners of the district, provided that it does not lie next to any other such street, and provided that a certain proportion of the property-holders along it are minded to follow a simple formula to procure the improvement. Improved road-beds are given to such streets, and they not only become neat and pretty, but enhance the value of all neighboring land. One boulevard in Chicago penetrates to the very heart of its bustling business district. By means of it men and women may drive from the southern suburbs or parks to the center of trade, perhaps to their office doors, under the most pleasant conditions. By means of the lesser beautified avenues among the dwellings, men and women may

Grand Boulevard.

sleep of nights and hide from the worst of the city's tumult among green lawns and flower beds.

"Chicago's park system is so truly her crown, or its diadem, that its fame may lead to the thought that enough has been said about it. That is not the case, however, for the parks change and improve so constantly that the average Chicagoan finds some of them outgrowing his knowledge, unless he goes to them as he ought to go to his prayers. It is not in extent that the city's parks are extraordinary, for, all told, they comprise less than two thousand acres. It is the energy that has given rise to them, and the taste and enthusiasm which have been expended upon them, that cause our wonder. Sand and swamp were at the bottom of them, and if their surfaces now roll in gentle undulations, it is because the earth that was dug out for the making of ponds has been subsequently applied to the forming of hills and knolls. The people go to some of them upon the boulevards of which I have spoken, beneath trees and beside lawns and gorgeous flower beds, having their senses sharpened in anticipation of the pleasure-grounds beyond, as the heralds in some old plays prepare us for the action that is to follow. Once the parks are reached, they are found to be literally for the use of the people who own them. I have a fancy that a people who are so largely American would not suffer them to be otherwise. There are no signs warning the public off the grass, or announcing that they 'may look, but mustn't touch,' whatever there is to see. The people swarm all over the grass, and yet it continues beautiful day after day and year after year. The floral displays seem unharmed; at any rate, we have none to compare with them in any Atlantic coast parks. The people even picnic on the sward, and those who can appreciate such license find, ready at hand, baskets in which to hide the litter which follows. And, O ye who manage other parks we wot of, know that these Chicago play-grounds seem as free from harm and eyesore as any in the land.

Boathouse in Lincoln Park.

"The best parks face the great lake, and get wondrous charms of dignity and beauty from it. At the North Side the Lincoln Park commissioners, at great expense, are building out into the lake, making a handsome paved beach, sea-wall, esplanade, and drive to enclose a long, broad body of the lake water. Although the great blue lake is at the city's edge, there is little or no sailing or pleasure-boating upon it. It is too rude and treacherous. Therefore these commissioners of the Lincoln Park are enclosing, behind their new-made land, a water-course for sailing and rowing, for racing, and for more indolent aquatic sport. The Lake Shore Drive, when completed, will be three miles in length, and will connect with yet another notable road to Fort Sheridan, twenty-five miles in length. All these beauties form part of the main exhibit at the Columbian Exposition. Realizing this, the municipality has not only voted five millions of dollars to the Exposition, but has set apart \$3,500,000 for beautifying and improving the city in readiness for the Exposition and its visitors, even as a bride bedecketh herself for her husband. That is well: but it is not her beauty that will most interest the visitors to Chicago. * * * *

"Whatever these visitors have heard or thought of Chicago, they will find it not only an impressive but a substantial city. It will speak to every understanding of the speed with which it is hastening to a place among the world's capitals. Those strangers who travel farther in our west may find other towns that have built too much upon the false prospects of districts where the crops have proved uncertain. They may see still other showy cities, where the main activity is in the direction of "swapping" real estate. It is a peculiar industry, accompanied by much bustle and lying. But they will not find in Chicago anything that will disturb its tendency to impress them with a solidity and a degree of enterprise and prosperity that are only excelled by the almost idolatrous faith of the people in their community. The city's broad and regular thoroughfares will astonish many of us who have imbibed the theory that streets are first mapped out by cows; its alley system between streets will win the admiration of those who live where alleys are unknown; its many little homes will speak volumes for the responsibility and self-respect of a great body of its citizens.

"The discovery that the city's harbor is made up of forty-one miles of the banks of an internal river will lead to the satisfactory knowledge that it has preserved its beautiful front upon Lake Michigan as an ornament. This has been bordered by park and parkways in pursuance of a plan that is interrupted to an important extent only where a pioneer railway came without the foreknowledge that it would eventually develop into a nuisance and an eyesore. Its splendid hotels, theatres, schools, churches, galleries and public works and ornaments will commend the city to many who will not study its commercial side. In short, it will be found that those who visit the exposition will not afterward reflect upon its assembled proofs of the triumphs of man and of civilization without recalling Chicago's contribution to the sum."

Libraries, Educational and Charitable Institutions.

It has been too generally the custom to regard Chicago exclusively in the light of its industrial activity, to note its commerce and manufactures without considering its humanitarian endeavors. Yet the latter by no means fall short of the city's achievements in purely material lines. When money getting is mentioned as a Chicago characteristic, liberality should be given as an equally prominent one. Aside from the great public charitable institutions of the city and county, there are almost countless hospitals, homes, asylums and missions supported wholly by private charity. To individual munificence also, are due Chicago's higher educational institutions, the great libraries, the Art Institute, and especially the new University of Chicago. In no city of the world are greater public spirit and private beneficence displayed than in restless Chicago. The number of these institutions makes it advisable to mention only the most prominent. First of all, from an educational standpoint, is the great University of Chicago, which received its first students in October, 1892. Its campus and buildings are on Midway Plaisance, its equipment complete and its endowment ample—$3,600,000 having been contributed to it by John D. Rockefeller alone.

All of the prominent colleges of America contributed to its faculty, and several of its professors came from Europe—among them being the distinguished German historian, Von Holst, of Freiburg. The dormitory system is used at the university, and the dormitories, already erected, will accommodate 2,000 students. The college fees and the actual living expenses of the students are remarkably small for so large an institution, and, in addition, scholarships are provided for deserving students. The university is co-educational, and a part of its faculty is engaged exclusively in the work of "university extension." The Northwestern University, with its college of liberal arts and theological and preparatory departments located in Evanston, a suburb of Chicago, has its professional schools in the heart of the city. The same is true also of Lake Forest University.

The Newberry Library, on the North Side, facing Washington Square, came to the city as the result of a clause in the will of Walter L. Newberry, which provided that if his two daughters should die without legal issue, then on the death of his wife his executors should divide one-half of his fortune among his brothers and sisters and their children, and should devote the other half to the foundation and support of a free public library. Both the Misses Newberry died without marrying, and on the settlement of the estate in 1886, $2,149,201 was turned over to the proper trustees for library purposes. This sum has increased to over three million dollars in the hands of the trustees, and the library building, erected at a cost of half a million dollars, is ready for occupancy. The building, which is 300 feet long and 60 feet deep, is a model of convenience, beauty and safety, and so designed that other buildings can be added to it from time to time as they may be found necessary. Dr. Wm. F. Poole, formerly of the Chicago Public Library, was made librarian of the new institution, and, with his assistant, Dr. Carl Pietsch, immediately began the purchase of books. An early and very valuable acquisition was that of the celebrated Probasco Library, in Cincinnati. The library now contains 107,157 bound volumes and 39,501 pamphlets. The great difference between the Newberry and the Chicago Public Library is that the former will contain fewer works of fiction and that none of its volumes can be taken from the library building. There will be, of course, many books written purely for amusement, but the specialty will be reference works for students and experts, rare volumes and costly editions. A recent accession to the library was the Robert Clarke collection on fish, fish-culture and fish-sport. This collection numbered 1453 bound volumes and 429 pamphlets. Many of the volumes are exceedingly rare and the bindings rich and elegant. Some of the accessions during the year 1892 are those on antiquities and folk-lore, 1063 volumes; on music, 7776 volumes; on language, 11,527 volumes; on medicine, 3081 volumes, and 324 dictionaries of various languages. Among the most valuable of the smaller accessions to the library are the "Basilica di San Marco," "Biblia Latina Argentorati," a four volume edition of the Scriptures published in 1480, and the first printed bible to have a commentary; a complete set of the "Astronomische Nachrichten," 135 volumes, running from 1823 to 1892, and two remarkably sumptuous and artistic volumes on the life of Christopher Columbus, printed in Barcelona in 1892. In the public reading room 338 of the best periodicals of the world can be found.

A third public library for Chicago was provided for by the will of the late John Crerar, who, after making bequests to the extent of $500,000 to various public and private charities, gave the remainder of his estate for "the erection, creation, maintenance and endowment of a free public library, to be called 'The John Crerar Library,' and to be located in the city of Chicago, the preference being given to the South Division of the city." This gift, now under the trusteeship of Huntington W. Jackson, will probably amount to $2,000,000. The Chicago Law Library, the establishment of which was due chiefly to the efforts of Julius Rosenthal, is the most valuable technical library in the city, and consists of 20,000 volumes.

The Chicago Historical Society, another of the humanizing institutions of the city, was founded in 1856, and at the time of the fire had a valuable collection of 20,000 volumes, numerous manuscripts, complete files of the local newspapers, the

original draft of the emancipation proclamation, and other treasures of Chicago's early days. All were destroyed, however, by the great fire, and a subsequent collection was destroyed by the second Chicago fire, in 1874. The society's endowment, however, was not lost, and under Judge John Moses, its curator, a new collection has been made, and the society is in flourishing condition. It will soon occupy the splendid building now (April, 1893) being erected for it.

A typical Chicago institution is the Armour Mission. It was established in November, 1886, and owes its origin to a provision in the will of Joseph F. Armour, bequeathing $100,000 for the founding of a free non-sectarian institution, which would provide the poor with such advantages as are to be derived from a day nursery, kindergarten, reading room, dispensary, bath-rooms, manual training school, Sunday school and lecture course. The work of carrying out his design Mr. Armour left to his brother, Philip, and that gentleman has added to the original endowment more than a million dollars from his own fortune. The mission building, on Thirty-third street and Armour avenue, is a handsome structure, and besides a creche, kindergarten room, library, kitchen, dispensary, bath-rooms and administration rooms, contains a main audience hall for social and literary purposes, that will hold an audience of 1300 persons. The Armour Institute, established in connection with the mission, was founded for the purpose of giving to young men and women the opportunity of securing a liberal education. It is not intended for the poor or the rich, as sections of society, but for all who are seeking practical education. Its aim is broadly philanthropic. The founder has conditioned his benefactions in such a way as to emphasize both their value and the student's self-respect. Armour Institute is not a free school, but its charges for instruction are merely nominal.

The Chicago Athenaeum, founded in 1871, is another institution devoted to the cultivation of body and mind. It has a

large library, pleasant reading-rooms, a well-equipped gymnasium and eight class rooms, where over a thousand pupils are taught daily. It is not a charity institution, but each beneficiary pays at least some part of the cost of the instruction and privileges given him. The Athenaeum building on Van Buren street, near Wabash avenue, is among the fine office buildings of Chicago.

Like every great city, Chicago has numerous hospitals, homes and charitable societies, dependent either on private munificence or supported by one or more of the many churches of the city; two only of these institutions are so peculiar to Chicago as to merit special mention: the Lincoln Park Sanitarium and the Flower Mission. The Lincoln Park Sanitarium is the outgrowth of a project originating in 1883, with Mrs Eleanore Shoneman. It is open only in summer, and is intended for infants and little children who are suffering from the numerous ailments incident to babyhood in warm weather. The sanitarium is in Lincoln Park, directly at the edge of Lake Michigan. Little ones are taken to it during the summer, and, aside from the fresh air and cool breezes from the lake, are given, gratis, the best medical attendance and proper nursing and food. The sanitarium is supported by individual contributions, collected and disbursed by a local paper. The Flower Mission has branches in every quarter of the city. Its members, women and girls, who give their services, collect flowers from the city parks and from country donors, and distribute them in the hospitals and among the poor and unfortunate of the city in general. Of all Chicago's charities, none is more gracious and kindly than the Flower Mission.

The Chicago Press.

The newspapers of Chicago, typical as they are of its push, energy and liberality, have been powerful factors in the development of the city. Their fearless criticisms and able and intelligent handling of the news, places them in the front rank of the journals of America, which means of the world. Without resorting to catch-penny methods, sensationalism or malignity, the typical Chicago paper of to-day is progressive and enterprising, and is unrivaled as a news collector. The influence of the Chicago press is not merely local, but extends over the whole northwest. As regards general appearance, typographical excellence and quality and quantity of newspaper illustrations, the Chicago press, as a class, is without equal. The average weekly cost of a great Chicago daily is $20,000, or $1,000,000 a year, and the daily telegraph tolls average $500.

The oldest of the morning papers is the Chicago Tribune, and its editor and proprietor, Joseph Medill, is the Nestor of Chicago journalism and the most reputably successful newspaper man on record. Mr. Medill belongs to the old school of journalists, like Thurlow Weed, Horace Greeley, Wilbur F. Storey and Charles A. Dana. He dominates his paper. His personal principles, not his counting-room, determine its policy. Thus, at the time the order of know-nothings was most powerful and influential, Mr. Medill violently and tirelessly opposed it. He pointed out the evils that would arise from checking immigration and to fight the new order on its own ground, established the "know-something order." This, in its time, did great service in protecting and encouraging immigration, and thus materially assisted in the development of the west in general and Chicago in particular.

The brightest newspaper men of the west have been, at various times, associated with the Tribune. Ex-Lieutenant-Governor Bross, Horace White, now of the New York Evening Post, Dr. Charles H. Ray and James W. Sheahan, George P. Upton, R. W. Patterson and Fred. H. Hall, have all served on its staff. Mr. Sheahan was at one time part owner of the Chicago Times, and wrote a "Life of Stephen A. Douglas," and various pamphlets and works of smaller scope. George P. Upton, art critic and litterateur, at present the senior editorial writer on the Tribune, is well known for his translations from the German—especially for his translation of Max Mueller's "Story of German Love"—for his art and literary criticisms and his connection with the various musical societies of the city. The Tribune has always been the leading organ of the Republican party in the northwest.

The Chicago Times, a Democratic organ, owed the period of its greatest prosperity, as well as of ill-fame, to Wilbur F. Storey, who concentrated in himself all that is characteristically good and bad in the modern American newspaper. He was as unscrupulous as fearless, as debauched as brilliant, as sensational as intelligent. Belying his venerable and respectable appearance, he was a journalistic Robespierre, guillotining the reputation of the decent by thousands. Feared, though despised, patronized and pandered to even by those he attacked, his death—the signal for rejoicing among all classes but the criminal—brought to an end a life certainly remarkable for brilliancy, audacity and intelligence, but misspent, inglorious, vicious. Mr. Storey opposed the war, not from principle, but for sensationalism, and his personal abuse of Lincoln and his attacks on Union soldiers so incensed the people that they broke into the Time's office, and the paper was suppressed for two editions. The worst feature of Mr. Storey's paper was the mingling of the good and the bad. Thus, while he prostituted the moral taste of the city and attacked the private lives of men who stood above

Lincoln Monument in Lincoln Park.

reproach, he also attacked various public abuses, and above all—printed the news. He gathered around him a staff of exceptional ability, including such men as Frank B. Wilkie, Andre Matteson, Alexander Botkin, Charles R. Dennet, Martin J. Russell and Horatio W. Seymour. Mr. Wilkie wrote "Sketches Beyond the Sea," and one or two other books, and made numerous translations from the French. Martin J. Russell, the present editor-in-chief of the Times, is remarkable for his terse, epigrammatical style. After the death of Mr. Storey, in 1884, the Times, theretofore highly successful, entered on its period of adversity. In November, 1891, Carter H. Harrison, the World's Fair mayor of Chicago, bought the paper, and since that time it has regained much of its lost prestige.

The Chicago Inter Ocean was founded in 1872 as a strictly Republican paper, and has always been a pronounced party organ. Financially, the paper was never remarkably prosperous until within the last three years, H. H. Kohlsaat, a successful business man, bought the controlling interest in it. Mr. Kohlsaat furnished the necessary capital to push the paper, and has made it one of the leading journals not only of the city but of the northwest. The editor-in-chief is William Penn Nixon, one of the best known of Chicago newspaper men and continuously identified with the Inter Ocean since its organization. One of the special features of the paper has been its dramatic department, under Elwyn A. Barron, a critic of intelligence and the author of several successful plays.

The Chicago Herald has achieved the most remarkable success of any of the recently-founded American newspapers. Its first number appeared in May, 1881, and for a time the paper was Republican. It is now, however, independently Democratic. At first the Herald did not prosper, but in 1883 John R. Walsh, James W. Scott and Martin J. Russell gained control of it. Since that time it has enjoyed unexampled prosperity, due in no small degree to the shrewd and at the same time liberal business policy pursued by James W. Scott, who has been its publisher since Mr. Walsh bought the controlling interest in the paper, and with his large fortune put it on a sound financial basis. The managing editor of the Herald is Horatio W. Seymour, one of the ablest writers connected with the Times under Storey. The Herald staff is very large, and its corps of special writers the brightest in the west.

The Chicago Evening Journal was established in 1844, and during its long career has been always prosperous. Andrew Shuman was its first editor, and was assisted by George P. Upton and Benjamin F. Taylor, the poet. Mr. Shuman continued to edit the paper until his death, in 1890. Aside from his newspaper work he held various public offices, among others that of Lieutenant-Governor of the state. John R. Wilson is the publisher of the Journal and Slason Thompson the present editor-in-chief. Mr. Thompson is one of Chicago's cleverest newspaper men, and, since getting control of the Journal, has, without changing its policy of respectability and reliability, infused into it something of his own intense energy and virility. Slason Thompson, and Martin J. Russell are the two most vigorous and forceful editorial writers of the city.

In 1875, the Chicago Daily News was founded as a one-cent, independent evening paper. For a time the new departure led a precarious existence, but in 1877 the enterprise of its controlling spirit, Melville E. Stone, put it on a sound basis, and its success has been so great that, from a purely commercial standpoint, it is probably one of the most profitable newspaper properties in the world. Mr. Stone was a practical newspaper man, and gave his personal attention to the editing of the paper. In 1876, Victor F. Lawson purchased a half interest in the News, assumed the business management, and, like Mr. Stone, proved remarkably successful in his line of work. In March, 1881, the News published a morning edition, which at first, although the most enterprising of all Chicago papers, and remarkably clever as a newspaper, was not financially successful. After Mr. Stone sold his interest in the paper to Mr. Lawson, the latter gentleman put the price of the paper down to one cent, cultivated a large out-of-town circulation, and, with Dr. F. W. Reilly as managing editor, put the morning edition on a paying basis. In 1892 he changed the name of the morning edition to the Morning News Record, and recently—to sharply distinguish it from the evening edition, with which it has no real connection—again changed it, this time to the Chicago Record. Under Mr. Stone's management, the Morning News, independent in politics, was a powerful factor in various local reforms. Perhaps the most enduring, and, as far as the public at large is concerned, profitable piece of work ever undertaken by the News, was when, under Dr. Reilly, it proposed and championed the drainage channel, which is at present being constructed. Mr. Stone was as prodigal of his money as of his own energy. He gathered about him a staff of exceptional ability—such men as Joseph K. C. Forrest, one of Chicago's oldest and brightest newspaper men; John Flynn, John F. Ballantyne, Slason Thompson, Eugene Field, Robert B. Peattie and Van Buren Denslow.

The Chicago Evening Post is one of the cleverest of the afternoon papers. It is independent, bright and newsy. Like the Herald, it is published by James W. Scott, while much of its success, from a newspaper standpoint, is due to the ability of its managing editor, Cornelius McAuliff.

The Chicago Mail is a one-cent evening paper. It gained considerable popularity under Joseph R. Dunlop, one of the best known of the Storey graduates of the Times, and one of the shrewdest of Chicago newspaper men. When Mr. Dunlop founded, recently, the Chicago Dispatch, Mr. Charles Almy was made managing editor of the Mail. The Dispatch is the last daily to appear in Chicago. Its publisher, Mr. Dunlop, has had sufficient experience in the business to warrant the prediction that it will achieve as great success as the other papers with which he has been connected.

Among the early Chicago newspaper men was Charles A. Dana, of the New York Sun, managing editor of the one-time Chicago Republican. The paper was backed by ample capital, was a handsome and attractive sheet, and had the best possible editorial ability, and still was a failure. Mr. Dana has never forgiven Chicago for not appreciating him, and the malignant but impotent attacks of his New York papers are undoubtedly due to this fact. Chicago reporters are among the brightest in the country, and scores of the best New York men received their training in Chicago.

In the difficult task of digesting and assimilating into the body politic the large numbers of non-English speaking immigrants who come to America, the "foreign" papers have rendered most efficient aid. The fact that they are published in a foreign tongue does not prevent them from handling the news substantially as do the papers printed in English, and in general, these foreign papers are animated by the same principles and follow the same general ideas as their English contemporaries. In this way they educate foreign immigrants to American modes of thought and life, and instruct them in the laws of the land and their duties as citizens, even before the newcomers master the English tongue. In this regard the German press deserves especial mention, and the best German dailies compare not unfavorably with papers of the same class printed in English.

In 1846 Chicago's first German paper, Der Volksfreund, was founded by a New York compositor named Hoeffgen. It was a weekly, and Mr. Hoeffgen wrote it exclusively with the shears. He did his own type-setting, printing and delivery of papers, and, despite his intense interest in his paper, it was not enthusiasm alone that prompted him to sleep on and under the "exchanges." Francis A. Hoffman, later Lieutenant-Governor of the state, at one time contributed to the Volksfreund, and his editorials exerted a marked influence upon the Germans. After a two years' struggle the paper died, but Hoeffgen at once founded, in connection with Dr. Helmuth, the Illinois Staats-Zeitung. Dr. Helmuth was a young physician just arrived from Germany, and, after a year, found his time so taken up with his practice that he resigned the managing editorship of the paper in favor of Col. Arno Voss. Helmuth did not entirely sever his connection with the Staats-Zeitung, however, and until 1852 wrote occasionally for it. Since then he has devoted himself exclusively to his profession. Up to this time the Staats-Zeitung had been a weekly, but now George Schneider came from St. Louis, assumed editorial charge of the paper and made it a daily. It was at once successful, and Schneider won a great reputation. He had been a revolutionist, and was condemned to death in Germany. During the stormy days preceding the war he took an active part in public affairs, and was a persistent and implacable foe to slavery. He gathered an excellent staff and the paper became the leading German organ of the northwest. At the close of the war, Mr. Schneider was sent to Denmark on a diplomatic mission, and, since his return, has been chiefly engaged in commercial life, being at present the president of the National Bank of Illinois. When Schneider went abroad, Lorenz Brentano purchased the paper, and afterwards sold a half interest to A. C. Hesing. Brentano was dictator of Baden during the German revolution, and had been a prominent statesman and jurist in Germany. In America he identified himself with German-American interests, and before and during the rebellion was a staunch supporter of the Republican party. In 1867 he sold his interest in the Staats-Zeitung to A. C. Hesing and went to Europe, where, owing to his influence with the European press, his knowledge of international law and his ability

Grant Monument in Lincoln Park.

as a jurist, he was able to create a favorable public opinion as to the rights of the United States in the Alabama claims. In recognition of his services, President Grant appointed him as consul to Dresden, in 1872, and in 1876, on his return to the United States, he was elected to Congress. He died in Chicago in 1891.

When he gained control of the Staats-Zeitung, A. C. Hesing exerted considerable influence in practical politics. He still owns a controlling interest in the paper, but pays little attention to its management. In 1866, Mr. Hesing brought Hermann Raster from New York, and made him managing editor. With him was associated Wilhelm Rapp, who, on Raster's death, in 1891, assumed full charge of the paper.

Hermann Raster was one of the foremost journalists of the country, and was a recognized power in political circles. He was a highly educated man, and, like many other of the prominent Germans of the past forty years, was a 48'er. Soon after his arrival in America he did such brilliant work on the New York press as to win an international reputation. He was active in the founding of the Republican party, and during the war created a European sentiment in its favor by his correspondence. His articles in the German press assisted the government in disposing of many of its bonds in Germany. The Staats-Zeitung achieved its greatest success under his editorship—his articles being copied by the German press of the whole country. In 1872 he was internal revenue collector, but later resigned to be able, more consistently, to advocate Grant's re-nomination. Raster was a member of the board of education, and held other offices of trust and honor, although he accomplished his greatest good as a journalist. He died in Germany, but was buried in America, being honored by one of the largest public funerals ever held in Chicago. William Vocke was formerly city editor of the Staats-Zeitung, but later resigned to practice law. He has written a popular work on American jurisprudence, has translated considerable classic poetry from German into English, and is a well-known leader of German thought in Chicago.

The Chicago Telegraph and the Union, General Lieb's paper, were two German ventures that proved unsuccessful.

In 1871, the Freie Presse was founded as an illustrated weekly, but later was published as a daily. Like the world, it was created out of nothing, but the latter creation was slow and tedious. Richard Michaelis was the editor and publisher, and was greatly assisted by his wife, a lady of considerable literary ability. Gradually, however, all difficulties were overcome, the paper became financially independent and prosperous, and very influential. It has five editions, two daily, two weekly and one Sunday. It is distinguished for its bitter fights against anarchy and all violent and radical labor movements. Aside from his reputation as editor of the Freie Presse, Mr. Michaelis gained considerable renown by his "Looking Further Forward," a reply to Edward Bellamy's "Looking Backward." Michaelis' book has been translated into various foreign languages, and has received excellent criticisms in all political science circles.

In 1889, Fritz Glogauer established the Abendpost, a popular independent evening paper, which from the first met with the most extraordinary financial success.

The Tageblatt is a more recent addition to the German press of the city, and is designed especially as the organ of the German Lutherans.

The National Zeitung led a brief but, from a literary standpoint, a glorious career. It was an exceptionally brilliant journal, but lacked subscribers and advertising patronage, and was forced to go under. Joseph Brucker was the publisher, and Paul Haedicke the managing editor. He was assisted by Dr. Edmund Markbreiter and Miss Dorothea Boettcher, a German writer of note in both prose and verse. When Mr Brucker retired from the paper and it ceased to appear as a daily, all was not lost, for it continued to appear as a weekly, and bids fair to become a success. Another German weekly of importance is the Rundschau.

Two well-known German writers, who occasionally contributed to the press, were Caspar Butz and Emil Dietzsch. Butz was a poet of real genius, helped to unify, by his writings, the German sentiment against slavery, and gained a reputation not only in America, but also in Europe. His poems have been printed in book form.

Emil Dietzsch was among the German pioneers of '48, and came to Chicago in 1853. He was a man of culture, a fine poet, a prolific writer on social and political topics, and an orator who could—and did—speak on all occasions with the greatest felicity. He was highly esteemed by his countrymen, over whom he exerted the greatest influence.

Of the Scandinavian papers, the most important is the Skandinaven, published by John Anderson. It has a daily and weekly edition, and not only goes to every state in the Union and to Canada, but also to Denmark, Sweden, Norway, Australia and the Sandwich Islands. The paper is well-edited, newsy and highly successful.

There are numerous other foreign papers published in Chicago, in Italian, Swedish, Polish, Bohemian, French and other languages, and all are doing a good work in teaching the newcomers something about American ideas, and the duties of American citizenship. In addition to the general press, Chicago has journals published in the interest of almost every large trade and industry.

Germans and German Influence in Chicago.

There is no other American city that has so large a German element as Chicago. The Germans are far stronger, numerically, than any other nationality in the city, but neither their political influence nor their social achievements are in proportion to this numerical strength. This is due to the peculiar individualism of the Germans—to their lack of harmony among themselves and their frequent inability to co-operate with each other in large enterprises. This national characteristic is being overcome, in a measure, by Germans both abroad and at home. Especially noticeable has been the reaction since 1870, when the unification of the German nation became the forerunner of unity among all Germans in both sentiment and interest. It is slow work, however, to change the habits of centuries, and the German element in Chicago is still suffering from the differences and dissensions of the past. None more keenly appreciate this fact than the Germans themselves, and they recognized their failing even before the reaction set in. It was in 1871 that Eduard Schlaeger, then editorial writer on the Staats-Zeitung, sharply criticized German customs in America. Mr. Schlaeger was a close student, and in his general characterization was correct, when, as the result of his twenty years' experience among the Germans of Chicago, he said: "The history of the development of the German-Americans can be divided into three periods ; or, better stated, perhaps, can be regarded from three main points of view. At first the German immigrants regard themselves as a German colony, as missionaries, as modern Greeks—the salt of the earth. America seems to them a very barbarous and unpleasant

country, as a colorless present, to escape from which—as soon as the necessary number of the almighty dollar can be procured—must be the first and highest aim of every sensible person. Until this end is attained they seek, as far as possible, to reproduce Germany in America, and the more exclusive and reserved they are in their conduct toward Americans, the more does everything go 'gerade wie in Deutschland' (just as in Germany). This reproduction of Germany has, of course, very different stages according to the education of each individual German 'missionary.' In little places in which the German element is represented by the simple, not to say simpletons the German colony confines itself to spending evenings and Sunday afternoons in some modest tavern over the foaming barley juice, to mocking the hypocritical Yankees, with their eyes turned heavenward and their thoughts otherward, and finally to singing some sentimental song of the fatherland. Where the Germans are more numerous and better educated they go a few steps further, build theatres, music halls, organize turning and singing societies, and regard these achievements as great deeds, entitling them to have their names entered in the book of history—especially the history of culture—in red ink. The highest performances in this line are the great saengerfests and productions of German opera by members of these singing societies. It is impossible to accurately set the time limits to this first period of the German colonists; each new relay goes through the same process of development and is fooled by the same delusions as its predecessors, which, meanwhile, have entered the second period—that of indifference to specific German endeavors and of approach to American methods. Of these, to be sure, the colonist learns only the disagreeable ones, the greed for gold and the business shrewdness, unrelieved by the other American traits—liberality, public spirit and interest in the affairs of the city, state and nation. * * *
These indifferent mules, who are neither donkeys nor horses,

The Humboldt Monument.

neither Americans nor Germans, offend the ear of the educated with their miserable English, and soon forget the magnificent German language and murder it as badly as they do English. Sometimes, however, these fellows of the second period fall back into the first period, when the number of their countrymen is so great as to bring some big political office into reach. Once elected, however, the 'professional Germans' immediately kick over the German ladder on which they have climbed into prominence.

"It is harder to trace the beginnings of the third period of the development of the German-American—when he is assimilated into American civic life, to which he contributes the desirable and adaptable characteristics of his nationality. Gradually, however, from the level mass of Germans some individuals spring forth into prominence, and each year more follow. Certain businesses fall entirely into the hands of these leaders—especially is this true of the wine and tobacco trade and of the handling of porcelain. In manufactures and the arts the Germans take a prominent place, and all the best gold and silver work is done in German work-shops. Of course it goes without saying that the Germans are at the head of the beer industry."

When this characterization of the Germans was written it was more or less true, but times have happily changed. In strong contrast with Mr. Schlaeger's pessimism the following optimistic quotation may be made from a biographical essay written by Emil Dietzsch: "It will be my especial contention," he wrote, "that it is the German element which has chiefly assisted the native Americans in the incomparably rapid development of the city, for although the Americans must, as a rule, be characterized as liberal and magnanimous, it is still, unfortunately, true that they are very loath to make the well-deserved public recognition of the services which the immigrants (and, most of all, their blood relations,

Distant View of the Schiller Monument in Lincoln Park.

the German immigrants) have everywhere rendered throughout the land. On this account the author feels especially called upon to assert that the labor of the actual erection of the miles of magnificent houses of our young metropolis on the shores of Lake Michigan, was, for the most part, performed by Germans. And this is true in spite of the fact that the number of the Germans has never exceeded one-third of the total population of the city.

"Yea, where the sparks fly and the bellows blow, where the hammer beats, and the anvil rings, where the dust falls from file and saw and the chips from chisel and plane, where carpenters and masons toil and sweat, in north, east, south and west of this great and glorious land, there for the most part is it the dextrous hand of the German which builds and shapes and makes real the great thoughts of the engineer and architect.

"And when far from out the thick, primeval forest, over the nodding heads of the wheat fields and through the climbing vines of the vineyard floats a joyous, touching melody, the listening wayfarer knows it is from the lips of a German, for with German hearts ever wander, over land and sea, music and German song. And the listener's heart rejoices and an inner voice whispers very gently to him: 'O, son of the Fatherland, what a precious factor thou hast become in the great folk-conglomerate of this nation! Thy reliability, thy sense of justice, thy industry and earnestness in home life and public life have made thee the kernel people of all the peoples of this republic, and in future time the fully developed American nation will itself have unmistakable characteristics, customs and methods of thought as witness of thy potent influence.'"

It is certainly due to the idealistic and philosophic influence of the Germans that life on this continent—and to a remarkable degree in cosmopolitan Chicago—has been relieved of its wearying monotony, its toil and burdens. In marked contrast

Entrance to the La Salle Street Tunnel.

to the Puritan, who tries to force everyone to be happy according to his own stern and sober notions, is the German with his light-hearted philosophy, strong love for music and art, and hearty enjoyment of the rational pleasures of life. The Germans aim at the broader development of man, and take life more easily and poetically, not allowing themselves to be totally absorbed in daily toils and money-getting. It were a mistake, however, to suppose that German influence upon the American people is due entirely to the Germans in America. It is from the great centers of German learning and culture that much of this influence comes, from German universities, music and art schools—from German prose, and German poetry. Thus, as has already been pointed out, in spite of many and manifold stimulating elements, and their numerical strength, the Germans in Chicago have not, as such, been able to exert due influence, either in the line of culture or politics. The inability to subordinate petty personal interests to great ends; that constant squabbling about personal rights, which the Americans call "Dutch quarrels," still stand in the way of full and free German-American progress. There are, however, many mitigating circumstances. Not all those who come from the other side appear in real life as they are depicted by Fourth of July orators or stump-speakers shortly before election. Not all of them are men, who, animated by a glowing impulse for freedom, have come here to escape the tyranny of bloody despots at home, and to develop, unhindered, their moral ideals in this land of freedom. Whoever has seen the steerage of an ocean steamer, knows this. Not the thirst for freedom, but the hunger for bread, brings most to America. Only the few come from intellectual or moral reasons; the many are moved by urgent necessity of a purely material nature.

The girl who has been working in almost slavish dependence, for a miserable pittance, hears from some friend in America of the great servant girl paradise across the seas;

the younger son of some petty farmer who has given his little all to his oldest boy on condition that he be cared for in his declining years, prefers going to America than serving his brother at home; the rural tradesman, a vegetarian against his will, who has heard that in America people have meat three times a day; the strong, vigorous day laborer, made stupid by too much work; the mill-hand grown stolid with more than his share of the burdens of life; the father of a big family who, on the evening of his life, tears himself from the dear old home, and with a heavy heart, transplants himself into foreign soil—solely for the sake of his children; the walking delegate, who, tired of working with his hands, wants to give his mouth a chance; the fellow who can't get along harmoniously with the state's attorney; the unappreciated genius who has striven in vain for recognition; the spendthrift fleeing from his creditors—all these are typical figures among immigrants, come they from Germany or elsewhere. And first of all, these people have to provide for their bodily wants—to earn bread. Only after they have lived in America and have laboriously worked out of their poverty, and have begun to read German papers, and gradually German books even, do any considerable number of them become good Germans—that is to say that they first learn to understand and appreciate German culture and German ways —in America. Some of them never get beyond the struggle for daily bread. Others again fail absolutely to comprehend the question of culture, intellectual and artistic endeavor and the feeling of nationality—they know only the "stomach question," and as between a sausage and a symphony, they would jump for the sausage. In addition to all this, even those Germans who are intelligent and in easy circumstances are politically unschooled, and prefer to leave governing to the government, and, much to their own detriment, take only a passive interest in politics, looking upon the doings of the politicians much as circus spectators look upon the performers—quite oblivious to the fact that they are in reality part of the political circus themselves.

All these considerations must be borne in mind in judging Chicago Germans; but despite these handicaps, the Germans will doubtless, in course of time, assume, both in politics and society, a position in accordance with their numerical strength.

In social life they have their own theatres and theatrical entertainments, their clubs, societies and charitable institutions. As a rule they attend their own churches, which are numerous and well supported. Their professional men stand well and their business men are successful. They form a large portion of the small tax-paying class, and, more than any other nationality of the city, the Germans own the homes they live in.

During the war the Germans proved themselves faithful to their new fatherland. As a class they are sound on matters of public policy, have always opposed the inflation of the currency, for instance, and no German paper ever dared, or wished to advocate "fiat" money or free silver coinage. During the last twenty years there has been a constantly recurring agitation as to the advisability of teaching the German language in the public schools. The desire of the Germans to have their language taught publicly is, they claim, often misunderstood. It is by no un-American spirit that the leaders in the movement are animated. They claim that the teaching of one of the great modern languages in the public schools of a cosmopolitan city like Chicago is of the greatest benefit to the children, that far from being a detriment to the teaching of English, the teaching of German is a positive help to it, that the cost of the instruction is insignificant compared to the benefit derived, and that were the teaching of German given up it would result in the removal from the public schools of thousands of children who would be sent to private schools, even though they should fail to there receive the thoroughly American education afforded by the public schools.

Population.

The last school census of the city of Chicago, taken May, 1892, showed a total population of 1,438,010, of which 760,143 were males, and 677,867 females. The present (estimated) annual growth of the city is 100,000 souls, so that with this increase and the thousands gained by annexation within the year, the present population of Chicago is estimated to be 1,618,010 souls.

The last general census (1890) showed a population of 1,208,669, of which there were 645,890 males, and 562,779 females. The different nationalities were represented as follows:

Germans	384,958	Dutch	4,912
Native-born Americans	292,463	Hungarians	4,827
Irish	215,534	Roumanians	4,350
Bohemians	54,209	Welsh	2,966
Poles	52,756	Swiss	2,735
Swedes	45,877	Mongolians	1,217
Norwegians	44,615	Greeks	689
English	33,785	Belgians	682
French	12,963	Spaniards	297
Scotch	11,927	Portuguese	34
Russians	9,977	West-Indians	37
Italians	9,921	Hawaiians	31
Danes	9,891	East-Indians	28
Canadians	6,989		

The third largest element of Chicago's foreign population are the Scandinavians—the Norwegians, Swedes and Danes. Thrifty and prosperous, the Scandinavian citizens of Chicago closely resemble, in general characteristics, their German cousins, and, like them, have their own churches, societies and newspapers. The Norwegians were among the first settlers of the city, and contributed largely to the development of lake navigation. The Bohemians of Chicago now number about 60,000 persons, equally divided between the Slavonic and the Germanic element. Of the 60,000 Poles in the city, most belong to the unskilled laboring classes.

For the last few years, Chicago has received an unusually large per cent of the total number of immigrants coming into the country. But of late, with the desirable immigrants, there has come a very undesirable class, hailing, for the most part, from the Polish provinces of Russia and the south-eastern part of Europe in general. The result of this latter class of immigration is that the people of the west have ceased to regard every increase in population as a necessary index to increased prosperity. They have learned to scrutinize the character of the immigrants and have found that, with the easily assimilated German, Scandinavian and Irish immigrant, come others whom it is almost impossible to assimilate into the body politic. The problem of governing the great American cities is becoming, therefore, alarmingly difficult. Under liberal naturalization laws, these undesirable elements enjoy all the rights and privileges of a citizenship for which they are totally unprepared and unfit. Local politics in Chicago are thus growing more demoralized year by year, and demagogues, who make it a business to organize these un-Americanized masses for selfish ends, are alarmingly prosperous. It is to be regretted that the courts are so notoriously lax in their examination of candidates for citizenship, and fail to make use of such means as are at their command for the exclusion of the vicious, ignorant and unfit applicants. The national laws in regard to pauper and contract-labor immigration would form a barrier to a great part of the undesirable influx from abroad, were they only rigidly and conscientiously enforced. And it is to be hoped that public opinion, already aroused on the question, will soon prove so strong as to force a remedy adequate to the evil.

Chicago River, Showing Clark Street Bridge.

Trade, Commerce and Manufactures.

Chicago is pre-eminently the American city. American enterprise, American methods, and the true American spirit have made it. As the typical city of progress, Chicago eagerly adopts every new invention, utilizes every new method, and encourages every new idea. Nowhere else in the world does life bear so plainly the stamp of progress; nowhere does the struggle for existence so plainly betray the changes brought about by the employment of modern machinery, which, replacing human labor, increases production a hundred-fold, nowhere can one obtain a glimpse into a happier industrial future. Civilization is striving for new forms, new methods, and it is no exaggeration to say, that the great problems with which the present age is struggling are seeking their solution here. The mere wish for it does not make progress, which is always the result of hard work—sometimes made easier, to be sure, by chance and circumstance. Thus, in Chicago, all conditions are favorable for rapid evolution. Modern industry and machinery necessitate a new order of things, and Chicago has more readily adapted itself to this new order than have the older cities of the world. This is one cause of Chicago's success, and also of the fact that so many energetic and progressive elements concentrate here. Another cause is the city's geographical position, lying in the line of all great trans-continental railways, in the centre of a fertile territory of thousands of miles in extent, and at the foot of Lake Michigan, which, connecting with the Atlantic ocean, affords the city a water commerce, equal in tonnage to that of London itself.

10,556 vessels, with an aggregate tonnage of 5,966,626 tons, arrived at the port of Chicago in 1892, and the clearances numbered 10,567 vessels, with a tonnage of 5,968,337 tons, giving a total tonnage of 11,934,963 tons for the year 1892, against 11,031,552 tons in 1891. Chicago's tonnage exceeds that of Liverpool, and also the combined tonnage of San Francisco, Boston and Havre, but does not quite equal that of New York. The most extensively used ship-canal of the world is within the commercial sphere of Chicago, the St. Mary's Fall's canal ("The Soo"). The tonnage carried on the great lakes aggregated 30,299,006 tons, comprising 28,295,959 tons in the United States coast-wise trade, and 2,003,047 tons in the United States foreign trade. The tonnage which passed through the St. Mary's Falls canal aggregated 8,454,435 tons, and that which passed through the Detroit river was 21,684,000 tons—the tonnage which at the same time passed through the Suez canal was 6,890,094 tons.

The number of vessels on the northern lakes June 30, 1891, was 3,600, aggregating a tonnage of 1,061,882 tons. Of these vessels 310 were steamers of more than one thousand net registered tons. The combined fleets of the Atlantic and Gulf coast, the Pacific coast and the western rivers, contained at the same date only 213 steamers of more than one thousand tons register. The aggregate tonnage of these steamers on the northern lakes was 512,787 tons, exceeding the combined tonnage of this class of vessels in all other ports of the United States by 193,000 tons. On December 31, 1891, there were eighty-nine steel vessels on the lakes, with a tonnage of 127,624 tons, and valued at about $14,500,000. Five years before there were on the great lakes but six steel vessels, with a total tonnage of 6,459 tons, and a total valuation of $694,000. Since 1891 over fifty steamers have been built, and others are now in process of construction. The deepening and improving of channels on the great lakes have brought about the construction of these enormous lake steamers, which, in turn, have been the cause of the reduction in lake transportation rates. In 1859, the cost of carrying a bushel of corn from

Chicago to Buffalo by water, was 15¾ cents; in 1890, the average rate was 1.9 cents; in 1891, it was carried at 1 cent per bushel, but during the latter part of the season rates advanced to about 3 cents per bushel. The commerce consists chiefly of grain, iron and copper ore and lumber, and, of course, the value of the cargoes carried by lake steamers is not nearly so great as of those carried by ocean vessels of the same kind.

Chicago's railway system developed with fabulous rapidity. About 1835 Chicago had to get the large part of its foodstuffs from other states. In the early 40's the neighboring farmers produced enough for themselves and Chicago. Soon the necessity was felt for an outside market for the surplus products. In the winter of 1842-3 the prices of all kinds of farm products fell below the cost of production. Dressed hogs, for instance, sold for 12 shillings a hundred pounds; lard, $3.50 per hundred; flour, $5.00 a barrel; oats and potatos, 10 cents a bushel; eggs, 4 cents a dozen; chickens, 5 cents apiece. These prices, of course, were ruinous, and caused the farmers to keep their surplus produce over winter and ship it to New York in the spring. Then the large freight to New York absorbed most of the profits. It took the farmers on the Rock river five days to get 30 bushels of wheat to the market, and then they never got more than $12 a load. During the early 50's farmers brought their products to Chicago from as far as 300 miles away, but never got in return more than enough to buy groceries with. They often camped east of State street, in large numbers. With the arrival of the first locomotive, of course, all things changed. Less than forty years have elapsed since then and Chicago to-day is the terminal of twenty-six trunk lines, and has various smaller branch roads. Over 90,000 miles of railroad now terminate in Chicago, connecting the city directly with the principal Atlantic, Pacific and Gulf ports, with Canada and Mexico. For the last ten years Chicago's east-bound freight has averaged 4,000,000 tons annually.

Scene on the Chicago River.

In 1892 Chicago received 256,000,000 bushels of grain (including flour in its wheat equivalent); the elevators, which are under the control of the Board of Trade, have a capacity of 30,325,000 bushels. One of these elevators holds over 3,000,000 bushels of grain. In 1892 there were received at the Chicago market 7,714,435 hogs, 3,571,796 cattle, 2,145,079 sheep, 149,496,436 pounds of dressed beef, 68,371,502 pounds of lard, 64,252,364 pounds of cheese, 134,196,828 pounds of butter, 5,500,000 bushels of potatoes, 18,000,000 pounds of broomcorn, 23,500,000 pounds of tallow, 104,688 barrels of oatmeal, 28,388,364 pounds of wool, 1,243,721 barrels of salt, and 2,203,874 feet of lumber.

While all else in Chicago was making rapid progress, the clearings of the Board of Trade fell from $104,083,529.67 in 1891 to $69,295,992.62 in 1892. This, however, simply shows that there has been less speculation on the board—not that less legitimate business was done. While the clearings of the Board of Trade showed this decided falling off, the bank clearings in Chicago showed an increase from $4,456,885,230.49 in 1891, to $5,135,771,186.74 in 1892.

Commenting on this falling off in the speculative business of the Board of Trade, its secretary, George F. Stone, in his annual report says:

"The business of buying and selling for future delivery was unsatisfactory throughout the year. Never was the speculative business of this board so harrassed. Legislative meddling (the Hatch and Washburn bills in Congress, proposing laws against 'dealings in futures') silver discussion, unfavorable weather conditions early in the year in the winter wheat belt region, despondent foreign markets occasioned by heavy stocks purchased at high prices, heavy failures in prominent continental markets, steady accumulations of grain at easily accessible points for shipments, all not only disturbed, but subdued the markets all over the world, and speculators grew weary waiting for business and distrustful of indications which under normal conditions would have infused animation to trade.

Every attempt to advance prices of wheat, the leading speculative cereal, was unsuccessful, and farmers rushed their grain to market, even while expecting the Hatch bill to become a law. They had joined the tirade against speculation, and could not withdraw; but however plausible the arguments of politicians, they knew that there was no hope for better prices should the Hatch heresy succeed. Hence the volume of receipts of grain at this great center was limited only by the capacity of transportation facilities to bring it hither. This was the real expression of the farmers' opinion of the Hatch bill, and which was diametrically opposite to his expression of that document as made known in some instances to his congressional representative."

A Chicago Elevator.

The value of foreign merchandise imported directly to the city was, in 1892, $17,388,496, and the duty on the same amounted to $7,490,578.91. In 1891 the duty on merchandise imported by Chicago amounted to only $5,983,589.72, and in 1890 to but $5,048,771.85.

Chicago's great factories, equipped with every modern appliance and machine, are principally due to the enterprising spirit of the capitalists, most of whom are native Americans. The skilled laborers in the factories are, however, chiefly foreigners. Chicago boasts, among its capitalists, more "self-made men" than any other city in the world. The city has quickly repaid the foreign and eastern capital which once ruled it and is now financially independent, being reckoned no longer as a debtor, but as a creditor city. In 1890 the factories of Chicago numbered 3250 and represented an investment of $190,000,000. They employed 177,000 men who received $96,200,000 in wages and produced merchandise to the amount of $558,000,000. The manufactures of Chicago include almost everything needed by man. The city contains 100,000 more males than females, which fact accounts, in part, for the very rapid growth of manufacturing and building industries, transportation facilities, wholesale trade and the banking business. Over 1000 firms and corporations are engaged in transportation. They employ about 60,000 persons, as follows: railways, 31,000; street railways, 8500; express companies, 1500; navigation companies, 8000; teaming and livery companies, 10,000 etc. The textile trades represent 1500 firms, employing 55,000 persons. Other trades and industries are represented as follows: clothing and furnishing goods, cloaks and millinery, dry goods and notions, 1000 firms, with 35,000 employees; hides, wool, leather, boots and shoes, harness, belting and other leather and rubber goods, 325 firms, with 12,000 employees; food, drink, tobacco, drugs and agricultural products 3300 firms, with 110,000 wage-workers, of whom

Scene in the Stock Yards.

the meat packers employ about 30,000, the hotels and restaurants about 10,000, etc.; lumber, wooden ware, furniture, boxes and cooperage, 7000 firms, with 45,000 employees; metal trades and manufactures, 1500 firms, with 88,000 employees—steel rails, machinery, stoves, heating apparatus, velocipedes, scales, tinware, brass goods, musical and electrical instruments and hardware being manufactured in large establishments; printing, publishing and paper, 1000 firms, with 26,-000 employees; building trades, 4000 firms, with 60,000 employees; dealers in coal and wood, 1000 firms, with 5000 employees; gas companies, with 2000 men; miscellaneous trades (chemicals, crockery, etc.) 200 firms, with 2000 employees; banking, real estate, insurance, amusements, etc., about 3500 firms and corporations, with 12,000 employees. Department stores are extending their trade in various lines and easy payments at installment stores, have revolutionized the retail business in household goods. Six of the large wholesale and retail department stores employ over 15,000 persons.

The industrial interests of the city are highly centralized; thus three foundries employ 1920 men; four machinery manufactories employ 6800 men; one glue works employs 600 men; three planing mills, 900 men; four musical instrument factories, 2000 men; three furniture factories, 2500 men; three carriage and wagon factories, 900 men; two soap factories, 1300 men; two electric works, 2500 men; one boot and shoe factory, 900 men; one cloak factory, 700 men and women; two millinery concerns, 800 persons; one retail store, 2200 persons; one bicycle factory, 1000 men; two brass factories, 1900 men; one car factory, 4500 men; one printing house, 1000 men; one restaurant, 325 men; three hotels 1550 persons; one brewery, 300 men.

In the retail business 33,000 firms and 135,000 persons are engaged. Among the retail business houses are 3500 grocery stores, 7000 saloons, 2200 meat markets, 1056 bakeries, 1385 barber shops, 1350 shoe stores, 561 blacksmiths and horse-

shoers, 175 book stores, 1400 confectionery and fruit stores, 1500 cigar stores, 1100 coal dealers, 231 crockery stores, 850 clothing and gentlemen's furnishing goods stores, 1430 dry goods and notion stores, 730 drug stores, 568 dentists, 141 dyers, 587 flour and feed stores, 240 florists, 700 hardware stores, 429 jewelers, 800 laundries, 1250 milk dealers, 570 millinery stores, 225 musical instrument stores, 600 plumbers, 400 furniture stores, 150 photographers, and 330 undertakers. This shows one person employed in retail business for every eleven of the city's inhabitants.

The foregoing figures were furnished largely by Joseph Gruenhut, city statistician, who makes the following comment on the industrial activity of modern cities: "In the large manufacturing establishments of to-day, the productive capacity of every workman is enormously increased by the use of steam and labor-saving machinery. One workman in a large modern factory can do from 5 to 10 times as much productive work as could the workman of 50 years ago, who performed in his own little shop, all the various processes of manufacture. Then the cost of the labor so increased the price of the manufactured articles as to limit demand, and few workmen were formerly employed in industries now using thousands of workers. Thus, for example, very few persons make all parts of a watch to-day; but each worker in a factory makes some one particular part of the completed product. The result is that the process has so cheapened the cost of watch production as to greatly increase the demand. Great factories mass people together in cities like Chicago, and the presence of factories of different kinds, so cheapens the cost of the production of the various articles manufactured, as to make them come within the reach of an ever increasing number of men, and thus an increasing population is easily cared for. Were this not true, no city would attract a population of 1,500,000 people. Liberal use of capital has made the great factories possible and increased the

Jefferson Park Fountain.

productivity of human labor, with the result that there has been an actual or real increase in the wages of the working classes.

"The distribution of merchandise to the consumer—the retail trade—is a personal service, and does not admit of the use of labor-saving machinery in any great degree. Stores increase with the increase and spread of the population, but the number of the great factories becomes less, and the small factories are no longer profitable. On the other hand, certain industries are absorbed into trusts, and thus all the benefits of competition are gradually lost. This modern tendency is noticed in the monopoly of gas-works, distilleries, petroleum and india rubber, and attempts have already been made to check the evil by a law, which shall not prevent the benefits of a centralization of interests, but will, nevertheless, secure to the general public the benefits of competition."

In his report for 1892, Secretary Stone, of the Board of Trade, touches on the same ground when he says:

"The crops of the country, which constitute the basis of all departments of business, have been large, and have given to the grain receivers a great activity and volume of business, which has been fairly remunerative. It is regretted that this prosperity has not been generally diffused, and that the business connected with the board has exhibited the prevailing tendency of the principal industries to concentration and monopoly, so that the comparatively small merchant has not met with that full participation in the advantages resulting from the heavy receipts of the year which he had a right to expect."

During the year 1892, 3,010,543⅜ barrels of beer were brewed in Chicago, and 2,875,818⅜ barrels were sold. The tax from this source amounted to $2,660,132. Overproduction and bad faith among the brewers in living up to their mutual agreements, have caused a great falling off in the brewing profits of Chicago. Capital in breweries is no longer regarded as a gilt-edged investment, and the English syndicates, who bought up so many American breweries, are still waiting for the fabulous profits they were promised. The Chicago production in distilled spirits in 1892 amounted to but 6,858,249 gallons, as against 8,979,958 gallons for 1891, and 10,778,000 gallons in 1890. Like the brewing industry, the distilleries are suffering from over-production.

Indian Group in Lincoln Park.

Chicago is the great market for small retail dealers of the west. The competition between the lake transportation companies and the railroads does much to keep freight rates down and to assist in making Chicago the great market for the "jobbing trade." In 1890, Chicago's business in this line amounted to $486,600,000. Of this sum there was expended $93,730,000 for dry goods, $56,700,000 for groceries, $25,000,000 for boots and shoes, $25,500,000 for paper and carpets, $22,000,000 for musical instruments, $20,035,000 for raw iron, $20,400,000 for jewelry, watches and diamonds, $15,580,000 for building iron, and $13,500,000 for spirituous liquors.

The suburban train service and the city street railway—both of which have their terminals in the down-town portion of Chicago—have contributed largely to the building up of great department stores, which tend to do away with the small retail stores throughout the city. In thirteen of these great central retail stores, lying between State and Wabash avenue, and Washington and Adams streets, over 12,000 persons are employed, three-fifths of the number being women. It is impossible for the smaller retail stores of the city to successfully compete with these great institutions. In thirteen of these large retail department stores are employed one-fifth of all the persons engaged in the city's retail trade.

Chicago's real estate and building interests are, of course, enormous. In the year 1890 the real estate transfers amounted to $227,000,000, but in 1891 and 1892 they fell off considerably. In 1886, they aggregated $86,000,000; in 1887, $95,000,000; in 1888, $93,000,000; in 1889, $135,000,000, and in 1891, $178,600,000. In building activity, the years 1891 and 1892 far surpassed all previous records. From 1881 to 1888, the average annual expenditure for new buildings was $19,000,000; in 1889 it was $25,065,000; in 1890, $47,322,000; in 1891, $55,360,000; in 1892, $64,740,800.

The banking business of the city is a simple index to its

business growth. The total capital of the twenty-six national banks in Chicago, in 1892, was $23,300,000, and of the twenty-three state banks $12,577,000, and in addition there were numerous private banks representing a large capital. In 1890, the clearings by the associated banks of Chicago were $4,093,145,904; in 1891, $4,456,885,230; in 1892, $5,135,771,186.

The increase in the deposits of Chicago banks is enormous, exceeding, in the last six years, the deposit increase in the New York banks by 125 per cent. This is a significant fact, and shows that Chicago's commercial development is more than twice as rapid as New York's, and that the financial center of the country is destined to be Chicago.

The Chicago post-office does an immense business. In 1892, 322,555,709 pieces of mail matter were received and handled at the post-office. The postal receipts for the year 1892 were $4,265,975.14, the expenditures were but $1,552,640.37, leaving the government a net income, from the Chicago post-office, of $2,713,334.77. In spite of the fact that it is far more than self-supporting, the national government does not see fit to equip the Chicago post-office with a force large enough to adequately perform the enormous amount of work to be done. In the year 1891 the Chicago post-office forwarded more printed matter than the offices at Boston, Cincinnati, New Orleans, Buffalo and Baltimore together, and more than all the post-offices of the thirteen southern states, including the St. Louis' office. Over 20,000,000 of Chicago newspapers were mailed in Chicago during the year 1892.

Miscellaneous Information.

Chicago's Municipal Resources—Statistics—Public Schools—Municipal Health Department—The Drainage Channel—The City Government.

Chicago is 850 miles, by the most direct rail communication, from Baltimore, the nearest sea-port, 1000 miles from New York, and 2,417 miles from San Francisco. Its mean height, above the lake level, is fourteen feet, and its altitude above the sea, 591 feet. The city contains 181 square miles, or 115,328 acres. The revenue of the city of Chicago for the year ending December 31, 1892, was $31,863,218.82, and the expenditures, $30,069,963.65. The principal sources of income were: general taxes, $10,260,036.70; special assessments, $6,600,310.69; water fund, $2,901,428.49; licenses, $3,908,948.96 (of which the saloon licenses amounted to $3,472,618.03); school fund, $2,657,328.90. The principal expenditures were for the department of public works, $2,422,085.07; for the fire department, $1,504,854.38; police fund, $3,008,990.39; school fund, $2,650,167; school tax fund, $4,229,974; special assessement fund, $6,799,094; street lamp fund, $1,015,410, and water fund, $3,330,342. The total bonded debt of the city is $18,476,450. The work of making special assessments in Chicago has so increased as to make this bureau the largest sub-department, in the magnitude of its work, in the city. The cost of such public improvements, as paving, sewer-building, street and alley-grading, sidewalk building, laying of water service pipes, and erection of lamp-posts, is defrayed by special assessments levied on the property most benefited by and lying nearest to the public improvement. In 1892, the assessments for wooden block pavement amounted to $6,056,442.19; for sewer construction,

Water Works Tower.

$3,864,714; for miscellaneous street and alley improvements, $1,301,491.99, which, with all other special assessments, made a grand total of $14,505,701.79, as compared with $42,635 in 1862, $62,222.25 in 1872, $1,227,169 in 1882, and $8,790,443 in 1892. This levy is made for improvements to be made during the year.

Chicago property is not taxed according to its value, but according to an absurd system of equalized valuation. The evils of this system are apparent, for it throws on the taxpaying property owners of to-day all the burden of improvements, the benefits of which will accrue to posterity. The actual value of property in the city cannot be less than two billion dollars, but the equalized valuation is only $243,732,138—$12,867,657 less than the equalized valuation of 1891 and almost $55,000,000 less than the property valuation in 1875, when the city comprised but thirty-seven square miles, as against the 181 square miles of to-day.

By the constitutional limit, city bonds can be issued only to the amount of 5 per cent on the assessed valuation of city property, as equalized. On a proper valuation bonds could be issued to the amount of from fifty to one hundred millions of dollars, at a low rate of interest, and the proceeds of the sale be used to make much needed improvements that are now entirely paid for by the heavily taxed property owner of to-day. The rate of taxation could be reduced, from its present figure—7 per cent, on the present valuation—to not over 2 per cent on a proper one. The rate in New York, in 1891, was 1.90.

Chicago's public and private school system is excellent. The enrollment of children in the public schools for the year 1891–92 was 157,743. The seating capacity of all city school houses was in February, 1893, 150,746, and of this capacity all but 10,455 were seats in buildings owned by the city. The city owns about 250 school buildings, twenty-five of which were opened during 1892. In addition to these 250, all other

La Salle Street. Front of the City Hall.

buildings are rented for school-house purposes. In February, 1892, 3,217 teachers were employed in the public schools, and during the same month in 1893, therewere 3,483 teachers.

The following figures are taken from such municipal reports for 1892, as have been published up to date (April, 1893):

Miles of street paved in 1892	108
Miles of paved street in the city	878
Miles of street in the city	2,370
Buildings erected in 1892	13,194
Their cost	$64,740,800
Miles of sidewalk built in 1892	799
Miles of sidewalk in the city	3,637
Gallons of water furnished in 1892	71,035,000,000
Miles of sewers in the city	992
Lumber received (in feet)	2,203,874,000
Lumber shipped (in feet)	1,060,017,000
Shingles received	395,206,000
Shingles shipped	140,227,000
Tons of coal received	5,529,468
Tons of coal shipped	942,068
Pounds of lard received	68,371,502
Pounds of lard shipped	398,915,558
Pounds of dressed meats received	179,965,327
Pounds of dressed meats shipped	1,212,344,343
Barrels of pork received	16,934
Barrels of pork shipped	294,781
Pounds of butter received	134,196,828
Pounds of butter shipped	140,494,155

The following figures are taken from the report of the preceding year:

Number of social clubs in Chicago	60
Number of churches	513
Number of railroads entering the city	35
Miles of street car tracks in the city	395
Miles of cable car tracks	68
Number of police	2,298
Number of fire engines	72
Number of fire boats	3
Number of chemical fire engines	23
Number of firemen	998
Number of bridges across the Chicago river	53
Number of viaducts over railroads	31

The high buildings in Chicago in 1892 were equipped with almost 7000 elevators. The number of daily suburban trains in 1880 was 128; in 1890, 670; the number of through passenger trains in 1880 was 260; in 1890, 940; number of hotels in 1880, 140; in 1890, 267. Since the great fire, 68,774 buildings have been erected in Chicago, at the cost of $320,000,000.

Chicago is the healthiest large city on the globe, having a death rate lower than any other city having a population of 500,000 persons or upwards. In 1892 there was an increase in population of 180,000, with a decrease of 1535 in the total number of deaths. The death rate per thousand in 1892 was 18.23 in Chicago and 24. in New York. Although there were several sporadic cases of small-pox in Chicago last year, no cases were communicated in the city itself, all cases being early diagnosed and removed to the municipal hospital before the contagion spread.

The drainage channel, now being constructed to connect Chicago with the Gulf of Mexico by means of the Illinois and Mississippi rivers, is intended to make Chicago a still healthier city by at once and forever settling the question of the city's sewage disposition. The primary object of the drainage channel is simply to dispose of Chicago's sewage, but it will incidentally open a waterway from the great lakes to the Gulf of Mexico and furnish a water power of the greatest value to the manufacturing interests along its proposed route. The simple drainage channel is to be built at the expense of the "Sanitary District of Chicago," the work being done under a legislative enactment of 1889, which created the sanitary district and gave the right, under certain limitations and restrictions, to cut a channel through the "divide" so that the sewage of Chicago could be discharged into the Illinois and Mississippi rivers. This act also provided for the issue of $15,000,000 of twenty-year bonds, and the levying of a tax of not over one-half of 1 per cent per annum on the assessable property in the district, with the further provision that special assessments could be levied on property especially benefited by the work. This tax of one-half of 1 per cent a year is to pay all the cost of making the channel —salaries, office expenses, construction expenses and principal and interest of the bonds. The bonds are issued and sold for the purpose of getting money with which to push the work to completion in four years, but the taxpayers will pay them off only at the rate of one-half of 1 per cent a year. The cost of the simple drainage channel is now estimated at about \$25,000,000. Over 80 per cent of the work has been contracted for, and it is expected that the channel will be completed by 1897. The cost to date has been \$1,500,000, and if the ship canal feature is carried out, the cost of the whole work will reach \$50,000,000—but for this latter feature the co-operation of city, state and nation must be secured.

Joliet first pointed out the commercial advantages of a canal connecting Lake Michigan with the Illinois and Mississippi rivers. Gallatin wrote about it and others urged it at various times. In the early 50's Col. J. D. Webster pointed out the fact that Chicago was emptying its sewage and filth into its drinking vessel—Lake Michigan—and urged the construction of the channel as the solution of the question of proper sewage disposition. City Engineer E. S. Chesbrough discussed the matter from an engineering point some years later, but it was 1885 before the agitation for a drainage channel was seriously regarded. August 3, 1885, there was a very heavy rainfall and the waters of the Chicago river reached the crib and polluted the city's water supply. L. E. Cooley, an engineer, Ossian Guthrie, a well-known geologist, and Dr. F. W. Reilly, of the Chicago News, discussed the situation, decided the drainage channel was the only proper (and sooner or later the inevitable) solution of the sewage disposal question, and at once began to agitate for legislative action, authorizing the organization of a drainage district with power to raise money

for the purposes of constructing a drainage channel. Mr. Stone, of the News, was induced to lend the influence of his paper to the scheme, but the greatest opposition was encountered in various quarters. Finally, however, the sanitary district was created, and the idea slowly became popular. September 14, 1892, seven years and seven days after the enterprise was first urged upon the people, the first shovelful of earth was turned in the great undertaking. In his address, delivered at that time, Trustee L. E. Cooley said:

> The work this day begun is to cover the Chicago Divide, forty miles from Lake Michigan to Lake Joliet, with over thirty miles of channel complete for navigation. The cost will be greater than to extend fourteen feet for 280 miles further to the Mississippi. The volume of water will give steamboat navigation in the lower river without obstructing locks and dams, in which nature, assisted by art, may develop increased depths. Permanent works are required for the gap of fifty-five miles between Joliet and Utica, but this problem is simpler than that of the Chicago divide.
>
> The policy underlying the law is an open river below Utica, to be improved progressively in conjunction with a water supply from Lake Michigan; works above Utica so designed as to permit future increase of capacity, and such a plan for the Chicago Divide as will facilitate enlargement to any requirement of water supply from the lakes to the Mississippi—the entire work to be carried out through the co-operation of city, state and nation. The augmented volume southward will raise the call down to the Gulf for all the lakes can spare. The lake region and the Mississippi Valley will join in the largest useful development. And so, the sanitary needs of that future which no man can now forsee, will surely become the incident of a commercial purpose that enlists the nation.
>
> This is the logic of our policy. To-day we cut the Chicago divide for an urgent sanitary need which rouses our city; and in so doing we sever the gordian knot which has fettered all projects, loosen possibilities of which statesmen have dreamed for a century; and in the manner of our doing, we set the gauge which shall govern the waterway of a continent. He who sets his conception as the limit of human achievement writes in his designs the obituary of his enterprises. This city, this state, this nation, are but in youth, and we can only dream of what they may seek to do in manhood and maturity. We do well if we work in the line of a continuing policy and construct no barriers.
>
> North to the frozen zone, east to the Alleghanies, south to the Gulf, west to the Rockies—an imperial domain of resources in forest, field and mine, as yet but scarcely opened—the population this may sustain, the civilization that may mature, is beyond prophetic ken. Point out the areas of richest soil, where food will be most abundant, and there ultimately will it be densest. Find the spot where the commerce of this people may be most cheaply handled, to which food, raw material and power shall most readily assemble, and from which manufactures may be best distributed, and there will be the chief city. No accident placed the urban population of the United States on navigable waters, determined wealth along their shores, and located the most valuable railway properties in competition therewith.
>
> Look at the position of Illinois in respect to these resources, in respect to transportation by rail and water, and in respect to climate—is she not to be the central ganglion of a marvellous growth? Look at her chief city; where is site more favored? Provide for health, develop the facilities which nature invites, follow a policy as though our estates were vested in one man, and that man's life prolonged through the generations, and we rise to the level of our opportunities. What we do to-day is but the beginning. An object vital in itself is to be attained as soon as practicable; yet, in achieving it, we but

Carter H. Harrison.

unfold larger purposes, purposes that, in their consummation, are but added resources, developing our estate to fuller fruitfulness by works that involve no tax for operation, maintenance and renewals, carvings on the bosom of mother earth that will persist in usefulness until nature in her cycles renews the face of continents.

Machines will vanish in rust, the proudest monument of man will sink to rubbish heaps, and his greatest work trail in curious mounds, while this goes on as nature's self, an added feature to mother earth as though it had always been.

The municipal government of Chicago is vested in executive and legislative departments. The mayor is at the head of the executive department, and also ex-officio chairman of the city council, the legislative department of the local government. The city council is composed of two aldermen from each ward in the city. All appropriations are made by this body. The mayor, in his executive capacity, is at the head of a great corporation. He has under his general control and supervision, the fire, police and water departments, the special assessment bureau, the health department, the legal department, etc. The present mayor of Chicago is the Hon. Carter H. Harrison. He has already filled the office for four terms—1879 to 1886—and his recent election by an overwhelming majority, in the face of the political or personal opposition of every prominent paper of the city—with but two exceptions—is a proof of his popularity. Mr. Harrison thoroughly understands the business of the city government, and is mayor in fact as well as in name. He is a gentleman of distinct social and literary attainments, and his broad, liberal, democratic public policy makes him a great favorite among the masses of the people—especially among the foreign-born citizens of the city, who have the greatest confidence that their rights and privileges will be protected under his administration.

The World's Fair.

CHICAGO, 1893.

Christopher Columbus.

April 25, 1890, Benjamin Harrison, President of the United States, approved an act of Congress providing for the celebration of the four hundredth anniversary of the discovery of America by Christopher Columbus, by holding an international exhibit of arts, industries, manufactures and the products of the soil, mine and sea, in the city of Chicago. Three years and a week after the act of Congress became a law, the greatest peaceful undertaking of modern times was an achieved fact. The history of the World's Columbian Exposition is a tale of miracles. It is a string of wonders that surpasses fiction in strangeness, and that will stand forever as a mighty monument to the admirable enterprise and indomitable spirit of Chicago and its people.

It was on the evening of July 22, 1889, that the first public step was taken in regard to securing the fair for Chicago, and then began the memorable struggle between New York and the city by the lake. The city council, on the date named, formally resolved that it would be good policy to make every effort to secure the fair, and took the initiative by authorizing Mayor Cregier to appoint a committee of 250 citizens to superintend the preliminary work. This committee was appointed by the mayor July 30, 1889, and held its first meeting in the council chamber at the city hall August 2. The best known, wealthiest and most truly representative citizens of Chicago attended that meeting, and not a man of all those called upon declined to serve. Before the meeting adjourned a stock company, with a capital of $5,000,000, had been started, and its affairs were placed in the hands of a small executive committee. Next day the work of the committee of 250 was divided among numerous sub-committees, and popular enthusiasm in the work began to develop. By September 20, the necessary funds had been subscribed. No sooner had the public announcement been made that the $5,000,000 was raised, than New York's opposition to Chicago developed. The tidings that the eastern city was a candidate for the fair came September 25, and it was said that it would raise the sum of $10,000,000 as a guarantee for the proper performance of its contract if given the fair. From September, 1889, to February, 1890, the fight between the rival cities was waged without ceasing, in and out of Congress, and there are few who forget the immense amount of wire-pulling and political maneuvering that marked the struggle. All the forces of the east were arrayed against the influence of the west, but Chicago won the fight.

The first congressional reports, made in the last week of October, 1889, were favorable to Chicago, but its representa-

George R. Davis.

tives relaxed no efforts until the great struggle finally ended in victory February 24, 1890, when Congress passed the act creating the World's Columbian Commission. Chicago had won its victory, but its difficulties were only just beginning. New York had agreed to raise $10,000,000 as a starting fund for the fair, and among the conditions imposed on Chicago by Congress was one to the effect that it must do as New York had promised to do. Consequently the next few months were spent in work among the aldermen of Chicago and the state legislators at Springfield, in an effort to secure the appropriation of the second $5,000,000 by the city. Finally a special session of the Legislature at Springfield, Illinois, called June 12, 1890, authorized the city of Chicago to increase its bonded indebtedness $5,000,000 in aid of the fair.

The Jackson Park site was first mooted February 25, the day after the national house of representatives at Washington had declared in favor of awarding the fair to Chicago, and the advantages of the site at once became so apparent that it was chosen. That brilliant and lamented genius John Wellborn Root, formulated plans for the building of the White City, and although he did not live to see them carried into execution, his successors found the conceptions of his master mind so perfect, that the fair, as it stands to-day, is practically what he pictured it before a spadeful of earth had been turned. Jackson Park has been transformed from a dismal morass into a city of white palaces, exemplifying the most perfect architecture, and conveying to the mind of the visitor profound admiration for the aggregated genius that has achieved so much in so short a time.

From the outset of the exposition undertaking, the women of America have exhibited the liveliest interest in it, and their co-operation was early invited. On the day after the election of George R. Davis as director-general, a board of lady managers was appointed, which, under the presidency of Mrs. Potter Palmer, of Chicago, has labored without ceasing for the

Mrs. Potter Palmer.

general good of the enterprise as well as in the specific direction of securing a complete representation of woman's work for the exposition. In every state of the Union, and in every country of the civilized world, the influence of the lady managers has been exerted, and as a consequence, one of the most interesting of all the buildings at Jackson Park is the woman's building.

Early in the history of the exposition, the Sunday-closing question began to be agitated. Various well-meaning but mistaken persons sought to influence public opinion by insisting that the fair should be closed on Sunday. They were so far successful as to induce Congress, when making its last appropriation of $2,500,000 for the fair, to insert a clause in the act providing that the gates of the exposition shall be closed Sunday.

THE FAIR MANAGEMENT.

The management of the fair is vested first, in a Board of Directors representing the Chicago stockholders of the corporation, which board provides the funds for constructing the buildings and preparing the grounds for the reception of exhibits; second, a National Commission, composed of two commissioners from each state in the Union, representing the United States government that took possession of the exposition after the dedication in October, 1892; and third, the Board of Lady Managers, a branch of the National Commission that has jurisdiction in woman's work the world over, and control of the woman's building. A list of the officers and members of these three bodies follows:

THE LOCAL BOARD

OFFICERS.

President............................H. N. Higinbotham.
Vice-Presidents......... { Ferd. W. Peck.   Treasurer........Anthony F. Seeberger.
                         { R. A. Waller.   Auditor..........William K. Ackerman.
Secretary...............H. O. Edmonds.   Attorney.................W. K. Carlisle.

DIRECTORS.

William T. Baker.	James W. Ellsworth.	Thies J. Lefens.	George Schneider.
C. K. G. Billings.	G. P. Englehard.	Andrew McNally.	Charles H. Schwab.
Thomas B. Bryan.	Lyman J. Gage.	Adolph Nathan.	Paul O. Stensland.
Edward B. Butler.	Chas. Henrotin.	Robert Nelson.	Henry B. Stone.
Benj. Butterworth.	H. N. Higinbotham.	John J. P. Odell.	Charles H. Wacker.
Isaac N. Camp.	Charles L. Hutchinson	Ferd. W. Peck.	Edwin Walker.
William J. Chalmers.	Elbridge G. Keith.	E. S. Pike.	Robert A. Waller.
Robert C. Clowry.	William D. Kerfoot.	Washington Porter.	Hempst'd Washburne
C. H. Chappell.	William P. Ketcham.	Alexander H. Revell.	John C. Welling.
George R. Davis.	Milton W. Kirk.	Edward P. Ripley.	Frederick S. Winston.
Arthur Dixon.	Edward F. Lawrence.	A. M. Rothschild.	Charles T. Yerkes.

THE NATIONAL COMMISSION.

OFFICERS.

President .... Thomas W. Palmer, of Michigan.
1st Vice-President..Thos. M. Waller, Conn. | 5th Vice-President, Alex. B. Andrews, N.C.
2d Vice-President...M. H. DeYoung, Cal. | Secretary........John T. Dickinson, Tex.
3d Vice-President..Davidson B. Penn, La. | Director-General.....George R. Davis, Ill.
4th Vice-President, Gorton W. Allen. N.Y. | Vice-Ch'm'n Ex.Com., Jas. A. M'Kenzie, Ky

STATES.	COMMISSIONERS.	
At Large..................	Bullock, Augustus G.	Massachusetts
	Allen, Gorton W.	New York
	Wiedner, Peter A. B.	Pennsylvania
	Palmer, Thomas W.	Michigan
	Furnas, R. W.	Nebraska
	Lindsay, William.	Kentucky
	Exall, Henry	Texas
District of Columbia........	McDonald, Mark L.	California
	Britton, Alex. T.	Washington
Alabama...................	Wilson, Albert A.	Washington
	Bromberg, F. G.	Mobile
Arkansas..................	Hundley, Oscar R.	Huntsville
	Clendenning, J. H.	Fort Smith
California.................	DeYoung, M. H.	San Francisco
	Forsyth, William	Fresno
Colorado..................	Goodell, Roswell E.	Leadville
	Smith, J. H.	Denver
Connecticut...............	Brainard, Leverett	Hartford
	Waller, Thomas M.	New London
Delaware	Massey, George V.	Dover
	Porter, Willard Hall	Wilmington
Florida....................	Bielly, C. F. A.	De Land
	Turnbull, Richard.	Monticello
Georgia...................	McLaws, Lafayette	Savannah
	Way, Charlton H.	Savannah
Idaho.....................	Manning, George A.	Post Falls
	Stearns, John E.	Nampa
Illinois...................	Deere, Charles H.	Moline
	Ewing, Adlai T.	Chicago
Indiana...................	Garvin, Thomas E.	Evansville
	Martindale, E. B.	Indianapolis
Iowa......................	Eiboeck, Jos.	Des Moines
	King, William F.	Mt. Vernon
Kansas....................	Holliday, C. K., Jr.	Topeka
	Barton, J. R.	Abilene
Kentucky	Bennett, John.	Richmond
	McKenzie, James A.	Oak Grove

389

STATES.	COMMISSIONERS.	
Louisiana	Penn, Davidson B.	Newellton
	Woodward, Thomas J.	New Orleans
Maine	Bxby, Augustus R.	Skowhegan
	Davis, William G.	Portland
Maryland	Hodges, James	Baltimore
	Lowndes, Lloyd	Cumberland
Massachusetts	Breed, Francis W.	Lynn
	Proctor, Thomas E.	Boston
Michigan	Lane, M. Henry	Kalamazoo
	Barbour, George H.	Detroit
Minnesota	Moore, M. B.	Duluth
	Tousley, O. V.	Minneapolis
Mississippi	Bynum, Joseph M.	Rienzi
	Saunders, Robert L.	Jackson
Missouri	Bullene, Thomas B.	Kansas City
	Jones, Charles H.	St. Louis
Montana	Hershfield, L. H.	Helena
	Mitchell, A. H.	Deer Lodge
Nebraska	Martin, Euclid	Omaha
	Scott, Albert G.	Kearney
Nevada	Haines, James W.	Genoa
	Russell, George	Elko
New Hampshire	Aiken, Walter	Franklin
	McDuffie, Charles D.	Manchester
New Jersey	Sewell, William J.	Camden
	Smith, Thomas	Newark
New York	Depew, Chauncey M.	New York
	Thatcher, John Boyd	Albany
North Carolina	Andrews, A. B.	Raleigh
	Keogh, Thomas B.	Greensboro
North Dakota	Rucker, H. P.	Grand Forks
	Ryan, Martin	Fargo
Ohio	Platt, Harvey P.	Toledo
	Ritchie, William	Hamilton
Oregon	Klippel, Henry	Jacksonville
	Wilkins, Martin	Eugene
Pennsylvania	Ricketts, R. Bruce	Wilkes-Barre
	Woodside, John W.	Philadelphia
Rhode Island	Goff, Lyman B.	Pawtucket
	Sims, Gardner C.	Providence
South Carolina	Butler, A. P.	Columbia
	Cochran, John R.	Walhalla
South Dakota	Day, Merritt H.	Rapid City
	McIntyre, William	Watertown
Tennessee	Baxter, Louis T.	Nashville
	Williams, Thomas L.	Knoxville
Texas	Cochran, A. M.	Dallas
	Dickinson, John T.	Austin
Vermont	McIntyre, Henry H.	W. Randolph
	Smalley, Bradley B.	Burlington
Virginia	Groner, Virginius D.	Norfolk
	Harris, John T.	Harrisonburg
Washington	Drum, Henry	Tacoma
	Hopkins, Charles B.	Spokane
West Virginia	Butt, James D.	Harper's Ferry
	St. Clair, J. W.	Fayetteville
Wisconsin	Allen, Philip, Jr.	Mineral Point
	Coburn, John M.	West Salem
Wyoming	Beckwith, Asahel C.	Evanston
	Hay, Henry G.	Cheyenne
Alaska	DeGroff, Edward	Sitka
	Williams, Louis L.	Juneau
Arizona	Coats, George F.	Phoenix
	Meade, W. R.	Tombstone
New Mexico	Gutierres, Thomas C.	Albuquerque
	White, Richard M.	Hermosa
Oklahoma	Beeson, Othniel	El Reno
	Gammon, F. R.	Guthrie
Utah	Kiesel, Frederick J.	Ogden
	Lannan, Patrick H.	Salt Lake City

BOARD OF LADY MANAGERS.

OFFICERS.

President................Mrs. Potter Palmer, of Chicago.

1st Vice-President, Mrs. Ralph Trautmann, of New York.	6th Vice-President, Mrs. Susan R. Ashley, of Colorado.
2nd Vice-President, Mrs. Edwin C Burleigh, of Maine.	7th Vice-President, Mrs. Flora Beall Ginty, of Wisconsin.
3rd Vice-President, Mrs. Charles Price, of North Carolina.	8th Vice-President, Mrs. Margaret Blaine Salisbury, of Utah.
4th Vice-President, Miss Katherine L. Minor, of Louisiana.	Vice-President-at-Large, Mrs. Russell B. Harrison, of Montana.
5th Vice-President, Mrs. Beriah Wilkins, of the District of Columbia.	Secretary, Mrs. Susan Gale Cooke, of Tennessee.

STATES.	MANAGERS.
At Large	Mrs. D. F. Verdenal................New York
	Mrs. Mary C. Cantrell.........Georgetown, Ky.
	Mrs. M. S. Lockwood.........Washington, D. C.
	Mrs. J. J. Bagley................Detroit, Mich.
	Miss E. A. Ford................Brooklyn, N. Y.
	Mrs. Mary S. Harrison..........Helena, Montana
	Mrs. I. A. E. Tyler............Philadelphia, Pa.
	Mrs. Rosine Ryan..................Austin, Tex.
Alabama	Miss H. T. Hundley..................Moresville
	Mrs. A. M. Fosdick......................Mobile
Arkansas	Mrs. J. P. Eagle....................Little Rock
	Mrs. R. A. Edgerton................Little Rock
California	Mrs. P. P. Rue......................Santa Rosa
	Mrs. J. K. Deane................San Francisco
Colorado	Mrs. R. J. Coleman................Buena Vista
	Mrs. S. R. Ashley......................Denver
Connecticut	Miss F. S. Ives....................New Haven
	Mrs. I. B. Hooker....................Hartford
Delaware	Mrs. M. R. Kinder....................Milford
	Mrs. J. F. Ball....................Wilmington
Florida	Mrs. M. C. Bell....................Gainesville
	Miss E. N. Beck........................Tampa
Georgia	Mrs. W. H. Felton..................Cartersville
	Mrs. C. H. Olmsted..................Savannah
Idaho	Mrs. A. E. M. Farnum..........Hanser Junction
	Mrs. J. C. Straughan................Boise City
Illinois	Mrs. R. J. Oglesby....................Elkhart
	Mrs. F. W. Shephard..................Chicago
Indiana	Miss W. Reitz........................Evansville
	Mrs. V. C. Meredith............Cambridge City
Iowa	Mrs. W. S. Clark..................Des Moines
	Miss O. E. Miller................Cedar Rapids
Kansas	Mrs. J. S. Mitchell....................Topeka
	Mrs. H. A. Hanback....................Topeka
Kentucky	Miss J. W. Faulkner................Lancaster
	Mrs. A. C. Jackson..................Covington
Louisiana	Miss K. L. Minor......................Houma
	Miss J. Shakespeare..............New Orleans
Maine	Mrs. E. C. Burleigh..................Augusta
	Mrs. L. M. N. Stevens................Portland
Maryland	Mrs. W. Reed........................Baltimore
	Mrs. A. Thomson................Mount Savage
Massachusetts	Mrs. J. H. French......................Boston
	Mrs. Rufus S. Frost....................Chelsea
Michigan	Mrs. E. J. P. Howes................Battle Creek
	Mrs. S. S. C. Angell................Ann Arbor
Minnesota	Mrs. F. B. Clark......................St. Paul
	Mrs. H. F. Brown..................Minneapolis
Mississippi	Mrs. J. W. Lee......................Aberdeen
	Mrs. J. M. Stone......................Jackson

STATES.	MANAGERS.
Missouri	Miss Phœbe Couzins............St. Louis
	Miss L. M. Brown..............Kirkwood
Montana	Mrs. Eliza Richards..........Butte City
	Mrs. C. L. McAdow..............Helena
Nebraska	Mrs. J. S. Briggs...............Omaha
	Mrs. E. C. Langworthy..........Seward
Nevada	Miss E. M. Russell...............Elko
	Mrs. M. D. Foley.................Reno
New Hampshire	Mrs. M. B. F. Ladd............Lancaster
	Mrs. D. Hall.....................Dover
New Jersey	Miss M. E. Busselle............Newark
	Mrs. M. B. Stevens.............Hoboken
New York	Mrs. R. Trautmann.........New York City
N. Carolina	Mrs. G. W. Kidder............Wilmington
	Mrs. Charles Price.............Salisbury
North Dakota	Mrs. S. W. McLaughlin.......Grand Forks
	Mrs. W. B. McConnell............Fargo
Ohio	Mrs. M. A. Hart..............Cincinnati
	Mrs. W. Heartpence.............Harrison
Oregon	Mrs. E. W. Allen...............Portland
	Mrs. M. Payton..................Salem
Pennsylvania	Miss M. E. McCandless........Pittsburg
	Mrs. H. A. Lucas...........Philadelphia
Rhode Island	Mrs. A. M. Starkweather.......Pawtucket
	Miss C. F. Dailey............Providence
S. Carolina	Miss F. Cunningham...........Charleston
	Mrs. E. M. Brayton............Columbia
South Dakota	Mrs. J. R. Wilson.............Deadwood
	Mrs. H. M. Barker...............Huron
Tennessee	Mrs. L. Gillespie..............Nashville
	Mrs. S. G. Cooke..............Knoxville
Texas	Mrs. M. A. Cochran..............Dallas
	Mrs. L. L. Turner.............Ft. Worth
Vermont	Mrs. E. M. Chandler............Pomfret
	Mrs. E. N. Grinnell..........Burlington
Virginia	Mrs. J. S. Wise...............Richmond
	Mrs. K. S. G. Paul.........Harrisonburg
Washington	Mrs. M. G. Owings..............Olympia
	Mrs. A. Houghton.........Spokane Falls
West Virginia	Mrs. W. N. Lynch...........Martinsburg
	Mrs. I. I. Jackson..........Parkersburg
Wisconsin	Mrs. F. B. Ginty..........Chippewa Falls
	Mrs. W. P. Lynde..............Milwaukee
Wyoming	Mrs. F. H. Harrison............Evanston
	Mrs. E. E. Hale................Cheyenne
Alaska	Mrs. E. K. Delaney...............Juneau
	Miss I. J. Austin................Sitka
Arizona	Mrs. I. J. Butler..............Prescott
	Miss L. Lovell..................Tuscon
New Mexico	Mrs. E. L. Allbright........Albuquerque
	Mrs. E. L. Bartlett...........Santa Fe
Oklahoma	Mrs. M. P. H. Beeson..........Reno City
	Mrs. G. Guthrie...........Oklahoma City
Utah	Mrs. T. A. Whalen...............Ogden
	Mrs. M. B. Salisbury.......Salt Lake City
District of Columbia	Mrs. J. A. Logan..............Washington
	Mrs. B. Wilkins..............Washington

The officials who have taken the most prominent part in the fair work are Director General Davis; Daniel H. Burnham, chief of construction; Thomas W. Palmer, president of the National Commission; Mrs. Potter Palmer, president of the Board of Lady Managers; Lyman J. Gage, the first, and

H. N. Higinbotham the last president of the Local Board; C. C. Bonney, president, and T. B. Bryan, vice-president of the World's Congress Auxiliary, and Moses P. Handy, chief of the Department of Publicity and Promotion. The fair itself speaks for the work of most of the officers, but the labors of Major Handy were unique. His was the duty to advertise the fair at home and abroad, to popularize it, to make success

Thomas W. Palmer.

possible. An old newspaper man, Major Handy understood the difficulties of the situation, organized his department at once, went over the United States and Europe in the interest of the exposition, and everywhere gave it a definite status, interested people of all classes in the enterprise, and in no small degree contributed to the great world co-operation that is making the fair a success.

Dr. T. W. Zaremba, of Mexico, proposed, as early as 1876, that an international exposition be held in America in 1892 in honor of Columbus' discovery of the new world, and in 1882 Dr. A. W. Harlan revived the idea in a letter printed in a Chicago newspaper. Thomas B. Bryan, of Chicago, was the first

Moses P. Handy.

man to make an energetic fight to secure the World's Fair for Chicago, and when the World's Fair Exposition Company was incorporated in 1889, Mr. Bryan was made chairman of the committee on national agitation and Lyman J. Gage chairman of the finance committee. In a debate before a congressional sub-committee, as to the site for the fair, Mr. Bryan argued in Chicago's behalf, and conducted the debate with such masterly skill as to completely defeat Chauncey M. Depew, who had spoken for New York. Mr. Bryan has thus been identified with the fair from the first, but his greatest services were his efforts to get the exposition for Chicago. The work of Lyman J. Gage was also of the highest value. His great ability as a financier helped to solve money difficulties and his

Thomas B. Bryan.

name lent the enterprise a standing in all financial circles. At the close of his term of office as president of the Local Board, Mr. Gage refused the salary attaching to the position, and also the renomination, which was unanimously tendered him. Thomas W. Palmer has served continuously as president of the National Commission and, like Mr. Gage, has never accepted any salary for his services.

THE GREAT BUILDINGS.

Daniel Hudson Burnham, the friend and partner of John Wellborn Root, built the White City. In so doing he has marked himself not only as a man possessed of the very highest order of executive talent, but also as one having the highest appreciation of every department of art, learning and

Lyman J. Gage.

science. Immediately on being appointed as chief of construction he adopted a general plan for the work, and assigned to the most prominent architects of the country the duty of designing the great buildings for the fair. The work was undertaken in the same generous spirit in which it was given, and only the hearty co-operation of America's leading architects made the great buildings a possibility. To Root, to Burnham and to Frederick Law Olmstead, the landscape gardener, chiefly belong the glory of the artistic success of the fair, as far as buildings and grounds are concerned.

The dimensions and cost of the great exposition buildings are indicated in the following table:

BUILDING.	Dimensions in feet.	Area in acres.	Acreage of floor space including galleries.	COST.
Manufactures and Liberal Arts	787x1,687	30.5	44.	$1,500,000
Administration	262x 262	1.6	4.2	435,000
Mines	350x 700	5.6	8.7	265,000
Electricity	345x 690	5.5	9.7	401,000
Transportation	256x 960	5.6	9.4	370,000
" Annex	425x 900	8.8	9.2	
Woman's	199x 388	1.8	3.3	138,000
Art Galleries	320x 500	3.7	4.	670,000
" Annexes (2)	120x 200	1.1	1.1	
Fisheries	165x 365	1.4	2.4	224,000
" Annexes (2)	135 diam.	.8	.7	
Horticulture	250x 998	5.7	6.6	300,000
" Greenhouses (8)	24x 100	.5	.5	25,000
Machinery	492x 846	9.6	17.5	1,200,000
" Annex	490x 550	6.2	6.2	
" Power House, etc.	100x 461			
" Pumping works	77x 84	2.1	1.9	85,000
" Machine shop	146x 250			
Agriculture	500x 800	9.2	15.	618,000
" Annex	300x 550	3.8	3.9	
" Assembly, etc	125x 450	1.3	1.9	100,000
Forestry	208x 528	2.5	2.6	100,000
Saw Mill	125x 300	.9	.9	35,000
Dairy	105x 200	.5	.8	30,000
Live Stock (3)	65x 200	.9	1.2	
" Pavilion	250x 440	2.8	2.8	335,000
" Sheds		40.	40.	
Casino	120x 250	.7	.7	210,000
Music Hall	120x 250	.7	.7	
		133.8	199.9	$7,041,000
U. S. Government	345x 415	3.3	6.1	400,000
" Imitation Battleship	69.25x 348	.3	.6	100,000
Illinois State	160x 450	1.7	3.2	250,000
" Wings (2)		.3		
		139.4	209.8	$7,791,000

The site of the fair buildings, Jackson Park, embraces 553 acres, with an added area of 80 acres in Midway Plaisance. All the buildings, with possibly one or two exceptions, will be at once torn down and removed on the closing of the exposition, October 30, 1893. Lumber, structural iron and "staff" are the building materials most used at Jackson Park—over

75,000,000 feet of lumber and 20,000 tons of iron being required for the work. Staff is a composition of plaster, cement and hemp or similar fibre. It is lighter than wood, is fire-proof, water-proof, and, if kept painted, will last for years.

The Agricultural building is located in the south end of the grounds, near the lake shore. The rotunda is surmounted by a glass dome 130 feet in height. Throughout the main vestibule statuary has been placed, illustrative of the agricultural industry. South of the Agricultural building is a spacious structure devoted chiefly to an assembly hall for conventions of live stock, agriculture and allied interests.

In the Agricultural building will be found, besides the vegetable products of the soil, the literature and statistics of agriculture, the preserved meats and foods preparations exhibit, pure and mineral waters, and the process of bottling and storing beverages. McKim, Mead & White, of New York, designed the building, and W. I. Buchanan is the chief of the department.

South of the Midway Plaisance entrance to the park, and facing the lagoon, is the Horticultural building. The plan is a central pavilion with two wings. From the centre of the structure rises a crystal dome 187 feet in diameter and 118 feet high, under which are exhibited the tallest palms, bamboos and tree ferns that can be procured. Here will be shown flowers, plants, vines, seeds and horticultural implements. The exhibits requiring sunlight will be arranged in the wings, which are almost entirely of glass. W. L. B. Jenney, of Chicago, designed Horticultural hall, and J. M. Samuels and John Thorpe have superintended the work of gathering the exhibit it contains.

The Fisheries building, designed by Henry Ives Cobb, is one of the most unique and characteristic structures of the fair. There is a circular main building with two tank annexes at either end, connected with the central structure by curving arcades. The whole building conforms itself to the banana-

The Horticultural Building.

shaped island on which it is located. The water capacity of the aquaria is 140,000 gallons, nearly one-third of which will be devoted to salt water fish. Captain J. W. Collins is chief of the fisheries exhibit.

The imposing building provided for the department of mining, designed by S. S. Beman, is simple and straightforward in construction, with wide galleries and sweeping ground spaces. The principal fronts show enormous arched entrances, richly embellished with sculptured decorations, emblematic of mining and its allied industries. This building contains everything pertaining to mines and metallurgy. Fred J. V. Skiff is chief of the department.

In Machinery hall, Lieutenant R. W. Robinson has charge of a marvellous exhibit. The building, designed by Peabody & Stearns, of Boston, measures 500 by 850 feet, and is spanned by three arched trusses. The interior presents the appearance of three railroad train houses side by side, surrounded on all the four sides by a gallery fifty feet wide. The trusses are built separately, so that they can be taken down and utilized. The power for the building is supplied from a power house adjoining the south side of the building. The floor area is 17.5 acres, an annex measuring 490 by 550 feet furnishing 6.2 additional acres. Adjoining Machinery hall is a machine shop 146 by 250 feet. There is a power house, 100 by 460 feet. In this structure are stationed the engines for the 24,000 horse-power provided for the exposition. One of these engines is about twice the size and power of the celebrated Corliss engine used at the Centennial Exposition, Philadelphia, in 1876. Oil is used for fuel.

Transportation building, designed by Alder & Sullivan, the architects of the Auditorium, is exquisitely refined and simple in architectural treatment. It is Romanesque in style, and the main entrance consists of an immense single arch enriched with carvings, bas-reliefs and mural paintings, the entire feature forming a beautiful color climax.

Machinery Hall.

The roof is in three divisions. The middle one rises much higher than the others, and its walls are pierced to form an arcaded clear story. The cupola, placed in the center of the building and rising 165 feet above the ground, is reached by eight elevators. These elevators naturally form a part of the transportation exhibit, and as they also carry passengers to the various galleries, a fine view of the interior of the building may easily be obtained. The main galleries of this building, because of the abundant elevator facilities, prove very accessible to visitors.

The main building measures 960 by 250 feet. From this extends westward to Stony Island avenue an enormous annex, covering about nine acres. This is one story in height. In it may be seen the more bulky exhibits. Along the central avenue of the nave the visitor may see scores of locomotive engines highly polished, and exceedingly novel. Willard A. Smith has directed the collection of the transportation exhibit.

The Manufactures and Liberal Arts building, George B. Post, architect, is the largest building in the world. The main roof of iron and glass spreads its giant spans 250 feet in air. The galleries, 50 feet wide, circle the entire building, and projecting from these main galleries are 86 smaller galleries, 12 feet wide, from which visitors may survey the vast array of exhibits on the 34 acres of floor space below. In the central hall of this building, which is without a supporting pillar under its roof, 75,000 persons could be seated, allowing each 6 square feet of space

Its unequalled size makes it one of the architectural wonders of the world. It is three times larger than the Cathedral of St. Peter, in Rome. It is four times larger than the old Roman Colosseum, which seated 80,000 persons. If the great pyramid Cheops could be removed to Chicago, it could be piled up in this building with the galleries left from which to view the stone. There are 7,000,000 feet of lumber in the floor, and it required five car-loads of nails to fasten the 215 car-loads of flooring to the joists. The Auditorium is the most notable building in Chicago, but twenty such buildings could be placed on this floor. There are eleven acres of skylights and forty car-loads of glass in the roof. The iron and steel structure of this roof would build two Brooklyn bridges, while there is in it 1400 tons more metal than in the Eads bridge at St. Louis. There are twenty-two main trusses in the roof of the central hall, and it required 600 flat cars to bring them from the iron works to Chicago. These trusses are twice the size of the next largest in existence, which are 90 feet high and span 250 feet. The latter are in the Pennsylvania Railroad depot at Jersey City.

Here are a few facts regarding the size of the building and its various parts: Dimensions, 1,687 x 787 feet; height of walls, 66 feet; height of four center pavilions, 122 feet; height of four corner pavilions, 97 feet; height of roof over central hall, 237.6 feet; height clear, from the floor, 202.9 feet; span of truss, 382 feet; width of truss at base, 14 feet; at hip, 32 feet; at apex, 10 feet; weight of truss, 300,000 pounds; floor area, including galleries, 44 acres; cost, $1,700,000; material, 17,000,000 feet of lumber; 12,000,000 pounds of steel in trusses of central hall; 2,000,000 pounds of iron in roof of nave. In the gallery space of this mammoth structure will be displayed the interesting and instructive exhibit of liberal arts, embracing education, music, hygiene, medicine and surgery, books and literature, engineering and architecture. James Allison and Selim B. Peabody have charge of the show in the manufactures and liberal arts departments.

In the Electrical building, where Prof. J. P. Barrett, Chicago's veteran electrician, has charge, Architects Van Brunt & Howe, of Kansas City, have provided a structure especially designed for illumination at night. There are ten towers and four domes, the tallest two towers being each 195 feet high. The floor area is 9.7 acres. A striking feature of this building is a heroic statue of Benjamin Franklin. The exterior of the building is richly decorated, and the pediments, friezes, panels and spandrils have received a decoration of figures in relief, with architectural motifs, the general tendency of which is to illustrate the purposes of the building. The display of electricity and electrical appliances presented in this building is the most complete exhibit of the kind ever made.

C. B. Atwood, designer-in-chief of the construction department of the fair, conceived the palatial Fine Arts building, where Halsey C. Ives has got together many of the great paintings of the world. Unlike the other exposition buildings, the Art Palace is constructed of brick, covered with staff. Although designed as a temporary structure, it is necessarily fire-proof, the walls being brick, and the roof, floors and galleries iron. The main building, which is Ionic in style, is entered by four great portals, richly ornamented with architectural sculpture, and approached by broad flights of steps. The walls of the loggia of the colonnades are highly decorated with mural paintings, illustrating the history and progress of the arts. The frieze of the exterior walls and the pediments of the principal entrances are ornamented with sculptures and portraits in bas-relief of the masters of ancient art.

In Administration building, the masterly conception of Richard M. Hunt, are located the offices of the exposition management. This noble achievement of modern architecture is universally admitted to be the artistic triumph of the fair. Connected with the grand central dome, which is coated with aluminium bronze, at a cost of $54,000, are four pavilions, four stories in height. Around the base of this dome, on the corners of the pavilions, are groups of statuary, emblematic of art and science. The general design of the building is in the style of the French renaissance. The first story is in the Doric order, the second the Ionic. The interior of the building exceeds in beauty and splendor even the magnificent exterior.

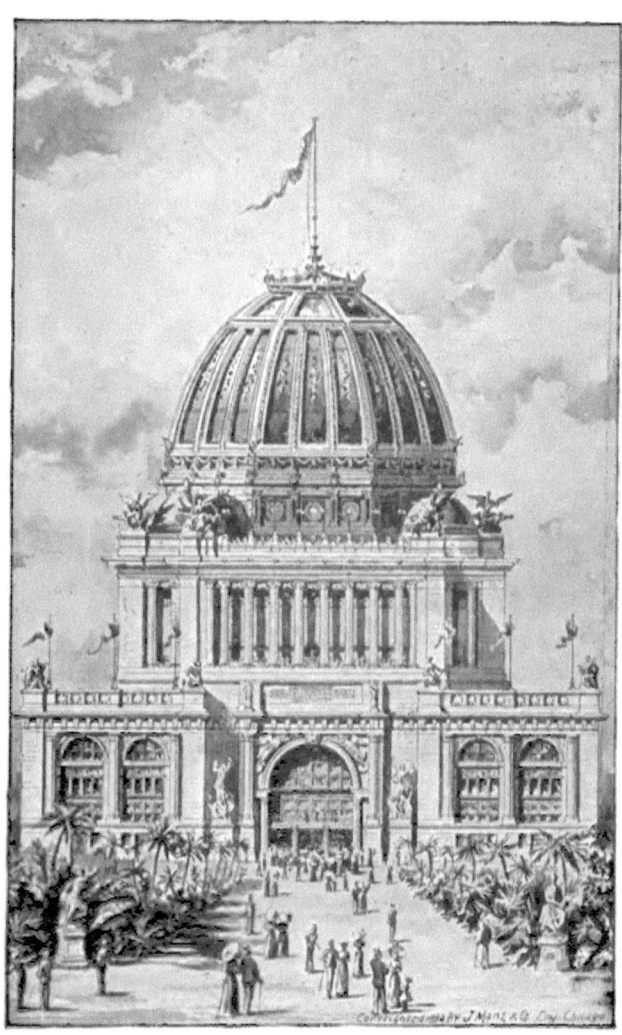

Administration Building.

The Government building, designed by Architect Windrum, does not meet with the favor of the critics. Its situation is one of the most delightful in the park. The organic lines are those of the capitol at Washington. Its central dome is imposing, but at a distance is lost in the magnitude of the structure. The dome is purely Roman and suggests that of St. Paul's Cathedral at London. Many features of the building suggest the Italian renaissance. The main and central entrances follow that period of architecture. The interior, or that portion devoted to artistic embellishments, is a comparative failure. The dome, or rotunda, is supported by columns of vivid and shaded green, in imitation of marble.

The Woman's building, designed by Sophia B. Hayden, is chaste and beautiful. On the first floor are located a model hospital and kindergarten, and much space is devoted throughout to reform and charity work. A feature is the roof garden and cafe.

The naval exhibit may be properly classed among the main buildings of the exposition. It consists of a structure that is to all outward appearance a full-sized model of one of the new coast line battle ships. It is erected on piling on the lake front in the northeast portion of the park. It is surrounded by water and has the appearance of being moored to a wharf. The structure has all the fittings that belong to an actual ship. Its dimensions are as follows: Length, 348 feet; width amidships, 69 feet 3 inches; from the main deck to water line, 12 feet.

HOUSES OF THE STATES.

All the states and territories participate in the exposition. The following thirty-one states and two territories have made appropriations through their legislatures:

Arizona	$ 30,000
California	300,000
Colorada	100,000
Delaware	10,000

Carried forward	$ 440,000
Idaho	20,000
Illinois	800,000
Indiana	75,000
Iowa	130,000
Kentucky	100,000
Louisiana	36,000
Maine	40,000
Maryland	60,000
Massachusetts	150,000
Michigan	100,000
Minnesota	50,000
Missouri	150,000
Montana	50,000
Nebraska	50,000
New Hampshire	25,000
New Jersey	70,000
New Mexico	25,000
New York	300,000
North Carolina	25,000
North Dakota	25,000
Ohio	125,000
Pennsylvania	300,000
Rhode Island	50,000
Vermont	15,000
Virginia	25,000
Washington	100,000
West Virginia	40,000
Wisconsin	65,000
Wyoming	30,000
Total	$3,441,000

These eight states have raised funds by stock subscriptions:

Alabama	$ 20,000
Arkansas	40,000
Florida	50,000
Georgia	100,000
Kansas	100,000
Oregon	50,000
South Dakota	25,000
Texas	30,000
Total	$415,000

Illinois furnishes by far the most pretentious of the state buildings, and it may be classed as one of the great exposition structures. The plan of the building forms a Greek cross, whose main axis is 450 feet long by 160 feet wide, while the shorter axis is 285 feet long with an average width of 98 feet. At the intersection of the arms of the cross rises the dome, with a diameter of 75 feet at the base, and a height of 152 feet at the top of the inner dome. At the east and west are two large entrances, at either side of which are rooms extending the entire width of the building, and about 29 feet deep, occupying the whole height, which is divided into three stories. The rooms at the east end are chiefly used for school exhibition purposes, a large one on the ground floor being fitted up as a model kindergarten. Beyond this extends the great exhibition hall, 381 feet long.

The design of the Arkansas building follows classic models, it being in the French "Rococo" style of architecture, as Arkansas was originally settled by the French. The exterior is in plaster and ornamental staff work, tinted in light color. The interior is tinted, and the ornamental work is brought out in gold. The building has a ground area of 66 by 92 feet. From a large circular veranda, which runs the width of the building, an elliptical entrance opens to the rotunda, 30 by 30 feet, lighted by a central dome. In the center of the rotunda is a fountain of Hot Springs crystals, lighted by electricity.

Next to Illinois California shows the largest state building at the fair. Its dimensions are 144 by 435 feet. It is in the style of architecture of the old California mission buildings. The exterior is of plain plaster, artificially seamed and cracked, giving it the appearance of the old mission buildings, while recessed entrances give the walls that appearance of depth and solidity characteristic of the old buildings. The south front is a reproduction of the old mission church at San Diego.

The Colorado building is in the Spanish renaissance style

Illinois State Building.

of architecture. The whole exterior is in staff of an ivory color, and in the salient features of the design profusely ornamented, the ornamentation comparing to fine advantage with the broad, plain surfaces of the building. The striking feature of the design is two slender Spanish towers, 98 feet high, rising from either side of the main entrance, on the east.

Connecticut shows a type of the old colonial residence, with circular windows and piazza, and Florida's building is a reproduction of Fort Marion, St. Augustine. Indiana's house is in the style of a French chateau. Iowa has a corn palace. Kansas builds a typical house, and Maine's home is of granite from the sea coast.

Massachusetts reproduces the historic John Hancock residence, which, until the year 1867, stood on Beacon Hill, Boston, near the state capitol. The building is three stories high, surmounted in the center by a cupola. The exterior is of staff, in imitation of cut granite. It follows the lines of the old house sufficiently to recall the original to the minds of those who have seen it. Like the original, it is surrounded by a terrace, raised above the street, and has in front and on one side a court, filled with old-fashioned flowers and foliage, in keeping with the character of the building.

Minnesota, Missouri, Montana and Nebraska have erected handsome structures after approved styles of architecture. The mountains of New Hampshire probably suggested the Swiss cottage for its club house. The architecture of New York's building is that of a big summer house, after the manner of an Italian villa. Among the state buildings it ranks in size next to Illinois and California. It is three stories high, being 57 feet from the ground to the cornice. The exterior is in staff, in imitation of marble, and in keeping with the style of the main exposition buildings. Its decked roof is surmounted and confined by a heavy balustrade. Each pedestal of the balustrade supports a large Italian vase, in which grows a bay-tree, giving the building, together with its other characteristics, the air of a Pompeiian house. On the north and south ends of the building are circular porticoes, in each of which is a fountain. The general dimensions are 160 feet front by 105 feet deep. A broad flight of steps, guarded by Roman lions, leads to the arched entrance.

Ohio shows a colonial house, and Pennsylvania's home is an exact reproduction of old Independence Hall, having its entrances, bell-tower, and spire. The famous independence bell hangs in the tower. The rotunda within the entrance is finished in tile and slate, like the old hall. The building is rectangular in form, two stories high, with a ground area of 110 by 166 feet. Piazzas 20 feet wide surround the building, and over them are verandas, with protecting balustrade. Outside staircases, right and left to the rear, lead to the garden on the roof. The outer walls to the roof line are of Philadelphia pressed brick. Above the main entrance is the coat of arms of the state, in bas-relief, and on either side of it are heroic statues of Penn and Franklin.

Rhode Island, South Dakota, Utah, Washington and West Virginia have characteristic houses. Wisconsin's house is of native marble.

In all, there are over 400 separate structures on the fair grounds, exclusive of booths, and there are 200 acres under roof, 150 of which belong to exposition buildings proper, the other 50 acres to concession buildings.

FINE ARTS AT THE FAIR.

The fine art collection at the fair not only far surpasses every former American exhibition of the kind, but equals the European standard of such exhibitions. There are several reasons for this. The amount of space granted to the artists of the world is but a fraction of what they desired and asked for—but this limitation of space has very largely enhanced the standard of excellence. It is no disparagement of the 10,000 works of art to say that they have been rejected by the World's Fair juries of selection. The works of art selected are representative. They are as numerous as such broad representation of the thousands of the world's artists made possible. Another reason is that there is a better representation from a greater number of nations than has ever been brought together at any previous exposition. The responses from foreign governments and the enthusiasm of foreign artists, when the World's Fair art exhibit was thrown open to them, far exceeded the most sanguine predictions of two years ago. World's Fair visitors will therefore see not only a great exhibit of American art, but the choicest productions of the world's great masters from across the sea.

The broad lines upon which the fine arts exhibit has been planned will dispel the impression that statuary, oil and water colors finish the category of fine arts. The application of sculpture to architecture is illustrated on a scale that will create admiration, and must prove educative to builders in this era of advanced architecture. The World's Fair fine arts exhibit of paintings is representative of all the different schools. Lovers of the finesse in the French school will see masterpieces by acknowledged leaders. The famous Dutch school, the Russian, the less known but powerful Scandinavian, the impressionist, and many others, will be represented by a selection of the choicest productions from leaders. A critical study of American art will not show characteristics of each of the foreign schools, but distinct individuality. The American section of the fine art exhibit will contain between 1500 and 2000 pieces, while Germany contributes 900 pieces, France 800, Dutch artists 300, England 600, Austria 300, Denmark 250, Sweden 200, Italy 600, Norway 180 and Belgium 400.

Foreign governments take care of the selection, installation and insurance of the exhibits from their own artists. The American artist exhibitors insure their own works. In the case of valuable loan collections from private galleries, the

Fine Arts Building.

exposition company carries the insurance. It were idle to speculate as to the monetary value of the art collections. Three paintings alone have been insured for $107,000, and the commercial value of one painting is placed at $70,000. There are, of course, hundreds of paintings that are not for sale at any price.

Germany, France, England, Holland, Belgium, Norway, Sweden, Denmark, Russia, Poland, Austria, Austria-Hungary, Italy and Spain, applied for 300,000 square feet of wall space at the World's Fair, but the total wall space in the art galleries amount to only 200,000 square feet. After reserving 35,000 square feet to American art, Chief Ives had 165,000 square feet of wall space to give foreign countries. Although little more than half what they asked for, this space is still more than double the foreign space in the Centennial art galleries of 1876.

The countries represented officially in the exhibit are Germany, France, Great Britain, Austria, Spain, Italy, Belgium, Holland, Norway, Sweden, Denmark, Russia, Canada, Mexico and Japan. Next to the United States comes France with 29,201 square feet, then Germany, Great Britain, Italy, Belgium, Austria, and so on down to Mexico, which received all it asked for—1,500 square feet. In previous art expositions, French art has been poorly represented when the exposition was held in Germany, and the Germans have withheld their art works when the exposition was held in France, but at Jackson Park there is nothing to interfere with a broadly representative foreign exhibit. Each of the foreign governments appointed its own art commission. In France, M. Proust, who was minister of fine arts under the Gambetta regime, headed the commission. H. W. Mesdag, the famous painter, headed the art commission for the Netherlands. For England the Royal Society of Arts, headed by Sir Frederick Leighton, president of the royal academy, undertook the World's Fair exhibit. The German commis-

The Woman's Building

sion is headed by Herr Schnars-Alquist, the Belgium commission by Professor Ernest Slingeneyer, the Italian commission by Signor Giulio Monteverde, the eminent sculptor. These commissions, in securing work by the leading European artists for the World's Fair, have had a dual success. Not alone the glory of achievement in a special school, or in a special line of art, has induced the foreign artists to send their best works. There is the ever present knowledge that within recent years the United States has become the greatest art market in the world and that the purchasing power of American art patrons seems illimitable.

In securing a good representation of American art, advisory committees were appointed in the leading art centers of the United States and in European centers where American art colonies flourished. By an interchange of service, these advisory committees became juries of selection. For a special exhibition of retrospective American art, a committee was appointed to solicit from private American owners and societies a loan collection that would best exhibit historical art in America. This committee has selected about a hundred pieces that will be hung together in one of the galleries. The collection will show the work of native artists from the earliest known specimens down to 1867.

One of the special noteworthy foreign exhibits is a collection of casts duplicating productions of monumental works shown in the Museum of Comparative Sculpture in the palace of Trocadero, Paris. This illustrates the history of French sculpture, and the development of fine arts in France in medieval and later times. There is also a collection of casts from ancient Greek sculpture, which has been sent as a special art exhibit by the Greek government. There is a loan collection of 150 foreign masterpieces, owned in America, which are hung in three adjoining galleries in the west end of the east pavilion. These are all the property of American collectors. They include all the illustrious names among artists, from the dawn of this century to the present time. From Boston and San Francisco, from New York, Chicago, Philadelphia and other centers, these pictures come. Millet, Rosa Bonheur, Carolus-Doran, John Constable, Millais, Meissonier, Alma Tadema and a score of other famous names are represented. There are also figures and groups in marble, casts from original works by modern artists, models, monumental decorations, figures and groups in bronze and bas-reliefs in marble and bronze.

The lighting arrangements of the galleries are well nigh faultless. All the pavilions, including rotundas, courts and galleries, are lighted from above. The modulation of natural light in the day-time is simple and effective. The system of artificial lighting at night will in itself be a work of art. Myriads of incandescent lamps will shed a mellow radiance over courts and galleries. The electric lamps are arranged in clusters above each court, and also in continuous rows around the galleries. The attractiveness of the art galleries at night will be one of the features of the exposition.

FOREIGN PARTICIPATION.

The lake shore, north of the big pier at Jackson Park, is studded with a number of beautiful buildings, the houses of the foreign nations represented at the fair. Interest in the exposition is general throughout the world. Appropriations by various countries amount to $6,589,779, as follows:

Argentine Republic $100,000	Hawaii $40,000
Austria 200,000	Hayti 25,000
Belgium 57,900	Honduras 20,000
Bolivia 30,700	Italy 35,000
Brazil 600,000	Japan 630,765
Colombia 100,000	Liberia 7,000
Costa Rica 150,000	Mexico 150,000
Denmark 67,000	Morocco 150,000
Danish West Indies 1,200	Netherlands 100,000
Ecuador 125,000	Dutch Guiana 10,000
France 733,100	Dutch West Indies 5,000
Germany 820,000	Nicaragua 31,000
Great Britain 201,050	Norway 56,280

Barbadoes	5,840	Orange Free State	7,500
Bermuda	2,920	Paraguay	100,000
British Guiana	25,000	Peru	140,000
British Honduras	7,500	Russia	400,000
Canada	100,000	Salvador	12,500
Cape Colony	50,000	San Domingo	25,000
Ceylon	65,600	Spain	214,000
India	30,000	Cuba	25,000
Jamaica	24,333	Switzerland	23,160
Leeward Islands	6,000	Sweden	108,000
New South Wales	243,325	Turkey	17,466
New Zealand	27,500	Uruguay	24,000
Tasmania	10,000	Venezuela	30,000
Trinidad	20,000		
Greece	57,900	Total	$6,589,779
Guatemala	200,000		

In all, 50 foreign nations and 37 colonies take part in the exposition. Germany, France, Spain, Russia and Japan make the finest displays. Germany's building is a work of the highest art. It is executed in polished woods, with a wealth of the most costly stained glass, and each detail worked out with the elaborateness and thoroughness characteristic of this government. The exterior decorations are equaled only by the interior, and the stately edifice, with its sightly turrets and graceful roof, will be a mecca for visitors. It is the costliest and generally conceded to be the finest foreign building on the grounds. In its dome the Society of Bochum have hung a chime of bells, intended, after the fair, for the use of the Cathedral of Mercy at Berlin. These bells are masterpieces of the German art of bronze founding. The walls of the building are partly of stone and partly of plaster and are elaborately decorated and painted with the escutcheons of the states of united Germany. In the Manufactures building 2500 exhibitors are representing Germany, especially in drugs, pottery, jewelry, glass, laces and musical instruments. The great Krupp gun exhibit is in a detached building, and, in addition to a monster 127-ton gun—the largest gun in the world—Krupp shows smaller guns, armor plates, shells, etc. The Krupp exhibit is one of the finest on the grounds and represents an outlay of half a million dollars. The German electricians—30 strong—have a splendid exhibit, including a 1000-horse power dynamo, enormous search lights, motors and instruments of applied science. The German mines are represented by selected ores forming the great Brandenburg gate, and by another exhibit showing a mine in detail, including smelters and all mining machinery. The German women, under the Empress Frederick, have shown great interest in the fair and have sent a fine collection of paintings, embroideries, laces, carvings, and illustrations of activity in educational and charitable matters. In the fine arts, transportation and horticultural lines the German display is complete and excellent.

Germany's Building.

Spain naturally takes a prominent place in a Columbus exposition. Its gorgeous building will contain an exhibition which promises to be unique as well as interestingly beautiful. The Columbus exposition held in Spain last year has given up all its treasures to make the show complete. Convents and monasteries have been pillaged in a friendly way and their treasures brought into the glaring light of a World's Fair. The forest and the field will add their quota to the list. Historic relics from a land teeming with romance will add a charm to the Spanish building. The latter itself is a poem in architecture and is a reproduction of the exchange at Valencia.

France sends the finest display the nation has ever shown outside its own borders. The surpassing exhibit in the Manufactures building will not overshadow the gay array of rich and rare gems in the white building by the lake. Here all that is delicate and artistic, all that is characteristic of La Belle France, will be displayed before those who have an eye for beauty in utility. It is said that there is a reason below the surface for this magnificent display. France's old foe on the

British Building.

battlefield and rival in arts and manufactures, Germany, is across the way with another brilliant display.

Italy, the land of olives, claims Columbus as a son, and therefore she has resolved to do him honor in the most beautiful way. Italy is rich in treasures of art, and many of these are shown in the building set apart for them. The subjects of King Humbert have been tardy in exhibiting, but their display will not lack anything by delay. The silver workers, the wood-carvers, the bronze-casters and the cameo-cutters will exhibit superb specimens of their handiwork.

The English display is not as extensive as it might be, but endeavors to show that England is still supreme in certain branches of manufactures. The Victoria house, standing on the edge of the lake, is meant for an exhibition of such furniture as one finds in typical English homes. It needs only the shady elms, the long avenue of beeches, a well-kept lawn with stretching fields to make it look like an English country house. In all the departments English exhibitors are well represented.

Japan's quaint little national houses are located on Wooded Island, in the lagoon, between Manufactures building and Horticultural hall. They are the only buildings that will be allowed to stand in the park after the fair, save perhaps the palace of Fine Arts. Russia, Denmark, Sweden, Austria, Switzerland, Greece, Bulgaria, Belgium, Holland and numerous other countries make splendid showings, both as nations and through their individual exhibitors. Canada, Brazil, Mexico and the South American countries are all excellently represented.

MIDWAY PLAISANCE.

The Midway Plaisance is the overflow from the regular fair grounds in Jackson Park. It is a strip of land 600 feet wide, almost a mile long, and connects Jackson with Washington Park. In the plaisance are located all the amusements and attractions outside of the exposition proper. In all, about 40 shows occupy the 80 acres of the plaisance. People from all the corners and ends of the earth will meet, exhibiting the characteristic manufactures and products of their distant homes, and their social, religious, domestic and business customs. As the more advanced nations are represented in the main exposition buildings, it has remained for exhibitors in the plaisance to show in miniature the life of many parts of the world about which little is practically known in America. This plaisance will be over a mile of wonders to the simply curious, an inexhaustible field for the student of sociology, and the most fascinating resort for thousands of visitors every day during the great fair.

Among the shows to interest the visitors will be the German village; the Austrian village; Bohemian glass factory; Dahomey village, with sixty native warriors of both sexes; the captive balloon, which carries twenty people to a height of 1500 feet; the ice railway, practically a toboggan slide of artificial ice; international beauty show, represented by women of various nations, wearing native costumes and busied with the occupations of their ordinary home life; the Japanese bazaar, with its peculiar fire department; the panoramas of the volcano Kilauea, and of the Bernese Alps; a Chinese village, with a native theatre and 200 native artists; the Hungarian dance hall, theatre and cafe; Lapland village; original model of St. Peter's at Rome; model of the Eiffel tower; Moorish labyrinth; the Turkish village, with horses from the Sultan's stables; the Barre Sliding railway, run by water power; natatorium; and the great Hagenbeck animal show from Hamburg. This exhibit consists of trained animals, including lions, tigers, dogs, cattle, horses, elephants, bears, etc., all of which go through various performances which exemplify wonderful results in scientific training. In addition to the other animals, there are 200 monkeys and 1000 parrots. The animal pavilion seats 5000 persons.

The German village consists of a group of houses representative of a German village of the present time, and, in connection with this, a German town of mediæval times. There are the houses of the Upper Bavarian mountains, the houses of the Black Forest, a Westphalian farm house and other typical scenes of German home life of various times and districts. In these houses is installed original household furniture, so characteristic as to be readily distinguished as belonging to particular classes. There are thirty-six different

Forestry Building.

buildings, all distinctively German. Emperor William gave his sanction for their construction, and also granted the promoters the privilege of recruiting two military bands from the German army. Besides the village there is a reproduction of a country fair, two German restaurants, a German concert garden, a water tower, and an ethnological museum. In the center is a castle, sixteenth century style, with moat and palisades. Inside this castle will be found the most famous collection of weapons in Germany. There are sixty iron dummies in uniform and equipment, giving a complete and true picture of the weapons and armor of Germany.

The town hall of the village will be used as a museum. Goods will be shown and sold in the village market place. In the concert garden, two military bands will furnish the music. These are composed of forty people from the Garde regiment and twenty-six from the Garde du Corps.

The street in Cairo is next to the German village, and will undoubtedly be one of the most entertaining and instructive shows on the plaisance. The street is lined with mosques, dance halls, and shops filled with wares from Arabia and the Soudan. There are many famous curiosities from the museums in Cairo and Alexandria in a special museum. Dogs and children and the general appearance will all remind the visitor of a street in Cairo, and fortune-tellers will be on hand.

The Irish village, just west of the glass exhibit, is intended principally for the sale of Irish laces and linens. These will be made by Irish women and exhibited in the building so the visitor may see for himself just how the famous Irish goods are made. The intention is to represent a perfect model of the ancient Castle of Donegal, famous in song and story, refitting some of the rooms in appropriate style to contain the exhibit. Besides the lace makers, there will be Irish girls spinning, weaving and making wool and butter.

The so-called Javanese exhibit—both people and things—

The United States Government Building.

come from the Fiji, Philippine, and Solomon Islands, Samoa, Java, Borneo, New Zealand, and the Polynesian Archipelago. Among other features of this exhibit will be a building sixty feet long, in which the people from the Philippine Islands will be employed in making cigars and peculiar kinds of cloth. A theater with dancing girls will be one of the shows. The Javanese inclosure and buildings are made of bamboo. All the houses were built in Java and had been left standing until the ship for Chicago was ready to sail. This village was gotten up by a syndicate of Dutch merchants. The great event in its history will be the visit of the Sultan of Johore, who will come to the fair during the month of July, with his suite of native Rajahs.

The Ferris wheel is an exhibit in itself. It is 250 feet in diameter, is swung on a 56-ton axle which is 36 inches in diameter, 45 feet long and is the largest piece of steel ever forged. It rests on steel towers 137 feet high and will be revolved perpendicularly by a 2000-horse power engine. On its perimeter will be hung 36 cars, each of which will hold 60 persons. On it 3000 incandescent lights will be used. The weight of the wheel complete is 2300 tons.

The end of the plaisance is devoted to an encampment for soldiers and for military display. In the plaisance also are located divisions of the police and fire departments.

THE EXHIBITS.

The interior view of the great Manufactures building is like a glimpse of wonderland. In the center of the building rises a clock tower 135 feet, from which float the sweetest peals of chimes to mark the passing hours. Around this clock tower are quartered the exhibits from the United States, France, Germany, Great Britain and the other great powers of the earth. Beyond lie exhibits not nationalized. France has a pavilion in this building, but neither the United States nor Great Britain are so represented. The German pavilion is the most beautiful thing in the great hall. Its corner entrance, facing the clock tower, is flanked by two monumental towers sixty feet high and surmounted by golden eagles, which arrest the attention even from a distance. But its most striking feature is the three ornamented iron gates, thirty feet high, in the center of the east front, which are certainly marvels in that line of art. There are also canopies, vestibules, colonnades, arches, statuary, painting, gilding, and marble work almost without end. In general, the articles in the Manufactures building are divided into 35 groups, 400 classes, and various sub-classes. All smaller manufactured articles not otherwise provided for are to be seen in this building. In the gallery of the Manufactures building are the exhibits of the department of liberal arts, chiefly educational and natural history exhibits. The department of Ethnology and Archæology is housed in a special building. Native American, Greek, Roman, Assyrian and Egyptian archæological exhibits are remarkably full. Collections are also seen from British Guiana, Africa, the West Indies, Mexico, Brazil, Paraguay, Honduras and various other places. Russia has a complete exhibit of customs and costumes of the Slavic races. The folk-lore division pays great attention to the evolution of modern games from those of barbarous races. The most interesting ethnological exhibit is made by the various tribes of North American Indians, including the Navajos, Apaches, Blackfeet, Flatheads, Penobscots, Sioux, Winnebagoes, Senecas, Mohawks, Iroquois and various other tribes. There are also cliff dwellers, Peruvian mummies, Esquimaux and Indians from the far north.

The department of mines presents an exhibit that is remarkable for its fullness and detail. The classification includes twenty-eight groups, embracing minerals, ores, native metals, gems, crystals and geological specimens; mineral combustibles, oils, natural gas; building, grinding and polishing stone, graphites, asbestos, limestones, salts, fertilizers, pigments, mineral waters, aluminum, tin, zinc, cobalt, antimony, arsenic, alloys and amalgams. All the processes for the extraction of the metals are shown, with practical illustrations in assaying. There are also miniature mining plants, with all the tools for boring, lighting, ventilation, hoisting, crushing, pulverizing, timbering. The history of mining and the literature of the industry are offered with great completeness, while models of early mining are shown in contrast to the improved machinery of to-day.

The electrical display is one of dazzling brilliancy. America leads in the extent of her exhibit, but France and Germany excel in the excellence of hand-made machinery. All the myriad phenomena of electricity and magnetism will be represented, including the electric telegraph, signals and cables; dynamical electricity, batteries, machines for the generation of electricity; appliances for the measurement of the force; for the transmission and storage; motors; telephones, phonographs, telautographs, kinetographs; plants for furnishing heat, power and light; appliances for use in surgical and dental work and in therapeutics; appliances that will relieve pain and others that will destroy life; appliances for use in chemistry, metalling, and kindred sciences; instruments for taking photographs of objects hundreds of miles away. The lighting of the grounds will in itself be the great electrical exhibit. Of the 24,000-horse power furnished for the exposition, 17,000 is used for electricity. In all, there are 2877 arc lights in the main buildings, and 56,622 incandescent lamps on all the grounds.

In Transportation building, the locomotive supply, especially the foreign one, is full and interesting. Every type of engine and car, now or formerly in use, is shown here. The exhibit includes street cars, vehicles for common roads, vessels, aerial, pneumatic and other forms of locomotion, and also models of the methods of naval warfare and coast defence.

In the Woman's building there is a model kindergarten, a

Transportation Building.

kitchen in which the latest methods of cooking are illustrated, and a magnificent collection of the work of women the world over.

The most striking feature of the Fisheries building is the exhibit made by the United States Fish Commission. One entire section of the building is given up to their aquaria, and in them are shown almost every species of salt and fresh water fish. In the main building the great sea-coast nations of the world make exhaustive exhibits of the products of their fisheries. Models of fishing fleets at their work and specimens of all manner of fish tackle and traps are also displayed.

In Machinery hall the great Allis engine is the chief attraction. While this engine is larger by many thousand horse power than that which furnished the motive power for the entire machinery at the Centennial Exposition, it is only one of nearly 50 of the great machines which drive the many wheels of the World's Fair.

The crowning glory of the fair is the view from the east front of the magnificent gilt-domed Administration building. Directly in front is the beautiful McMonnies fountain, on either side of which are electric fountains, throwing prismatic streams 150 feet high. Then the grand basin, dotted with electric launches and gay gondolas, flanked by patches of green-sward, and rows of great figures of animals. At the farther end of the basin stands French's golden statue of the Republic; on either side are the Manufactures and Agricultural buildings, the latter surmounted by the beautiful Diana; beyond all these the white peristyle, its columns supporting heroic statues and flanked on either side by the Casino and the Music hall, and then, last of all, the great blue lake melting in the distance with the blue of heaven.

Almost in front of the Manufactures building is the brick ship—the model of a United States cruiser—that contains the government naval exhibit.

Fisheries Building.

WORLD'S CONGRESS AUXILIARY.

The World's Congress Auxiliary constitutes the intellectual and moral branch of the exposition. It is organized to provide for the presentation, by papers and discussion, of the mental and moral status and achievements of the human race. Under its auspices a series of congresses will be held in Chicago during the progress of the fair, in which will participate the leading professional men and women of the world. The congresses will meet in the permanent Memorial Art Palace, which the Chicago Art Institute and the exposition directory have erected on the lake front at the foot of Adams street. This will contain two large and several small audience rooms, and, on occasion, the Auditorium will also be used.

The department of woman's progress will hold the first general congress of representative women of all countries, in the middle of May. It will be followed at intervals one week apart by the public press congress, the department of medicine congress, the temperance congress, congress of the department of moral and social reform, and also of commerce and finance.

The department of music includes the general divisions of orchestral art, choral music, songs of the people, organ and church music, musical art and literature, musical criticism and history, opera houses and music halls. The congress of this department will be held during the week commencing July 3, 1893.

The department of literature includes the general divisions of libraries, history, philology, authors, folk-lore and copyright. The congress of this department will commence on July 10, 1893.

The department of education includes the general divisions of higher institutions of learning and university extension; public instruction, the kindergarten, manual and art training, business and commercial education, education in civil law and

Hall of Mines and Mining.

government, instruction of the deaf, education of the blind, representative youth of public schools, college and university students, college fraternities, psychology, experimental and rational, physical culture, domestic and economic education, agricultural education, authors and publishers. The congresses of these general divisions will commence on July 17, 1893, and will be followed by the general educational congress, in which all the departments of education will be properly represented.

The department of engineering includes the general divisions of engineering; that of art includes the general divisions of architecture, painting, sculpture, decorative art, photographic art, government patronage of art. The art congress will begin July 31, 1893.

The department of government includes the general divisions of jurisprudence and law reform, political and economic reform, city government, executive administration, intellectual property, arbitration and peace. Other congresses will be held in the department of science and philosophy, labor, religion, agriculture and public health, including the general divisions of sanitary legislation, public health authorities, governmental administration in relation to epidemics and contagions, food inspection and other food problems.

FINANCES OF THE FAIR.

The value of exhibits at the fair undoubtedly exceeds $200,000,000 and the cost of making the display is estimated at $60,000,000. This sum includes the amount expended in preparing the grounds and main buildings, the foreign and state buildings in making the foreign, state and individual exhibits and the general expenses of conducting the fair.

The last statement of World's Fair finances submitted before the opening of the gates on May 1 was issued by Auditor Ackerman, of the local directory, April 15. This report

Electricity Building.

showed that up to April 1, 1893, there were spent in building the fair $16,708,826.48—a sum equal to twice the total cost of building the Paris exposition—and at least $2,000,000 more were spent during April. Of this enormous outlay, $14,411,-506.74 have gone into the fair buildings proper, while $2,206,-644 were spent in general expenses, salaries and dedication day expenditures. Following are the figures let on contracts made for work for the exposition proper:

CONTRACTS LET.	AMOUNT OF CONTRACT.
Administration building	$ 463,213
Agricultural building	658,687
Galleries of fine arts	737,811
Dairy building	29,308
Electricity building	423,350
Mines and Mining building	266,530
Forestry building	82,018
Fisheries building	217,672
Grounds and buildings office	61,665
Horticultural building	298,649
Machinery hall and boiler house	1,173,897
Manufactures and Liberal Arts building	1,727,431
Art building, Lake-Front	200,000
Transportation building	483,183
Women's building	135,399
Propagating houses	3,651
Pumping station	36,736
Live Stock Exhibit building	62,259
Filters	20,000
Fencing	26,144
Water and sewer pipe and laying same	293,760
Water tank for locomotive and railroad material	174,863
Perron and train sheds	54,710
Railway terminal station	225,384
Bridges	57,289
Grand fountains	122,500
Pumping works, city of Chicago	200,000
Choral hall	86,743
Anthropological building	85,666
Installing tools	7,350
Fire and police houses	75,813
Police station, Hyde Park	47,569
Fire hydrants	17,400

CONTRACTS LET.	AMOUNT OF CONTRACT.
Fire and police alarm system	$ 19,043
Hose and hose reels	75,305
Statue of Columbus	65,112
Statue of Benjamin Franklin	3,000
Statue of the Republic	9,467
Sculpture models and statuary	159,390
Piers and breakwaters	321,565
Accounting building	33,290
Finishing terraces and interior docking	197,979
Sewerage cleansing works	54,895
Sewerage ejectors	66,425
Ejector pits and stop gates	25,526
Roadways and sidewalks	193,000
Roadway drainage	139,429
Warehouse for packing cases	35,863
Rent of land	75,000
Seats and band stands	21,700
Rubber-covered wire and conductors	75,000
Electric motors	5,500
Electric light plant	448,201
Arc lights and telephone circuits	213,282
Board of Architects	124,050
Garbage crematory	2,341
Children's building	22,218
Shoe and Leather building	89,442
Boiler plant	164,184
Music hall, Casino, and Peristyle	366,253
Oil plant	16,962
Saw mill	21,794
Uniforms for guards	30,000
Colonnade and Obelisk	98,945
Elevation of Illinois Central tracks	200,000
Temporary viaducts	28,600
Fire boat	7,050
Monastery La Rabida	24,302
Public Comfort Building	26,828
Launches	12,625
Runways and traveling cranes	136,500
Machinery, belting, and shafting	55,753
Entrances and ticket booths	88,500
Coloring and decorating	158,216
Total	$12,469,201

In addition are the costs of foreign and state buildings, foreign, state and individual exhibits, and of general running expenses of the fair, including police, fire, janitor service, salaries, music, etc.

Exclusive of the money spent by individual exhibitors, the following is a statement of moneys raised for the exposition:

Appropriated by foreign governments	$ 5,675,298.00
The compilation made by the Department of Publicity and Promotion, from all sources	896,231.00
Contributions by states of the Union	6,020,850.00
Original appropriation by United States government	1,500,000.00
Appropriation by government of five million souvenir coins	2,500,000.00
Appropriation by government for bronze medals and diplomas	103,000.00
Appropriation for government board, 1892	408,250.00
Appropriation for government board, 1893	150,750.00
Appropriation for national commission, 1891	95,500.00
Appropriation for national commission, 1892	230,000.00
Appropriation for national commission, 1893	211,375.00
Receipts from stockholders	5,553,760.80
City of Chicago	5,000,000.00
Six per cent debenture bonds, due January 1, 1894	4,094,500.00
Gate receipts to April 1	234,853.00
Interest	88,963.00
Miscellaneous receipts	295,504.75
Grand Total	$33,248,930.55

As the stockholders are, almost without exception, Chicagoans, it will be seen that the city has thus directly contributed $10,553,760.80 to the fair, besides purchasing debenture bonds and paying an enormous amount of the installation costs. At first fostered and agitated in Chicago, the great enterprise, although largely conducted under national auspices, is, as these figures prove, essentially a Chicago institution.

Manufactures and Liberal Arts Building.

DEDICATION AND OPENING CEREMONIES.

[Opening chorus of Harriet Monroe's "Commemoration Ode," read and sung at the dedicatory ceremonies, October 21, 1892.]

Columbia! Men beheld thee rise
   A goddess from the misty sea.
Lady of joy, sent from the skies,
   The nations worshiped thee.
Thy brows were flushed with dawn's first light;
By foamy waves with stars bedight
   Thy blue robe floated free.

Now let the sun ride high o'erhead,
   Driving the day from shore to shore.
His burning tread we do not dread,
   For thou art evermore
Lady of love whose smile shall bless,
Whom brave deeds win to tenderness,
   Whose tears the loss restore.

Lady of hope thou art. We wait
   With courage thy serene command.
Through unknown seas, toward undreamed fate,
   We ask thy guiding hand.
On! though sails quiver in the gale!—
Thou at the helm, we can not fail.
   On to God's time-veiled strand!

Lady of beauty! thou shalt win
   Glory and power and length of days.
The sun and moon shall be thy kin,
   The stars shall sing thy praise.
All hail! we bring thee vows most sweet
To strew before thy winged feet.
   Now onward be thy ways!

The fair was formally dedicated October 21, 1892, and opened May 1, 1893—each occasion being marked by appropriate ceremonies. Wednesday, October 19, there was a grand ball, reception and banquet at the Auditorium, given in honor of the invited guests—President Harrison's cabinet, Vice-President Morton, the Supreme Court of the United States, the foreign diplomatic corps, many senators and members of the House of Representatives, ex-President Hayes, the

Agricultural Building.

governors of nearly all the states and territories, with their official staffs, many specially commissioned representatives of foreign countries, the high officers of the army and navy, and thousands of the most distinguished citizens of the several states of the Union.

Thursday was marked by an imposing civic parade, and Friday was dedication day proper.

One hundred thousand persons witnessed the dedicatory exercises in Manufactures and Liberal Arts building. Director General Davis opened the ceremonies. He said:

LADIES AND GENTLEMEN: By virtue of my official position, it is my pleasurable duty to present the noted personages who, at this hour, in their several functions, are to contribute to the exercises with which we here dedicate the grounds and buildings of the World's Columbian Exposition. Of the great nations of the world, the United States is the youngest; our resources are equal to those of any other nation. Our sixty millions of people are among the most intelligent, cultured, happy and prosperous of mankind. But what we are and what we possess as a nation is not ours by purchase, nor by conquest, but by virtue of the rich heritage that was spread out beneath the sun and stars, beneath the storms and rains and dews, beneath the frosts and snows, ages before a David, a Homer, or a Virgil sang, or before Italy's humble and immortal son had dreamed his dream of discovery. This rich heritage is ours, not by our own might, not even by our own discovery, but ours by the gift of the Infinite. * * * A single century has placed this people side by side with the oldest and most advanced nations of the world; nations with a history of a thousand years. But in the midst of our rejoicing, no American citizen should forget our national starting point, and the quality of the manhood on which was laid the very foundation of our government. Our fathers were born under foreign flags. The very best brain, and nerve, and muscle, and conscience of the older governments found their way to this western continent. Our ancestors had the map of the world before them; what wonder that they chose this land for their descendants! * * * The World's Columbian Exposition is the natural outgrowth of this nation's place in history. Our continent, discovered by Christopher Columbus, whose spirits were revived as his cause was espoused by the generous-hearted Queen of Spain, has, throughout all the years from that time to this, been a haven to all who saw here the promise of requited toil, of liberty and of peace. The ceaseless, restless march of civilization, westward, ever westward, has reached and passed the great lakes of North America, and has founded on their farthest shore the greatest city of modern times. Chicago, the peerless, has been selected for the great celebration which to-day gives new fire to progress, and sheds its light upon ages yet to come. Established in the heart of this continent, her pulse throbs with the quickening current of our national life, and that this city was selected as the scene of this great commemorative festival was the natural outgrowth of predestined events. Here all nations are to meet in peaceful, laudable emulation on the fields of art, science and industry, on the fields of research, invention and scholarship, and to learn the universal value of the discovery we commemorate; to learn, as could be learned in no other way, the nearness of man to man, the fatherhood of God and the brotherhood of the human race. This, ladies and gentlemen, is the exalted purpose of the World's Columbian Exposition. May it be fruitful of its aim, and of peace forever to all the nations of the earth.

Following the Director General, Mayor Hempstead Washburne delivered an address of welcome and tendered the freedom of the city to the guests. Then the Director of Works, D. H. Burnham, delivered the buildings to President Higinbotham of the local directory, who in turn delivered them to President Thomas W. Palmer of the National Commission. In the absence of the President of the United States, Vice-President Levi P. Morton then formally declared the fair to be

H. N. Higinbotham.

dedicated. Henry Watterson, Chauncey M. Depew and Mrs. Potter Palmer also spoke, Cardinal Gibbons prayed, and after the benediction had been spoken, the booming of the cannons firing the national salute announced to the world that Chicago's great work was done, the fair was dedicated and ceased to be a local and became an international institution.

On Monday, May 1, 1893, Grover Cleveland, President of the United States, formally opened the fair. An immense crowd, estimated at from 300,000 to 500,000, filled the grounds. Spectators there were from every country on the globe, and almost every country was officially represented. In front of the great stand before the Administration building, where the representatives of over fifty nations, the World's Fair officers, the President and his cabinet, the United States Supreme Court, the diplomatic corps and other distinguished guests had gathered, there was a great mass of men, blending together all the races of humanity from orient and occident, from north and south, from races new and vigorous, and from races old and disappearing.

First came a grand crash of martial music, when 600 musicians, at the nod of Theodore Thomas, began John R. Paine's "Columbian March." Then after a prayer, the reading of a poem in honor of Columbus, and the orchestral overture of Wagner's "Rienzi," Director General Davis spoke as follows:

The dedication of these grounds and buildings for the purpose of an international exhibition took place on October 21 last, at which time they were accepted for the objects to which they were destined by the action of the Congress of the United States.

This exposition is not the conception of any single mind; it is not the result of any single effort; but it is the grandest conception of all the minds and the best obtainable result of all the efforts put forth by all the people who have in any manner contributed to its creation.

The great commanding agencies, through which the government has authorized this work to proceed, are the National Commission, the corporation of the state of Illinois, known as the World's Columbian Exposition, consisting of forty-five directors, and the Board of Lady Managers, consisting of 115 women. To these great agencies, wisely selected by Congress, each performing its special function, the gratitude of the people of this country and the cordial recognition of all these friendly foreign representatives are due.

The department of works and its many bureaus of artists, architects, engineers and builders, have transformed these grounds, which twenty-one months ago were an unsightly, uninviting and unoccupied stretch of landscape, into the beauty and splendor of to-day. They have conspicuously performed their functions, and these grand avenues, these Venetian waterways, the finished landscape, the fountains and sculptures and colonnades, and these grand palaces stand out as a monument to their genius and their skill, supplemented by the labor of that great army of skilled artisans and workmen, all citizens of this republic.

The chiefs of the great departments, who have exploited this mighty enterprise and gathered here the exhibits forming the picture that is set in this magnificent frame, have confirmed the wisdom of their selection. No state or territory in the Union has escaped their voice; no land on the globe that has a language but has been visited, and the invitation of the President of the United States personally presented. Fortunately, at the inception of this enterprise, our government was, and still is, at peace with the whole world. Commissioners were sent to Europe, to Asia, to Australia, British North America, and to the islands of the seas; so that to-day the whole world knows and is familiar with the significance of the great peace festival we are about to inaugurate upon this campus, and all the nations join in celebrating the event which it commemorates.

This enclosure, containing nearly seven hundred acres, covered by more than four hundred structures, from the small state pavilion occupying an ordinary building site, to the colossal structure of the Manufactures and Liberal Arts building, covering over thirty acres, is filled and crowded with a display of the achievements and products of the mind and hand of man such as has never before been presented to mortal vision.

The habits, customs and life of the peoples of our own and foreign lands are shown in the variegated plaisance; those stately buildings on the north are filled with the historical treasures and natural products of our several states. The artistic, characteristic and beautiful edifices, the headquarters of foreign commissions surrounding the gallery of fine arts, which in itself will be an agreeable surprise to the American beholder, constitute the grand central zone of social and friendly amenities among the different peoples of the earth. * * * * *

To the foreign nations who have a representation upon these grounds never before witnessed at any exposition, as shown by the grand exhibits they have brought here, and the hundreds of official representatives of foreign governments who are present on this occasion, we bow in grateful thanks. More than $6,000,000 have been officially appropriated for these commissions in furtherance of their participation in the exposition. The great nations of Europe and their dependencies are all represented upon these grounds. The governments of Asia and of Africa and the republics of the western hemisphere, with but few exceptions, are here represented.

To the citizens and corporation of the city of Chicago who have furnished $11,000,000 as a contribution, and in addition have loaned the management $5,000,000 more, are due the grateful acknowledgement of our own people, and of all the honored guests who share with us the advantages of this great international festival.

To the tens of thousands of exhibitors who have contributed on a larger amount than all others combined, we are under the deepest obligations for their interest and co-operation.

To the women of Chicago and our great land, whose prompt, spontaneous and enthusiastic co-operation in our work turned the eyes of the world towards the exposition as toward a new star of the east—an inspiration for womanhood everywhere—we extend our cordial and unstinted recognition.

It is our hope that this great exposition may inaugurate a new era of moral and material progress, and our fervent aspiration that the association of the nations here may secure not only warmer and stronger friendships, but lasting peace throughout the world.

The grand concerted illustration of modern progress which is here presented for the encouragement of art, of science, of industry, of commerce, has necessitated an expenditure, including the outlay of our exhibitors, largely in excess of $100,000,000. We have given it our constant thought, our most devoted service, our best energy; and now, in this central city of this great republic on the continent discovered by Columbus, it only remains for you, Mr. President, if in your opinion the exposition here presented is commensurate in dignity with what the world should expect of our great country, to direct that it shall be opened to the public, and when you touch this magic key, the ponderous machinery will start in its revolutions and the activities of this exposition will begin.

When the Director General had finished speaking, President Cleveland arose and said: "I am here to join my fellow-citizens in the congratulations which befit this occasion. Surrounded by the stupendous results of American enterprise and activity and in view of magnificent evidences of American skill and intelligence, we need not fear that these congratulations will be exaggerated. We stand to-day in the presence of the oldest nations of the world and point to the great achievements here exhibited, asking no allowance on the score of youth. The enthusiasm with which we contemplate our work intensifies the warmth of the greeting we extend to those who have come from foreign lands to illustrate with us the growth and progress of human endeavor in the direction of a higher civilization. We who believe that popular education and the stimulation of the best impulses of our citizens lead the way to a realization of the proud national destiny which our faith promises, gladly welcome the opportunity here afforded us to see the results accomplished by efforts which have been exerted longer than ours in the field of man's improvements, while in appreciative return we exhibit the unparalleled advancement and wonderful accomplishments of a young nation, and present the triumphs of a vigorous, self-reliant and independent people. We have built these splendid edifices, but we have also built the magnificent fabric of a popular government, whose grand proportions are seen throughout the world. We have made and here gathered together objects of use and beauty, the products of American skill and invention; but we have also made men who rule themselves. It is an exalted mission in which we and our guests from other lands are engaged, as we co-operate in the inauguration of an enterprise devoted to human enlightenment; and, in the undertaking we here enter upon, we exemplify in the noblest sense the brotherhood of nations. Let us hold fast to the meaning that underlies this ceremony, and let us not lose the impressiveness of this moment. As by a touch the machinery that gives life to this vast exposition is set in motion, so at the same instant let our hopes and aspirations awaken forces which in all time to come shall influence the welfare, the dignity and the freedom of mankind."

With the concluding words, President Cleveland touched the electric switchboard and inaugurated the World's Columbian Exposition. It was a grand transformation scene. The great machinery was set in motion, thousands of flags and silken banners flashed and floated on the breeze, great jets of water burst forth from silent fountains, the drapery that had hidden the great golden statue of the Republic fell, cannons thundered, bells pealed, a chime of steam whistles blew, and then the great orchestra and the greater chorus gave Handel's "Hallelujah Chorus," and the fair was open.

During the afternoon the Woman's building was formally dedicated by Bertha Honore Palmer, president of the Board of Lady Managers. After an elaborate musical and literary program, Mrs. Palmer spoke as follows:

The moment of fruition has arrived. Hopes, which for more than two years have gradually been gaining strength and definiteness, have now become realities. To-day the exposition opens its gates. On this occasion of the formal opening of the Woman's building, the Board of Lady Managers is singularly fortunate in having the honor to welcome distinguished official representatives of many of the able foreign committees and of the state boards which have so effectively co-operated with it in accomplishing results now disclosed to the world.

We have traveled together a hitherto untrodden path; have been subjected to tedious delays and overshadowed by dark clouds, which threatened disaster to our enterprise. We have been obliged to march with peace offerings in our hands lest hostile motives be ascribed to us. Our burdens have been greatly lightened, however, by the spontaneous sympathy and aid which have reached us from women in every part of the world, and which have proved an added incentive and inspiration. . . . .

It is not our province, however, to discuss these weighty questions, except in so far as they affect compensation paid to wage-earners, and more especially that paid to women and children.

Of all existing forms of injustice, there is none so cruel and inconsistent as is the position in which women are placed with regard to self-maintenance; the calm ignoring of their rights and responsibilities which has gone on for centuries. If the economic conditions are hard for men to meet, subjected as they are to the constant weeding out of the less expert and steady hands (who are thereby plunged into an abyss of misery), it is evident that women, thrown upon their own resources, have a frightful struggle to endure, especially as they have always to contend against a public sentiment which discountenances their seeking industrial employments as a means of livelihood.

The cry which exists among conservative people that the sphere of woman is her home; that it is unfeminine, even monstrous, for her to wish to take a place beside, or to compete with men in the various lucrative industries, tells heavily against her, for manufacturers and producers take advantage of it to disparage her work and obtain her services for a nominal price, thus profiting largely by the necessities and helplessness of their victim. That so many should cling to respectable occupations while starving in following them and should refuse to yield to discouragement and despair, shows a high quality of steadfastness and principle. These are the real heroines of life, whose handiwork we are proud to install in the exposition, because it has been produced in factories, workshops and studios under the most adverse conditions, and with the most sublime patience and endurance.

Men of the finest and most chivalric type, who have poetic theories about the sanctity of the home and the refining, elevating influence of woman in it—theories which we have inherited from the days of romance and chivalry, and which we wish might prevail forever—these men have asked many times whether the Board of Lady Managers think it well to promote a sentiment which may tend to destroy the home, by encouraging occupations for women which take them out of it. We feel, therefore, obliged to state that in our opinion, every woman who is presiding over a happy home is fulfilling her highest and truest function, and could not be lured from it by temptations offered by factories or studios. Would that the eyes of these idealists could be thoroughly opened that they might see, not the fortunate few of a favored class, with homes they possibly are in daily contact with, but the general status of the labor market throughout the world, and the relation to it of women. They might be astonished to learn that the conditions under which the vast majority of the "gentler sex" are living are not so ideal as they assume, that each is not "dwelling in a home of which she is the queen, with a manly and loving arm to shield her from rough contact with life."

Because of the impossibility of reconciling their theories with the stern facts, they might possibly consent to forgive the offense of widows with dependent children, and of wives of drunkards and criminals who so far forget the high standard established for them as to attempt to earn for themselves daily bread, lacking which they must perish. The necessity for their work under present conditions is too evident and too urgent to be questioned. They must work or they must starve. * * * *

We observe that there are two classes of the community who wish to restrain women from actual participation in the business of the world, and that each gives, apparently, very strong reasons in support of its views. These are, first, the idealists already mentioned, who hold the opinion that woman should be tenderly guarded and cherished within the sacred precincts of the home which alone is her sphere of action. Second, certain political economists, with whom may be ranged most of the men engaged in the profitable pursuit of the industries of the world, who object to the competition that would result from the participation of women, because they claim it would reduce a general scale of wages paid and lessen the earning power of men, who require all their present income to support their families.

Plausible as these theories are, we cannot accept them without pausing to inquire what then would become of all women but the very few who have independent fortunes or are the happy wives of men able and willing to support them. The interests of probably three-fourths of the women in the world would be sacrificed. Are they to be allowed to starve, or to rush to self-destruction? If not permitted to work, what course is open to them? Our oriental neighbors have seen the logic of the situation far more clearly than we, and have been consistent enough to meet it without shrinking from heroic measures. The question is happily solved in some countries by the practice of polygamy, which allows every man to maintain as many wives as his means permits. In others etiquette requires that a newly-made widow be burned on the funeral pyre with her husband's body, while the Chinese take the precaution to drown surplus female children. It would seem that any of these methods is more logical and less cruel than the system we pursue of permitting the entire female population to live, but making it impossible for those born to poverty to maintain themselves in comfort, because they are hampered by a caste feeling almost as strong as that ruling India, which will not permit them to work on equal terms with men. These unhappy members of an inferior class must be content to remain in penury, living on the crumbs that fall from the tables spread from those of another and higher caste. This relative position has been exacted on the one side, accepted on the other side; it has been considered by each an inexorable law. We shrink with horror from the unjust treatment of child-widows and other unfortunates on the other side of the globe, but our own follies and inconsistencies are too close to our eyes for us to see them in proper perspective.

Sentimentalists should have reduced their theories to set terms and applied them.

They have had ample opportunity and time to provide means by which helpless women could be cherished, protected and removed from the storms and stress of life. Women could have asked nothing better. We have no respect for a theory which touches only the favored few who do not need this protection and leaves unaided the great mass it has assisted to push into the mire. Babble it not, therefore, until it can be uttered not only in polite drawing-rooms, but also in factories and workshops, without a blush of shame for its weakness and inefficiency.

But the sentimentalists again exclaim: "Would you have women step down from their pedestal to enter practical life?" Yes, a thousand times, yes. If we can really find, after a careful search, any women mounted upon pedestals, we should willingly ask them to step down in order that they may meet and help to uplift their sisters. Freedom and justice for all are infinitely more to be desired than pedestals for a few. I beg leave to state that, personally, I am not a believer in the pedestal theory—never having seen an example of it—and that I always suspect the motives of any one advancing it. Is it not the natural and fine relation between husband and wife, or between friends, that they should stand side by side, the fine qualities of each supplementing and assisting those of the other? Men naturally cherish high ideals of womanhood, as women do of manliness and strength. These ideals will dwell with the human race forever without our striving to preserve and protect them.

If we now look at the question from the economic standpoint, and aside for good and logical reasons, that women should be kept out of industrial fields in order that they may leave the harvest for men, whose duty it is to provide for women and children, then, by all laws of justice and equity, these latter should be provided for by their natural protectors, and, if deprived of them, should become wards of the state and be maintained in honor and comfort. The acceptance of even this doctrine of tardy justice would not, however, I feel sure, be welcomed by the women of to-day, who, having had a taste of independence, will never relinquish it. They have no desire to be helpless and dependent. Having the full use of their faculties, they rejoice in exercising them. This is entirely in conformity with the trend of modern thought, which is in the direction of establishing proper respect for human individuality and the right of self-development. Our highest aim now is to train each to find happiness in the full and healthy exercise of the gifts bestowed by a generous nature. Ignorance is too expensive and wasteful to be tolerated. We cannot afford to lose the reserve power of any individual.

We advocate, therefore, the thorough education and training of woman to fit her to meet whatever fate life may bring, not only to prepare her for the factory and workshop, for the professions and arts, but, more important than all else, to prepare her for presiding in the home. It is for this, the highest field of woman's effort, that the broadest training and greatest preparation are required. The illogical, extravagant, whimsical, unthrifty mother and housekeeper belongs to the dark ages; she has no place in our present era of enlightenment. No course of study is too elaborate, no amount of knowledge and culture too abundant to meet the actual requirements of the wife and mother in dealing with the interests committed to her hands.

Realizing that woman can never hope to receive the proper recompense for her services until her usefulness and success are not only demonstrated but fully understood and acknowledged, we have taken advantage of the opportunity presented by the exposition to bring together such evidences of her skill in the various industries, arts and professions as may convince the world that ability is not a matter of sex. Urged by necessity, she has demonstrated that her powers are the same as her brother's, and that like encouragement and fostering care may develop her to an equal point of usefulness. The fact that the Woman's building is so small that it can hold but a tithe of the beautiful objects offered has been a great disadvantage. The character of the exhibits and the high standard attained by most of them serve, therefore, only as an index of the quality and range of the material from which we have drawn.

Japan, under the guidance of its liberal and intelligent empress, has promptly and cordially promoted our plans. Her Majesty, the Queen of Siam, has sent a special delegate with instructions that she put herself under our leadership and learn what industrial and educational advantages are open to women in other countries, so that Siam may adopt such measures as will elevate the condition of her women.

The exposition will thus benefit women, not alone by means of the material objects brought together, but there will be a more lasting and permanent result through the interchange of thought and sympathy among influential and leading women of all countries, now for the first time working together with a common purpose and an established means of communication. Government recognition and sanction give to these committees of women official character and dignity. Their work has been magnificently successful, and the reports which will be made of the conditions found to exist will be placed on record as public documents among the archives of every country. Realizing the needs and the responsibilities of the hour and that this will be the first official utterance of women in behalf of women, we shall weigh well our words—words which should be so judicious and convincing that hereafter they may be treasured among the happy influences which made possible new and better conditions.

We rejoice in the possession of this beautiful building in which we meet to-day; in its delicacy, symmetry and strength. We honor our architect and the artists who have not only given their hands, but their hearts and their genius to its decoration. For it, women in every part of the world have been exerting their efforts and talents; looms have wrought their most delicate fabrics; the needle has flashed in the hands of fair maidens under tropical suns; the lacemaker has bent over her cushion weaving her most artful web; the brush and chisel have sought to give form and reality to the visions haunting the brain of the artist; all have wrought with the thought of making our building worthy to serve its great end; we thank them all for their successful efforts.

The eloquent president of the commission last October dedicated the great exposition to humanity. We now dedicate the Woman's building to an elevated womanhood, knowing that by so doing we shall best serve the cause of humanity.

FORMER FAIRS.

There is every reason to believe that the World's Columbian Exposition will far outshine all preceding world's fairs. The number of acres under roof is equal to that of Paris in 1889, Philadelphia in 1876 and Vienna in 1873 combined. There are more exhibitors, more interesting and numerous exhibits, finer buildings, more spacious and beautiful grounds.

In London, in 1851, there were 6,039,195 visitors; in Paris, in 1855, there were 5,162,330 visitors; in London, in 1862, 6,250,000 visitors; in Paris, in 1867, 10,200,000; in Vienna, in 1873, 7,254,687; in Philadelphia, in 1876, 9,910,966; in Paris, in 1878, 16,000,000, and in Paris, in 1889, 28,149,353 visitors. The largest attendance any single day in Philadelphia was 274,919, and in Paris, 1889, 400,000. The total outlay for buildings and grounds in Paris in 1889 was $8,300,000—in Chicago it will exceed twice that amount, and it is to be assumed that the attendance will be in accordance with this increased expenditure. The fair has aroused the greatest interest among the people, not only of the United States, but also of the whole world. But more interesting to the visitor from abroad than even the beauties and splendor of the White City in Jackson Park, will be the development and progress of a typical American city as exemplified in Chicago, the wonder city on the shores of Lake Michigan.

www.ingramcontent.com/pod-product-compliance
Lightning Source LLC
Chambersburg PA
CBHW022110300426
44117CB00007B/654